CHRISTOPHER WREN

CHRISTOPHER WREN

IN SEARCH OF EASTERN ANTIQUITY

VAUGHAN HART

PAUL MELLON CENTRE FOR STUDIES IN BRITISH ART
Distributed by Yale University Press • New Haven and London

First published in 2020 by the
Paul Mellon Centre for Studies in British Art
16 Bedford Square, London, WC1B 3JA
paul-mellon-centre.ac.uk

Copyright © 2020 by Vaughan Hart

All rights reserved. This book may not be reproduced or transmitted
in any form or by any means, electronic or mechanical, including
photocopy, recording or any other information storage and retrieval
system, without prior permission in writing from the publisher.

ISBN 978-1-913107-07-9 HB
Library of Congress Control Number: 2019947814

British Library Cataloguing-in-Publication Data
A catalogue record for this book is available from the British Library

Origination by Evergreen Colour Management Ltd
Printed by C&C Offset Printing

Frontispiece: St Stephen Walbrook, London (see fig. 138)

CONTENTS

ACKNOWLEDGEMENTS		*vii*
PREFACE	*Towards a New History of Architecture*	*ix*
INTRODUCTION	*East Meets West at the Royal Society*	*1*
1	*Classical Orders and Lanterns*	19
2	*Gothic Arches and Towers*	45
3	*Greek Crosses and Domes*	69
4	*Monumental Columns and Colonnades*	119
CONCLUSION	*Eastern Wonders and National Identity*	147
NOTES		151
BIBLIOGRAPHY		185
PHOTOGRAPH CREDITS		203
INDEX		204

In memory of my father

ACKNOWLEDGEMENTS

I would like to thank the following for their advice at various stages in writing this book: Professor Andrew Ballantyne (Newcastle University), Dr Peter Fane-Saunders (Birkbeck, London University), Professor Peter Hicks, Professor Michael Hunter (Birkbeck, London University), Professor Tim Ibell (Bath University), Dominique Lazanski (Bath University), Dr Peter Lindfield (St Andrew's University), Professor Fabrizio Nevola (Exeter University), Dr Juliet Odgers (Newcastle University), Dr Robert Proctor (Bath University), Professor Fiona Robertson (Durham University), Professor Ingrid Rowland (Notre Dame University), Professor Joseph Rykwert, Dr Julia Snape (Westminster Abbey Library and Archive), Tim Tatton-Brown, Professor Robert Tavernor, Dr Edmund Thomas (Durham University), Nicola Thwaite (National Trust), Mark Wilson Jones (Bath University), Mark Wray, and the late Professor Lisa Jardine (formerly of London University) and Professor David Watkin (formerly of Cambridge University).

I would also like to thank the librarians at Bath University and Cambridge University, especially at the Rare Books Department of the University Library but also at Gonville and Caius College, Christ's College and Trinity College, in Oxford at All Souls College and Merton College, and in London at the British Library, the British Museum, the Royal Society, the Warburg Institute, Lambeth Palace, St Paul's Cathedral and Westminster Abbey. I have received funding for travel both in England and in Istanbul from the Department of Architecture and Civil Engineering at Bath University. The Paul Mellon Centre for Studies in British Art provided funding for illustrations. An earlier version of Chapter One was delivered at a workshop entitled 'Classicism and the East' held in the Durham Centre for Classical Reception in Durham University in July 2014; a version of part of Chapter Four was delivered as a keynote paper at a symposium entitled 'Emblems and Enigma: The Heraldic Imagination', at the Society of Antiquaries of London in April 2014, and to the Oxford History Society in November 2015. And themes discussed in the Preface were aired in a seminar on Vitruvius held at Merton College in April 2017.

Finally I would like to thank Gillian Malpass, formerly of Yale University Press, who commissioned and was a constant supporter of this book, and Emily Lees, my editor at the Paul Mellon Centre. And I should also like to express gratitude to my wife, Charlotte, for her encouragement and patience.

PREFACE

TOWARDS A NEW HISTORY OF ARCHITECTURE

Christopher Wren is England's most famous architect (fig. 1). His genius was recognised from an early age, with John Evelyn describing him at twenty-two as 'that miracle of a Youth'.[1] Wren was born in 1632, one year before Inigo Jones started his ill-fated refacing of old St Paul's Cathedral, and died in 1723 at the grand age of ninety-one. He would carry to completion the centrepiece of his age, a new cathedral built on the ashes of the old. Unlike Jones, Wren never visited Rome to study its antiquities, but his brief visit to Paris to escape the plague between July 1665 and March 1666 allowed him to meet leading continental architects including Gian Lorenzo Bernini. Having become the Professor of Astronomy at Gresham College at the tender age of twenty-five, in 1657, his early achievements were not in fact in architecture at all but in the sciences. When Wren turned to architecture five years later, it represented more a change in employment than in intellectual outlook. He served at Gresham until 1661 when he was appointed the Savilian Professor of Astronomy at Oxford, and held the post until 1673 while also serving as the Surveyor-General of the King's building Works from 1669.[2] His first architectural commissions – the supervision of the construction of the fortification at Tangier in Morocco (which he declined) and the repair of old St Paul's – were a result of his acknowledged ability with geometry and mechanics in their relation to building, rather than any proven mastery of the much debated rules of classical architecture derived from the Roman author Vitruvius.

Wren went on to design some of the country's best-recognised buildings. Nearly all of these survive, unlike much of the work of his predecessor Jones, and are among the most popular tourist attractions in Cambridge, Oxford and London. When designing these buildings, Wren frequently departed from classical precedents and norms. Sometimes the novelty of his work produced contemporary opposition, such as with the initial design for a cathedral in the form of a Greek cross with dome that was disliked by the traditionally minded clergy. He often fused antique forms with more modern inventions, as for example at the Sheldonian in Oxford, with its plan adapted from the ancient theatre and Renaissance ceiling structure, or at St Paul's, with its traditional Latin cross plan and novel dome.[3] Wren and his pupils Nicholas Hawksmoor and John Vanbrugh would also experiment with a much wider palate of ornament and forms than those surviving from ancient Rome and recorded by Vitruvius and his Renaissance commentators.[4] Broken entablatures and split pediments, paired columns and flamboyant lanterns, all signalled a break with antiquity and the work of Jones, in the manner sometimes referred

1 Sir Christopher Wren, Royal Society portrait by John Closterman, c.1690. Oil on canvas, 143 x 121 cm. Royal Society, London

to as 'Baroque'. In justification, Wren observed that: 'MODERN Authors who have treated of Architecture' have 'little more in view' than to 'set down the Proportions of Columns, Architraves, and Cornices, in the several Orders'; however, 'in these Proportions finding them in the ancient Fabricks of the *Greeks* and *Romans*, (though more arbitrarily used than they care to acknowledge) they have reduced them into Rules, too strict and pedantick, and so as not to be transgressed, without the Crime of Barbarity'.[5] Instead, what might be seen as Wren's freer approach to designing with the Orders (the classical columns) prioritised the observer's perception of geometry, which Wren regarded as the 'natural' basis of beauty, and was justified by him with reference to a wider view of historical precedents.[6]

Due to the influence of Vitruvius's unique description of classical, or Graeco-Roman, architectural principles and the limited nature of travel, Renaissance architectural commentators had for the most part focused on his text and on surviving Roman buildings in Europe. This reliance on architectural models centred on Roman antiquity and the supposed 'strict' rules for designing classical architecture based on it, never in fact fully agreed, was being increasingly undermined in Wren's day by travel and the growing awareness of the broader nature of the ancient world.[7] Ancient buildings in India and China lay beyond the limits of the classical world but nonetheless had admirable qualities of proportion and monumentality, while non-Roman buildings in Asia at places like the Persian capital of Persepolis, and even further east in India and China, boasted novel yet classical attributes (see figs 16 and 164–6). For example, Wren himself commented on how 'odd a Figure' was the '*Indian* Pagod[a]'.[8] He discussed Chinese buildings with John Aubrey, who recorded Wren's belief that 'the *Chineses* have great Mausolea of Earth, which fashion is more ancient than the Romans'.[9] In being introduced to Turkish mosques and Chinese buildings, he became one of the earliest European architects to be aware of such structures. Limited descriptions of Turkish and Egyptian architecture were emerging through popular travel accounts, such as Henry Blount's *Voyage into the Levant*, with its exotic tales of robbery and slavery, which passed through no less than eight editions in English between 1636 and 1671. Wren's awareness was for the most part through such travellers, who like Blount were associated with the Royal Society. In some cases these are identifiable, as with John Chardin who described Persepolis to Wren; in others they are not, Wren merely referring to information from 'modern travellers' concerning antiquities at Ephesus, Alexandria, Palmyra and Jerusalem.[10] Like Chardin (1643–1713), many travellers to the Levant and India were French, most notably Jean-Baptiste Tavernier (1605–1686), François Bernier (1620–1688), Jean de Thévenot (1633–1667) and Guillaume-Joseph Grelot (*c*.1630–*c*.1680). The curiosity of Louis XIV would lead him to dispatch expeditions to Greece, Egypt, Syria and Persia in order to record their ancient buildings.[11] It would lead to the building of the Chinese-inspired Pavillon de Porcelaine in 1670 at Versailles.[12] Charles Perrault proposed in 1697 that in the completion of the Louvre in Paris, the interiors should not be restricted to the French classical style but, together with their furniture, should be decorated not only in the Italian, Spanish and German manners but also in the Turkish, Persian, Mongolian and Chinese styles – that is, in 'an exact imitation of all the ornaments with which these nations variously embellish their Palaces'. As a result, 'all foreigners would have the pleasure of finding in us, as it were, their own country, and all the magnificence of the world enclosed in one Palace'.[13] Thus with expanding geographical horizons came equally expanding architectural ones.

An important outcome of this 'shock of the new' in France was the debate in the second half of the seventeenth century between the 'Ancients' and 'Moderns'.[14] Here the 'Ancients' were akin to Wren's pedants in regarding the authority of Vitruvius and ancient models as absolute in matters of architectural taste. This group was represented by Roland Fréart de Chambray and François Nicolas Blondel. Condemning the 'licentious' use of the Orders by modern architects and citing Greek monuments as the source for architectural principles, Fréart proposed the Greek Doric, Ionic and (particularly) the Corinthian Orders as the ultimate models of beauty in architecture. In contrast, the 'Moderns' regarded ancient teaching as relative and subject to further enquiry, in the light of new architectural and scientific discoveries. Most notably, Perrault's brother, Claude, rejected the Renaissance notion of absolute beauty assured by 'perfect' proportions and cited instead custom and habit as determinants of a changeable beauty in architecture. The conservative side of this debate found voice in England through the work of Evelyn in particular. When republishing his 1664 translation of a work by Fréart, Evelyn observed in 1707 concerning Perrault's invention of a 'Gallic Order' that the French were 'the fondest of their own Inventions' in seeking 'to alter and change what for almost Two Thousand Years, none has been so bold to Attempt with that Exhorbitance: For they have Garnish'd this *Capitel*

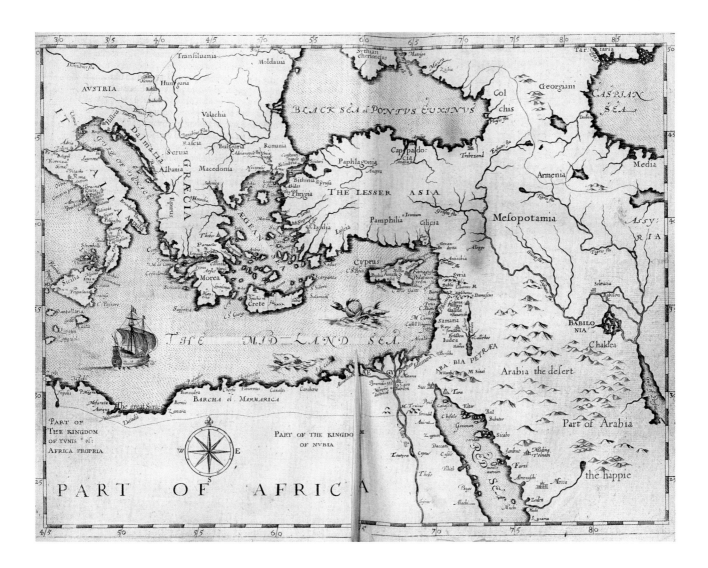

with *Cocks-Feathers* and *Cocks-Combs* too among the *Flowrdeluces*, ridiculously enough'.[15] Of fundamental importance to this debate was the search for a new, necessarily classical architecture of universal validity, to which the emerging knowledge of Eastern, Indian and Chinese architecture contributed.

As Wren's comments on the architectural pedants indicate, for the most part he took the side of the 'Moderns'. He too sought the basis for a universal, classical architectural style involving the use of novel ornament and building types. Wren produced designs for a wide variety of building types using classical forms that were new to England, all of which designs were to be found in London. These included colonnaded hospitals and an observatory, churches with domes as well as classically inspired lanterns and steeples, a memorial column and a cathedral also with a dome and even a plan for an entire city after the Great Fire of London.[16] When accounting for Wren's innovations, considerable emphasis has been placed on his interest in ancient and modern classical Rome, as mediated through the Renaissance treatises, as well as in the Baroque buildings of Paris witnessed at first hand.[17] The importance to his work of these cities is undeniable, and has been amply studied in the books by Margaret Whinney and Kerry Downes. This book will look further east, however, for sources of these forms and to understand the wider meaning of his work. It will examine Wren's awareness of the ancient Phoenicians, Syrians, Babylonians, Persians, Greeks and Egyptians, as well as of the dominant culture of his day, that of the Ottomans. The book will follow Wren and his contemporaries in referring to the region as the 'East' and the 'Eastern nations', or under the name of the Levant (fig. 2).[18] Clearly, Wren did

2 Map of the Levant region, from George Sandys, *A relation of a Journey begun an: Dom: 1610. Foure bookes. Containing a description of the Turkish Empire, of Ægypt, of the Holy Land* (1615), facing p. 1

3 Jerusalem, showing its sacred sites. Etching by Jacques Callot after engraving by Antonio de Angelis (published in Rome in 1578), from Bernardino Amico, *Trattato delle piante et imagini de sacri edificii di Terra Santa, disegnate in Gierusalemme secondo le regole della prospettiua, & vera misura della lor grandezza, etc.* (1620 edn), fig. 44

not copy sphinxes and minarets in his work or create an 'exotic' style. He was first and foremost a classicist. Rather, his very use of the classical language, and his questioning of Vitruvius, was based on his belief that its origins lay in the East on biblical buildings such as Solomon's Temple in Jerusalem and ancient structures like the legendary Mausoleum at Halicarnassus.

Wren found Eastern buildings particularly important and meaningful due to their links with biblical antiquity, as well as with early Christianity and great civilisations.

The Levant had once formed a major part of the Roman Eastern provinces, as well as the Byzantine and then the Ottoman empires. The Ottomans controlled much of the Levant in Wren's day, from Greece in the north through modern-day Turkey (a name used by travellers such as Tavernier for westernmost Asia or Anatolia), Syria and the Holy Land to Egypt in the south. They controlled the great Judaeo-Christian capitol of Jerusalem, with what remained of Solomon's Temple, and the early Christian one of Constantinople, with Hagia Sophia (figs 3 and 4). Constantinople held an obvious appeal to Wren and his contemporaries as the Christian, not pagan, capital of the later Roman Empire. Here was to be found a repository of Christianised antique forms. Equally, most of the legendary 'Wonders' of antiquity had stood in the East. The Great Pyramid was built at Giza, the Lighthouse at Alexandria, the Hanging Gardens at Babylon, the Temple of Diana (Artemis) at Ephesus, the Colossus at

Rhodes and the Mausoleum of Mausolus at Halicarnassus. Renaissance architectural commentators had been made aware of these and other legendary antiquities from the East through descriptions in the Bible, as too by Pliny the Elder, Herodotus, the Romano-Jewish scholar Josephus and Philo (as republished in the modern era by Leone Allatius or Allacci).[19] Antonio di Pietro Averlino (known as Filarete), in his treatise of the early 1460s, drew on Pliny and the Bible when discussing the Halicarnassus tomb and Solomon's Temple.[20] The *Hypnerotomachia Poliphili* of 1499, thought to be by Francesco Colonna, referred via Herodotus to the lost 'famous labyrinth of Egypt' and 'solid statue of Hercules in Tyre'.[21] And Cesare Cesariano illustrated the Mausolus tomb, again based on Pliny, in his Italian translation of Vitruvius of 1521 (fig. 5).[22] When it came to surviving Eastern antiquities like the pyramids, Renaissance treatise writers had on the whole to rely on these ancient sources, without the assistance of first-hand

4   Constantinople, from George Braun and Frans Hogenberg, *Civitates Orbis Terrarum*, vol. 1 (1572)

reports from travellers that were becoming available to Wren. But Sebastiano Serlio was made aware of Egyptian monuments through the travels of his friend Marco Grimani, the Patriarch of Aquileia. In the third book of his treatise of 1540, on Roman antiquities, Serlio illustrated one of the pyramids at Giza and a sphinx, as well as a royal tomb in Jerusalem, and added at the end a section on 'Some of the Marvels of Egypt' based on descriptions by Diodorus Siculus (fig. 6).[23] He also illustrated a number of Egyptian obelisks, the form having become part of the repertoire of classical elements in the Renaissance. Squeezed into a book on Roman monuments, such Eastern wonders were starting to undermine the Graeco-Roman classical paradigm.

Eye-witness reports such as that by Grimani were still relatively rare when Serlio wrote in the mid-sixteenth century, but their lack would not necessarily prohibit the influence of more modern Eastern buildings. For example, the grandeur of mosque architecture had not escaped the attention of Anglican divines in the seventeenth century in their consideration of church buildings. When lauding Solomon's Temple as 'the stateliest structure that ever

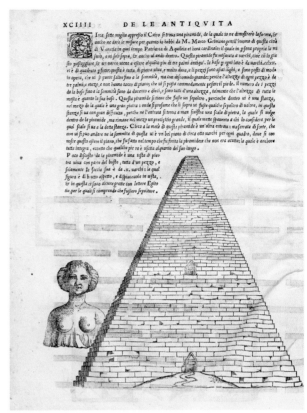

was or shall be in the world', the preacher Thomas Fuller in his *The Holy State and the Profane State* (1642) could not deny that there had been larger temples: by way of comparison he listed five great edifices chronologically – the Temple of Diana at Ephesus, Constantine's Church of the Holy Sepulchre in Jerusalem, Justinian's Hagia Sophia in Constantinople, Ethelbert's St Paul's in London and the 'Turkish mosque' at Fez.[24] Fuller had not visited any of these sites but cited Joannes Leo Africanus's *Totius Africae Descriptio* (1556) as his source for the dimensions of the mosque.[25] In a similar way, Anglicans knew of Hagia Sophia through descriptions by Procopius and Paul the Silentiary.[26] In the case of the holy sites of Palestine, accounts by medieval pilgrims such as John Phocas and Burchard of Mount Sion (both entitled *Descriptio*

LEFT 5   The Mausoleum at Halicarnassus reconstructed by Cesare Cesariano, from Vitruvius, *Di Lucio Vitruvio Pollione De architectura libri dece traducti de latino in vulgare* (1521), fol. XLIv

RIGHT 6   The Great Pyramid at Giza and the Sphinx, from Sebastiano Serlio, *Il terzo libro di Sebastiano Serlio Bolognese* (1540), p. XCIIII

terrae sanctae) had been published in various editions in the sixteenth and seventeenth centuries. The account of Niccolò da Poggibonsi (*Libro d'oltramare*) was published in 1500 with woodcuts of the sacred buildings and cities of the Holy Land. The most vivid visual reconstruction of the early Christian churches in Jerusalem and that at Bethlehem, which were then under Ottoman control, was to be found in Bernardino Amico's *Trattato delle piante et imagini de sacri edificii di Terra Santa, disegnate in Gierusalemme secondo le regole della prospettiua, & vera misura della lor grandezza, etc*. This eye-witness account was published first in Rome in 1609 and then in expanded form in Florence in 1620, with detailed engravings that served as an on-site guide to the sacred structures as well as a kind of imaginary pilgrimage for readers back home (fig. 7; see figs 3 and 132).[27]

Thus a body of literature by European merchants, pilgrims and clergy had built up in Wren's day that gave patchy eye-witness accounts of Eastern buildings, but when it came to long-lost and more enigmatic antiquities Wren followed in the footsteps of the Renaissance theorists and turned to ancient sources. He owned the 1693 illustrated English edition of Josephus's *The Antiquities of the Jews* (as recorded in a sale catalogue of his library, Lot 255),[28] although his references in works

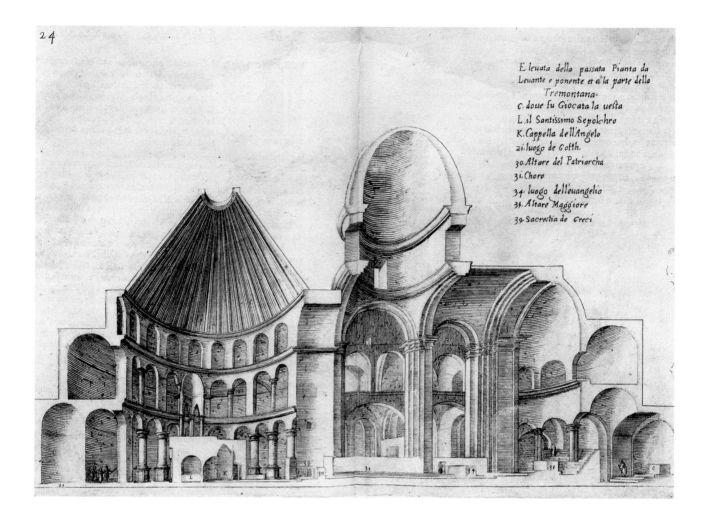

before that date show that he owned or had access to an earlier edition as well.[29] This may well have been the 1580 illustrated Latin edition owned by his friend Robert Hooke.[30] Hooke mentioned in his Diary in April 1676 that he 'saw new edition of Josephus', probably referring to the English translation (from French) published in London in that year.[31] This edition had illustrations of the Tabernacle of Moses and a map of the Holy Land that Wren may well have also seen. In addition Wren owned a 1635 Latin edition of Pliny's *Natural History* (Lot 188) and a further Latin edition published in the year of his death (1723, Lot 292), but he acknowledged having consulted many editions in his writings.[32] As Hooke recorded in his Diary, Pliny formed an active topic of conversation among members of the Royal Society.[33] Wren owned the illustrated 1592 Latin translation (with the original Greek) of Herodotus's *Histories* (Lot 122, with woodcuts of Babylon and its Hanging Gardens; see fig. 148). He was not an uncritical student of these ancient authors, however; he observed on the Tower of Babel that while 'Herodotus gives us a surprizing Relation of it', how he 'had his Measures, I question, for He flourish'd but *100* years before Alexanders Conquest of Babylon, so It was then *1500* years old'.[34]

Drawing on sources both ancient and modern, Wren attempted nothing short of a comprehensive re-evaluation of the history of classical architecture as the essential basis for re-formulating its use. Up to this time, no single source had offered such a coherent history. This is to be found in a series of four Tracts and, most clearly, in an incomplete 'Discourse on Architecture' sometimes identified as Tract five.[35] The first four were eventually published in 1750 by Wren's grandson in *Parentalia: Or, Memoirs of the Family of Wrens*, and the 'Discourse' survives as a

7 Section through the Church of the Holy Sepulchre, Jerusalem. Etching by Jacques Callot, from Bernardino Amico, *Trattato delle piante et imagini de sacri edificii di Terra Santa, disegnate in Gierusalemme secondo le regole della prospettiua, & vera misura della lor grandezza, etc.* (1620 edn), fig. 24

PREFACE xv

manuscript, in the hand of Wren's son, bound in a copy of the book now held in the Royal Institute of British Architects in London.[36] They are thought to date from the mid- to late 1670s and were worked on over time, with the 'Discourse' written slightly earlier than the fourth Tract, but their intended audience is unclear.[37] Wren sought in these Tracts the universal laws or what he termed the 'Grounds of Architecture' as a theoretical basis for the classical style of his own buildings.[38] This was much like his attempt to return to first principles in the study of nature at the Royal Society, and the Society's quest for other universal forms such as of speech and writing.[39] He noted in the 'Discourse' that his ambition was 'to endeavor to reform the Generality to a truer taste in Architecture by giving a larger Idea of the whole Art, beginning with the reasons and progress of it from the most remote Antiquity; and that in short, touching chiefly on some things, which have not been remark'd by others'.[40] As an aspect of this novelty, Wren's 'larger Idea' necessarily embraced 'the most remote Antiquity' of the East that pre-dated the Greek and Roman eras. The Orders were seen as originating not in Greece or Rome, as Vitruvius had maintained, but with the older Phoenician, or Tyrian, civilisation centred on Tyre in modern-day Lebanon, as well as with several of the ancient 'Wonders'. These buildings were, to Wren's mind, logical precursors to those of the Greeks and Romans, and he discussed these and other structures more or less chronologically in the Tracts. Hence he began his 'Discourse' with the legendary monuments cited in Genesis and for the most part described by Josephus – the first city, Enos in Syria inhabited by Noah, the two columns erected by the sons of Seth, Noah's Ark, the Tower of Babel as the 'first Peece of Civil Architecture' and the Great Pyramids of Egypt; he continued with what he regarded as monuments built with the Tyrian Order, which were also mentioned in the Bible – the temple of Dagon in Gaza destroyed by Samson and, in Jerusalem, the tomb of Absalom in the Kidron Valley and the Temple of Solomon. He moved on to Babylon and then to other early classical structures this time mentioned by Pliny, which were also supposedly built in the Tyrian style. Notable were the tomb of Mausolus (the king of Caria) at Halicarnassus that he understood as built in a Tyrian form of Doric, as well as that of the Etruscan king Lars Porsenna at Clusium in Tuscany with which the 'Discourse' abruptly ends. In Tract four Wren discussed the Greek Temple of Diana (in fact Artemis) at Ephesus that was credited with pioneering the Ionic, and the evocative forms of the Roman temples of Peace and War (Mars) in the Forum that displayed the Corinthian.[41]

Also mentioned in the Tracts, although not explicitly as part of this historical narrative, were the Roman Empire's first Christian cathedral, Hagia Sophia in Constantinople, the Holy Sepulchre in Jerusalem and the Byzantine churches in the Ottoman empire.[42] These surviving Byzantine domed buildings were particularly significant at this time because Anglican theologians were identifying them with original, or so-called 'primitive', Christianity (whose period in fact predated Constantine's foundation of Constantinople in 330): these Anglicans looked not to Rome and her Catholic churches, ties to which had been severed by the Reformation, but to the Eastern Church and its Byzantine buildings, as well as to Solomon's Temple, for Christianity's origins. Ancient Eastern cities too featured in Wren's Tracts as examples of the use of the colonnade in forming early urban settlements, notably at Alexandria in Egypt and Tadmor (Palmyra) in Syria identified with Solomon. Even though they were not mentioned in the Tracts, Persepolis and the Assyrian city of Nineveh were also known to Wren through travel accounts.

Wren most likely produced drafts of Solomon's Temple, since the minutes of the Royal Society meeting on 25 June 1712 recorded that: 'A letter was read from Dr. [William] Musgrave concerning Dr. [J.] Hudson's new designed Edition of Josephus. Mr. [Abraham] Hill said that Sir Christopher Wrenn had made severall draughts of Buildings mentioned in Josephus.'[43] In addition, he appears to have drawn, or supervised Hawksmoor in drawing, the tombs of Absalom, Porsenna and Mausolus, as well as the Ephesus temple and, by recent attribution, Hagia Sophia (see figs 28, 36, 42, 98 and 99).[44] He was particularly attracted to these tombs because of their structural complexity as recorded, in the case of the last two, by Pliny. Wren seems to have drawn them not only as an abstract exercise in structural logic but as inspiration for his work. When attempting their reconstruction as accurately and logically as possible, he united his knowledge of structural engineering with his antiquarian interests. In the spirit of contemporary natural and experimental philosophy, his acceptance of these and other enigmatic structures in the East was at all times conditioned by the need to explain them.[45] For example, one such practical problem that fascinated Wren was how the stones for the Temple of Solomon could have been transported, 'in an uneven Craggy Country as it is about Jerusalem' (asserted despite having never visited the Holy Land).[46] Wren went on in the 'Discourse' to calculate the capacity of each workman. And on the Tower of Babel he observed: 'it consisted of Eight several Stories'

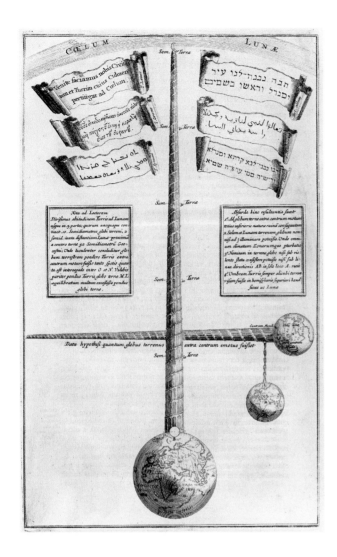

LEFT 8 The Tower of Babel and the earth, from Athanasius Kircher, *Turris Babel* (1679), p. 38

BELOW 9 Noah's Ark, from Athanasius Kircher, *Arca Noë* (1675), facing p. 117

but 'if they were all equal with the First would amount to *2,500* foot, which is not credible: the Form must be therefore Pyramidal'. Since the pyramid was the preferred form of the tomb in antiquity, it was reasonable to suppose that 'the Successors of Belus the son of Nimrod probably finish'd It, and made it His Sepulchre upon his Deification'.[47]

In this regard his attraction to the East was clearly not because of the exotic qualities commonly associated with it (they had been contrasted with the austerity of Rome in Shakespeare's *Antony and Cleopatra*, 1607, for example). Wren's explanation of legendary Eastern structures was similar to that of the hermetic philosopher Athanasius Kircher. In *Turris Babel* (1679) Kircher attempted to show how the Tower of Babel and the earth were counterbalanced, in the wake of the 'advances' in mechanics and physics that called into question the biblical structure (fig. 8). Equally, in *Arca Noë* (1675) he offered a rational interpretation of the miraculous ark in attempting to demonstrate how it worked (fig. 9).[48] And Wren's re-evaluation of architectural history to take account of Eastern buildings and cities, and to arrange them in some

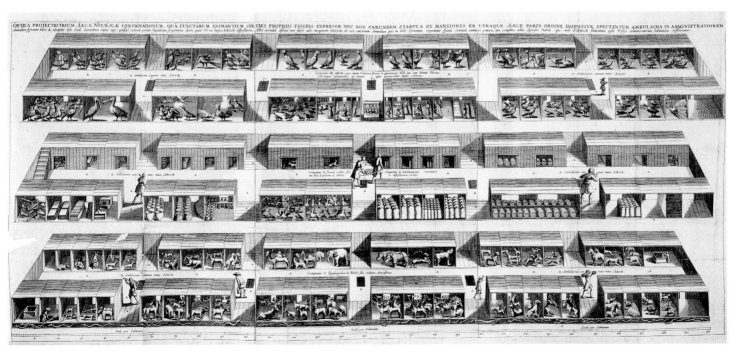

PREFACE xvii

kind of stylistic sequence, foreshadowed Fischer von Erlach's *Entwurff einer Historischen Architectur*, which was started in 1705, presented in manuscript to Charles VI in 1712 and published in Vienna in 1721.[49] This work was a radical departure from the Renaissance treatise, one now grounded in comparative studies of the hitherto largely neglected monuments of a wide range of cultures. Assyrian, Egyptian, Phoenician, Persian, Arabian, Turkish and Chinese monuments were imaginatively reconstructed from travel accounts, and were placed on an equal footing with the monuments of classical antiquity (fig. 10).

Although Wren's principal interest was in the origins of classical architecture and civilisation, the Gothic did not escape his attention. Despite the consensus among architectural theorists at the time disparaging Gothic,

10 'Mosque built by Sultan Orcanus II in Bursa', Turkey, and 'A mosque at Pest in Hungary', from Johann Bernhard Fischer von Erlach, *Entwurff einer Historischen Architectur* (1721), Book II, pl. 2

and Wren's own preference for the classical, he approved of the use of Gothic on a number of projects related to situation and function. This book will discuss how, in the context of his work at Westminster Abbey and some of his church towers with their pointed arches and spires, he sought to justify the Gothic style as a legitimate, Christian one by imagining its origins to lie in the Holy Land (albeit in buildings of the Arabs or 'Saracens'). Thus Wren will be shown to have attempted to trace the origins of both the classical and Gothic styles to the East. In this regard, his understanding of the region was shaped as much by his imagination as it was by the patchy physical evidence.

As this book will also show, Wren's view of architectural history not only justified the classical and Gothic styles but also directly informed his buildings, since he drew on legendary and surviving Eastern antiquities that featured in it, and in the Tracts more generally. Tyre and Jerusalem were home to the 'Tyrian' column that he saw as having formed a prototype for the Doric Order used on his hospital colonnades; Halicarnassus to the mausoleum that, when reconstructed by Wren, formed a 'Tyrian' model for novel church lanterns and steeples; Constantinople and Jerusalem to monumental columns, domes and churches based on the Greek cross, which informed his own versions in London; and Alexandria and Palmyra to urban colonnades of a type he would also propose. In the case of the dome in particular, ancient Rome provided only the Pantheon as a large-scale model.[50] Its dome rested on a drum; for ancient originals of domes on pendentives (which allowed them to sit on four columns and thereby cover square forms), examples had to be found further east. There were more modern examples of dome construction in Europe, such as at St Mark's in Venice, the medieval baptistery in Padua, Filippo Brunelleschi's Pazzi chapel in Florence and the early Baroque churches in Paris. But irrespective of Wren's knowledge of any or all of these, he was especially interested in the origins of the structural form in the ancient world. Equally, he was interested in the role of long colonnaded streets in laying out the first ancient cities, discussed at some length in the Tracts, rather than any particular European Renaissance colonnade. The urban role of the colonnade was far more evident in Roman cities of the East than it was in Rome itself, whose colonnades such as that of Pompey mentioned by Vitruvius (V.ix.1) had long disappeared.[51]

Wherever possible this book will draw on Wren's theoretical ideas as evidenced in his limited writings on architecture. These comprise his letters (written in 1665 from Paris on French architecture and in 1711 on the new Queen Anne churches), his reports on Salisbury Cathedral and Westminster Abbey, and most importantly his Tracts from the mid- to late 1670s.[52] Although these Tracts are the principal record of Wren's historical studies, his awareness of ancient writers started much earlier since they were essential to a classical education (which Wren had firstly at home, then briefly, or so it is thought, at Westminster School and subsequently at Wadham College in Oxford).[53] He went on to rely on Vitruvius and Herodotus for parts of his inaugural lecture in 1657 as Professor of Astronomy at Gresham College.[54] This too was published in *Parentalia*, as were reports by Wren's son of his father's views on ancient London as well as on Freemasonry and its role in the origins of Gothic architecture. While these second-hand reports should be treated with some caution, especially given that the book itself was not published until 1750, the first manuscript version (in the British Library) is dated 1719, that is four years before Wren's death, and he therefore had ample chance to approve its contents.[55]

Wren never saw any of the Eastern cities that interested him. In fact Paris was the only major foreign city he visited, despite the growing fashion to visit Rome on a Grand Tour.[56] Instead, he studied the ancient and modern buildings of the East from afar: he discussed them in meetings with the authors of travel books and fellow members of the Royal Society, and saw often sketchy descriptions and illustrations in the books in his library. This library is recorded in a sale catalogue of 1748.[57] The sale's lot numbers are referred to throughout this book, since the library is an important source of information on Wren's interests. Also examined is Hooke's library, to which Wren would have had easy access, as he would have to that of Evelyn, who like Hooke was a friend and colleague at the Royal Society.[58] Wren and Hooke collaborated particularly closely after the Fire on the City churches and the Monument as well as on the repair of Westminster Abbey.[59] Wren would have had equally easy access to the Society's library (the former Arundel library), catalogued by Hooke, as too to the collection of manuscripts of Robert Cotton focused on English Church chronicles and tales of chivalry (and occasional works on the East, most notably the twelfth-century 'Descriptio Constantinopolis').[60] Hooke's Diary (written in note form from 1672 to 1693 with a missing section between 1683 and 1688), together with the more famous and complete contemporary ones by Samuel Pepys and John Evelyn, provide important evidence as to the emerging knowledge of Eastern antiquity at this time.[61] These diaries testify to the flow and exchange of this knowledge in the 1670s and 1680s, from and between a multitude of sources including travellers, diplomats, clergymen, merchants and natural philosophers. They also record the discussions between Wren, Hooke and Evelyn, often within the Royal Society, concerning Eastern architecture. Hooke took a keen interest in Eastern cultures throughout his life, and he and Wren were active collaborators in the study of its antiquities: Hooke's Diary records them avidly discussing the form of the Temple of Solomon and of Hagia Sophia, for example.[62] In the course of studying the impact of Islamic culture on British art from 1500, John Sweetman observed in 1988 that, 'the amount of information about Islamic lands was building up prodigiously in both France and Britain during the last 40 years of the seventeenth century'.[63] Nevertheless it is important to emphasise that much of what was known was sketchy and often inaccurate, and with few illustrations. This led in some instances to misinterpretations (as particularly with Hagia Sophia) and, in Wren's case, to his imaginative reconstructions of (surviving and lost) buildings based on structural logic alone. But the absence of information and the fanciful nature of details recorded by ancient authors seem to have only stimulated his curiosity, not diminished it. On at least two occasions concerning the style of surviving structures (the Palmyra colonnades and the tomb of Absalom), inaccuracies in eye-witness reports fortunately helped Wren's argument rather than hindered it. His interest in the East was as much about the meaning of forms as it was about their dimensions: indeed, the relative obscurity of Eastern antiquity actively facilitated his narrative on the pre-Greek origin of the Orders, just as vagueness as to the style of Arab buildings facilitated his argument that the pointed arch had originated in the Holy Land.

While historians have focused on particular strands of Wren's interest in the East, be it the Tyrian or the Arabian, this study is the first to draw his concerns together to form a coherent picture and fully to acknowledge the importance of these concerns to his understanding of architecture's origin and meaning. It is also the first to relate this interest in the East to practice, that is, to explore its implications for the study of Wren's design of particular architectural forms and his conception of their meaning. The influence on him of the architecture of the Levant region was early overlooked, with Downes asserting in 1959 for example that 'exotic sources probably found no practical application in Wren'.[64] Over time, the importance of Eastern antiquity to Wren has gradually received greater recognition, alongside the growing awareness of the influence of the East on early modern Britain more generally. Lydia Soo, when republishing Wren's Tracts and other writings in 1998, studied his Tyrian theory and mentioned his ideas on Gothic's roots in the East.[65] In an article on the English in the Levant published in 2012, Soo briefly discussed the influence of Byzantine designs on Wren's City churches, explored much more fully here in Chapter Four.[66] When examining the Levant Company chaplain John Covel's journal record of Ottoman splendour, in an article published in 2017, Soo concluded by noting the influence of this splendour on Wren's ambition to 'nation build' through architecture.[67] She points out that the great empires of the East such as the Persian under the Shah or Sophy, the Indian under the Great Mogul, and especially the Ottoman under the Sultan, were of particular fascination at this time as models for the developing idea of a British nation. Pierre de la Ruffinière du Prey, when discussing Hawksmoor's churches in 2000, considered as a prelude Wren's interest in Solomon's Temple and Hagia Sophia in the context of the contemporary theological fascination with the Eastern Church and its Byzantine legacy. This understanding is developed further and applied here in Chapter Four by tracing the influence of Byzantine churches on Wren's own church domes and plans. For it was felt by Anglicans at the time that the closer English churches and liturgy were modelled on these buildings, the more legitimate would be the architectural and liturgical experience. Hence this study will go further than Soo and du Prey by suggesting that the consequences of expanding geographical horizons were immediate, not just profound. Du Prey was somewhat dismissive of Wren's historical narrative, observing that the last two Tracts 'embark on a more or less tortuous route through the history of architecture loosely organised around the evolution of a proto-Doric order to which Wren gave the name Tyrian'.[68] Chapter One demonstrates just how fundamental the Tyrian Order was for Wren in justifying classical architecture in general and specific structures, used as models for his steeple designs, in particular.

Wren's wider interest in the East is also placed for the first time in the context of the growing contemporary awareness of Arab and Turkish culture, as too in Freemasonry and its own cultivation of Eastern roots. This book is equally novel in examining the parallels made in the seventeenth century between the Stuart kings and Eastern rulers, in particular Solomon and Constantine, and between London and Eastern Christian centres, in particular Jerusalem and Constantinople. It serves as the prequel to my two monographs on Wren's pupils, and their esoteric and sometimes 'Gothic' style, entitled *Nicholas Hawksmoor: Rebuilding Ancient Wonders* (published in 2002 and in paperback in 2007) and *Sir John Vanbrugh: Storyteller in Stone* (published in 2008). Both these volumes examined the influence of Wren's theories, as well as that of mosques in Hawksmoor's work and Mogul buildings in Vanbrugh's. And the book also serves as a companion to my earlier *St Paul's Cathedral: Sir Christopher Wren* (1995) that explored the application of Wren's Tracts in the design of St Paul's.

Wren's interest in the East found a wider context in the profound impact of the Muslim world on early modern Britain. The work of John Sweetman, Nabil Matar and Gerald MacLean has shown the extent to which English-speaking men and women knew about Muslim culture and societies in this period. Awareness of the East, especially of Ottoman and Persian society, was actively promoted through the by then well-established links with Muslim traders in such commodities as carpets, coffee and silk.[69] Marble too was imported from the Levant, and its quality meant that it was proposed as the source for the columns in Wren's design for a mausoleum for Charles I at Windsor Castle in 1678.[70] This trade with the Ottomans, notably in Egypt, the Holy Land, Syria and with Turkey itself, was facilitated primarily by the Levant Company after its foundation in 1581; and with Persia and India, by the East India Company after 1600.[71] When it came to trade and other relations with the Muslims, Britons did not express the tendency towards possessiveness, or domination, that later gave rise to what Edward Said termed 'Orientalism'.[72] Said's seminal, if controversial, work of 1978 traced the image of Muslims and Arabs in European culture from the second half of the eighteenth century until the twentieth and illustrated how European writers 'constructed' and 'defined' the 'natives' in order to prepare for, and justify, the process of colonisation of the Levant and North Africa. His was a study of the West's *image* of the East from Napoleon's invasion of Egypt in 1798 to the present, during which time the Ottoman empire began its decline both militarily and intellectually: he did not deal with the earlier, Renaissance reception of the East or that by later inquisitors such as the merchants, clergymen, travellers and scientists discussed here. During Wren's lifetime, the Ottoman empire was feared (militarily), admired (commercially and culturally) and condemned (theologically) but was not the object of British colonial ambition.[73] Matar and MacLean have also recognised the 'allure' of Islam for significant numbers of Christian converts during the seventeenth century and that, because of its magnitude and civilisation, the Turkish empire played a significant role in the formation of British history and identity.[74] Equally, they have pointed out the over-arching impact of Arabic civilisation on England at this time. As will be seen, Wren's understanding of the development of the Gothic, based on an imaginary world of Arab mosques and a much more real one of Arabic learning, formed part of this influence.

For Wren and many of his contemporaries, the concept of a 'renaissance' of antiquity was thus a wholly different affair to that of his forerunner in the royal Office of building Works, Inigo Jones. Whereas Jones more often than not turned to Vitruvius and the Renaissance architect Andrea Palladio in search of the rules of classical architecture, Wren embraced a much wider range of ancient and modern sources. Nor for that matter did he prioritise visiting Rome as Jones had done. When building the dome at St Paul's he even sought the advice of a merchant with first-hand knowledge of Turkish structures, meeting him on site. In so doing and in tracing the origins of architecture beyond the canonical Greeks and Romans to the Phoenicians and later Saracens, Wren's approach reflected the emerging view of the world encouraged by the Royal Society in which the exotic would become familiar. As the following chapters will show, Wren formulated what he regarded as a plausible history of classical architecture – one which took account of surviving and legendary buildings of ancient civilisations other than the Roman and of Roman structures further east than the shores of Italy (that were not necessarily identified as Roman): this led him to the domes of Jerusalem and Constantinople, the Solomonic colonnades at Palmyra and the Tyrian-styled tombs of the Levant. His parallel interest in the origins of natural history and experimental philosophy equally embraced the East, and particularly the ancient civilisations of the Chaldeans, Syrians and Egyptians. The insights of these cultures only served to underline the sophistication, as he saw it, of their architecture. Wren thus identified the East as nothing less than the cradle of classical civilisation. In this book, each chapter will take as its theme an element or elements whose introduction or development in English architecture was encouraged by Wren – the Orders and classical church lanterns and steeples, Gothic churches with towers and pointed arches, classical churches with domes and plans based on Greek crosses, and finally city plans with colonnades and triumphal columns. They will examine the extent to which these elements were inspired and given meaning, or assisted in a practical way, by Wren's knowledge and imagination of their ancient originals in the East.

INTRODUCTION

EAST MEETS WEST AT THE ROYAL SOCIETY

'That which the Eastern Nations used'

One of the main stimuli for the interest of Wren, Evelyn and Hooke in the East was the Royal Society, of which they were founding Fellows. Indeed, Wren serves as its President from 1681 to 1683. Although the Society's study of Eastern architecture was only one concern among many, as with architecture more generally, it formed part of the quest for 'universal' knowledge. The interest in the East also had an economic motivation, since it was a major source of trade. In the Society's early years it elected a sizeable group of Fellows on the basis of their first-hand knowledge of the East, notably Henry Blount, John Chardin, George Wheler, Thomas Smith, Paul Rycaut, Francis Vernon and André de Monceaux (fig. 11).[1] Fellows paid particular attention to the antiquities of Greece, Egypt and Syria, and to the modern cultural practices of the Ottoman empire and Persia.[2] This reflected the wider realisation in the early modern period that there were 'several different Orients' – from Turkey in the north and Egypt in the south to China in the more distant east – and a consequent desire to distinguish

11 Sir John Chardin, with a globe indicating the Arabian Sea, portrait by John Michael Wright, *c.*1690. Oil on canvas, 124 x 100 cm. British Embassy, the Hague: Government Art Collection

between them.[3] The 1686 issue of the Society's *Philosophical Transactions* was entirely dedicated to China, for example, in the wake of the well-known studies by Jan Nieuhof and Athanasius Kircher.[4] Fellows were also interested in the East as the source of natural and experimental philosophy, or what might be termed early science. Wren was for example well aware of the arcane medical and astronomical practices of the ancient Egyptians and Chaldaeans, located in Mesopotamia. As this introduction will show, he cited these practices in his inaugural lecture as Professor of Astronomy at the Society's forerunner, Gresham College, in 1657. However, the Society's information on the civilisations of the East was sketchy. Sources took the form of a limited number of letters to the Society from travelling Fellows and Levant Company diplomats, a few journals of their expeditions, face to face meetings between Fellows and visiting or returning travellers, and most important of all, travel literature that was sometimes illustrated.

In 1682 Hooke was urging the Society's Fellows to collect as many travel books as possible in order to aid the enquiry into Eastern civilisations.[5] Whereas the library of Inigo Jones had for the most part been limited to books on Italy and its history,[6] Wren and Hooke's collections reflected the more extensive travels of their contemporaries in including works on the peoples and

trades of many countries in Europe and beyond.[7] Wren owned works on Denmark, Germany, Bohemia and Switzerland,[8] not to mention those on countries further afield such as in Africa, the South Seas, Chile, Peru, Argentina, Brazil and America, the East Indies, Guinea and Ethiopia.[9] He collected a large number of popular travel books on the Eastern Mediterranean and its ancient civilisations, including those by George Sandys on Egypt and the Holy Land (1670), Jacob Spon and George Wheler on Greece and the Levant (1678 and 1682), Guillaume-Joseph Grelot on Constantinople (the English translation of 1683 and a French edition of 1689), Chardin on Turkey and Persia (1686), Jean de Thévenot on the Levant (1687), Cornelis de Bruyn (or Le Brun) also on the Levant (1702) and Henry Maundrell on the pilgrimage route from Aleppo in Syria to Jerusalem (1703; fig. 12; see fig. 14).[10] Grelot's work was particularly well illustrated and offered the most reliable views of Constantinople and the Hagia Sophia to date (see figs 106–13 and 117–18). Hooke too owned editions of Sandys (1627), Grelot (1681), Chardin (1686), and Thévenot (1665 and 1681), all of which were illustrated, as well as other popular volumes on the Levant including those by Blount (1669) and François Savinien d'Alquié (1671).[11] His Diary provides an important record of his long-running interest in travel books. For example, in May 1673 Hooke noted that he had 'read Monconys voyage', referring to Balthasar de Monconys's *Journal des Voyages* (1665), volume one of which included Egypt, Syria and Constantinople.[12] Some sixteen years later, in December 1689 he recorded that he had 'borrowed *Thevenots Voyages*' from the astronomer and Royal Society Fellow Edmond Halley, and that he had transcribed alphabets from it.[13]

Travel writers were, however, often distrusted and presumed guilty of exaggeration. Thomas Fuller in 1642 had cautioned against relying too heavily on the accounts of travellers, who were liable to exaggeration and 'usually count the best they ever saw to be the best that was ever seen; yea, in charity will lend a church some hundreds of feet to help out the dimensions thereof'.[14] By way of example he referred to Pierre Belon, a sixteenth-century traveller or 'modern eye-witness', who had 'counteth three hundred and sixty-five doors in the present church of Sophia, which hath but four, as an exact traveller hath observed' (with a footnote referring his reader to Sandys's *Travels: containing an history of the original and present state*

12 Aleppo, from Henry Maundrell, *Journey from Aleppo to Jerusalem at Easter, A.D. 1697* (1703), p. 1

of the Turkish Empire). Given the difficulty of travelling to countries in the Levant, reports from the region were frequently inaccurate. Hooke recorded in his Diary in July 1693, for example: 'News of uprore at Constantinople' involving a false account of the strangulation of the Grand Signior, the Grand Vizier (Prime Minister) and the French ambassador, as well as the plundering of the Topkapi Palace.[15] The Royal Society's aim at all times was for accuracy, prioritising eye-witness reports over more romanticised publications or second-hand accounts.[16]

From its foundation in 1660, the Society had been particularly interested in promoting the discovery and dissemination of 'useful' knowledge. The albeit still limited studies of the East played a part in this purpose. As a tangible expression of this aim, the Society's early members – in particular Hooke and Evelyn, as well as Robert Moray and Henry Oldenburg (the Society's first Secretary and editor of the *Transactions* until his death in 1677) – proposed to complete nothing less than a collaborative 'history' of all trades: this project (only partially realised) aspired to produce comprehensive descriptions of trade processes, and owed its origins to Francis Bacon's proposal for a technological counterpart to his projected 'natural history' of minerals and materials.[17] Information about technical processes such as tanning and salt-making was collected, to serve as data for experiments and so that improvements in one area could inform another. Practical information from the East, via merchants and diplomats, fed into these utilitarian aims, especially since the protagonists of the trade histories were also among the Fellows most keen to gain insight into Eastern cultures. As will be seen in Chapter Three, Wren enquired after Ottoman building practices via one such merchant and in so doing fell in line with the Society's interest in craft processes. Its more general interest in the architecture of the East, still only sketchily understood, not only stimulated enquiries into the ancient tombs and temples Wren mentioned in the Tracts, as will be seen in the following chapter, but also modern trade buildings. For example, the buildings used to organise domestic trade in the Ottoman empire were brought to the attention of the Society through travelling Fellows such as Rycaut. Concerning market halls he observed in 1667: 'in these Buildings the *Turks* are extraordinary Magnificent in most parts of the Empire, having united to many of them a stately *Mosch* [mosque], Baths, and Shops for Artisans and Trades-men to supply all the necessities of the Travellers'. He continued that the 'form of these Buildings is for the most part according to the model of the highest and stateliest of our Halls, covered with Lead, though not altogether so high Roofed' and that 'in a few of them are Apartments for different Companies'.[18]

Related to this concern with trade was the Society's ambition to improve agriculture. Botany formed an aspect of this, and Evelyn was particularly interested in the plants of the East.[19] He produced a list of 'Coronarie Flowres for the parterr & Bordures' consisting of fifty species of which more than half came from Turkey.[20] In line with the Society's practical aims, and botanist travellers in the Levant such as Leonhard Rauwolf (1537–96), Evelyn sought to understand the health benefits of foreign horticultural practices. For example, he noted in his Diary in September 1683 that, as regards 'the *Zinnar Tree* or *Platanus*', his neighbour Christopher Boone (a merchant and member of the board of the East India Company) 'told me that since their falling to plant this Tree about the City of *Ispahan* in *Persia*, the Plague (which formerly much infested that place) has exceedingly abated of its mortal effects, & rendered it very healthy; & that they impute it to the salutary shade of this Tree'.[21] Ways to alleviate the plague would have had particular potency in the light of London's experiences in 1665.

The Society also looked beyond the East in its quest for useful knowledge such as this. In July 1670 the traveller André de Monceaux sent Oldenburg a copy of François Bernier's work on his encounter with the Mughal emperors, asking to 'know the sentiment, your Illustrious Society hath of this Piece'; the work proved interesting enough for Oldenburg to translate it into English.[22] Commanded by Louis XIV to purchase ancient Eastern manuscripts and coins, de Monceaux had also travelled extensively in the Levant in 1668–9, including to Constantinople, Aleppo and Baalbek in Lebanon. Writing to Oldenburg in October 1670, the Dutch poet and composer Constantijn Huygens reported that de Monceaux 'has these last years travelled in the Levant and has made very interesting observations everywhere that he has been, especially concerning buildings and ancient ruins, of which he has brought back an incredible quantity of drawings which deserve to be published and will be one of these days'. Moreover, since de Monceaux wanted to visit England, Huygens asked Oldenburg to be 'so good as to make him acquainted with Mr. Wren, I am sure you will give pleasure to both, since they both delight in architecture, about which this traveler is very learned'.[23] Oldenburg replied in November that he would indeed make de Monceaux 'known to Mr. Wren, who will be very glad to discuss with him Persian architecture and so on'.[24] During his visit, de Monceaux was made a Fellow of the Society, on 15 December 1670, but it is not known whether the meeting with Wren actually took place.[25]

As this introduction will illustrate, the study of Persian, Egyptian, Syrian and most of all Ottoman cultures provided the Society with the raw material for theoretical reflection. Wren's refashioning of the history of architecture and his search for its origins in Eastern civilisations formed part of this.

'THE EASTERN FASHION, AFTER THE PERSIAN MODE': EASTERN TRAVELS AT THE ROYAL SOCIETY

With its mighty pyramids and mysterious sphinxes, Egypt posed a particular challenge to the classical ideal. The Royal Society took a keen interest in Egypt, especially its antiquities with their non-classical forms and decoration. A description of Egyptian temples was published in the *Transactions* in May 1671,[26] while a challenge by Robert Huntington to the accuracy of Johann Michael Vansleb's 1677 account of Egypt appeared in July 1684; this formed part of a description of two porphyry obelisks that were illustrated in December 1685 and cannot have escaped Wren and Hooke's attention.[27] Hooke owned the major contemporary studies of Egyptian (and also of Chinese) antiquity published by Kircher, noting in his Diary in March 1676 that he 'saw Kircher's sphinx' in reference to the *Sphinx Mystagoga* published that year (fig. 13).[28] Hooke many times recorded his interest in Egypt, as for example in April of the following year when he 'discoursed' about the Egyptians or in February 1690 when he went with Henry Hunt to see 'a fair mummy 5⅔ high, head & face bare & entire, hieroglyphyck, much the same as in Repository'.[29] The Repository of the Royal Society was a collection of exotic objects, from fossils to specimens, representing a kind of cabinet of curiosities that was eventually transferred to the British Museum.[30] It also had a practical purpose, housing minerals that the trade historians had collected.[31] Hunt was its Keeper, having gone to work for Hooke in 1672 as an illustrator and become the Society's Laboratory Operator in 1676.[32]

The pyramids were of especial interest within the Society, having been the most illustrated of Egyptian antiquities. As the Preface pointed out, Serlio had included a woodcut of a pyramid at Giza together with a sphinx in the third book of his treatise of 1540, as had Sandys in his *Travels* of 1615 (fig. 14; see fig. 6). The astronomer and traveller John Greaves illustrated the Great Pyramid in his *Pyramidographia: or a description of the pyramids in*

Egypt (1646), a work praised by Oldenburg and a model for imaginative reconstructions of the type undertaken by Wren (fig. 15).[33] In the spirit of Kircher's studies, Wren attempted in his 'Discourse on Architecture' to explain the construction of the pyramids as part of what he termed his 'larger Idea of the whole Art':

> I proceed next to those mighty Works of Antiquity, the Wonderful *Pyramids* of Egypt, yet remaining without considerable decay after almost *4000* years: for *2000* years agoe, they were reckon'd by Historians of uncertain Original. I cannot think any Monarch however Despotick could effect such things meerly

13 Fanciful view of the Pyramids and the mummy crypt (after Giovanni Battista Balatri) by Coenraet Decker, from Athanasius Kircher, *Sphinx Mystagoga* (1676), title-page

4 CHRISTOPHER WREN

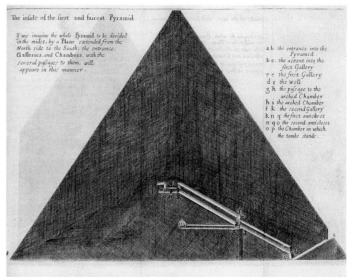

for Glory; I guess there were reasons of State for it. Egypt was certainly very early Populous, because so Productive of Corn by the help of the Nile, in a manner without labour. They deriv'd the River, when it rose, all over the Flat of the Delta, and as the People increas'd, over a great deal of Land that lay higher.[34]

Wren reflected the Society's interest in the Nile, which formed part of its aim to understand irrigation in order to improve agriculture. In this vein a Fellow of the Society, Peter Wyche, produced *A Short Relation of the River Nile, of its Source and Current, and of its overflowing the Campagnia of Egypt* (1669). Hooke had a copy, which he lent to Abraham Hill, the Society's Treasurer, in December 1673.[35] This work was a translation by Wyche of a Portuguese manuscript by a Jesuit, Jerónimo Lobo, made at the request of Society Fellows and most notably Robert Southwell (the ambassador to Portugal) who had obtained the work from Lobo.[36] At the outset of his translation, Wyche praised the Portuguese for their daily discoveries of 'the Wonders and Mysteries of the *East*'.[37] Wren continued with apparent reference to this work on the Nile, as also to Genesis on Joseph (41:48), in noting that:

LEFT 14   The Pyramids and the Sphinx, from George Sandys, *A relation of a Journey begun an: Dom: 1610. Foure bookes. Containing a description of the Turkish Empire, of Ægypt, of the Holy Land* (1615), Book II, p. 128

RIGHT 15   The Great Pyramid at Giza, from John Greaves, *Pyramidographia: or a description of the pyramids in Egypt* (1646), between pp. 70 and 71

The Nile did not always Flow high enough for a great Part of the then inhabited Country, and without the Nile They must either starve or prey upon those who had Corn; This must needs create Mutiny and Bloodshed, to prevent which it was the Wisdom of their Ancient Kings and Priests to Exact a certain Proportion of Corn, and lay it up for those who wanted the benefit of the River when it disappointed their sowing. Thus Joseph lay'd up for Seven Years; and sur'ly He was not first: this Provision being ever so essentially necessary to support the Popularity, and consequently the Grandure of the Kingdom; and continu'd so in all Ages, till the Turks neglected all the upper Canales, except one which still supply's Alexandria. Now what was the consequence? It was not for the Health of the Common People, nor Policy of the Government, for them to be fed in Idleness; great Multitudes were therefore imploy'd in that which requir'd no great Skill, the Sawing of Stone square to a few different Scantlings; nor was there any need of Scaffolding or Engines, for hands only would raise them from Step to Step: a little teaching serv'd to make them set Line: and thus these great Works in which some Thousands of hands might be imploy'd at once, rose with Expedition.[38]

For Wren, the act of building and of royal statecraft, whether by ancient Egyptians or modern Englishmen, went hand in hand. He would have found this view reinforced in his copy of Jean Foy-Vaillant's study of Egyptian monarchy and its coins entitled *Historia Ptolemaeorum Ægypti Regum* (1701; Lot 110), as too in an

earlier companion volume on Syrian monarchy entitled *Historia regum Syriae* (1681; Lot 70).[39]

Fellows of the Society were also interested in the remains of ancient cities in the East, especially the Assyrian city of Nineveh and the Persian capital of Persepolis (fig. 16). Persepolis was understood by contemporaries to be exceedingly ancient, John Webb having observed in 1669 that some would have an 'inscription at *Persepolis* more ancient than the Flood'.[40] In this regard, the first-hand experience of the city by John Chardin attracted the attention of Hooke, Wren and Evelyn (see figs 165–6). Chardin was a merchant adventurer and, like his fellow countryman Jean-Baptiste Tavernier, a trader in precious stones who had arrived in England in August 1680. He spent most of the remainder of his life in the country, and in November 1681 was knighted by Charles II for services to the East India Company (or, it has been argued, on payment of a fee).[41] On 17 July 1680 Hooke recorded a visit to the celebrated French traveller.[42] Five days later he reported to the Royal Society, with Wren in the chair (as Vice President) that 'moʳ. Chardin was in Town and that he had spoken wth him. he was desired to Indeavour to bring him the next Day to the Society'.[43] This meeting did not take place, however, and the following month Evelyn and Wren with John Hoskins (the Society's future President) visited Chardin as emissaries of the Society. There was no shortage of suitable candidates for this meeting among the Fellowship, so Wren's presence indicates both his keen interest and the expected architectural content of the conversation. According to Evelyn's account, faithfully recorded in his Diary, both Nineveh and Persepolis were avidly discussed: the entry is quoted at some length for its details of this meeting between Wren and the great traveller resplendent 'in his Eastern habite':

> I went to visit a French Stranger, one Monsieur *Jardine*…I was desir'd by the *Ro. Society* in their name, to salute him, & to let him know how glad they should be to receive him, if he pleased to do them that honour: &c. There were appointed to accompanie me Sir *Jo[hn]. Hoskins* and Sir *Chr. Wren* &c. We found him at his lodging, in his Eastern habite…After the usual Civilities, we told him, we much desired an account of the extraordinary things he must have seene; having (as we understood) traveld over land, those places, where few, if any *northern Europeans* used to go, as the Black & Caspian Sea, *Mingrelia, Bagdat, Nineve[h], (Persepolis),* &c: He told us the things most worthy of our sight, would be, the draughts he had caused to be made of some noble ruines &c: for that (besides his little talent that way) he had carried two very good Painters along

16 The Tachara (Palace of Darius the Great), completed in 486 BC, Persepolis in Persia

with him, to draw Landskips, Measure, and designe the remainders of the *Palace* which *Alexander* burnt in his frolique at *Persepolis*, with divers Temples, Columns, Relievos, & statues, yet extant, which he affirm'd were Sculptures far exceeding, any thing he had observ'd either at *Rome*, Greece or any other part of the World, where Magnificence was in estimation: That there was there an Inscription, of Letters not intelligible, though exceedingly intire; but was extreamely sorry he could not gratifie the Curiosity of the *Society*, at present, his things, not being yet out of the ship.[44]

Chardin's emphasis that the monuments in Persepolis eclipsed anything that Rome or Greece had to offer can only have further whetted Wren's appetite for information on Eastern antiquities. Just before this meeting, on 9 August Hooke had reported to the bookseller Octavian Pulleyn that Chardin 'carried with him a painter who hath drawn all things that were curious that he [met] with as particularly the Ruins and inscriptions and Basso relives of Chilmenr, supposed to be Persepolis' (see figs 165–6).[45] The painter in question was Grelot, and his on-site drawings, unavailable on this occasion, were of especial interest to the Society. One of its chief concerns was with the accuracy of such reports, in avoiding romantic descriptions found in some travel literature, and the drawings would have helped corroborate Chardin's account.[46] Evelyn continued his entry by explaining: 'so we failed of seeing his Papers; but it was told us by others, that he durst indeede not open or show them, 'til he had first shew'd them to the French King; though of this he himself said nothing'. The interest of Louis XIV in Persian antiquities has already been noted.

The three men also discussed with Chardin the city of Nineveh in upper Mesopotamia that, like Persepolis, was one of the oldest cities in antiquity: 'On farther discourse, he told us that *Nineveh* was a vast Citty, all now buried in her ruines, and the Inhabitants building on the subterranean Vaults, which were (as appeared) the first stories of the old Cittie; That there were frequently found, huge Vases of fine Earth, *Columns*, & other Antiquities &c:'.[47] Evelyn had prior knowledge of Nineveh, having recorded in his Diary in December 1673 a meeting with some unidentified Syrian visitors:

> I had some discourse with certain strangers, not unlearned, who had been born not far from old *Nineveh*: They assur'd me the ruines being still extant, & vast, wonderfull was the buildings, Vaults, Pillars, & magnificent fragments now buried, & remaining: but little could they say of the Toure of *Babel* that satisfied me: but the description of the amœnitie and fragrancy of the Country for health, & cheerfulnesse, did almost ravish me; so sensibly they spake of the excellent aire & climat, in respect of our cloudy & splenetic Country.[48]

Given that the ruins of ancient cities in Greece and Italy for the most part lay unexplored, this excitement at eye-witness reports of two ancient Eastern cities is hardly surprising. First-hand accounts would have been much more powerful than any written descriptions. Such excitement must have been heightened by the fact that the architectural forms there were non-classical (that is, not Graeco-Roman). Take for example the monumental free-standing columns at Persepolis, with their non-Vitruvian capitals illustrated by Chardin in 1711 (as previously by Thomas Herbert in 1634 and 1665, see figs 163–4).[49] Moving from architectural matters, Chardin also spoke to Wren and Evelyn about the peoples he had seen on his travels: according to Evelyn, the Frenchman reported: 'That in *Persia* are yet a race of *Igniculi*, that still Worship the Sunn, & the fire as Gods', and finally 'he spake also of Japon, & China, & of the many greate errours of our late Geographers &c'.[50] The latter addressed one of the key concerns of the Society. Two years after this visit, in 1682 Chardin was elected a Fellow of the Society on Wren's nomination, bringing him into further contact with Wren and Hooke. In December 1683 Evelyn recorded another visit to Chardin, and then in March 1684 he noted that he 'dined at my L.[ord] *Keepers*' (of the Great Seal) 'and brought to him *Sir John Chardin*: who shewed him his accurate draughts of his travels in Persia &c'.[51] Evelyn was at pains to emphasise the accuracy of these drawings, finally available, in order, perhaps, to elicit support for their publication (in 1686). The Lord Keeper in question was Francis North, the brother of the architect Roger North and of the Levant merchant Dudley North. Chardin's entry into London society was thus facilitated by Evelyn and Wren, and for both the Frenchman was clearly an intriguing source of information, beyond the still-limited publications on Ottoman and Persian buildings and cities. It is no surprise therefore that when his *Journal du Voyage du Chevalier Chardin en Perse et aux Indes Orientales* eventually appeared in London in 1686 in parallel French and English editions, Chardin presented Evelyn with a first edition with the inscription 'Pour Monsieur Evelin par son tres humble et tres obeissant serviteur Chardin'.[52] Wren had the French edition and Hooke had both. These editions contained Chardin's journey from Paris to Isfahan, which included

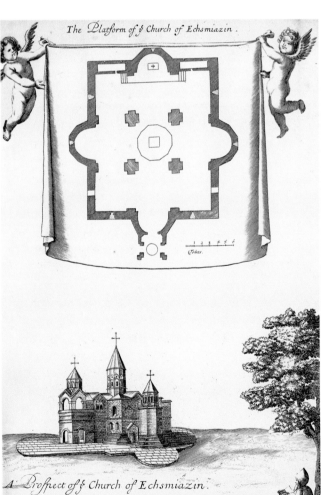

ABOVE 17 View of the Cathedral of Echmiadzin, Armenia, from John Chardin, *Travels* (1686), between pp. 244 and 245

LEFT 18 Plan of the Cathedral of Echmiadzin, Armenia, from John Chardin, *Travels* (1686), between pp. 248 and 249

BELOW 19 Funerary chamber of Shah Safi at his mausoleum at Qom in Persia, from John Chardin, *Travels* (1686), between pp. 398 and 399

Constantinople, and contained images of the Kara Koyunlu mausoleum at Yerevan and the Byzantine Cathedral of Echmiadzin, both in Armenia, and Shah Safi's tomb at Qom with its pendentives and dome (figs 17–19). The more complete version, describing further south in Persia and including detailed views of Persepolis, finally appeared in 1711 (see figs 165–6).

Persian culture – or what passed for Persian, both ancient and modern – had already featured in publications during the English Renaissance.[53] Johann Sleidan's work on the ancient kingdom was translated in 1563 as *A Briefe Chronicle of the foure principall Empyres. To witte of Babilon, Persia, Grecia and Rome*, and was republished in 1627. Herbert, who accompanied Dodmore Cotton's diplomatic mission to Persia in 1627–8, had published an account of the country and its monarchy in his *Relation of some Yeares Travaile* of 1634 (Evelyn owned a 1638 edition and Hooke the enlarged, 1667 one).[54] With the illustrations were descriptions of some of the novel antique forms at Persepolis, including for example, 'a *Daemon* of as uncouth and ugly a shape as well could be imagined…and of a gigantick size…discovering a most dreadful visage 'twixt Man and Beast' (see fig. 164).[55] On his return, Herbert was painted in Persian dress.[56] Chardin and he were not the only figures to dress in 'Eastern habite'. Turbans had been worn in the Tudor court, and when Pepys visited Philip Howard in November 1666 he found him dressed in a 'night-gown and turban like a Turk'.[57] Eastern clothing, in the form of the Persian vest, influenced even Charles II. Evelyn recorded in October 1666:

> to Court, it being the first time his *Majesties* putting himselfe solemnly into the *Eastern fashion* of Vest, changing doublet, stiff Collar, [bands] & Cloake &c: into a comely Vest, after the *Persian* mode with girdle or shash, & Shoe strings & Garters, into bouckles, of which some were set with precious stones, resolving never to alter it, & to leave the French mode, which had hitherto obtained to our great expense & reproach.[58]

Evelyn went on to imply that this change was in part a result of his publication of *Tyrannus, or the Mode* (1661). This was a pamphlet in which, rather than recommending French fashion, he 'tooke occasion to describe the Comelinesse & usefulnesse of the Persian clothing in the very same manner, his Majestie [would] clad himself'.[59] It has been suggested that this apparent knowledge of Persian costume during the reign of Charles II was acquired via their miniatures, as well as through Eastern subjects in plays, but Persian dress had enjoyed a fairly high profile in the first Stuart court.[60] In his role as court architect, Jones had designed masque costumes of 'A Noble Persian Youth' and 'Queen Zenobia', a third-century queen of the Palmyrene empire.[61] The adventurer Robert Shirley and his wife were painted in Rome by Anthony van Dyck in 1622, both resplendent in Persian costume (fig. 20).[62] Shirley and his brother, Anthony, had travelled extensively in Persia from 1599 on a mission to promote trade with England and persuade the Persian king to ally himself with the Christian princes of Europe against the Turks. Their experiences were published in *Sir Antony Sherley His Relation of His Travels into Persia. The Dangers, and Distresses, which befell him* (1613).[63]

Like Evelyn, Hooke was also interested in the Persians, both ancient and modern. He owned many books on their culture to which Wren would have had easy access. For example, in January 1689 Hooke borrowed (and subsequently bought) Joseph Labrosse's *Gazophylacium Linguae Persarum, Clari Italicae, Lat. & Gallicae Linguae reseratum* (1684), which was the first accurate Persian dictionary composed using the knowledge of missionaries, merchants and other travellers in Persia.[64] He owned some of the main works by travellers in Persia, not only the copies of Chardin's *Travels* (1686) but also Adam Olearius's *The Voyages and Travels of the Ambassadors sent by Frederick Duke of Holstein, to the Great Duke of Muscovy, and the King of Persia* (1662, first published in 1647), and Jean-Baptiste Tavernier's *Voyages thro' Turkey into Persia and the East Indies, with Figures* (1678 edition; fig. 21).[65] The content of Tavernier's work had been reported to the Royal Society and published in the *Transactions* in November 1676.[66] Hooke noted keenly in his Diary in September 1677 that 'Taverniers voyages first sold' and early in the following year bought this copy of the English translation.[67] In November 1688 he recorded that he had read Henry Lord's *A Display of two forraigne sects in the East Indies: sect of the Banians…and sect of the Persees* (1630), the title-page of which illustrated a Persian 'Daroo' (or ancient priest), and in June 1689 that he had bought the French translation of Jan Struys's *Voyages* (1681) which included travels in Persia and a fanciful illustration of Persepolis.[68]

The Turks held a particular fascination for Wren's contemporaries, due to their power in matters of commerce and war. Their empire could hardly be ignored, as a powerful enemy of Christians from the Crusades onwards. Pepys observed in his Diary, for example, in September 1663 that, 'Every day brings newes of the Turke's advance into Germany, to the awakening of all the Christian Princes thereabouts.'[69] Oldenburg wrote to Robert Boyle on 24 August 1665 to assure him that

following the reported conquest of Mecca by the Messianic pretender Sabbatai Sevi, 'now ye Christians need not fear ye Turks any more, there being work enough cut out for ym at Meccah'.[70] Well-known illustrated works on the Turks had been published in the previous century, notably those in French by Nicolas de Nicolay (owned by Hooke),[71] and in Italian by the Venetian historian Francesco Sansovino.[72] More limited essays on the 'wicked' Turks had also appeared in English, by John Foxe in 1570, William Biddulph in 1609 and Henry Marsh in 1633.[73] These were followed by a much less prejudiced view offered by Blount in 1636 based on careful observation, befitting a future Fellow of the Royal Society: he went so far as to describe the Turks as 'an other kind of civilitie, different from ours, but no less pretending'.[74] As will be seen, Wren reflected this open-mindedness with regard to Turkish achievements when enquiring about their dome construction. An important English study of the military and political aspects of the Ottoman empire was Richard Knolles's *The Generall Historie of the Turkes*, which first appeared in 1603 and ran to many editions. A further major study appeared during Wren's lifetime, written by the Society Fellow Rycaut. The work's title expressed its wide scope and anti-Islamic polemic: *The Present State of the Ottoman Empire containing the maxims of the Turkish politie, the most material points of the Mahometan religion, their sects*

LEFT 20   Sir Robert Shirley in Eastern dress, portrait by Sir Anthony van Dyck, 1622. Oil on canvas, 214 × 129 cm. Petworth House, West Sussex

RIGHT 21   Jean-Baptiste Tavernier, portrait by Nicolas de Largillière, c.1678. Oil on canvas, 212 × 121 cm. Herzog Anton Ulrich Museum, Braunschweig

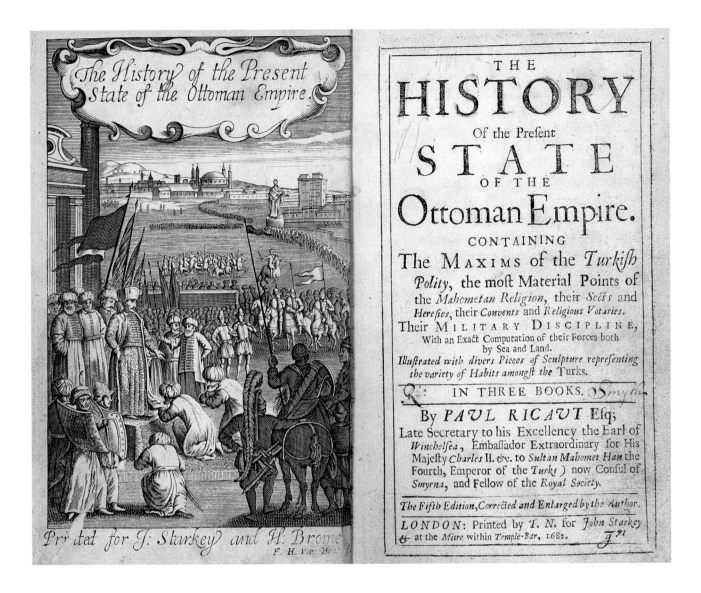

and heresies, their convents and religious votaries, their military discipline…illustrated with divers pieces of sculpture, representing the variety of habits among the Turks (1667). One such illustration was of the Sultan or Grand Seignior, who appeared in a scene opposite the book's title-page (fig. 22), while others featured courtiers such as a 'Black Eunuch'. These images provided readers with tantalising glimpses of Turkish buildings in the background, including their domes and minarets. Rycaut was the leading authority on the Ottoman empire, having spent seventeen years in Turkey during which he served as the Levant or 'Turkey' Company's consul in Smyrna (now Izmir; fig. 23).[75] Pepys

ABOVE 22 The Sultan or Grand Seignior, from Paul Rycaut, *The History of the Present State of the Ottoman Empire. Containing the maxims of the Turkish politie* (1682 edn), title-page

RIGHT 23 Smyrna (Izmir), from George Wheler, *A Journey into Greece by George Wheler, Esq., in Company of Dr Spon of Lyons in Six Books* (1682), Book III, p. 240

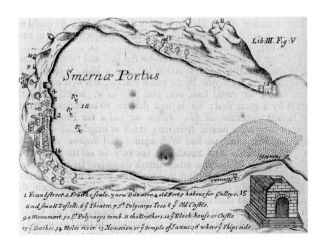

read his book in the year of its publication, enthusiastically noting in his Diary in May 1667: 'down to my chamber and made an end of Rycaut's History of the Turks, which is a very good book'.[76] Hooke too owned a 1668 edition and Evelyn a 1670 one.[77] Evelyn was especially interested in Turkish culture. He noted in his Diary in September 1668 that he had had 'much discourse with Signor *Pietro Cisij* a *Persian* Gent: about the affaires of *Turky* to my infinite satisfaction'.[78] This formed part of his research for *The history of the three late, famous impostors, viz. Padre Ottomano, Mahomed Bei and Sabatai Sevi the one, pretended son and heir to the late Grand Signior, the other, a prince of the Ottoman family, but in truth, a Valachian counterfeit, and the last, the suppos'd Messiah of the Jews, in the year of the true Messiah, 1666* (1669). Included at the end was a brief account of the current war between the Turks and the Venetians, as well as of the exile of the Jews from Persia.

Rycaut was not the only officer of the Levant Company to channel news of Turkey to the Society. The Company had organised English trade with Turkey from 1581 through its offices in Smyrna and Constantinople, as well as in Aleppo in Syria (a link in the silk route to China).[79] In noting details of the Turkish armada sent to attack Malta in 1645, Samuel Hartlib (who was influential in the Society's formation) recoded that news 'was brought from Smyrna by Mr William Bastwick Turkey merchant who was an eye witnes of much'.[80] Oldenburg, in seeking information 'for ye use of ye R. Society' in 1672, urged the newly appointed ambassador to the Sultan and Society Fellow, John Finch, to 'excite the English Consuls, Vice-consuls, and Factors' who 'reside in the Turkish Dominions in the Levant and in Egypt' so that they could 'impart all the Observables of Nature and Art, yt have already occurr'd or may henceforth occur to their Observation'.[81] Company chaplains wrote important accounts of their missions at its main stations, notably Thomas Smith (Constantinople, 1668–70), John Covel (Constantinople, 1670–6), Henry Maundrell (Aleppo, 1695–1701) and Edmund Chishull (Smyrna, 1689–1701).[82] Ambassadors too such as Finch's kinsman, Heneage Finch (the second Earl of Winchelsea and ambassador in 1661–7), published accounts of the court in Constantinople.[83] The role of these English ambassadors and consuls was principally to encourage and safeguard trade with the Sultan.[84] During a mission led by John Finch in 1675 to Adrianople (Edirne), Covel recorded observations in a journal of two festivals as well as an audience with the Grand Vizier and, eventually, the Sultan to ratify trading rights.[85] Back home, such Ottoman spectacles and their architectural setting were condemned and admired in equal measure.[86] Trade and cultural exchange with the Ottoman empire had been encouraged from the time of Elizabeth I, when Turks had started to settle in England.[87] In London they worked as tailors, cobblers, button-makers and even lawyers.[88] By the end of the century, trade with Turkey accounted for a quarter of all England's overseas commercial activity, according to Chardin.[89] As a result, Wren's contemporaries drank Turkish coffee in the many coffee houses in London, bathed in Turkish baths, decorated their homes with Turkish carpets and on occasions even dressed as Turks.[90] As will be seen, Wren's desire to gain knowledge of the domed buildings of Constantinople, as examined in Chapter Three, was stimulated by this diplomatic and commercial exchange.

The emphasis from Evelyn that Chardin had been to places 'where few, if any *northern Europeans* used to go' underlines the difficulty of travelling in the East at this time. Indeed, in June 1645 Evelyn had himself attempted to sail from Venice in order to visit the East, only to fail when his ship was requisitioned.[91] The title of William Lithgow's book describing his experiences in the Levant in 1612, *Rare Adventures, and Painfull Peregrinations* (1632), is particularly telling.[92] Given that the Holy Land and Jerusalem had been under the control of the Ottoman empire since 1517, a pilgrimage to the city was not without risk.[93] The explorer Laurence Aldersey was there in 1581; another traveller, Anthony Shirley, had arrived at Antioch in 1599 with the intention of visiting (although he appears to have been diverted to Babylon); an accountant to the Levant Company, John Sanderson, went there in 1601; and the merchant adventurer Henry Timberlake was in the city in 1602, having been arrested and freed through the help of his companion, a Muslim from Morocco (fig. 24).[94] Biddulph (the Company's chaplain in Aleppo) went to Jerusalem also in 1601, when he visited the Kidron Valley and the 'Sepulchre of the Kings'.[95] Sandys visited the city in 1611 and published some of the earliest illustrations in England of its ancient churches in his *Travels* of 1615 (fig. 25; see figs 85–9). But English pilgrims to the Levant remained few before 1650: on average only fifteen Britons travelled to Palestine annually between 1583 and 1632.[96]

The Royal Society was fully aware of these difficulties. Rycaut, for example, mentioned the problem of returning to remote sites to check details, in a letter of November 1667 that was sent from Smyrna to Oldenburg and which was read to the Fellows. Rycaut noted that although he had often seen the aqueducts near Constantinople, built by Suleiman the Magnificent, 'the measure of them, I must confess, I never was so curious as to take, and being at this distance now from thence, I conceive, that I shall never again have the opportunity to do it'.[97] Before he left England, Rycaut had been issued by the Society with a list of 'Inquiries for Turky' that included aqueducts as well as mummies, inscriptions and opium.[98] The Society was also well aware that Eastern travels could be dangerous, especially for Christians intent on visiting Muslim sites such as mosques.[99] Hooke recorded in his Diary in March 1676 that Oldenburg had 'read Mr. Vernons Letter from Smyrna of January last'.[100] Francis Vernon was a Fellow who had travelled from Venice through Dalmatia, then Greece and Smyrna to Persia where he had been killed. He had left London in 1673, and by July 1675 had met up en route with the English clergyman George Wheler, the French antiquarian Jacob Spon and Giles Eastcourt.[101] Vernon eventually parted company with Wheler and Spon, who travelled on to Constantinople (and stayed in the Levant Company's embassy there), while he returned to Athens. Here he measured the monuments and checked the veracity of previous reports, most notably the inaccurate one by Georges Guillet entitled *Athènes Ancienne et Nouvelle* (1675). Vernon then journeyed to Smyrna alone, following a brief detention by pirates between the Greek islands of Siphnos and Nisos (Eastcourt had already died en route, further underlining the perils of such easterly travels). Vernon's letter to Oldenburg from Smyrna, dated 10 January 1676, was published in the Society's *Transactions* in April that year as 'Observations made during Travels from Venice through Dalmatia…to Smyrna' and contained the critique of Guillet.[102] Vernon then went on to Constantinople in early April. He moved on to Persia around July where, in the spring of the following year, he was murdered after an argument over a penknife: Hooke noted in May 1677 'the ill news of poor Fr. Vernon's death, killed by Turks with cimeters at Ispahan'.[103] While at Split (Spalatro), Vernon had begun a journal, which obviously stopped, all too abruptly, at Isfahan: it was eventually found among Hooke's papers.[104] In October 1677 Hooke also received (from Francis's younger brother, James) Vernon's letters from Cephalonia, Constantinople and Trapezeum, and he went on to transcribe these over the following two weeks.[105] This material might well have been shared with Wren given their joint interest in the cities of the East and the open discussion within the Society of Vernon's voyage.[106] Although of limited practical use, the journal would have interested Wren given that Vernon had sketched the plan of the Propylaea, the Erechtheion and the Odeon of Herodes Atticus in Athens (fig. 26), as well as making notes on Hagia Sophia and the opulence of the Seraglio.[107]

Not surprisingly, Fellows of the Society did not admire every aspect of the diverse cultures of the East. In July 1659 Oldenburg had written to Hartlib on the subject of Eastern manuscripts and printing, and observed that,

> No question, but the Great Turk is an Ennemy to learning…in regard of his subjects, because he finds it his advantage, to have such a people, on whose ignorance he may impose. Whence it is, that he will indure no printing, being of this opinion, that printing and learning, especially such as is found in universities

24   Henry Timberlake, *Two journeys to Jerusalem Containing First A Strange and True Account of the Travels of Two English Pilgrims* (1685 edn), title-page

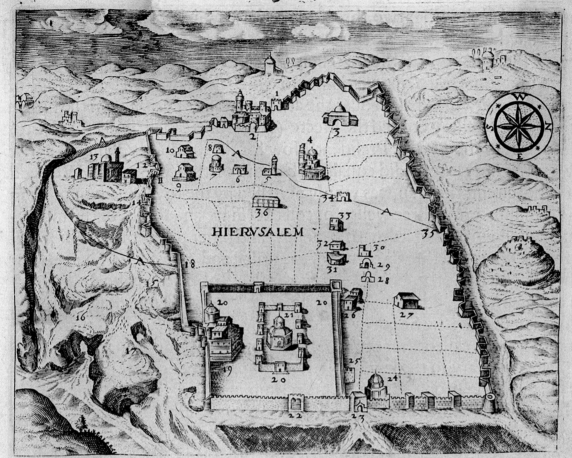

1. The gate of Ioppa.
2. The Castle of the Pisans.
3. The Monastery of the Franciscans.
4. The Temple of the Sepulcher.
5. A Mosque once a collegiat Church where stood the house of Zebedeus.
6. The iron gate.
7. The Church of S. Marke where his house stood.
8. A Chappell where once stood the house of S. Thomas.
9. The Church of S. Iames.
10. The Church of the Angels, where once stood the palace of Annas the High Priest.
11. The port of Dauid.
12. The Church of S. Sauiour, where stood the palace of Caiphas.
13. A Mosque, once a goodly Temple there standing, where stood the Coenaculum.
14. Where the Iewes would have taken away the body of the Blessed Virgin.
15. Where Peter wept.
16. The fountaine Siloe.
17. The fountaine of the Blessed Virgin.
18. Port sterquiline.
19. The Church of the Purification of the Blessed Virgin, now converted into a Mosque.
20. The court of Salomons Temple.
21. A Mosque, where stood the Temple of Salomon.
22. The Golden gate.
23. The gate of S. Stewen.
24. The Church of Anna, now a Mosque.
25. The Poole Bethesda.
26. Where the palace of Pilat stood.
27. Where stood, as they say, the palace of Herod.
28. Pilats arch.
29. The Church of the Blessed Virgins swowning.
30. Where they met Simon of Cyrene.
31. Where the rich Glatton dwelt.
32. Where the Pharise dwelt.
33. Where Veronica dwelt.
34. The gate of Iustice.
35. Port Ephraim.
36. The Bazar.
A. The Circuite of part of the old City.

Hugo Grotius's *De Veritate Religionis Christianae* (*On the Truth of the Christian Religion*) in 1660 by Edward Pococke (chaplain in Aleppo in 1630–5) that, according to Evelyn, 'he caused to be dispersed in the Eastern Countries'.[109] Less seriously, aspects of Eastern cultures were the cause of ridicule. Thomas Sprat, writing to Wren in 1663 on the subject of the wit of conversation, observed concerning the full royal titles (which were historical accumulations expressing claims to subdued states) of the Persian Sophy and the Turkish Grand Seignor that 'the Eastern Wit in all Ages has been principally made up of lofty and swelling Comparisons' but 'to our Understanding, they require the Assistance of Mahomet's Dove to make Sense of them'.[110] Many facets of 'Eastern wit' were nonetheless clearly becoming better understood and even admired at this time through the agency of the Royal Society, and Wren, Hooke and Evelyn played a prominent role in this process of enlightenment.

'FROM THE EASTERN PARTS OF THE WORLD': EASTERN ASTROLOGY AT GRESHAM COLLEGE

More often than not commentators have emphasised Wren's role in the development of natural and experimental philosophy (the foundation of the sciences), and his rational application of mathematical and geometric methods to the practice of architecture.[111] This may be because he is seen as looking forward to the new era of experimentation, rather than back to the old one of superstition. Wren certainly played a central role in the development of the 'scientific' project at the Royal Society, during a key period of the transition from a metaphysical to a mechanical view of nature.[112] Nevertheless he was also interested in more esoteric and arcane practices, commonplace in hermetic and Neoplatonic philosophy, which traced their origins to Arabia and the wider East.[113] For example, the search for the original arcane or 'primitive' language, spoken before the building of the Tower of Babel and the confusion of tongues, inevitably led Hooke and others in the Royal Society east to Egyptian hieroglyphics (and even further east, to Chinese characters).[114] And the alchemist Paracelsus was thought to have travelled in Egypt, Arabia and the Holy Land where he learned the secret of the 'alkahest', the substance believed to transform base metal into gold.[115] Paracelsus's ideas informed those of Hartlib, with whom Wren was closely associated in his formative years at Oxford; Wren was also in close contact with

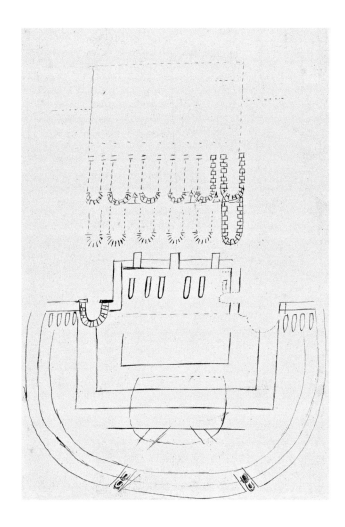

...are the chief fewell of division among Christians. Whence he binds his priests to no more, than to be able to read the Alcoran, and to interpret it in Turkish. Though I heare, that they begin to give themselves somewhat to the study of philosophy, Astronomy and poetry.[108]

Some Fellows even aspired to convert the Turks to the Christian faith or, more accurately, to Anglicanism. Boyle promoted and partly funded a Turkish translation of the Scriptures undertaken by William Seaman (who had travelled in Turkey in the late 1620s) and an Arabic one of

OPPOSITE 25 Jerusalem, from George Sandys, *A relation of a Journey begun an: Dom: 1610. Foure bookes. Containing a description of the Turkish Empire, of Ægypt, of the Holy Land* (1615), Book III, p. 158

ABOVE 26 Francis Vernon's plan of the Odeon of Herodes Atticus in Athens, from his 'Journal of Travels in the Eastern Mediterranean' (1675–6), fol. 31v. Royal Society, London, MS 73

John Wilkins, who maintained many interests and ideas inspired by Neo-platonism.[116] Wren's curiosity to trace the cultures that had influenced Greek architecture, in order to inform his 'larger Idea of the whole Art' outlined in the Tracts, was mirrored by his early interest in the origins of Greek 'science' in the mysterious practices of ancient Eastern civilisations. This interest is particularly evident in his inaugural lecture at Gresham College in 1657. Here he spoke of the 'Aphorisms' (concise statements of natural principles) of Hippocrates:

> let me seriously ask the most rational philosophical Enquirer into Medicine, whether those Aphorisms, wherein Hippocrates hath marshal'd Diseases under the Seasons of the Year, and the several Winds, and the Varieties of Weathers, have not as much of the Aphorism in them, as the rest?…But it may be objected, that these astrological Aphorisms savour much of the Chaldean & Syrian, from whom it appears the Graecians receiv'd much of their Art of healing, as they did almost all their other Learning.[117]

Thus despite possible 'objections', with the help of Herodotus, Wren traced the origins of Greek medicine – and indeed other 'learning' – to the Syrians and Chaldaeans or southern Babylonians. The Chaldaeans were renowned astrologers and astronomers, as well as innovators in the arts.[118] Giorgio Vasari drew on Herodotus and Pliny when observing in the preface to the 1568 edition of his *Lives* that the arts of sculpture and painting were first discovered 'by the people of Egypt, and that there are certain others who attribute to the Chaldaeans the first rough sketches in marble and the first reliefs in statuary'.[119] Their achievements were inevitably compared to modern ones by Wren's contemporaries as an aspect of the 'Ancients' versus 'Moderns' debate. For example, in 1665 Hooke boasted that

> in *Coelestial Observations* we have far exceeded all the Antients, even the *Chaldeans* and *Egyptians* themselves; whose *vast Plains*, *high Towers*, and *clear Air*, did not give them so great advantages over us, as we have over them by our *Glasses*. By the help of which, they have been very much outdone by the famous *Galileo*, *Hevelius*, *Zulichem*, and our own Countrymen, Mr. *Rook*, [and] Doctor Wren.[120]

Wren's interest in the astronomy and astrology of the Chaldaeans, as precursors to Greek 'science', was also informed by his reading of Vitruvius. In this Gresham lecture he identified a miraculous dial described in 'Holy-Scripture' (the Dial of Ahaz) with 'that which the Eastern Nations used, and which Vitruvius tells us, Berosus Chaldaeus brought into Greece'.[121]

A further instance of Wren's interest in hermetic superstitions with Eastern origins was his faith in dream prophecy. This idea had been cultivated during the Renaissance in the popular beliefs of magic and alchemy, and was justified with reference to the Egyptian magi and the great prophets of Hebrew scripture.[122] Early members of the Royal Society shared this interest. Among the Hartlib papers there is a 'Treatise' by John Beale, an early Fellow, entitled 'A Severe Enquyry After the Patriarchicall & Propheticall Arte Of Interpreting dreames by the Light of the Holy Scriptures, Of Uncorrupted Antiquity, & of Constant Experiences. It beeing a chiefe branch of the most famous & soundest Learning of the Children of the Easte, The Abrahamites, Hebrewes, Egyptians, Arabians, & Chaldeans'.[123] Aubrey recorded in his *Miscellanies*, eventually published in London in 1696 and owned by Wren (Lot 17), a number of instances of Wren taking seriously the prophetic power of his dreams.[124] *Parentalia* too reported that when Wren was in Paris in 1665 he was taken ill but 'that Night he dreamt that he was in a Place where Palm-trees grew, (suppose Egypt) and that a Woman in a romantick Habit reach'd him Dates. The next Day he sent for Dates, which cur'd him of the Pain in his Reins.'[125]

Wren continued his Gresham lecture with a further observation on the medical practices and astrology of the Babylonians, observing that 'the great Learning of these Nations being Astrology, we may imagine that they made good Observations of epidemical Diseases from the Distempers of the Air, from the coelestial Influxes, which are now either wholly lost, or deprav'd, or useless, as not suited to our Climate'.[126] Befitting his new Chair in astronomy, he concluded the lecture with a panegyric on London seen in astrological terms. He recalled the Egyptian astrological art of drawing down influences from the stars (the 'coelestial influxes') to favour cities.[127] Wren identified the classic characteristics of the seven planets with various qualities of London:

> Saturn hath given it Diuturnity, and to reckon an earlier *Aera ab Urbe conditâ* ['Airs from the founding of the city'] than Rome itself. Jupiter hath made it the perpetual Seat of Kings, and of Courts of Justice, and fill'd it with inexhausted Wealth. Mars has arm'd it with Power. The Sun looks most benignly on it, for, what City in the World so vastly populous, doth yet enjoy so healthy an Air, so fertile a Soil? Venus hath given it a

pleasant Situation, water'd by the most *amaene* River of Europe; and beautify'd with the external Splendor of Myriads of fine Buildings. Mercury hath nourish'd it in mechanical Arts and Trade, to be equal with any City in the World…Lastly, the Moon, the Lady of the Waters seems amorously to court this Place.[128]

Just as Mercury 'nourished' the old city's trade, so markets would be identified by the symbol of Mercury on the revised version of Wren's plan for the new City after the Fire. This Egyptian hermetic idea of drawing down favourable influences from the stars had informed the Renaissance practice of commissioning astrological calculations of auspicious dates and times for building foundations, a practice adopted by the early Society Fellow Elias Ashmole and Wren on a number of occasions.[129]

Wren's admiration for these aspects of ancient Eastern practices shows that, despite promoting a questioning methodology, he was by no means an out-and-out 'Modern'.[130] In fact, founding members of the Royal Society emphasised a continuity with ancient learning, and that of ancient Eastern civilisations in particular, rather than a break with the past. Theirs was a project of rediscovery as much as it was one of rejection. Thus Sprat in his *The History of the Royal Society of London, For the Improving of Natural Knowledge* (1667) echoed Wren when noting:

> It is evident, from the universal Testimony of *History*, that all Learning and Civility were deriv'd down to us, from the *Eastern* parts of the World. There it was, that Mankind arose: and there they first discovered the wayes of living, with safety, convenience, and delight. It is but just, that we should attribute the original of *Astronomy*, *Geometry*, *Government*, and many sorts of Manufactures, which we now enjoy, to the *Assyrians*, the *Chaldeans*, and *Egyptians*.[131]

Sprat continued that 'into the *East*, the first Inquisitive Men among the *Grecians* traveled: By what they observed there, they ripened their own imperfect Conceptions, and so return'd to teach them at home'.[132] Wren had a copy of Sprat's book (Lot 365). Oldenburg, writing in a preface to the *Transactions* of 25 March 1671 celebrating the seventh year of their publication, defended the Society's approach to promoting the 'New Philosophy'. To disparage it was an error, since ''tis so old as to have been the Discipline in Paradise' and was confirmed by the example of the Eastern sages, 'as in Noah, Moses, Solomon, Daniel, and others'.[133] Nor should the modern philosophers neglect antiquities, according to Oldenburg. Indeed the moderns had not been negligent in the study of the actual remains of the ancient world, he maintained, citing the works of recent travellers and geographers. And following the example of John Greaves, others should study ancient authors 'to give us an accurate Accompt of the Temple of Belus, the Gardens of Semiramis [the hanging gardens of Babylon], the Bridge over Euphrates, the Walls and Towers in Babylon and Ninive, and the Obeliskes and other Wonders of the Assyrian Monarchy'. This was the challenge that Wren would accept in his Tracts.

In this way, firstly Gresham College and then the Royal Society played their part in advancing knowledge of ancient and modern Eastern cultures. The impact of these expanding horizons on contemporary society was far-reaching, with books published for the first time in English on Turkey, Persia and Egypt, and with the king, no less, taking to appearing at Court dressed 'after the Persian mode'. As the following chapters will show, Wren and Hooke discussed Eastern buildings with their Royal Society friends in the many Turkish-inspired coffee shops, while there was abundant opportunity to enjoy Turkish bathing under Eastern-style domes in the London of the 1680s. This growing awareness and the concerns of the Royal Society provide a context for Wren's interest in Eastern architecture and its influence on his novel designs for lanterns and domes, colonnades and monumental columns.

CHAPTER ONE

CLASSICAL ORDERS AND LANTERNS

'The most observable Monument of the Tyrian Style'

Wren observed in the second of his Tracts that 'curiosity may lead us to consider whence' the use of classical columns 'arose originally', and that during the Renaissance 'those who first labored in the Restoration of Architecture, about three Centuries ago, studied principally what they found in *Rome*, above-ground'.[1] However, he would take a different approach. This chapter examines Wren's argument that classical architecture and the columns by which it was composed had originated not in Rome or Greece but further east.[2] Rather than archaeology, this view was based on his study of ancient authors, stimulated by contemporary reports of travels to Turkey, Egypt and the Holy Land. It is not of minor importance since it underpinned his belief in the authenticity of the classical style, as well as his willingness to depart from Roman principles and models when using it. Moreover, as this chapter will also show, ancient structures that featured in Wren's study, as well as others from the Levant region, went on to directly inform a number of his unprecedented and unorthodox classical lanterns and steeples on the churches he built in the City of London after the Fire of 1666. Most notable are those on the Great Model for St Paul's (1673), St Dunstan-in-the-East (1695–1701; fig. 27) as well as St Michael Paternoster Royal (1713–17),
St James Garlickhythe (1714–17) and St Stephen Walbrook (1713–14) (see figs 49, 52, 139). While the dramatic lanterns and steeples on the Queen Anne churches designed by Hawksmoor have been much discussed, these earlier ones by Wren have been less well studied.[3]

'NOT ONLY ROMAN AND GREEK, BUT PHOENICIAN': THE TYRIAN ORDER

Wren understood from Vitruvius that Greece was the source for Roman architectural principles and that, as he put it in Tract two, most ancient architects had 'their Education in Greece'.[4] He made passing reference to 'the ancient Fabricks of the *Greeks*' and knew that in his day, 'among the *Greeks* little was then remaining'.[5] In May 1676 Hooke recorded being 'at Sir Chr. Wren with him to Mr Montacues, then to Corners. Saw scetches of Athens.'[6] These lost sketches may possibly have been by Francis Vernon, since he had been in Athens between October and November the year before, had served as secretary to Ralph Montagu mentioned here and is known to have sent letters to others describing his experiences in the city.[7] (Indeed, Hooke himself received letters from Vernon in February 1676.[8]) In any case, Wren would have seen Vernon's description of the Erechtheion, the Temple of Hephaestus and the Parthenon in his letter published in the Royal Society's *Transactions* in April 1676, and would

27   The tower and steeple at St Dunstan-in-the-East, London (1695–1701)

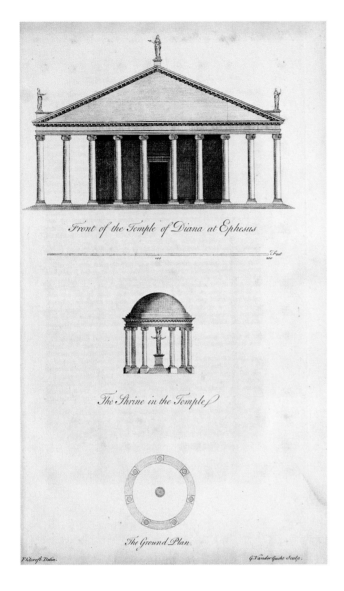

eventually have had access via Hooke to his journal, with its much more detailed Athenian observations (see fig. 26).[9] Wren also owned a 1551 Latin edition of Pausanias, with its account of ancient Athens (Lot 132). In his fourth Tract he described the ruined Greek temple of Diana (more precisely, of Artemis) at Ephesus in modern-day Turkey, one of the ancient Seven Wonders. His description was based on the account in Pliny (Lots 188 and 292) supplemented by those of what he referred to as 'modern travellers', and a reconstruction of the ruined temple, engraved by Henry Flitcroft after Wren's lost drawings, was eventually published in *Parentalia* (fig. 28).[10] The unidentified travellers could have included Robert Huntington, who visited Ephesus some time between 1670 and 1681 while serving as the chaplain in Aleppo.[11] They might also have been Vernon's companions Jacob Spon and George Wheler, both of whom published reports

LEFT 28 Wren's reconstruction of the temple of Diana (Artemis) at Ephesus, engraved by Henry Flitcroft from Stephen Wren, *Parentalia: Or, Memoirs of the Family of the Wrens* (1750), between pp. 250 and 251

OPPOSITE

TOP 29 Ephesus, from George Wheler, *A Journey into Greece by George Wheler, Esq., in Company of Dr Spon of Lyons in Six Books* (1682), Book III, p. 253

MIDDLE 30 Athens, from Wheler, *Journey* (1682), Book V, p. 338

BOTTOM 31 The Parthenon, from Wheler, *Journey* (1682), Book V, p. 360

of their travels in Ottoman-held Greece and the Levant, including of Ephesus, in 1678 and 1682 respectively.[12] Their books contained views of Greek buildings that were among the first, including of the ruins in Ephesus and, in Athens, the Parthenon and the Tower of the Winds built by Andronicus of Cyrrhus (a town in Syria) (figs 29–31). Both accounts were in Wren's collection (Lots 114 and 318), and were widely studied: Evelyn recorded in December 1683 that he had met 'that most ingenious and learned Gent: Sir Geo: Wheler, who has publish'd that excellent description of Attica & Greece'.[13] Wheler had become a Royal Society Fellow in 1677, where he could easily have met Wren. In this way, knowledge of Greek architecture and its role in the development of the Orders, although still sketchy, was gradually becoming more comprehensive.

When opening the third Tract Wren observed from Vitruvius on the Doric style (IV.i.3) that 'the first Temple of that Order was built at *Argos*'.[14] Yet the image of the Greek temple was so complete that, to an enquiring mind like Wren's, its origins in turn demanded an explanation.[15] Just as he had looked beyond the Greeks in highlighting the influences on them of the hermetic arts practised by the Eastern civilisations of Syria and Chaldea, so he now looked for Eastern influences on Greek architecture. More specifically, he sought a columnar prototype that was simpler than the Greek Orders from which their temples were composed (that is, in displaying the ever-more decorative Doric, Ionic and Corinthian Orders or 'styles', as they were also called).[16] Wren fully understood that, although more plain, the Tuscan style was Roman and thus came later. His coherent, if personal, view as to the origin of the Orders was centred on Tyre in Phoenicia, as well as on monuments that he identified as using what he calls the 'Tyrian' Order or style and that were built within the eastern Mediterranean, in the region broadly called the Levant.

In the spirit of the increasing awareness in Europe of Eastern classical, as well as non-Roman, antiquities, Wren observed right at the start of his first Tract that, 'the *Orders* are not only *Roman* and *Greek*, but *Phoenician*, *Hebrew*, and *Assyrian*; therefore being founded upon the Experience of all Ages'.[17] But it was a so-called Phoenician, or Tyrian, Order that he singled out as the prototype of the Doric Order of the Greeks. He noted in Tract four (and repeated in the 'Discourse') that, 'from these *Phoenicians* I derive, as well the Arts, as the Letters of the *Grecians*, though it may be the *Tyrians* were Imitators of the *Babylonians*, and they of the *Ægyptians*'.[18] In this way, Wren proposed a development of classicism that embraced the Babylonians and originated with the earliest known civilisation, the Egyptians. He elaborated in the opening of the third Tract that the Tyrian Order was originally of timber and, on being adopted by the Greeks, was initially used on porticoes and colonnades, only later becoming petrified in the form of the Doric temple:

> THE Tyrian *Order* was the first Manner, which, in *Greece*, was refined into the *Dorick* Order, after the first Temple of that Order was built at *Argos*: but if we consider well the *Dorick* Order, we manifestly may trace the same to be but an Imitation in Stone, of what was usually done in Timber, in the long Porticoes they used to build in Cities, by which they tolerated the Heat of the Day, and conversed together.[19]

Wren's identification of the Phoenicians as the precursors of the Greeks in the invention of the Orders was in no way dependent on Renaissance architectural treatises. These works were largely silent as to the origins of the Greek Orders, much as Vitruvius had been on the Doric, and only implied Egyptian or Asian roots.[20] For example, Leon Battista Alberti in the sixth book of his treatise *De re aedificatoria* condemned the kings of Asia for 'the folly of constructing pyramids' and observed that 'Building, so far as we can tell from ancient monuments, enjoyed her first gush of youth, as it were, in Asia, flowered in Greece, and later reached her glorious maturity in Italy.'[21] The idea of a Tyrian Order was equally unique in architectural writing in Wren's day. As such it represented a fundamental aspect of the broader reappraisal by Wren of Vitruvius and his Graeco-Roman understanding of the Orders. While this need to find an origin for the Doric was rational, the choice of the Phoenicians as the originators of classicism was perhaps less obvious.

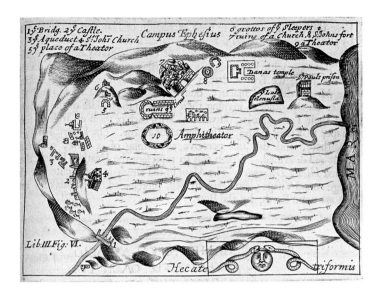

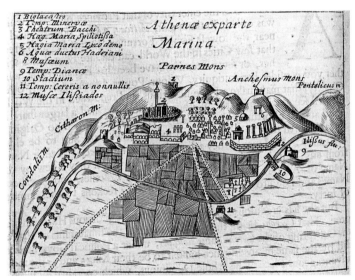

CLASSICAL ORDERS AND LANTERNS

'TYRE HAD ALREADY STOOD FOR TWO THOUSAND THREE HUNDRED YEARS': WHO WERE THE PHOENICIANS?

The Phoenicians occupied the coast of the Levant. Unlike the peoples of neighbouring inland states such as Assyria or Babylonia, Phoenicia was a confederation of fiercely independent coastal cities populated by maritime traders. The principal Phoenician cities were Tyre, Sidon, Byblos and Arwad.[22] Phoenician merchants are thought to have been the first to navigate the Mediterranean waters and they also founded colonies on the Greek coast and neighbouring islands of the Aegean Sea, on the northern coast of Africa at Carthage, in Sicily and Corsica, in Spain at Tartessus, and even beyond the pillars of Hercules (Gibraltar) at Gadeira in Cadiz. Wren mentioned in his Gresham College lecture of 1657 the explorations of one such Carthaginian, Hanno, who had discovered 'the Errors of the Ancients about Africk'.[23] According to Herodotus, the Phoenicians were enemies of Greece and had come from the coasts of the Indian Ocean: 'and as soon as they had penetrated into the Mediterranean and settled in that part of the country where they are to-day, they took to making long trading voyages. Loaded with Egyptian and Assyrian goods, they called at various places along the coast, including Argos.'[24] But the Phoenicians were not just great merchants, since their artisans were skilled in wood, ivory and metalworking, as well as in textile production.

Tyre on the Lebanese coast was famous throughout the ancient East, and the Old Testament refers to it several times.[25] Herodotus recorded that the city was founded around 2750 BC, and its name appeared on monuments from around 1300 BC. He described Tyre in the mid-fifth century BC, including its sanctuary of Melqart (or Hercules as he called it, believing the two deities to be identical), in the second book of the *Histories*.[26] Other ancient sources too described the city. Josephus chronicled its history in *The Antiquities of the Jews*, as well as the Phoenician builders of Solomon's Temple in Jerusalem (it was noted in the Preface that Wren owned a 1693 edition of Josephus and probably an earlier one too; Lot 255).[27] And the Greek historian Strabo reported in his *Geography* that despite an earthquake and being besieged by Alexander the Great, the city 'overcame such misfortunes and restored itself' by means of 'the seamanship of its people, in which the Phoenicians in general have been superior to all peoples of all times'. Strabo added that 'the number and the size of their colonial cities is an evidence of their power in maritime affairs. Such, then, are the Tyrians.'[28] Wren owned the 1620 Latin edition of Strabo, which was a complete version translated (from the Greek) by the classical scholar Isaac Casaubon;[29] and, as also noted in the Preface, he owned a 1592 edition of Herodotus's *Histories* (Lots 122 and 131). Hooke, too, owned two editions of Herodotus and studied them carefully, noting for example in his Diary in September 1680: 'At home, read Herodotus'.[30] And he owned the 1674 Latin edition of Stephanus of Byzantium's *De urbibus et populis fragmenta*, which contained entries on Tyre and the Phoenicians (as well as geographical details of the ancient cities of Byzantium in the sixth century AD).[31]

Wren's reading of these ancient authors was no doubt an important source of his admiration for Phoenician antiquity, although its ancient civilisation featured in various works in England at this time. As noted in the Preface, the *Hypnerotomachia Poliphili* (1499, translated into English in 1592) referred to a statue of Hercules in Tyre. From the time of the early Stuarts it had been understood that Tyre was a significant centre in antiquity, as *Pericles, Prince of Tyre* (1607) by Shakespeare (and his collaborator) shows. Phoenician command of the seas was also recognised, which was referred to in *Antony and Cleopatra* (1607, III.7). Wren's contemporaries were also interested in the Phoenicians. The Oxford medical student Edmund Dickinson's *Delphi Phenicizantes* (or 'Delphi derived from the Phoenicians') had been published in the city in 1655 and then in Frankfurt in 1669. The purpose of this work was to question the cultural claims of the pagan Greeks, or as its lengthy subtitle has it, to show *by not inelegant arguments, that the Greeks made up whatever was famous at Delphi (whether you look at the story of Apollo and the Python, or the Paeanic contests and prizes, or the original form of the Temple and its inscription or the Tripod, the Oracle, etc.) from the story of Joshua and the Sacred Scriptures*. It is not known if Wren was aware of this work, but it made a similar case to his in claiming Phoenician influence on Greek architecture. The 1655 edition was in Hooke's library, to which Wren had easy access.[32] Evelyn too was well aware of Phoenician achievements in navigation and trade, observing in his *Navigation and Commerce* (1674) that they were 'the first *Merchants* in the World since the deluge'.[33]

Strabo suggested that either Phoenicians or Syrians had settled in Britain, and this idea was picked up by a number of early English antiquarians. In 1590 John Twyne published a symposium-style dialogue in which the Phoenicians were said to have arrived in the country some time between its legendary founding by giants and its invasion by Trojans.[34] A much more notable work on these

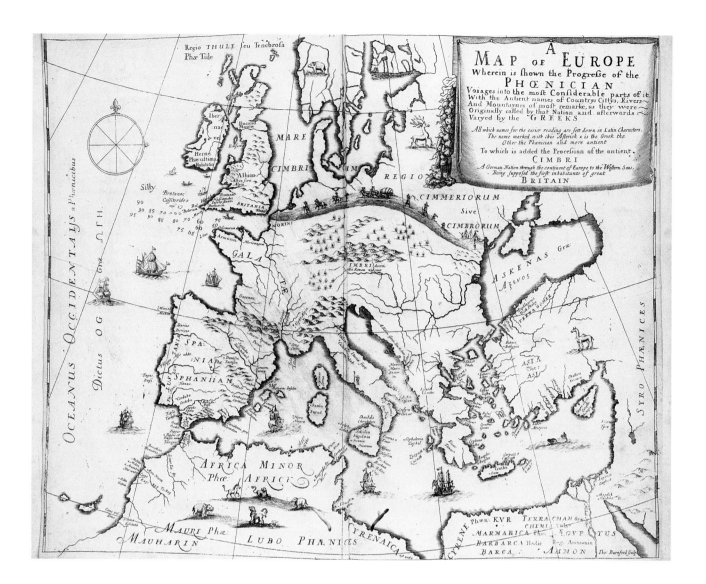

British Phoenicians was that by Wren's contemporary, Aylett Sammes. His *Britannia Antiqua Illustrata, or the Antiquities of Ancient Britain derived from the Phœnicians: wherein the original trade of this island is discovered…with the antiquities of the Saxons, as well as Phoenicians, Greeks, and Romans* (1676) could be found in Wren's library (Lot 287). The book did not go unnoticed, being favourably reviewed in the Royal Society's *Transactions* in April 1676.[35] It contained 'A map of Europe wherein is shown the progresse of the Phoenician Voyages into the most Considerable part of it' that included 'Albion' (fig. 32). As the *Transactions* pointed out, Sammes drew heavily on the work of the Protestant biblical scholar Samuel Bochart, who had identified Phoenician origins even in Celtic words (for example, Britain was supposedly from the Phoenician 'Bratanac' meaning 'land of tin'). The title of Sammes's map made clear the early date of Phoenician culture in noting that 'the Antient names of Countries' were 'afterwards Varyed by the Greeks'. Whether or not Wren accepted Sammes's case for a Phoenician ancient Britain, his study would certainly have highlighted their supposed achievements, including those as builders. Sammes argued for a Phoenician Stonehenge, for example, and this idea persisted: William Stukeley, who had information from John Harwood (a Royal Society Fellow from 1686), recorded that 'Sir Christopher Wren says, there are such works as Stonehenge in Africa & that they are temples dedicate[d] to Saturn[.] He well may mean they were made by the Phoenicians, and by Saturn Shad[da]i [God Almighty] is meant.'[36]

32 Map of Europe showing Phoenician voyages, from Aylett Sammes, *Britannia Antiqua Illustrata, or the Antiquities of Ancient Britain derived from the Phœnicians* (1676), facing title-page

CLASSICAL ORDERS AND LANTERNS   23

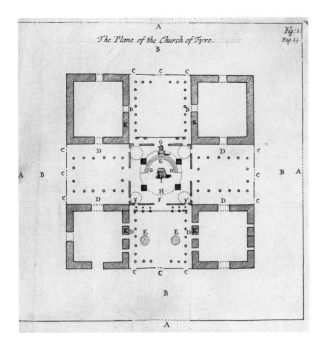

33   Plan of the early Christian church at Tyre (destroyed), from George Wheler, *An Account of the Churches, or Places of Assembly, of the Primitive Christians from the churches of Tyre, Jerusalem, and Constantinople described by Eusebius... with a Seasonable Application* (1689), between pp. 12 and 13

Wren's interest in Tyre also reflected that of another major group, this time theologians who studied the early, or 'primitive', Christian Church. The traveller and priest Wheler (who took Holy Orders in 1683) published *An Account of the Churches, or Places of Assembly, of the Primitive Christians from the churches of Tyre, Jerusalem, and Constantinople described by Eusebius...with a Seasonable Application* (1689), which had a description and plan of the early church at Tyre (fig. 33).[37] As the title indicated, this plan followed Bishop Eusebius (c.260–c.341, from Caesarea in Judaea) and his *Historia Ecclesiastica* (Book 10, ch. 4). Wren would surely have been familiar with Eusebius through his father and uncle Matthew, both Deans of Windsor and well-versed in Church history, as well as through the English translation of the *Historia Ecclesiastica* by Meredith Hanmer that had first appeared in 1577 and been republished in six editions by 1663. Indeed, Wren owned a 1606 edition of Eusebius's *Thesaurus temporum, Eusebii Pamphili Caesarae Palaestinae Episcopi, Chronicorum canonum ominimodae historiae libri duo* (Lot 130).[38] A church had been dedicated at Tyre in 317 by Eusebius himself in the presence of Constantine, whilst St Paul, on his return from his third missionary journey, had spent a week in conversation with the disciples there. Tyre thus acquired a prominence among Anglicans, since by focusing on such early churches the intention was to provided a pure, non-Catholic model (as a 'seasonable application' as Wheler's title put it) for the form of Anglican churches around the same time as Wren was designing them. The similarities between some of these churches and Byzantine examples, both real and imaginary, will be examined in Chapter Three.

It should also be noted that Wren's Tyrian theory concerning the Orders may well have influenced, or even been influenced by, the brothers Roger and Dudley North. Writing in an unpublished manuscript entitled 'Of Building', thought to date to about 1690 but possibly earlier, the architect Roger North echoed the idea that the Orders originated in the East. When discussing the theory that their form had stemmed from timber construction, he noted in passing that his brother 'hath informed me of the method of building in the Easterne parts, which in this theory is chiefly to be regarded, because the 5 orders are fetch't or derived from thence'.[39] By 'Easterne parts' North meant the Levant region, not Greece, since Dudley, also known as 'Turkey' North, had been the most important English merchant in Constantinople.[40] Having established himself as the Factor for the Levant Company in Smyrna in 1661, and thereafter in Constantinople where he was also the Company's treasurer, Dudley returned to London with a fortune in 1680 and continued to trade with the Levant. Roger referred to him here as 'My worthy and curious friend at Stambole' (or Istanbul). Both brothers were on friendly terms with Wren, visiting the building site at St Paul's on Saturdays which, according to Roger, 'were Sir Christopher Wren's days, who was the Surveyor', and when 'we commonly got a snatch of discourse with him'.[41] This report thus placed an expert with first-hand experience of Ottoman architecture at the Cathedral during its construction, and one who agreed with Wren on the Eastern origins of the Orders being used there.

'THE TYRIAN ORDER WAS THE FIRST MANNER': TYRIAN TEMPLES AND TOMBS

In identifying the Phoenicians as the forerunners of the Greeks in the development of the Orders, their artistic prowess and travels in the pursuit of trade furnished Wren with a plausible explanation for the supposed use of the Tyrian manner on some of the greatest early Greek and non-Greek buildings scattered across the eastern

Mediterranean and in territories such as Etruria with settlers from the East. Those early structures described by Wren as built in the Tyrian style easily outnumbered the later Greek and Roman buildings also discussed in the Tracts. The physical properties of these structures had been recorded in the Bible and by the ancient authors Josephus and Pliny, as well as the Roman scholar Varro. As such they were among the legendary and most enigmatic in the history of architecture. They included the temple or 'theatre' of Dagon in Gaza, the tomb of Mausolus (the king of Caria) at Halicarnassus in modern Turkey, that of Absalom in the Kidron Valley as well as of Lars Porsena at Clusium in Italy. Even the Temple of Solomon was understood by Wren to have been built in the Tyrian style. Of these five, only the tomb of Absalom remains standing today (see fig. 37). While that tomb appeared to provide a degree of proof of Wren's Tyrian vision of antiquity, though inaccurately described by his sources, the fact that the remainder of these buildings no longer existed allowed him maximum leeway in identifying their structural and proto-Doric virtues. As the Preface noted, most of them were also the subject of speculative reconstructions by Wren or his associates.[42]

At the start of the fourth Tract, Wren described the early use of Tyrian timber columns at the temple of Dagon. Samson's famous destruction of the temple was achieved by his pushing over the two central columns, as recorded in Judges (16:25–30), and its structure and plan evidently fascinated Wren: 'AN Example of *Tyrian* Architecture we may collect from the Theatre, by the fall of which, *Sampson* made so vast a Slaughter of the *Philistines*, by one Stretch of his wonderful Strength'. This Tyrian attribution was given credence through a logical identification of the structure with timber construction: 'In Considering what this Fabrick must be, that could at one Pull be demolished, I conceive it an oval Amphitheatre, the Scene in the Middle, where a vast Roof of Cedar-beams resting round upon the Walls, centered all upon one short Architrave, that united two Cedar Pillars in the Middle.'[43]

The most prominent example of Wren's association of (pre-Greek) buildings mentioned in the Old Testament with the Tyrian style was his presentation of Solomon's Temple, although its columns were not timber but made of stone (fig. 34).[44] This link between the two helped give the Tyrian Order an unquestionable biblical virtue, even a divine origin, and was not without evidence. One of the Temple's supporters, King Hiram I, was the Phoenician king of Tyre who reigned from 980 to 947 BC. The king was a contemporary of David and Solomon, as recorded in 2 Samuel (5.11), 1 Kings (5.1) and 1 Chronicles (14.1). And according to the Bible, and then Josephus, Hiram supplied materials and Phoenician workmen for the Temple, which included its architect who was somewhat confusingly also called Hiram. Wren observed in his fourth Tract, in a passage repeated almost word for word in the 'Discourse', that 'it is to be wished, some skilful Artist would give us the exact Dimensions to Inches, by which we might have a true Idea of the ancient *Tyrian* Manner; for, 'tis most probable *Solomon* employed the *Tyrian* Architects in his Temple, from his Correspondency with King *Hiram*'.[45] His case for this plain Order was despite well-known arguments by other commentators for the much more decorative Greek Corinthian Order on the Temple. Best-known was that by the Jesuit

34 Reconstruction of the Temple of Solomon in Jerusalem, from Juan Bautista Villalpando, *In Ezechielem Explanationes et Apparatus Urbis ac Templi Hierosolymitani*, vol. 2 (1605), facing p. 145

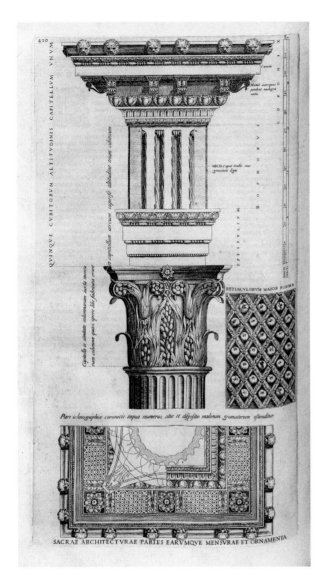

35 Solomonic Corinthian Order, from Villalpando, *In Ezechielem Explanationes*, vol. 2 (1605), p. 420

Juan Bautista Villalpando in a magnificent Temple reconstruction published between 1596 and 1605 (see fig. 34); however, the capital was modified with lilies and palm leaves replacing acanthus since, according to the Bible, the interior of the temple was decorated with palm (Kings 6:29; fig. 35).[46] In proposing a logical, chronological development of the Orders, from plain to decorative, Wren continued that:

> *Villalpandus* hath made a fine romantick Piece, after the *Corinthian* Order, which, in that Age, was not used by any Nation: for the early Age used much grosser Pillars than the *Dorick*: in after Times, they began to refine from the *Dorick*, as in the Temple of *Diana* at *Ephesus*, (the united Work of all *Asia*) and at length improved into a slenderer Pillar, and leafy Capital of various Inventions, which was called *Corinthian*; so that if we run back to the Age of *Solomon*, we may with Reason believe they used the *Tyrian* Manner, as gross at least, if not more, than the *Dorick*, and that the *Corinthian* Manner of *Villalpandus* is mere Fancy.[47]

Wren was clearly keen to argue that Solomon's Temple, as the greatest building in the Bible, should be recognised as Tyrian work. He would have seen Villalpando's modified, 'Solomonic' Corinthian in both Roland Fréart's *Parallèle de l'Architecture antique et de la moderne* published in 1650 and Evelyn's translation of it in 1664: Evelyn gave a copy of this to Wren, and the later edition of 1707 was also in his collection (Lot 567).[48] Hooke probably owned a copy of the Jesuit's work, since he mentioned in his Diary in January 1676, 'Villalpandus 30sh' bought from the bookseller Robert Boulter (although the book is not listed among those in his library).[49] Hartlib recorded a copy in the Bodleian.[50] Of some encouragement to Wren, the Fréart–Evelyn works were also not fully supportive of Villalpando over Vitruvius, observing, 'it were very unjust that the particular conceit of a modern Writer should prevail above the Authority of so grave an *Author*'.[51] Nevertheless, Wren shared with Villalpando the fundamental desire to distance the Orders from paganism through their Solomonic pedigree.

Both Wren and Hooke were fascinated by the Temple. For example, Hooke recorded in his Diary in September 1675: 'With Sr Chr. Wren. Long Discourse with him about the module [model] of the temple at Jerusalem'.[52] This refers to a model exhibited in London in that year by a Dutch rabbi called Jacob Judah Leon and that had no doubt just been seen by both men (and which Hooke unsuccessfully attempted to revisit in January the following year.[53]) Wren may well have met Leon, after a letter of introduction sent to him by Huygens on 7 October 1674.[54] Solomonic imagery from the Temple was used by Wren and his office most notably in various tomb designs. In particular, his design of 1678 for a monument within a proposed mausoleum for Charles I at Windsor included palm branches (see fig. 175).[55] Somewhat inevitably given the role of the Temple as the ultimate model for all church architecture, the old and new St Paul's were both seen as its natural successor. Practically all public sermons in favour of Jones's restoration of old St Paul's undertaken in the 1630s were animated by the conception of it as the rebuilt Temple and of Stuart London as the prophesied New Jerusalem.[56] Consequently James I would be identified with Solomon and Charles II was also on occasions seen in this way.[57] At his coronation in 1661, for example, the congregation 'Prayed for the Peace of Jerusalem' and that he might 'govern with the Mildness of Solomon', while 'the *Choir* sung this *Anthem: Sadoc the Priest*, and *Nathan* the Prophet, anointed *Solomon* King: and all the People rejoiced, and said, GOD SAVE THE KING'.[58] Similarly, at the consecration of Wren's new Cathedral on 23 December 1697, the sermon by Bishop Henry Compton was based on Psalm 122: 'I was glad when they said unto me, Let us go into the house of the Lord / Our feet shall stand within thy gates, O Jerusalem'.[59] The fact that the Cathedral's classical style found its origins in the biblical Temple's Tyrian columns can only have helped this association.

Wren completed the development of the Tyrian column, from timber to stone, by identifying it in the fourth Tract with the Doric Order as supposedly used on the tomb of Mausolus, built in 350 BC at Halicarnassus. This was the first of three tombs identified with the Tyrian style. A drawing of Mausolus's tomb, in the hand of Hawksmoor, is bound at the end of the 'Discourse' in the copy of *Parentalia* held at the Royal Institute of British Architects in London (fig. 36). Seemingly in reference to this drawing, Wren observed that 'The Sepulchre of *Mausolus* is so well described by *Pliny*, that I have attempted to design it accordingly, and also very open, conformable to the Description in *Martial*. Aëre vacuo pendentia Mausolèa [Mausolea poised on empty air].[60] And yet it wanted not the Solidity of the *Dorick* Order, which I rather call the *Tyrian*, as used in that Age.'[61] In fact Pliny gave no details as to the monument's style, Tyrian or otherwise. Wren justified his association of the Doric or Tyrian Order with the monument through chronology, and details of its sculptors taken from Pliny: 'The Skill of four famous Artists, *Scopas, Briaxes, Timotheus,* and *Leochares,* all of the School of *Praxiteles*, occasioned this Monument to be esteemed one of the seven Wonders of the World.' Because these lived 'before the Time of *Alexander*, and before the Beginning of the Temple of *Diana* at *Ephesus*', when 'the *Ionick* Order was first in Use', so 'I conclude this Work must be the exactest Form of the *Dorick*'. Wren continued by describing the tomb's physical characteristics as indicated in the drawing, particularly the steps at its base and the triumphal chariot of Mausolus at its apex.[62] The use of the refined Tyrian, or Doric, on the ancient warrior's tomb would have been given credence by Serlio's association of the Doric Order in his fourth book with buildings for those who 'professed to be soldiers', and helped justify Wren's own use of the Doric on the colonnades at Greenwich and Chelsea military hospitals (see figs 147, 155–6).[63]

In the fourth Tract, Wren identified a further biblical structure as built in the Tyrian style, although here again with Doric attributes. This was the tomb of Absalom, which was mentioned by Josephus (Book VII, 10) and survives to this day (fig. 37). Absalom was the rebellious son of king David (described in 2 Samuel 14–18). For this reason Jews and Muslims were known to throw stones at the tomb, according to the traveller George Sandys writing in 1615.[64] Absalom's story also had potency closer to home in Wren's day, since it was famously the subject of John Dryden's poem entitled *Absalom and Achitophel* published in November 1681: this was an allegory of the Duke of Monmouth's attempt to gain the throne from Charles II and his Roman Catholic brother, the future James II.[65] It may have helped draw Wren's attention to the monument. He commented on the tomb that 'the most observable Monument of the *Tyrian* Style, and of great Antiquity, still remaining, is the Sepulchre of *Absalom*'.[66] A marginal note identified the tomb's location as '*Over against* Jerusalem *eastward, in the Valley of* Jehosaphat', that is, in the Kidron Valley. The tomb lies on the approach from the Mount of Olives to the site of the Temple of Solomon. Wren continued:

> the Body of this Structure is square, faced on every Side with Pillars, which bear up an hemispherical *Tholus* solid; a large Architrave, Freeze, and Cornice lie upon the Pillars, which are larger in proportion to their Heighth, than what we now allow to the *Tuscan* Order; so likewise is the Entablature larger. This whole Composition, though above 30 Feet high, is all of one Stone, both Basis, Pillars, and *Tholus*, cut as it stood out of the adjacent Cliff of white Marble.[67]

He was clearly eager to emphasis the tomb's monolithic, proto-Doric qualities (here contrasted with the Tuscan), in keeping with his view as to the plain character of Tyrian-style buildings. However, although he knew that the monument had survived, he was unaware that it has a Doric frieze unconventionally supported by pilasters of the more elaborate Ionic Order. This ignorance was

FOLLOWING PAGES

LEFT 36 The Mausoleum at Halicarnassus reconstructed by Hawksmoor, bound with Wren's 'Discourse on Architecture' in the Royal Institute of British Architects' 'Heirloom' MS copy of *Parentalia* (1750).
RIBA, London

RIGHT 37 The tomb of Absalom, Jerusalem, c.1000 BC

(24)

will appear half the Face, or like the Façade of a Tuscan Temple, to which the Breadth of the Brim of the Petasus, & the Bells, supply the Place of an Entablature.

I have been the longer in this Description, because the Fabrick was in the Age of Pythagoras and his School, when the World began to be fond of Geometry, and Arithmetick.

NB. In all the Editions of Pliny for Tricenûm read Tricentenûm, as the Sense requires.

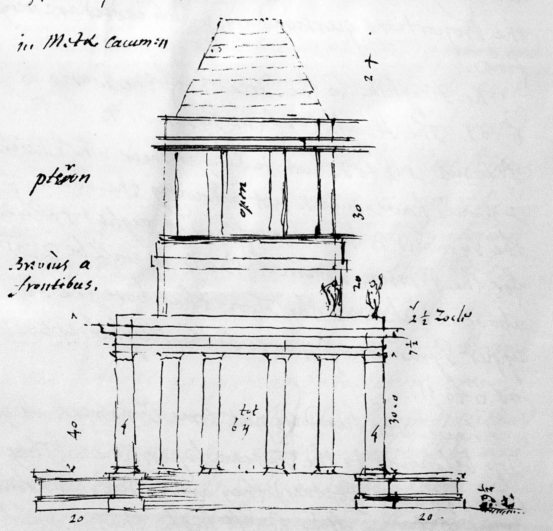

Statue of Mausolus
in Metâ Cacumiñ
pteron
Brevius a frontibus.

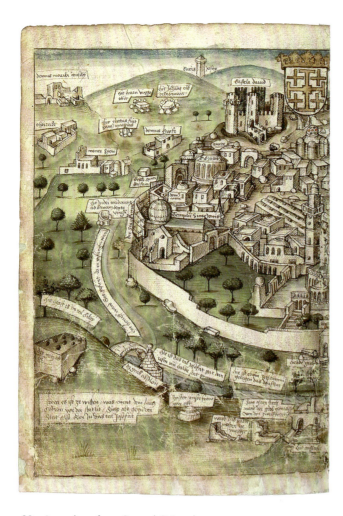

38 Jerusalem, from Conrad Grünenberg, 'Beschreibung der Reise von Konstanz nach Jerusalem' (1487), fol. 35v (detail, the tomb of Absalom in the foreground). Badische Landesbibliothek, Karlsruhe MS Cod. St. Peter, pap. 32

certainly convenient as far as his purpose is concerned, since the presence of the Ionic made the tomb much less Tyrian in character.

Wren also mentioned the tomb in his 'Discourse' (referred to as the 'pillar' of Absalom), where in place of the correct observation that the monument is square and faced with pilasters, the text noted that 'by the description given of it, and what I have learnt from Travellers who have seen it, we must allow it to be very Remarkable, though not great [i.e., large]. It is compos'd of seven Pillars, six about in a Hexagon, and one in the middle, which Bear up an Hemispherical Tholus solid'.[68] This error might reflect the fact that early topographical views of Jerusalem, such as Conrad Grünenberg's of 1487, gave the impression that the tomb was circular (fig. 38). Faynes Moryson (who had died in 1630 long before Wren's interest) visited the Mount of Olives in 1596 and equally incorrectly reported in his *An Itinerary…containing his ten yeeres travell* of 1617:

> Here be two old Sepulchers, almost of a round forme, built of Free-stone, or rather cut out of the living stone, wherof the one is called the Sepulcher of Absolon, the sonne of David, the other of King Manasses (or as others say, of the King Ezektas.) And considering the antiquitie, they seeme no Plebean Sepulchers, but stately and fit for Princes, being foure Elles from the ground in height.[69]

The inaccuracy of these sources serves to demonstrate the unreliability of information on Eastern antiquities at this time.[70]

As with Wren's account of the temple at Ephesus, the identity of his informants is unclear. One candidate is Isaac Basire, who was in Jerusalem in 1652 (during his mission to introduce Anglicanism to the Eastern Church).[71] Basire was fairly well-known. Evelyn noted in his Diary on 10 November 1661 that he had spent the afternoon at the Abbey with 'Dr. Basiere (that greate Traviller, or rather French Apostle, who had ben planting the Church of England, in divers parts of the Levant & Asia)' and who had shown 'That England was the very land of Goshen'.[72] In the following year, on 29 October, he further noted that 'I went to Court this Evening and had much discourse with Dr. Basiers one of his Majesties Chaplains the greate Travellor, who showed me the Syngraphs [signed contracts] & original subscription of divers Eastern Patriarchs & Asian Churches to our Confession &c'.[73] Another candidate for information on Absalom's tomb is the Quaker George Robinson, who had travelled to Jerusalem in 1657 (although he seems to have had little actual contact with the holy sites).[74] Yet another is Robert Frampton, the Bishop of Gloucester from 1681, who served as the chaplain at Aleppo from 1655 to 1666 and stayed there until 1670: according to Evelyn, Frampton had been to Jerusalem twice.[75] And a subsequent chaplain at Aleppo, Robert Huntington, visited not only Ephesus but Jerusalem, also twice, during his office between 1670 and 1681.[76] Two travellers to the Levant published brief accounts of the monument that we know Wren could easily have studied, namely Sandys in his *Travels* (1615, of which Wren owned a 1670 edition, Lot 109) and eventually, much later than the Tracts, de Bruyn in his *Voyage to the Levant* (first published in Dutch in 1698, of which Wren owned the 1702 English edition, Lot 140).[77] Sandys's description of the tomb was of an exclusively

LEFT 39 The tomb of Absalom (detail, left edge), from George Sandys, *A relation of a Journey begun an: Dom: 1610. Foure bookes. Containing a description of the Turkish Empire, of Ægypt, of the Holy Land* (1615), Book III, p. 189

BELOW 40 The tomb of Absalom (top right, bottom left), from Cornelis de Bruyn, *Voyage to the Levant* (1702), pp. 119–20

Doric structure, which tended to support Wren's stylistic attribution of it as Tyrian and was therefore a more likely source for this aspect at least. His accompanying illustration was small and only of one corner of the tomb (confusingly with what looks like a Corinthian column), whereas de Bruyn's was complete and accurately showed a square structure with Ionic pilasters (figs 39 and 40). Incidentally, the differences between Wren's two descriptions of the tomb seem to confirm that the manuscript 'Discourse'

CLASSICAL ORDERS AND LANTERNS

preceded the more accurate fourth Tract eventually published in *Parentalia*. Wren had attempted to draw this monument too, probably in the late 1670s: Aubrey observed in the third part (on mausoleums) of his 'Monumenta Britannica' (1663–93): 'Absalom's Pillar, wch was cutt out of a Rock; wch Sir Christ Wren says 'twas a pretty thing: insert *his* draught of it here'.[78]

Wren's Tyrian manner thus became the first, simple antique column in a story of architectural development that moved from the plain to the decorative, as different cultures adapted the Orders to their needs. It started life as a Phoenician timber column (as eventually used at Dagon), although the Phoenicians had been influenced by the Babylonians and they in turn by the Egyptians. The column then became stone (as at Solomon's Temple, built with Phoenician help under divine instruction) and developed into an early example of Doric (as at Halicarnassus). The Halicarnassus mausoleum (after Pliny) formed Wren's model for the Doric (although a Tyrian form of Doric), just as the Greek temple of Diana at Ephesus (again after Pliny) represented his model for the Ionic, while the Roman Temple of Mars Ultor (after Palladio) formed his preferred model for the Corinthian (see figs 28 and 36). In this way the Greek Orders were identified in Wren's fourth Tract with some of the most magnificent buildings of antiquity – two of which, the Doric mausoleum and the Ionic temple, were among the legendary Seven Wonders of the ancient world. This was a progression that required the Temple of Solomon to be a simple Tyrian, rather than a Corinthian, structure.

'A STUPENDIOUS FABRICK, OF TYRIAN ARCHITECTURE': THE TYRIAN TOMB OF PORSENNA

The fifth and final example of Tyrian-style architecture can only be found in the 'Discourse' and seems to have held a special significance for Wren and Hooke as a 'stupendious fabric, of I think also Tyrian architecture'. This was the now destroyed tomb of Lars Porsenna, King of Etruria. The tomb was built around 500 BC at the ancient city of Clusium in Tuscany and, as Wren emphasised, was thus 'standing before the absolute conquest of Etruria by the Romans'.[79] This dating allowed the tomb to be a Tyrian prototype for the Tuscan style, invented by the Romans, befitting its Etruscan location and the influences on the region of the pre-Roman Phoenicians (according to Herodotus, the Etruscans originally came from the kingdom of Lydia in modern Turkey).[80] Although long-lost, the tomb was described by Varro (who Wren felt the need to emphasise was a 'diligent and therefore credible Author') in a work that is now also lost but whose description survives as quoted by Pliny.[81] As Wren's detailed study of the temple at Ephesus and the tomb of Mausolus shows, he was a keen student of Pliny (Lots 188 and 292).

Pliny was by no means in awe of the tomb of Porsenna, however, regarding its structural complexity as a lesson in the folly of vanity: 'It is only proper that I should make some mention of it, if only to show that the vanity displayed by foreign monarchs, great as it is, has been surpassed.' But as 'the fabulousness of the story connected with it quite exceeds all bounds', Pliny proceeds by quoting Varro's lost passage:

> Each side of this monument was three hundred feet in length and fifty in height, and beneath the base, which was also square, there was an inextricable labyrinth, into which if anyone entered without a clew of thread, he could never find his way out. Above this square building there stand five pyramids, one at each corner, and one in the middle, seventy-five feet broad at the base, and one hundred and fifty feet in height. These pyramids are so tapering in their form, that upon the summit of all of them united there rests a brazen globe ... Upon this globe there are four other pyramids, each one hundred feet in height; and above them is a single platform, on which there are five more pyramids.

Pliny concluded that 'Varro has evidently felt ashamed to add' the height of this final element, but that 'according to the Etruscan fables, it was equal to that of the rest of the building. What downright madness this, to attempt to seek glory at an outlay which can never be of utility to any one; to say nothing of exhausting the resources of the kingdom, and after all, that the artist may reap the greater share of the praise!'[82] However, it was the tomb's apparent plainness and structural virtuosity that no doubt made it an ideal candidate to be a Tyrian-style monument as far as Wren was concerned. Although he mentioned as an aside in the 'Discourse' that Pliny had considered it a monument to vanity, he quickly passed over this and concentrated on its physical properties. Wren described these twice, at first basing himself on Pliny and then giving

41   The tomb of Porsenna at Clusium, Italy, from John Greaves, *Pyramidographia: or a description of the pyramids in Egypt* (1646), between pp. 64 and 65

Porsena's Tombe at Clusium in Italy consisting of many Pyramids.

his own interpretation. Wren seems to have approached the task of such reconstructions as if designing the monument himself from first principles, by devising a logical structure, much as he went back to first principles in his architectural history and in the natural sciences. Taking into account issues of structural stability, as with the Temple of Dagon, he considered the tomb's 'pyramids', or pinnacles:

> Now how These could be borne is worth the consideration of an Architect. I conceive it might be thus perform'd secur'ly. Set half Hemispherical Arches, such as we make the heads of Niches, but lay'd back to back, so that each of these have its Bearing upon 3 Pyramids of the Lower Order, that is 2 Angular ones and the Middle Pyramid; and These cutting one another upon the Diagonals will have a firm Bearing for all the Works above. Pliny mentions a Brass Circle and Cupola, lay'd upon the Five Lower Pyramids, not I suppose to bear any thing, but chiefly for Ornament, and to Cover the Stone Work of the Arches, upon the strong Spandrells of which if another Platform were rais'd, upon That might the upper Structure be built; and the whole have a stupendious effect, and seemingly very Open.[83]

Despite Pliny's scorn, the complexity of Porsenna's tomb and the fact that it had been described in some detail, much like that of Mausolus, seem to be why it caught Wren's attention. A well-known reconstruction interpreting Pliny's description of the tomb had already been published at the end of Greaves's *Pyramidographia* of 1646 (fig. 41). Oldenburg praised the work, as noted earlier, and Evelyn and Hooke both owned copies: Evelyn annotated his copy and Hooke mentioned the book in his Diary a number of times, the first in October 1673.[84] Like Wren, Greaves had no doubt been intrigued by the tomb's structural complexities. He was Professor of Geometry at Gresham in 1630–1 (a post Hooke himself later held in 1664) and travelled in the Levant from 1637 to 1640 (including in Turkey and Egypt). Hooke too was interested in the tomb and would have studied it via his four editions of Pliny (an Italian of 1573, a Latin of 1606, a French of 1622 and an English of 1635).[85] According to his Diary, he met Wren on at least three separate occasions in October

42 Wren's reconstruction of the tomb of Porsenna as sketched by Robert Hooke in his Diary (17 October 1677). London Metropolitan Archives, MS 01758

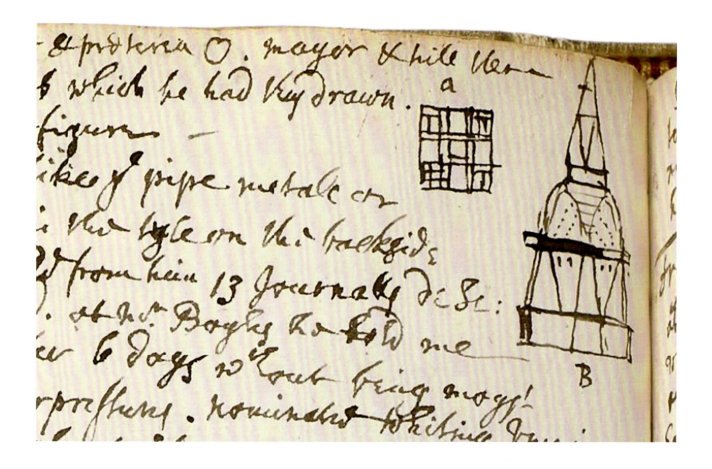

1677 and 'Discoursd with him long of Porsena's tomb'.[86] On the 4th he noted that Wren had given a 'description' of the tomb, probably with a drawing, although he added with possible reference to Pliny that 'comparing it with the words it agreed not. I found the form of it quite otherwise and describd it.'[87] Wren certainly produced a drawing, since on the 17th Hooke met Wren again and sketched his friend's reconstruction in his Diary entry for the day (fig. 42). This small sketch indicates that Wren took Pliny's central dome as suggestive of the presence of arches or niches. In structural terms the sketch resembled a type of Gothic steeple known as an 'imperial crown', where four flying buttresses spring from the corners of a tower and meet in the centre to support a spire.[88] Aubrey, who was living with Hooke at Gresham College at the time of these discussions with Wren, recorded in the 'Monumenta Britannica' that Wren's drawing was an 'excellent draught' and 'about four foot long', although he had not seen it.[89] The following day found Hooke drawing his own 'rationall porcenna',[90] which was eventually presented to the Royal Society in July 1684. The minutes recorded: 'Mr Hooke read a discourse concerning the form of PORSENN'S tomb, described in PLINY. He also shewed a scheme of it different from that of Mr. GREAVES, of which he was desired to leave a copy.'[91] This drawing is also lost, although Aubrey (a Fellow of the Society) sketched what he noted was 'Porsenna's Monument according to Mr Rob. Hook R.S.S.' in his 'Monumenta Britannica' (fig. 43).[92]

Hooke and Wren continued their discussion of the tomb on Saturday 20 October 1677 at Man's coffee house near Charing Cross.[93] This interest may have been prompted by Wren's imminent project to design the mausoleum for Charles I at Windsor, drawn up the following year, although this design was for a rotunda and therefore bore no similarity to the Porsenna tomb.[94] The tomb's more certain influence can be seen in his design for a wooden catafalque for Mary II at Westminster Abbey of 1695 (fig. 44; chosen in preference to that by Grinling Gibbons).[95] What is clear is the long-running interest of both men in this tomb. It equally fascinated Hawksmoor, since a sale catalogue of his books and drawings recorded no less than twenty-eight reconstructions of it by him.[96] He commended the tomb in a letter to Lord Carlisle in 1726 concerning the mausoleum at Castle Howard and a

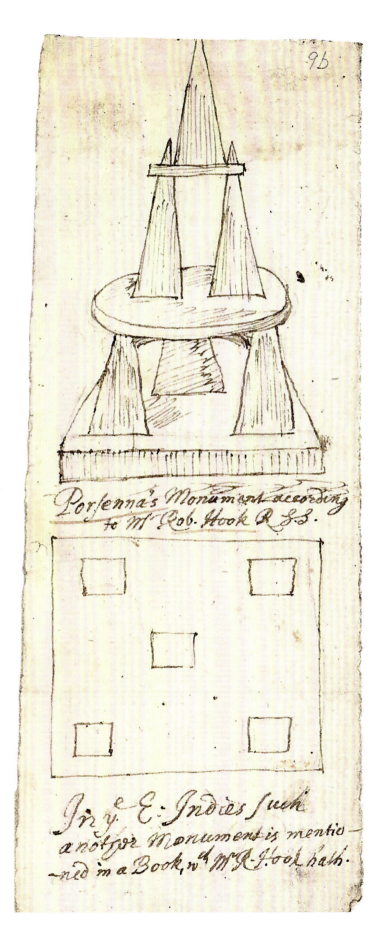

43 Hooke's reconstruction of the tomb of Porsenna as sketched by John Aubrey in his 'Monumenta Britannica' (1663–93), fol. 9br. Bodleian Library, Oxford, MSS Top. Gen.c.24–25

CLASSICAL ORDERS AND LANTERNS 35

year later sent Carlisle 'a Mosoleum like the Tomb of King Porsenna'.[97] There is a clear resemblance between the pyramidal forms on Hawksmoor's Carrmire Gate at Castle Howard (fig. 45) and Greaves's Porsenna illustration.

Wren's view of architectural history was of no minor significance to his practice, since it supplied the theoretical legitimacy for his inventive use of the classical language and, through hypothetical reconstructions of Tyrian-style structures, some of the actual models on which

ABOVE 44 Wren's wooden catafalque for Mary II in Westminster Abbey, etched by Romeyn de Hooghe in Samuel Gruterus, *Funeralia Mariae II Britanniarum* (1695), n.p.

RIGHT 45 The Carrmire Gate at Castle Howard, by Hawksmoor

his architecture depended. As will now be seen, such a dependency was especially the case with classical versions of forms like church lanterns and steeples, where surviving antique examples were elusive and a degree of invention was necessary to fill the archaeological void.

'SEEMINGLY VERY OPEN': LEVANT TEMPLES AND TYRIAN TOMBS AT THE LONDON STEEPLES

When advising the Commission for building the Queen Anne churches in 1711, Wren reflected the advice of Alberti that towers 'provide an excellent ornament, if sited in a suitable position and built on appropriate lines'.[98] Wren recommended that, together with porticoes, 'handsome Spires, or Lanterns, rising in good Proportion above the

46 The 'Warrant' design for St Paul's Cathedral, c.1675, south elevation drawn by Wren. All Souls College, Oxford

neighbouring Houses, (of which I have given several Examples in the City of different Forms) may be of sufficient Ornament to the Town, without a great Expence for inriching the outward Walls of the Churches, in which Plainness and Duration ought principally, if not wholly, to be studied'.[99] 'Plainness and duration' were, after all, good Tyrian qualities. Wren was evidently proud of the many 'different forms' of his spires and lanterns. While these were established features of English Gothic churches, they had no precedents on antique temples. Evelyn had emphasised that the lantern was a contemporary feature, not an ancient one, when discussing the lighting of domes in Italy and further north in 1664.[100] Wren can be seen to have 'reinvented' these elements through the use of proto-classical and, on occasions, exotic forms. A pine cone was proposed for the 'lantern' to the dome in the pre-Fire design for old St Paul's, for example (see fig. 76), as well as for the steeple of St Augustine Old Change designed by Hawksmoor.[101] The steeple in the later 'Warrant' design for the Cathedral of around 1675 even resembled a Chinese pagoda (fig. 46).[102] The octagonal Tower of the Winds as illustrated (inaccurately) in Cesariano's 1521

CLASSICAL ORDERS AND LANTERNS 37

ABOVE LEFT 47   The Tower of the Winds in Athens, illustrated by Cesare Cesariano, from Vitruvius, *Di Lucio Vitruvio Pollione De architectura libri dece traducti de latino in vulgare* (1521), fol. XXIIIIv

ABOVE RIGHT 48   The steeple at St Bride Fleet Street, London (1701–3)

RIGHT 49   The steeple at St Michael Paternoster Royal, London (1713–17), possibly designed by Hawksmoor

Italian translation of Vitruvius (I.vi.4, and republished in Ryff's Vitruvius of 1575, owned by Hooke), appears to have formed the basis for the steeple at St Bride Fleet Street (1701–3; figs 47 and 48).[103] The Athens tower was a natural antique model for a steeple, and all the more so when represented taller than in reality by Cesariano and Ryff. Its octagonal form and the pine cone both had Christian associations with rebirth and resurrection, which the presence of flaming urns on Wren's church towers only served to enhance.[104] A pine cone was used in the courtyard of the Triconchos of the Great Palace at Constantinople where the emperor enacted the part of Christ in the Entry on Palm Sunday, for example, as well as in the atrium at St Peter's (again mentioned by Cesariano).[105] Jones used one as a model for his finials in the refacing of old St Paul's. Hawksmoor followed suit in using novel classical forms, and tomb architecture in particular, for his own towers and steeples in Oxford and London.[106]

In addition to these proto-classical and exotic models, a temple in the Levant may well have influenced the design of various lanterns on the Wren churches. Above the tower at St Michael Paternoster Royal, a circular lantern forms the lower stage of the steeple added in 1713–17, possibly to Hawksmoor's design (fig. 49).[107] The lantern stage has a 'serrated' entablature, unorthodox in Vitruvian terms, which cuts back between each of the protruding Ionic columns. Each projection is given added emphasis through being capped by a vase. This type of entablature was novel in England up to this time, although it was also being used on the contemporary lantern stages of the spires at St James Garlickhythe (1714–17) and St Stephen Walbrook (1713–14), albeit that these are square and have paired columns at the corners (see fig. 139). Such an entablature had been illustrated on a variety of fanciful antique structures in Giovanni Battista Montano's *Li Cinque Libri di Architettura* (1691).[108] But for a built example, and on an antique building with Christian associations to boot, Wren and Hawksmoor would have had to look to the Levant. It could be found on the circular Temple of Venus at Baalbek (old Heliopolis) in Lebanon, a temple that had been consecrated by the time Europeans first visited it in the second half of the seventeenth century (fig. 50).

50   The Temple of Venus at Baalbek (Heliopolis), Lebanon (early 3rd century AD)

Baalbek was of much interest to the Royal Society. Phoenicians were thought to have founded it and, like Tadmor (or Palmyra) in Syria, it had long been associated with Solomon (as Hooke would have seen in his study of de Monconys's *Journal des Voyages* of 1665, although he died in 1703 well before these steeple designs). In a letter of 1672 requesting information on behalf of the Society from John Finch, the newly appointed Levant Company ambassador and Society Fellow, Oldenburg asked for 'a particular description of ye remainder of ye Castle and Temple of [Bacchus at] Balbecc, said by Monsr [André de] Monceaux, (a great Traveller and very skilfull Architect,) to be the best piece of Architecture, he ever saw; not far distant from Damascus in a fair plaine'.[109] It was noted in the Introduction that de Monceaux had travelled extensively in the Levant in 1668–9. Baalbek continued to be topical in Wren's circle during the period when these steeples were being designed and built. Henry Maundrell's *Journey from Aleppo to Jerusalem at Easter, A.D. 1697*, first published in Oxford in 1703, contained a view of Baalbek that included the Temple of Venus and its 'serrated' entablature (fig. 51). As the Introduction also noted, it was this first edition that was in Wren's collection (Lot 471). Maundrell mentioned the Temple's consecration, and drew attention to its unusual entablature (or 'cornish'):

51 Baalbek, from Henry Maundrell, *Journey from Aleppo to Jerusalem at Easter, A.D. 1697* (1703), p. 135 (the Temple of Venus in the centre)

Coming near these ruins, the first thing you meet with is a little round Pile of building, all of Marble. It is encircled with Columns of the Corinthian order, very beautiful, which support a Cornish that runs all round the structure of no ordinary state and beauty. This part of it that remains is at present in a very tottering condition, but yet the Greeks use it for a Church.[110]

The third edition of 1714 contained Hawksmoor's reconstruction of the Temple of Bacchus at Baalbek (based on that by Jean Marot).[111] Hawksmoor recorded in 1732 that he had discussed the measurements of the temples at Baalbek with one of Maundrell's successors as the Levant Company chaplain in Aleppo, Samuel Lisle (who was the chaplain first at Smyrna and then at Aleppo in 1710–19) and he may even have earlier discussed them with Maundrell himself.[112] This was probably some time before 1714, the date of his reconstruction, and therefore of the design of the lantern at St Michael Paternoster Royal with its similar cornice of 'no ordinary state and beauty'. He was certainly not averse to using the temples at Baalbek as models for works in both London and Oxford.[113] Kerry Downes has pointed to the Temple of Venus as Hawksmoor's possible model for a design of about 1723–4 for the Temple of the Four Winds (Belvedere) at Castle Howard.[114]

Moreover, given the lack of antique precedents for lanterns and steeples, these elements provided Wren with a particular opportunity for the re-creation of structures mentioned in his history of classical architecture. For

example, both he and Hawksmoor used the mausoleum at Halicarnassus as the basis for these forms. In Wren's case, the Tyrian-style mausoleum was used as the model for the lantern of the vestibule dome in the Great Model for St Paul's of 1673 (with a crowning statue of St Paul), and in Hawksmoor's, for the steeple built at St George in Bloomsbury of the later 1720s (with a crowning statue now of George I; figs 52 and 53).[115] The ancient tomb of the king of Caria was thus converted into a Christian monument to British monarchy (St Paul was after all a 'Prince' of the Anglican Church). Wren's use of the mausoleum here proves just how early he was interested in its form. In addition, four 'Wren Office' designs for an unidentified

ABOVE 52   The Great Model for St Paul's Cathedral, 1673 (the lantern of the vestibule dome modelled on the Mausoleum at Halicarnassus). St Paul's Cathedral, London

LEFT 53   The steeple at St George, Bloomsbury (from 1723), by Hawksmoor

CLASSICAL ORDERS AND LANTERNS   41

church of about 1711–14 in Hawksmoor's hand have steeples inspired by the mausoleum.[116]

Following this use of the Halicarnassus mausoleum in a lantern design, Wren's version of another tomb in the Tyrian style, in the form of Porsenna's tomb as sketched by Hooke in 1677, resembles the striking steeple designed above the tower of St Dunstan-in-the-East from 1695 to 1701 (see figs 27 and 42).[117] This has four corner pinnacles, detailed in the Gothic manner, which anchor pointed arches that cross to support a much larger, central pinnacle or spire. Both Hooke and Hawksmoor worked on this steeple.[118] In July 1693 Hooke recorded in his Diary, for example, 'viewed St Dunstans, S. Vedast towers, with J.[ohn] Oliver': his Diary equally recorded that he was discussing Pliny in the early 1690s and that he lent his copy of Greaves's *Pyramidographia*, with its reconstruction of the tomb, in March 1693 (to the Royal Society's printer, Samuel Smith).[119] The tomb continued to fascinate Hooke way beyond his frequent discussions with Wren in 1677 and reconstruction in 1684, as well as Wren's own consideration of it 'as an architect' in his Tracts. In April 1693 (just a few months before visiting St Dunstan) Hooke noted that he had been at Jonathan's coffee house with a group that included Benjamin Woodroffe, Francis Lodwick, Richard Waller and John Houghton, all of whom were Fellows of the Royal Society, and that their conversation included 'Turris Beli' (the Tower of Babel), 'Arab Library, Learning Antient modern' and 'Porsenna'.[120] The tomb was also in Wren's mind around 1695 when the steeple at St Dunstan was being designed, since this was the same year it formed the basis for Mary II's catafalque (see fig. 44).

In structural terms, the steeple and Hooke's Porsenna sketch clearly both reflected the Gothic 'imperial crown' as used, for example, in the steeple of St Mary-le-Bow destroyed in the Fire.[121] However Wren's steeple has few Gothic details, is lighter in form and the central octagonal spike looks more like an obelisk than a Gothic spire. It is both plain and structurally coherent, qualities identified by Wren with the Tyrian style. The form of the steeple is structurally efficient, as the four corner needles help anchor the outward thrust of the supports for the central obelisk in a way that must have appealed to Wren. The structural similarities between Wren's steeple and Hooke's sketch are obvious, one the 'rational' (to use Hooke's own term) version of the other. Even if the tomb as imagined by Wren was not the steeple's primary model, this likeness cannot have gone unnoticed. In describing the steeple, we might aptly borrow Wren's own words on the tomb in the 'Discourse', where the arches 'cutting one another upon

54 Scheme for St Peter's, Rome, by Antonio da Sangallo the Younger, engraving by Antonio Labacco and Antonio Salamanca, 1547, published in *Speculum Romanae Magnificentiae* (1553–63), variously bound

the Diagonals will have a firm Bearing for all the Works above' and will 'have a stupendous effect, and seemingly very Open'.[122] It will be remembered that the tomb of Mausolus was also 'very open' according to him and as such was equally ideal as a model for a lantern such as that proudly crowning St Paul's. Much like this lantern, the St Dunstan steeple is perhaps best understood as a quotation or interpretation of the Tyrian-styled structure, rather than as a reconstruction of it.

Nor would this have been the first instance where the ancient tomb had been used as inspiration for a modern church tower. It was so used by Antonio da Sangallo the Younger in the giant model for St Peter's in Rome (built over the saint's tomb) made by Antonio Labacco in 1539–46.[123] Wren may well have seen the 1547 engravings of this model, by Labacco and Antonio Salamanca, bound a few years later in the *Speculum Romanae Magnificentiae* ('The Mirror of Roman Magnificence'; fig. 54).[124] There is also the case of San Biagio outside Montepulciano, a centrally planned church begun to Sangallo the Elder's design in 1518, where four obelisks stand beside the octagonal stage of the bell-chamber in probable allusion to the pyramids of Porsenna's tomb: indeed, according to legend, Porsenna had founded Montepulciano and so its use here would have been seen to relate to local antiquity more than to the Catholic denomination of the church.[125]

Wren ended his discussion of the Porsenna monument by repeating his admiration for it, noting that in his version, 'the Bases of the 5 upper Pyramids would be contiguous, and thus would be of the same shape and as high as the same below as Varro asserts with some suspicion, fearing how they would stand, but I with confidence, the Proportions perswading, which indeed are very fine'.[126] Tyrian-style buildings could not be anything other than of fine proportions, given that they had informed the Greeks, according to Wren. For he made clear that these structures had coincided with the first age of geometric, and therefore artistic, achievement under the Greeks. On the Tomb of Porsenna he concluded that 'I have been the longer in this Description, because the Fabrick was in the Age of Pythagoras and his School, when the World began to be fond of Geometry and Arithmetick.'[127] And on the Halicarnassus mausoleum he observed that its artists were 'contemporary with the School of *Plato*', a fact that explained its 'harmonick Disposition'.[128] Although the audacious structure of Porsenna's tomb had represented extravagance for Pliny, it thus took on a more profound meaning for Wren as a monument not only to ancient kingship but also to a pure classical style formed at the very birth of the sciences of geometry and arithmetic. As such Wren's Tyrian structures served a similar function to how the early churches that had been built in the East at places such as Tyre by the 'primitive' Christians, untainted by later Catholic corruption, were being viewed by Anglican divines keen to find a basis for Protestant Church ritual, iconography and architecture. When seen in this context, it was perfectly fitting that the two tombs in the Tyrian style, as well as a Greek tower and Levant temple, should inform Wren's church lantern and steeple designs. These designs in turn set the pattern for Hawksmoor's equally inventive forms, not least in Bloomsbury where his Halicarnassus steeple can now be seen to represent a late manifestation of Wren's Tyrian ideal.

CHAPTER TWO

GOTHIC ARCHES AND TOWERS

'The Saracen Mode of Building seen in the East'

Wren is most commonly described as an architect who worked in the classical tradition, or sometimes that of the Baroque in line with the style of St Paul's. When his attitude to the Gothic is discussed, he is more often than not understood to have held a negative view of the style (fig. 55).[1] This is perhaps not surprising, given that the rejection of the Gothic by Renaissance theorists had, bar a few exceptions, been commonplace.[2] Serlio dismissed it as 'German work' and pointed out in his third book of 1540 that it was the Goths and Vandals who had sacked Rome in 1527.[3] Giorgio Vasari noted in the preface to the 1568 edition of his *Lives* that what he called 'new architects' had 'brought from their barbarous races the method of that manner of buildings that are called by us to-day German'.[4] Francesco Sansovino observed in his Venetian encyclopaedia entitled *Venetia città nobilissima et singolare* (1581) that 'the Goths remained in Italy for many years, filling everything with their barbarian and corrupt customs, extinguishing almost completely Roman beauty'.[5] And closer to home, the poet Ben Jonson in the Stuart masque *Prince Henry's Barriers* (1610) wrote that during Britain's legendary antiquity 'More truth of *architecture* there was blaz'd, Than liv'd in all the ignorant *Gothes* have raz'd' (fig. 56).[6]

55 The tower of St Alban Wood Street, London (1697–8)

As the signature form of the Gothic, the pointed arch was singled out for special criticism during the Renaissance. The origin of its form had been identified as resulting from uneducated German tribes bending trees together to form shelters: the letter to Leo X of about 1519 concerning the monuments of Rome, probably written by Raphael and Baldassare Castiglione, noted that 'the Germans would bend the branches together and bind them to form their pointed arches'.[7] In England the diplomat Henry Wotton, while advocating the classical in 1624, noted the 'naturall imbecility' of pointed arches and advised that they 'ought to bee exiled from judicious eyes, and left to their first inventors, the *Gothes* or *Lumbards*, among other *Reliques* of that barbarous *Age*'.[8] Members of the Royal Society followed suit. John Aubrey in his unpublished 'Chronologia Architectonica' of about 1671 called Gothic 'the Barbarous Fashion'.[9] And John Evelyn in the 1707 expanded version of 'An Account of Architects and Architecture' appended to *A Parallel of the Ancient Architecture with the Modern*, described buildings by the Goths and Vandals 'and other barbarous Nations' as 'congestions of Heavy, Dark, Melancholy and *Monkish Piles*, without any just Proportion, Use or Beauty, compar'd with the truly *Ancient*'.[10] He also objected to Gothic's 'non-sense Insertions of various Marbles impertinently plac'd' and its 'turrets, and pinacles thick set with *Munkies* and *Chimeras*' along with 'other Incongruities'.[11] Indeed, Gothic buildings abounded in

56 Inigo Jones, 'St George's Portico', from *Prince Henry's Barriers* (1610). Devonshire Collection, Chatsworth

'slender and Misquine [petty] *Pillars*' and 'ponderous Arched Roofs'.[12] The message was clear: Gothic architecture was barbaric while classical architecture was civilised. Not only was the 1707 edition in Wren's collection (Lot 567) but this version of the 'Account' was also dedicated to him (which was dated 21 February 1697). Although Wren would disagree with Evelyn on the virtues of Gothic (as he did concerning the supremacy of ancient architectural rules), as the book's dedicatee he could have been left in no doubt as to what Evelyn regarded as the style's heathen ancestry and its more recent Catholic associations via the 'Monkish Piles'.[13]

To view Wren's attitude to Gothic as equally hostile places into shadow a body of work by him that might reasonably be called Gothic in style: at Tom Tower over the entrance gate to Christ Church in Oxford in 1681, at Westminster Abbey principally from 1698 and, perhaps most notably, at his London churches from the 1670s. These churches are, as a group, often described as classical, but they do not boast porticoes or pediments in the manner of a classical temple.[14] Rather, they invariably have towers that recall those of the English parish church, with or without a spire or steeple, rather than any classical prototype. For while these towers had ample medieval precedents, they had no antique ones on temples.[15] Moreover, some of Wren's churches had quintessential Gothic elements such as spires, pinnacles and even pointed arches. To help justify his use of Gothic forms on churches and cathedrals, and in parallel to his tracing of the origin of the Orders, Wren developed a theory as to the origins of Gothic that did not involve the heathen Goths. In common with his understanding of the birth of classical architecture in Tyre and the Levant, and the use of the first, Tyrian column on the great biblical structure of Solomon's Temple, he traced the later Gothic style to Arab or what he calls 'Saracen' builders in the Holy Land.[16] Knowledge of their buildings had, he maintained, been brought to England by the returning Crusaders and in this way the style acquired a Christian gloss. This view, and the approval of Gothic architecture that it implies, was articulated in unpublished remarks made in private correspondence and played no part in the public effort by Wren and Evelyn to promote the virtues of harmony and proportion synonymous with classical architecture.[17] As this chapter will show, Wren's understanding of an Eastern origin for medieval masonry practices fell in line with reconstructions by contemporary Protestant theologians of the Temple in Jerusalem complete with medieval church towers and Gothic details, as well as with ideas developing in Freemasonry concerning the origins of medieval masonry at the Temple. Before examining Wren's Gothic narrative, his approach to using the style should be explored.

'THE WHOLE PILE IS LARGE & MAGNIFICENT': RESPECTING MEDIEVAL ARCHITECTURE

There can be no doubt that Wren's early statements on the Gothic presented it as decidedly inferior to the classical. He noted on his proposal to re-case the inside of old St Paul's in 1666, for example, that 'it will be as easy to perform it, after a good *Roman* manner, as to follow the *Gothick* Rudeness of the old Design' (see fig. 76).[18] Nevertheless there is an obvious discrepancy between his theory and practice concerning Gothic. He advised in Tract one (which was started, it has been suggested, in the mid-1670s) that '*Gothick* Buttresses are all ill-favoured, and were avoided by the Ancients',[19] yet he used them (albeit concealed) later at St Paul's. He added that 'no sort of Pinnacle is worthy enough to appear in the Air, but Statue. Pyramids are *Gothick*',[20] yet he used pinnacles extensively on his London church towers. Take, for example, those at St Olave, Old Jewry of 1677–9, St Mary Somerset of 1685–94 (fig. 57), and All Hallows Bread Street of 1697–8 (demolished in 1877–8). All these designs therefore departed from advice he recorded in the Tracts. This discrepancy can perhaps best be seen in Wren's attitude to spires and steeples: he wrote in 1666 that his proposed

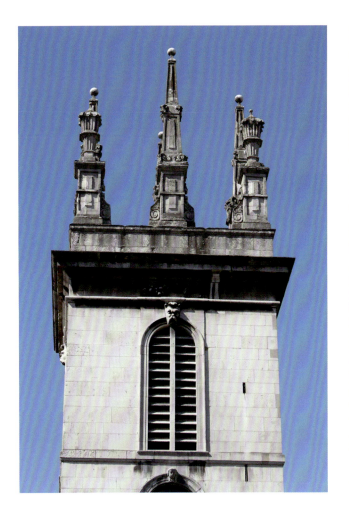

57 The tower of St Mary Somerset, London (1685–94)

58 The tower of St Antholin (1686, demolished in 1874), engraved by Archelaus Cruse, from Thomas Shepherd, *London and its Environs in the Nineteenth Century* (1829), pl. 71

'*Rotundo* bearing a *Cupola*' at old St Paul's (see fig. 76) had 'incomparable more Grace in the remoter Aspect, than it is possible for the lean Shaft of a Steeple to afford', yet by the time of the proposed Queen Anne churches in 1711, he was recommending 'handsome Spires'.[21]

Wren used conventional Gothic spires and steeples, of various forms, to cap a number of his church towers. St Lawrence Jewry of 1671–80 has a faceted, lead-covered spire; St Martin Ludgate of 1677–82/6 (designed with major input from Hooke) has a slender lead-covered spire on an arcaded lantern above an octagonal cupola; St Antholin Budge Row of 1686 was demolished in 1874 but had what *Parentalia* described as 'a neat Spire Steeple' that was faceted and in stone (fig. 58);[22] and St Mary Abchurch of 1681–6 has a lead-covered spire that rises from a square base.[23] Wren's church towers were decorated with a mix of Gothic and classical elements. Some have predominantly classical details, as at St Bride in Fleet Street (1671–8) with its Corinthian pilasters; some, although medieval in tone, have round-headed windows rather than pointed ones, as at St Mary Aldermanbury (1671–5); and others are more Gothic still, in including pointed arches such as at St Dunstan-in-the-East of 1695–1701 and St Alban Wood Street, of 1697–8 that also boasted what *Parentalia* described as Gothic pinnacles (see figs 27 and 55).[24] Initially Wren repaired the Gothic tower at St Mary Aldermary in 1674, only to rebuild it extensively in 1701–4 complete with pointed arched windows (fig. 59).[25] He had already used this type of arch on Tom Tower in Oxford in 1681 (see fig. 61). And he also sometimes used crenellations on his towers, of no use defensively but strong in medieval associations, as with his reconstruction of the tower at St Mary-at-Hill of 1670–4.

GOTHIC ARCHES AND TOWERS   47

Clearly, Wren had a more positive appreciation than Evelyn of Gothic forms, and this attitude is evident as early as 1668 in his report on Salisbury Cathedral to Bishop Seth Ward. Here he observed that 'the whole Pile is large & magnificent, and may be justly accounted one of the best patterns of Architecture in the age wherein it was built'. He went on to comment on 'the first Architect whose judgmen[t] I must justly commend for many things', adding 'for here the breadth to the hight of the Navis, and both to the shape of the Iles beare a good proportion' and 'the Mouldings are decently mixed with large planes, without an affectation of filling every corner with ornaments'.[26] As this report and those on the repair of old St Paul's (1666) and Westminster Abbey (1713) testify, Wren fully acknowledged that medieval architecture represented an important national building tradition and, as such, an unbroken link with British history and Christianity. At the Abbey, for example, he recognised the work done by Henry III on the nave and, subsequently, 'the Abbots and Monks towards the West'.[27] The Gothic cathedrals, together with the ruins of monasteries and abbeys, signified the continuity of the Christian faith in England stretching back, through the legend of St Paul's visit to the country (recounted by Wren's son in *Parentalia*), to the times of Christ himself.[28] No one with Wren's interests in architectural history and construction could fail to be captivated by these monumental buildings. Despite the adoption of the classical style for court buildings during the reign of the first Stuarts, the Gothic had continued to be used for church buildings.[29] Peterhouse College chapel in Cambridge was built in 1628, with the maligned pointed windows, under the guidance of Wren's uncle, Matthew (fig. 60). It stood as an example of 'Laudian Gothic', a style promoted by Archbishop William Laud that was consistent with Peterhouse's medieval foundation and as such was possibly seen as signifying a continuity with the college's Catholic origins.[30] Wren's respect for Gothic buildings, when faced with the task of restoring or adding to them, may well have been influenced by Laudian attitudes via his father and uncle.

The sensitivity of Wren to repairing medieval buildings – and, as will be seen, to designing in their proximity – should be understood in the context of a growing interest in Gothic architecture at this time.[31] This interest was a further symptom of the emerging pluralistic approach to architectural history, embracing not just classical buildings, discussed in the Preface. Mirroring contemporary developments in taxonomy in the natural sciences, Wren came to see Gothic as a further 'species' of architectural styles, albeit one that was, for

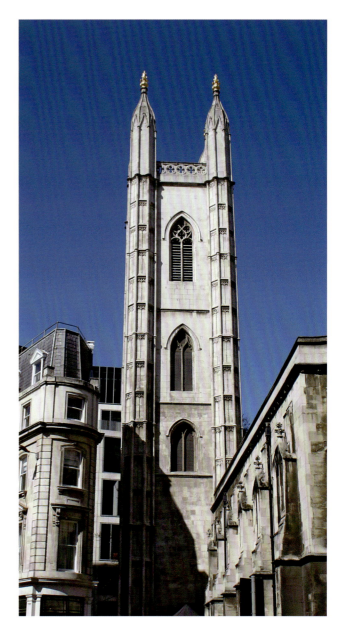

59 The tower of St Mary Aldermary, London (1701–4)

the most part, inferior to the classical. This recognition was stimulated by the Royal Society, which had helped foster the growth of antiquarianism. The objective of early antiquarians such as William Camden (1551–1623) to chronicle a legendary antiquity for Britain centred on Roman occupation gave way to the desire to develop an 'accurate' (or dispassionate) British history, shorn of its need to underpin the monarchy and Church. Given the non-classical character of churches and castles, as well as of ruined monasteries and manors, this reformulation of British history was necessarily medieval in tone. Prominent contemporary antiquarians included William

Dugdale (1605–1686) and John Aubrey (1626–1697), and slightly later Browne Willis (1682–1760) and William Stukeley (1687–1765).[32] Wren's library contained books on England's cathedrals and abbeys by the leading antiquarians of the day, which he collected throughout his life. He owned the main works by Dugdale, notably *The History of St Paul's Cathedral* (1658; Lot 251) in which he would have seen the medieval cathedral celebrated in the plates by Wenceslaus Hollar, *The Antiquities of Warwickshire* (1656; Lot 252) and *Monasticon Anglicanum* in the form of both the abridged edition of 1693 and the expanded version by John Stevens of 1718 (Lots 253 and 254).[33] Indeed, Wren knew Dugdale: Aubrey recorded a conversation between them about the 'Fraternity of Architects or Free-Masons' who were given a licence by the Pope in Henry III's time for the building of churches.[34] Wren also owned Richard Rawlinson's *The history and antiquities of the Cathedral-Church of Salisbury, and the abbey-church of Bath* (1719; Lot 277). In addition, the medieval fabrics of the institutions of London, including the City's livery company halls and its churches, colleges and libraries, were outlined in his copy of Edward Hatton's *A New View of London* (1708; Lot 484). As will now be seen, this interest in medieval buildings and a contextual approach to working on them compelled Wren to view the Gothic as a viable – and even in some situations, preferable – alternative to classical architecture, but one whose origins were therefore equally in need of explanation.

'OF A STYLE WITH THE REST OF THE STRUCTURE': NATURAL BEAUTY AND CONTEXT

Wren's approach to the appropriate use of Gothic can be found in his reports on the medieval fabrics of two of England's most important religious centres, namely Salisbury Cathedral in 1668 and Westminster Abbey in 1713, and in letters, once again to a senior cleric, concerning his new works at Tom Tower at Christ Church in Oxford in 1681. This use was in practice restricted to such ecclesiastical establishments or foundations, be

60 Peterhouse College chapel, Cambridge (1628)

it in repairing or adding to their existing buildings or in building the new parish churches. Whereas the early practitioners of classicism, Jones and Webb, had dealt with decay at old St Paul's by refacing its façades with a classical 'skin', albeit with due regard to the underlying Gothic proportions, Wren came to deal with the repair of medieval buildings in a different way.[35] His choice to use Gothic was justified in terms of context, that is the pre-existing, medieval fabric of the surrounding ecclesiastical buildings.[36] In this he followed Hugh May's remodelling of Windsor Castle for Charles II from 1675, where a similar sensitivity to medieval context was expressed through the use of crenellations and round-headed windows.[37] In seventeenth-century Italy, prominent designs for new façades to existing medieval buildings such as those for Milan Cathedral and S. Petronio in Bologna had bowed to context.[38] The classical theory of architectural decorum emphasised the importance of matching the style of ornament (from plain to flamboyant) to its setting (from town to country and affluent to poor).[39] Evelyn in both editions of his 'Account' (1664 and 1707) defined appropriate decorum as 'where a *Building*, and particularly the *Ornaments* thereof, become the *station*, and *occasion*'.[40]

Wren explained the choice of Gothic in his design for Tom Tower (so-called because it housed a bell called 'Tom') at Christ Church in a letter of May 1681 to John Fell, the Bishop of Oxford and Dean of the College (fig. 61; see fig. 68). Here he stated: 'I resolved it ought to be gothic to agree with the Founders worke' but qualified this by observing, 'yet I have not continued soe busy as he began'.[41] The 'founders work' in question was the gate built by Cardinal Thomas Wolsey and the partly built Gothic Tom Quadrangle (three of the four sides were almost completed, with the chapel on the fourth side still to be started at the time of Wolsey's fall from power in 1529).[42] Wren's tower sits on the gate and its two mini-towers either side, and bows not only to the principle of stylistic uniformity with them but to Wolsey's Gothic vision for the quadrangle as a whole. In this vein *Parentalia* emphasised continuity when describing Tom Tower as the 'Campanile, or Bell-tower, over the Gate, in the Front and principal Access to the great Quadrangle-court of Christ-church, Oxon, in the Gothick Stile; begun on the old Foundation (laid by Cardinal Wolsey) in June 1681, and finished November 1682'.[43] However, while the style of the tower is Gothic, it is relatively plain (or not 'so busy', as Wren put it) and the underlying arrangement – in its symmetry and use of pure geometric forms – is perfectly compatible with the classical.

In December 1681, when building operations were well under way, Fell suggested using Wren's top storey (housing the bell) as an astronomical observatory; this additional function would have required a change in height. Wren's rejection of the idea is revealing in terms of his belief in stylistic integrity and uniformity. If alterations to the design were to be made at this late stage, he felt, 'it will necessarily fall short of the beauty of the other way', namely the Gothic, 'for having begun in the Gothick manner, wee must conclude above with flats and such proportions as will not be well reconcilable to the Gothic manner wch spires upward & the pyramidal forms are essential to it'. The latter was in reference to the pinnacles terminating the buttress 'columns'. Thus, Wren continued to Fell, 'this proposition had been much better effected had not the parts formerly built diverted us from beginning after the better forms of Architecture', in reference to the classical style. Wren was equally against a stylistic mixture at Tom Tower, for 'I feare wee shall make an unhandsome medly this way'.[44]

Wren's acceptance of Gothic at Tom Tower and elsewhere was facilitated by his preference for composition over outward style, given that the use of an underlying order or geometry was just as fundamental to Gothic works as it was to classical ones. He observed in the second Tract that, 'it seems very unaccountable, that the Generality of our late Architects dwell so much upon this ornamental, and so slightly pass over the geometrical, which is the most essential Part of Architecture'.[45] And he also noted that 'geometrical Figures are naturally more beautiful than other irregular; in this all consent as to a Law of Nature. Of geometrical Figures, the Square and the Circle are most beautiful.'[46] At Tom Tower, for example, its three upper storeys are composed of simple regular forms overlaid with minimal Gothic ornament. The lowest section (with its window) sitting over the existing gate is square in plan and supports an intermediary storey (with its square panels), which in turn supports the buttressed octagonal (bell) lantern that is crowned by an octagonal dome. In the first of his Tracts Wren recognised two 'causes' of what the observer perceives as beautiful in architecture, 'natural' and 'customary'. While the natural cause of the perception of beauty in an object 'is from *Geometry*, consisting in Uniformity' and included proportion and symmetry, the customary cause is 'begotten by the Use of our Senses to those Objects

61 Tom Tower at Christ Church, Oxford, by Wren (1681–2)

which are usually pleasing to us for other Causes, as Familiarity': thus 'particular Inclination breeds a Love of Things not in themselves lovely. Here lies the great Occasion of Errors; here is tried the Architects Judgement: but always the true test is natural or geometric beauty.'[47] This distinction between intrinsic or primary qualities and customary or secondary ones in the human perception of 'objects' resonated with ideas developed by John Locke, a Fellow of both the Royal Society and Christ Church at the time Wren was designing Tom Tower there.[48] His *Essay Concerning Human Understanding* was begun many years before its first publication in 1690, probably around 1671, and it has been used to help understand Hawksmoor's drawing technique in the 1690s.[49] Locke noted in chapter eight of the second book that 'Qualities thus considered in bodies are: First, such as are utterly inseparable from the body, in what state soever it be', which he called 'real' and 'original or *primary qualities* of body' that included 'solidity' and 'figure'.[50] And he also continued in a similar vein to Wren when distinguishing, 'Secondly, such *qualities* which in truth are nothing in the objects themselves but powers to produce various sensations in us by their primary qualities' that include 'colours, sounds, tastes, etc. These I call *secondary qualities*…we may conceive that the *ideas of secondary qualities* are also *produced*, viz. by *the operation of insensible particles on our senses*'. In fact, Wren's definition of customary beauty further resonated with Locke's idea that 'fashion and the common opinion having settled wrong notions, and education and custom ill habits, the just value of things are misplaced and the palates of men corrupted. Pains should be taken to rectify these.'[51]

Tom Tower might reasonably be considered in these terms, given that it was designed at the same time as both men were formulating them. It can be seen to cause the perception in the onlooker of natural beauty based on 'primary qualities' such as its simple geometric forms. These fundamental geometric attributes are further enhanced, in terms of natural beauty, by strict symmetry. The unifying presence of the dome might be understood to resolve the design, much as that at St Paul's would do: the circular form (to which the octagon tends) represented a universal form of unity and, for Wren, the most powerful of geometric forms guaranteeing beauty. Locke too had observed that 'among all the *ideas* we have…there is none more simple, than that of unity, or one: it has no shadow of variety or composition in it'.[52] Moreover, the tower can be seen to have conveyed a sense of 'customary beauty' to the onlooker through the superficial (or surface) characteristics of its architectural style ('familiar' or 'customary' quasi-Gothic details): these were as a direct result of the less universal, more specific requirement of matching the tower's medieval context. When seen in Lockean terms, the tower's primary qualities are its conveyance of the sense of what he terms 'solidity' (enhanced by its massiveness and relatively plain detailing in contrast to the fussy pre-existing adjoining towers) and clarity of 'figure' (as expressed through its symmetry and geometric profile); and its secondary qualities are its ability to evoke the sensation of familiarity through Gothic decoration applied to the surface. Thus Wren's emphasis on the geometric quality of objects, both natural and built, as the basis of the perception of their beauty, further liberated him from Vitruvius and the obligation to use classicism; while it greatly assisted his freedom to use Gothic, when context demanded, given its quintessential geometric qualities.

In Wren's proposals in 1713 for repairs and additions to Westminster Abbey, made to the newly appointed Dean, Francis Atterbury, he again emphasised context when suggesting the use of Gothic. Wren and Hooke worked together on the fabric during 1693 and Wren became responsible for it in the newly established role of Surveyor from 1698 until his death in 1723.[53] Concerning a proposed new central tower and spire he observed in his report to Atterbury:

> I have made a Design, which will not be very expensive but light, and still in the *Gothick* Form, and of a Style with the rest of the Structure, which I would strictly adhere to, throughout the whole Intention: to deviate from the old Form, would be to run into a disagreeable Mixture, which no Person of a good Taste could relish.[54]

Wren's scheme, complete with windows in the form of the much-maligned pointed arch, had been represented in a timber model of 1710.[55] With the help of his assistant, William Dickinson, Wren went on to remodel the north transept façade from around 1719 in a symmetrical Gothic style (now much altered but compare Dickinson's drawing for the scheme and Hollar's engraving of the medieval north façade; figs 62 and 63).[56] Here, according to Wren's report, 'the Stair-cases at the Corners must be new ashlar'd, and Pyramids set upon them conformable to the old-Style'. The intention once again was 'to make the Whole of a Piece'. The removal of the fourteenth-century Solomon's Porch and other alterations aimed to regularise the transept façade and 'to restore it to its proper Shape first intended'.[57] Dickinson's drawings even recorded the use once again of pointed-arched windows; and they

re-occurred in drawings by him of a further proposal by Wren for a central tower and spire, this time of 1722.[58] The key priority to avoid a mixture of styles, Gothic and the classical, was emphasised a number of times by Wren to the Dean:

> For all these new Additions I have prepared perfect Draughts and Models, such as I conceive may agree with the original Scheme of the old Architect, without any modern Mixtures to shew my own Inventions: in like manner as I have among the Parochial Churches of *London* given some few Examples, (where I was oblig'd to deviate from a better Style) which appear not ungraceful, but ornamental, to the East part of the City; and it is to be hoped, by the publick Care, to the West part also, in good Time, will be as well adorned; and surely by nothing more properly than a lofty Spire, and Western-towers to *Westminster-abbey*.[59]

62   The north façade of Westminster Abbey, engraved by Wenceslas Hollar, 1654, from William Dugdale, *Monasticon Anglicanum*, vol. 1 (1655), pl. 56

While the classical, as the 'better style', had the potential for a purer expression of the qualities of 'natural' beauty sought by Wren, the Gothic was evidently perfectly capable of grace and ornament. It is interesting that in the case of his Gothic churches, he again saw himself as 'obliged' to use the style, rather than preferring to do so. This use was most probably also due to context. As previously noted, these 'few examples' – the vast majority of designs were evidently seen as classical – that are indisputably in the Gothic style with pointed-arched windows are St Alban, St Dunstan and St Mary Aldermary (see figs 27, 55, 59). St Alban was rebuilt using as much as possible of the surviving walls, St Dunstan was no more than a repair and reconstruction of the damaged building and St Mary Aldermary was a repair and reconstruction of the late medieval fabric.[60]

The western towers at the Abbey to which Wren referred were eventually added by Hawksmoor from 1734, in a style that once again matched the Gothic façade.[61] Hawksmoor echoed Wren's respect for context when working once more in Oxford, this time at All Souls, and providing an 'explanation' of his Gothic design for the north quadrangle to his patron George Clarke in 1715.

He noted: 'I must ask leave to say something in favour of ye Old quadrangle, built by your most Revd. founder for altho it may have some faults yet it is not without its virtues', adding that 'I am confident that much conveniency and beauty, may be added to it, whereas utterly destroying or barbarously altering or mangling it, wou'd be using ye founder cruelly, and a loss to ye present possessours.'[62] It thus appears likely that Gothic was considered by both architects, at least when used in the context of Oxford colleges, as symbolising the ancient virtues of the building's foundation. Hawksmoor also followed his master in regarding the Gothic as especially appropriate to ecclesiastical and semi-ecclesiastical buildings such as colleges (rather than, say, country houses, a building type of which he was certainly experienced). At All Souls, his drawing for a Gothic west gate to the north quadrangle was labelled 'after ye Monastick Maner'.[63] And to a later Dean of Westminster, Joseph Wilcocks, he commented: 'this is the most Antient style in the Gothick or Monastick manner, as they call'd it'.[64] This 'monastic' description seems to have been coined to convey Gothic's associations with Christian buildings, rather than any specific monastic qualities it may or may not have had, and was much in line with Wren's pattern of use of the style. Given this use, the need to trace a Christian origin for Gothic, or at least one that was more virtuous than the traditional heathen explanation, was no doubt of some importance to him. Significantly enough, as will now be seen, Wren's case for the origins of Gothic was not made in abstract but formed part of his justification to Dean Atterbury for its proposed use at the Abbey.

'CALLED THE SARACEN STYLE': GOTHIC AND THE HOLY LAND

Wren's acceptance of Gothic as a viable building style in certain circumstances motivated him to come up with a rational theory as to its origins. This was in common with the general purpose of his enquiry into the history of architecture or what he called his 'larger Idea of the whole Art'. Unlike the Renaissance view of Gothic in Britain and France as having originated with the buildings of the uncouth Goths, and thereby as morally corrupt, Wren's view of the style was necessarily more positive.[65] Evidence for his understanding of Gothic's origins comes in its earliest form from the Tracts, in reference to what he calls the 'Saracen Style'. However, the main explanation is to be found in the Abbey report of 1713 to Atterbury, with additional, second-hand material within the defence of Wren's ideas by his son in *Parentalia* and remarks by his erstwhile assistant, Hawksmoor. As noted, it was in the context of this practical work at the Abbey, and elsewhere on medieval cathedral fabrics, that Wren considered the origins of Gothic. As his son put it in *Parentalia*, 'these Surveys, & other occasional Inspections of the most noted cathedral Churches & Chapels in England' induced 'the Surveyor to make some Enquiry into the Rise and Progress of this Gothick Mode'.[66]

The Abbey had been rebuilt by Henry III from 1245 with the help of a French mason, Henry of Reyns, using a pointed-arch style now known as 'Early English'.[67] Wren argued in his report that it was built

> according to the Mode, which came into Fashion after the Holy War. This we now call the *Gothick* Manner of Architecture (so the Italians called what was not after the Roman Style) tho' the *Goths* were rather Destroyers than Builders; I think it should with more Reason be called the *Saracen* Style; for those People wanted neither Arts nor Learning; and after we in the West had lost both, we borrowed again from them, out of their *Arabick* Books, what they with great Diligence had translated from the *Greeks*.[68]

Here Wren repeated the Renaissance topos of the Goths as a barbaric people; nevertheless, they were becoming better understood through Olaus Magnus's study of 1555, translated as *A compendious history of the Goths, Swedes, & Vandals, and other Northern nations* (1658: this was mentioned in Hooke's Diary and was in his library).[69] Wren continued by proposing that Henry III's use of Gothic at the Abbey had come about as a result of earlier contact between Christian knights and the East during the Crusades.[70] He reported to the Dean concerning the pointed arch that 'the *Crusado* gave us an Idea of this Form; after which King *Henry* built his Church', adding that 'the *Saracen* Mode of Building seen in the East, soon spread over *Europe*, and particularly in *France*; the Fashions of which Nation we affected to imitate in all Ages, even when we were at Enmity with it'.[71] Wren's son, writing in *Parentalia*, gave a slightly more coherent account of his father's apparent understanding of the Christian refinement of the style: for he 'was of Opinion'

63 Wren's scheme for remodelling the north transept of Westminster Abbey, 1719, drawn by William Dickinson. Westminster Abbey, WAM (P) 900

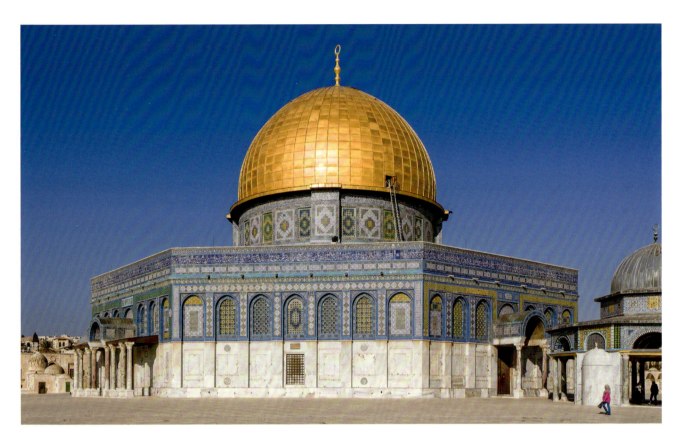

that what we now vulgarly call the Gothick ought properly and truly to be named the Saracenick Architecture refined by the Christians; which first of all began in the East after the Fall of the Greek Empire by the prodigious Success of those People that adhered to Mahomet's Doctrine, who out of Zeal to their Religion, built Mosques, Caravansaras, & Sepulchres, wherever they came.[72]

As its name suggests, the 'Saracen style' was thus not one used by Christian builders at the time when Wren understood it to have first flourished in the East. Nevertheless, Gothic became Christianised in his account through the agency of the Crusaders (whose very purpose had been the overthrow and conversion of the Saracens, or Arabs and Turks, as the Muslim occupiers of Jerusalem). The style's Christian credentials were further enhanced by its birth in the Holy Land, much as those of the classical style had been (via its use on Solomon's Temple). The migration of style was explained not this time by Phoenician merchants but by Crusading knights returning to England after 1096.

In fact, Gothic is thought to have been introduced into England by masons from France, although it may well have had Eastern roots.[73] A shallow pointed arch is a feature of the Muslim Dome of the Rock built on Temple Mount in Jerusalem (completed in 691 on the site of Solomon's Temple and with an inner arcade of pointed arches; fig. 64).[74] The 'Syrian' pointed arch is to be found in the Al-Aqsa mosque in Jerusalem (as rebuilt in 1035; fig. 65) and the fortress of Al-Ukhaidir in modern-day Iraq (775), while the Armenian Cathedral of Ani in modern-day Turkey (early eleventh century) is credited with influencing the development of Gothic.[75] A Gothic form that had more certain Eastern origins than the pointed arch was the ogee (which, like an 'S', is a double continuous curve passing from convex to concave).[76] This form was used for arches, domes and openings throughout the East. The arches on the Green mausoleum of Mehmed I at Bursa in Turkey (1421) have this form, as does the dome to the Fatima Masumeh Shrine at Qom in Iran (rebuilt from 1519) that was illustrated, together with pointed arches, by Chardin in 1686 (figs 66 and 67).[77] The spread of this ogee form in the West has

OPPOSITE ABOVE 64   The Dome of the Rock, Jerusalem (completed in 691)

OPPOSITE BELOW 65   The Al-Aqsa mosque, Jerusalem (as rebuilt in 1035)

BELOW LEFT 66   The Green mausoleum of Mehmed I at Bursa, Turkey (1421)

BELOW RIGHT 67   The dome to the Fatima Masumeh Shrine at Qom, Persia, from John Chardin, *Travels into Persia and the East Indies, with Figures* (1686), between pp. 390 and 391

indeed been linked with the returning Crusaders, and to Western eyes it could convey strong Eastern associations: it formed part of a style that came to be called 'Arabesco' or 'Saracenic'.[78] The distinctiveness of the form and its identification by the term 'ogee' were fully recognised in seventeenth-century England.[79] Small domes of this kind had sometimes been used in medieval, and especially in Elizabethan, architecture.[80] At Tom Tower, the domes on

GOTHIC ARCHES AND TOWERS   57

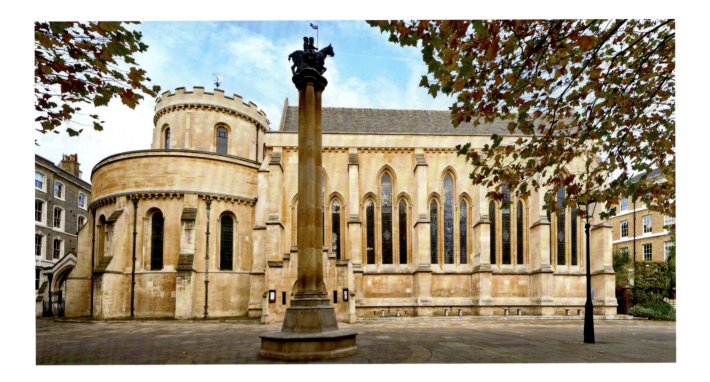

the two existing side towers, built under Wolsey, took this ogee profile (fig. 68; see fig. 61). The crowning octagonal dome on Wren's central tower followed suit and he also used the form for the main window. In addition, four 'onion' half-domes fill the recesses created between the square and octagonal stages of the tower.[81]

It is, however, unclear if Wren knew of any actual examples of Eastern pointed arches and ogee domes before designing Tom Tower in 1681: this was certainly possible via the travellers to Jerusalem to whom he alluded in the Tracts or via Rycaut and Chardin, or other Royal Society Fellows who had spent time in Turkey before 1680 (discussed in Chapter Three). The meeting with Chardin recorded by Evelyn was around the same time as Wren designed Tom Tower and used the term 'Saracen' for its style in the Tracts. Nevertheless, he would have found evidence for his understanding of Gothic's origins and migration to England, if not of its Saracen creators, closer to home. At Westminster Abbey, the north transept entrance cast as Solomon's Porch, the Jericho Parlour and Jerusalem Chamber all associated the Gothic fabric with biblical sites.[82] Legend has it that in 1413 Henry IV, on his deathbed and having been told he was in the Jerusalem Chamber, exclaimed: 'his prophecie sayde "he schulde make an ende and deye yn Jerusalem"'.[83] In crediting the introduction of the Gothic to the Crusaders when reporting to the Abbey's Dean, Wren was implying that his own work using the style, most notably in remodelling the north transept façade, should been seen as a further celebration of these links with the Holy Land made through the Abbey's monumental Gothic fabric.

Such links were to be found in London even more directly still, at the Temple Church in the Inns of Court that had been built in the late twelfth century by the Knights Templar (fig. 69).[84] Wren was familiar with this church, having reported on its condition in May 1682 and subsequently refurbished it, as well as proposing a new cloister (an arcade running south from the west porch).[85] In its original form, the church was a free-standing rotunda (called the 'Round'), which was intended to recall the rotunda of the fourth-century church of the Holy Sepulchre in Jerusalem (rebuilt in 1027–48), which contained the empty tomb of Christ (called the Anastasis Rotunda, see figs 7, 84–7).[86] The protection of Christ's tomb had been tasked to the Templars, as Ashmole made clear in his *The Institution, Laws & Ceremonies of the Most Noble Order of the Garter* (1672 and reissued in 1715, both editions owned by Wren [Lots 259, 412 and 478]).[87] The influence of the Holy Sepulchre on the Temple Church was well known, the traveller George Sandys noting in

OPPOSITE 68   The domes on Tom Tower at Christ Church, Oxford, by Wren (1681–2)

ABOVE 69   The Temple Church, London (late 12th century)

GOTHIC ARCHES AND TOWERS   59

1615, for example, that the London church had been 'built round in imitation' of that in Jerusalem.[88] Moryson visited the Holy Sepulchre in 1596, as did Biddulph in 1601.[89] And Wren was well aware of its prominence in Jerusalem, as the next chapter will show. While it was the Holy Sepulchre's form that had influenced the Temple Church rather than its style, which was Byzantine with shallow pointed arches, there was evidently some confusion in Wren's day regarding this style. Amico and Sandys showed the church with round arches, while Evelyn identified it with the Gothic (see figs 7, 87). In Evelyn's 1707 'Account', following the list of the defects of the Gothic such as 'Clumsy Buttresses, Towers' and 'sharp pointed Arches', he gave examples of Gothic buildings 'not Worthy the Name of *Architecture*'; these included the cathedrals at Canterbury and Salisbury in England, Strasbourg and Basel then in Germany, Amiens and Lyons in France, as well as 'the *Santa Sophia* at Constantinople' and 'the Temple of the *Sepulchre* at *Jerusalem* (at the Decadence at least of the Art)'.[90] Irrespective of whether or not Wren was aware of the Holy Sepulchre's pointed arches, its historic connections with the Temple Church would certainly have offered him direct evidence of links between English Gothic architecture and the Holy Land via Crusading knights (in this case the Templars).[91] Wren may also have been aware that the Crusaders had been active builders while in the Levant, constructing fortifications and religious structures in a style dubbed 'Crusader Gothic'. For example, the Chapel of the Ascension on the Mount of Olives (*c*.328) as rebuilt by them in the twelfth century (some time before 1188 when it became the Ascension mosque under the Turks), has pointed arches (fig. 70).[92] His identification of the Crusaders as builders reflected the historic links between the Orders of Chivalry (such as the Templars and Hospitallers) and the craft guilds (particularly Masons), both of whom for example cultivated Solomon as their patron.[93]

Various reconstructions of Solomon's Temple published by Protestant theologians in the second half of the seventeenth century had equally implied Gothic's Eastern roots.[94] John Lightfoot in *The Temple: Especially as it stood in the Days of Our Savior* of 1650 described Herod's Temple as resembling not so much a classical temple as a medieval church complete with a steeple.[95] Hooke owned a copy of this, the first edition of Lightfoot's book.[96] In the 1684 edition within Lightfoot's collected *Works*, the Temple was illustrated with towers with crenellations and arrow slits, and quoins round the main door (fig. 71). He noted that the Temple 'did very truly resemble one of our churches', except that the tower, 'like

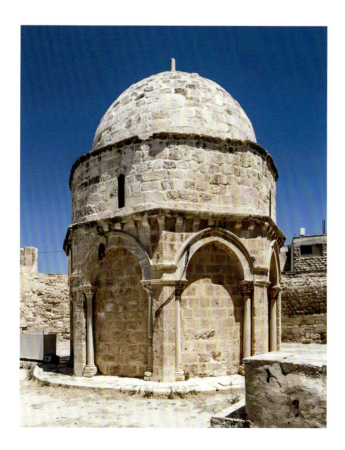

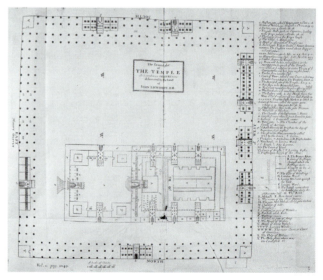

LEFT 70 The Chapel of the Ascension, Jerusalem (12th century)

ABOVE 71 Reconstruction of Solomon's Temple, Jerusalem, as rebuilt in the time of Christ, from John Lightfoot, *The Works of the Reverend and Learned John Lightfoot*, vol. 1 (1684), facing p. 1049

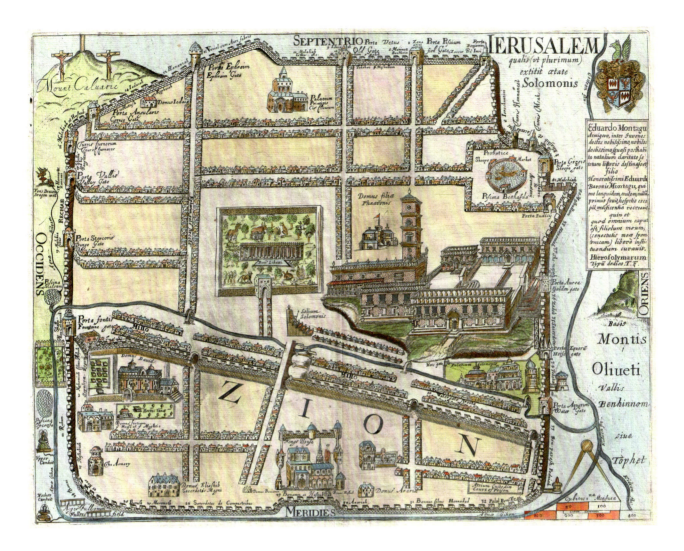

one of our high steeples', stood at the east rather than at the west end.[97] Equally, Thomas Fuller represented the Temple, this time the original in the days of Solomon, with an English-style church tower in his *Pisgah-sight of Palestine and the confines thereof* (1650; fig. 72). Hooke also owned a first edition of Samuel Lee's *Orbis Miraculum; or, the Temple of Solomon, pourtrayed by Scripture-light: wherein all its…buildings* (1659), which likewise portrayed the Temple with an English-style church tower (fig. 73) of the type that Wren and Hooke were soon designing.[98] Hooke

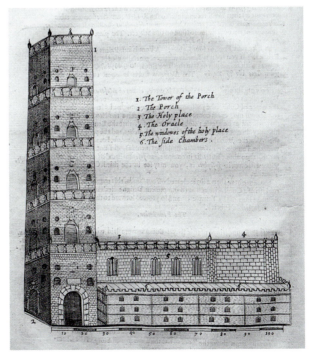

ABOVE 72 Map of Jerusalem at the time of Solomon (with the Temple in the middle right), from Thomas Fuller, *Pisgah-sight of Palestine and the confines thereof* (1650), facing title-page

RIGHT 73 Reconstruction of the tower of Solomon's Temple, from Samuel Lee, *Orbis Miraculum; or, the Temple of Solomon, pourtrayed by Scripture-light* (1659), chapter 2, p. 20

GOTHIC ARCHES AND TOWERS

owned a first edition of this too. Lee was a Puritan divine who had been in Wren's and John Wilkins's Oxford circle.[99] The effect of these various reconstructions was to justify familiar elements of English medieval buildings such as church towers in Solomonic terms. In addition, German Renaissance artists such as Albrecht Dürer and Lucas Cranach the Elder had been especially fond of depicting fanciful biblical landscapes that included Northern European medieval buildings recognisably Gothic in character.[100] Regardless of whether Wren was familiar with these Temple reconstructions and biblical fantasies, they clearly would have lent a Christian virtue to the Gothic, as a style originating in the Holy Land, when viewed by clerics such as the Dean of Westminster alongside Wren's justifications for its use.

'OUT OF THEIR ARABICK BOOKS':
CONTEMPORARY ARABIAN STUDIES

In fact, Wren was not the first to suggest that the Gothic style's roots lay in Arab (or 'Saracen') buildings. The idea had featured in a history of the Hieronymite order by José de Sigüenza, which appeared in Madrid in 1600.[101] François Fénelon, the Archbishop of Cambrai, observed in 1679 that 'this architecture which we call Gothic came down to us from the Arabs; their type of mind, very lively and unrestrained by rules or culture, could not do otherwise than plunge into false subtleties. Thence comes poor taste in all things.'[102] Evelyn was a more immediate source. He commented in the 'Account' of 1707 that 'it was after the Irruption, and Swarmes of those Truculent People from the *North*', namely the Goths as well as 'the *Moors* and *Arabs* from the *South* and *East*, over-running the Civiliz'd World', that 'wherever they fix'd themselves, they soon began to Debauch this Noble and Useful art' (referring to classical architecture).[103] Later, around 1734, Hawksmoor noted to the new Dean of Westminster, Wilcocks, concerning the 'sharp pointed Arches' of the Abbey that 'this manner of Building Mr Evelyn, Sr Chrisr: Wren and other regular Artists, beliv'd was brought from ye Saracens (in the holy war) by some of the Curious of the time'.[104]

Evelyn's view of the Moors and Arabs as uncivilised was in line with the perception held by many Englishmen since the Crusades, and further popularised by Protestant theologians such as John Foxe.[105] As part of his mission to promote Christianity, Biddulph had included a highly prejudiced description of contemporary Arab culture as wicked and backward in his travel account of 1609.[106]

Returning knights had included the menacing head of a Saracen on their armorial bearings, which became transferred, alongside the Turk's Head, to inn and alehouse signs (by report Wren himself used a house next to an inn called the Saracen's Head, in Friday Street, Cheapside, during the construction of St Paul's).[107] Wren must have read Evelyn's comment, given that the 'Account' was dedicated to him. However, his much more positive view of the Saracens, or Arabs, as the inventors of Gothic arose, as has been seen, from the need to find a more civilised origin than the Goths for the style whose use was imposed on him by context. He therefore emphasised the Saracen's virtues, presenting them as ciphers of Greek, or what we would call Byzantine, antiquity. His method of associating the virtues (or vices) of an architectural style with those of its inventor was nevertheless the same as Evelyn's. Presumably, the unidentified Arabic books that Wren's Crusaders supposedly copied had been on the subject of stereotomy, or descriptive geometry, fundamental to Gothic practice. As Wren's son re-emphasised in *Parentalia*, 'the Arabians wanted not Geometricians in that Age, nor the Moors, who translated most of the most useful old Greek Books'.[108] Their mastery of geometry had produced the dome, as Wren was well aware. His identification of the Saracens as the originators of Gothic – a style fundamentally based on geometry – was to his mind logical in that, while 'those People wanted neither Arts nor Learning', at the same time 'we in the West had lost both' (due to the rise of the Goths and Vandals) and so via the Crusades 'we borrowed again from them, out of their *Arabick* Books'.

Wren's citation of Arabic learning coincided with a growing contemporary interest in wider Arab culture, both ancient and modern, although knowledge was still sketchy. As Nabil Matar has shown, the recognition of Arabs' learning continued well into the seventeenth century.[109] They had long been seen as the originators of the hermetic and esoteric arts, of alchemy in particular, still of interest to early natural scientists. Hooke, for example, had a 1545 copy of *Alchemia* by 'Geber Arabs' (Jabir ibn Hayyan).[110] Wren must have known the astronomical tables of Ulugh Beg, used as a textbook at Oxford when he was the professor of astronomy there.[111] John Milton praised the Arabs when observing, 'I must not, however, omit to mention that the Saracens...enlarged their empire as much by the study of liberal culture as by the force of arms.'[112] Following the notable translation work of Stuart scholars such as William Bedwell, the academic study of Arabic was also becoming more established at this time.[113] In 1632 Thomas Adams (the Lord Mayor of London in

1645), gave to Cambridge University the money needed to create the first Chair in Arabic in England. The new professor's task was recoded as,

> the advancement of good Literature by bringing to light much knowledge which as yet is lockt upp in that learned tongue; but also to good service of the King and State in our commerce with those Easterne nations, and in Gods good time to enlarging the borders of the Church, and propagation of Christian religion to them who now sitt in darkeness.[114]

A corresponding Chair in Arabic at Oxford was established in 1636 by Laud, who had amassed a large collection of manuscripts in Arabic including Korans.[115] Laud's interest in a rapprochement with the Eastern Orthodox Church as well as in records of early Christian teaching stimulated the study of Eastern religions and languages, including Arabic, as it would with such later advocates as the clergyman William Beveridge and the scholar Henry Stubbe (who promoted the unitarianism of Islam as a model for Protestant reform).[116] Arabic even featured in the curriculum of schools, notably at Westminster where Evelyn recorded in his Diary in May 1661: 'I heard, & saw such Exercises at the Election of *Scholars* at *Westminster Schoole*, to be sent to the Universitie, both in *Lat[in]: Gr[eek]: & Heb[rew]: Arabic* &c in Theames & extemporary Verses, as wonderfully astonish'd me.'[117] Arabic manuscripts were of interest to the Royal Society, as a necessary element in their search for the universal, 'primitive' language. It was noted in the previous chapter that while discussing Porsenna's tomb in 1693 with a group of Fellows, Hooke had also talked about 'Arab Library, Learning Antient modern' and the Tower of Babel.[118] In his letter to Samuel Hartlib in July 1659, Oldenburg had reported that 'They say, there is at the Escurial in Spaine, a brave Library, which belonged formerly to the king of Marocco'. This referred to a vast collection of Arab manuscripts in the library of the Escorial in Madrid that was acquired in 1572 and 1614.[119] Oldenburg continued on the subject of Arab manuscripts:

> Olearius in his voyage of the Levant affirms, that at Ardebil in Persia, the city of the sepulchers of the Persian kings, there is in a vault a huge and excellent library consisting all in manuscripts, most Arabian, and some Persian and Turkish, bound in Spanish leather, covered with lames of gold and silver, most historians and philosophers.[120]

Oldenburg's source was Adam Olearius's *Beschreibung der muscowitischen und persischen Reise* (1647 and later in enlarged editions, with the English translation of 1662 owned by Hooke).[121]

Despite Biddulph's prejudices, more accurate details as to the Arab way of life were emerging during Wren's lifetime via travellers and Royal Society members.[122] Writing again in his Diary, Evelyn recorded a visit on New Year's Day of 1651 from John Wandesford, who had been Consul at Aleppo and 'told me many strange things of those Countries, the Arabs especialy'. One of these was that they 'dwell in long black Tents, made of a wooll like felt, that resists all weather'.[123] Rycaut discussed Arabian burial practices in his letter, sent to Oldenburg from Smyrna in November 1667, that was read to the Royal Society.[124] As a Fellow of the Society, Rycaut could easily have passed information about the Saracens to Wren via its meetings. Like Hooke, Wren took an interest in Arabic culture. He owned a copy of the first volume of Simon Ockley's *Conquest of Syria, Persia, and Egypt by the Saracens...Giving an account of their most remarkable battles, sieges...Illustrating the religion, rites, customs and manner of living of that warlike people*. This had been *Collected from the most Authentick Arabick Authors, especially Manuscripts, not hitherto publish'd in any European language*, and appeared in 1708 (and was generally known as *The History of the Saracens*, with a second volume appearing in 1718; Lot 195). Here Wren would have read of Constantine's observation that 'the *Arabs* and *Greeks* were near kindred, and that it was pity they should make War one upon other'.[125] In 1711 Ockley was appointed to the Chair of Arabic at Cambridge and his work could only have reinforced Wren's positive view of the Saracens outlined a few years later to Atterbury. Ockley wrote a further work on the Muslim kingdom of Morocco, which Wren also owned (Lot 195): the offer of a commission to fortify the British garrison at Tangier in 1661 would have made him particularly aware of the threat posed by Muslim forces in the country.[126] Wren would have been fully aware of the fact that the Saracens 'adhered to Mahomet's Doctrine', as his son put it. On the subject of Islam, or rather Christian superiority, he owned two copies of the Hebraist Humphrey Prideaux's *The true nature of imposture fully display'd in the life of Mahomet with a discourse annexed for the vindicating of Christianity from this charge* (1697; Lots 28 and 180). Hooke even lent a work on Islam to Wren, which illustrates their sharing of books: on 17 December 1678 Hooke noted in his Diary that he had borrowed from John Martin, the Royal Society printer, 'Mahomets book'; three days later he referred to this again, now 'at Westminster Hall with Sir Chr. Wren, dined with him promised Lady Wren, Mahomets booke'; and it was mentioned once more, this time in January the following year – 'Book of Mahomet from Martin' and 'Gave Mahomet to Sir Chr. Wren'.[127] This was probably referring to the Koran. Hooke owned a copy in French, translated in 1647 by the French Consul in Egypt, André du Ryer, as well as the first English translation, based on it, by Alexander Ross published two years later (with 'A Summary of the Religion of the TURKS').[128]

'THEIR CARRIAGE WAS BY CAMELS': SARACEN MOSQUES AND THE RISE OF THE POINTED ARCH

Having praised the Saracens, Wren continued his report on Westminster Abbey in 1713 with a brief history of the form and structure of their mosques. Here he followed the method of his Tracts in offering a rational explanation for stylistic developments in architecture: in this case, he explained the Saracen's preference for the (Gothic) pointed arch over the (Roman) circular one with keystones:

> the old Quarries whence the Ancients took their large Blocks of Marble for whole Columns and Architraves, were neglected, and they [the Saracens] thought both impertinent. Their Carriage was by Camels, therefore their Buildings were fitted for small Stones, and Columns of their own Fancy, consisting of many Pieces; and their Arches were pointed without Keystones, which they thought too heavy. The Reasons were the same in our Northern Climates, abounding in Free-stone, but wanting Marble.[129]

Yet again, the logic of construction and the transport of materials (here by camel) played an important part in determining the structure of buildings (here Saracen) and, it followed in Wren's imagination, the development of an architectural style (here Gothic). Concerning the form of these prototype 'Gothic' buildings, Wren added with a further nod to the logic of construction that the Saracens 'were Zealots in their Religion, and where-ever they conquered, (which was with amazing Rapidity) erected Mosques and Caravansara's in Haste; which obliged them to fall into another Way of Building; for they built their Mosques round, disliking the *Christian* Form of a Cross'.[130] Wren's Crusading builders not only copied the Arabic books on Gothic principles but must have seen these buildings as well. He would have admired this preference for the circle over the cross, given his strictures on the most natural form of beauty based on circles and squares outlined in the first Tract and put into practice in his early plan for a circular (and centralised) St Paul's of 1670–5.[131]

In *Parentalia* Wren's son made the obvious next step by linking the 'round' form with the dome, in emphasising that, 'affecting the round Form for Mosques', the Saracens 'elevated Cupolas in some Instances, with Grace enough'.[132] Of course, mosques are not in general circular – their perimeters are for the most part rectangular – but contemporary accounts were often vague and sometimes made them circular. Sandys described the mosques of Constantinople in 1615 as 'magnificent…all of white marble, round in forme, and coupled [domed] above; being finished on the top with gilded spires, that reflect the beams they receive with a marvelous splendor'.[133] Wren owned the sixth, 1670 edition of Sandys (Lot 109). Thomas Herbert, when recalling his visit to Shiraz in Persia in the late 1620s, in the fuller 1667 edition of his *Relation* (owned by Hooke), had observed that, 'fifteen Mosques express their bravery here, which in shape are round (after the *Alkaha* in *Mecca*)'. The most prominent of Shiraz's mosques, the Atigh Jame, is decidedly rectangular. Herbert too used the language of Gothic to describe these mosques' features, noting on the minarets that two mosques 'are especially note-worthy in their steeples, (so some call them) being small but exceeding high Towers'.[134] This may well have caught Hooke's and Wren's attention, given their design of churches with steeples. Perhaps the most prominent example of Arabic sacred architecture actually nearest the circular is the Dome of the Rock. This is octagonal, however, and was identified as Solomon's Temple in panoramas of Jerusalem such as that by George Braun and Frans Hogenberg of 1575. And equally some domed mausoleums were octagonal, such as the Green mausoleum of Mehmed I at Bursa (see fig. 66) – it will be remembered that round sepulchres were mentioned by Wren's son. Some map views of the city represented mosques as round, as for example that by Jaspar Isac made some time before 1654, and in 1721 Fischer von Erlach illustrated a fanciful view of a 'Mosque built by Sultan Orcanus II in Bursa' that was circular (see fig. 10). Prior to Grelot and Chardin, illustrations of Arab and Turkish architecture, and of mosques and mausoleums in particular, were diagrammatic, and lack of clarity together with unreliable descriptions clearly helped Wren's argument rather than hindered it. His search for architectural origins in the

Holy Land was, in this case at least, a triumph of need and imagination over actual evidence.

There is, moreover, an all too obvious discrepancy between Wren's Gothic buildings in the East, that is, circular mosques with domes, and the characteristics of those in the West, namely cruciforms with towers and spires. As Wren's son acknowledged in *Parentalia*, Gothic builders 'affected Steeples, though the Saracens themselves most used Cupolas'.[135] In fact, with no mention of flying buttresses or spires, the only Gothic characteristic of Saracen buildings mentioned by Wren was that 'their Arches were pointed'. His son explained this anomaly by suggesting that the Christian builders 'refined upon' Saracen works 'every Day, as they proceeded in building Churches', an understanding which may or may not have reflected Wren's own.[136] He seized on the Byzantine example of St Mark's in Venice (from 1063) – with its ogee gables, cruciform plan based on a near-perfect Greek cross and central dome – which he said 'is built after the Saracen Manner' (fig. 74).[137] Somewhat ironically, the plan for St Paul's started life as a circle and ended up as a cruciform, a change that met with a degree of disapproval by Wren.

74 The west façade of St Mark's, Venice

One of Wren's comments in the Tracts on the various forms of vaults suggests that his identification of the Saracens as the originators of Gothic was in fact made much earlier than in his report on the Abbey in 1713. In the second Tract (probably begun in the mid- to late 1670s) he suggested that 'the different Forms of Vaultings are necessary to be considered, either as they were used by the Ancients, or the Moderns, whether *Free-masons*, or *Saracens*'.[138] After going on to make comparisons, he concluded that 'the *Gothick*, or *Saracen* Way' was the best, it 'being evidently the least and lightest', and that 'I have therefore followed in the Vaultings', or saucer domes, 'of *St. Paul's*, and, with good Reason, preferred it above any other Way used by Architects'.[139] Here in passing we learn that what he considered originally to have been Eastern building practices influenced his design of the great Cathedral, a source examined in more detail in the following chapter. This reference to St Paul's is likely to date from the end of the 1680s, given the construction process there, and suggests not only that the Tracts were worked on over time but that Wren's interest in the Saracens dated back to this formative period. As such it would have informed his choice of the Gothic style for his churches with their towers, and not least their pointed arches so ill-favoured by the likes of Evelyn but traced by Wren to the Holy Land.

'WHETHER FREE-MASONS, OR SARACENS': FREEMASONRY AND THE EAST

Wren's identification of the East as the place where the sciences and the art of building had originated found a curious contemporary parallel in the lore of the emerging fraternity of speculative Freemasonry.[140] This lore was based on that of medieval 'operative' stonemasons (who it has just been seen Wren referred to as 'Free-masons').[141] The principal source for the origins in Britain of Gothic Masonry, as practised by guilds of stonemasons, was a group of medieval manuscripts called the *Old Charges* or *Gothic Constitutions* of Freemasonry.[142] These documents related the Eastern origins of the craft. The earliest date from about 1450 (although they are possibly earlier still) and begin by describing how Euclid of Alexandria established the craft of geometry in Egypt and called it Masonry.[143] This craft was taught to the children of the Egyptian nobility. The manuscript went on to recount the spread of the art of geometry abroad and how the craft was brought to England during the reign of King Athelstan (924–39). Other manuscripts in the *Old Charges* elaborated on this, drawing on Genesis in relating how Lamech's eldest son Jabal discovered geometry and became Cain's Master Mason.[144] Knowledge of geometry and Masonry was eventually passed down through Pythagoras and Nimrod, the king of Babylon and master builder of the Tower of Babel (who was accordingly himself a Mason), to Abraham. Abraham taught this knowledge to the Egyptians, including Euclid, who in turn taught Masonry to the children of the nobility. The craft was then taught to the children of Israel and, via the Temple of Solomon, whose builders had been instructed by Euclid while in Egypt, it found its way to France and thence once again to Saint Alban's England.[145] In a variant version, a Mason called Naymus Grecus was credited with being present at the building of the Temple and teaching Masonry to Charles Martel before he became King of France, and thereby brought it to Europe.[146] Solomon's Temple was thus supposed to have been built using the best geometric practices later evident in the Gothic cathedrals of Europe. Wren also regarded the Temple as the archetypal structure that bore witness to the design qualities he admired the most, namely geometry and logical structure applied to Masonry construction. Although the Masonry manuscripts were not concerned with the Gothic style of pointed arches *per se*, nonetheless as with Wren's account they all advanced the idea that Gothic principles of Masonry construction originated in the Holy Land.

So, given that aspects of this history were reflected both in Wren's letter to Atterbury concerning the Gothic and in his Tracts, how might he have become aware of the lore of Freemasonry? Certainly, he knew many early Freemasons, including Ashmole who joined a Masonic lodge as early as 1646.[147] And both Wren and Hooke were friends with one of the first Freemasons (from 1641), Robert Moray, meeting particularly through Gresham College and then the Royal Society of which Moray had likewise been a founding Fellow (as an enthusiastic 'Chymist').[148] Hooke recorded in his Diary in May 1673 that he had 'read Sir R. Moray of Masonry &c', probably referring to a work on masonry craft that formed part of the Society's 'history of trades' programme.[149] Wren's own membership of a lodge has been the subject of much debate, ranging from those who think he was never a speculative Freemason to those, like James Anderson in 1738, who have argued that he was a Grand Master of a lodge.[150] Most recently James Campbell has concluded on the evidence of two obituaries and a note by Aubrey that Wren did indeed become a member in 1691, but that there is nothing to support the idea that he was ever a Grand Officer.[151] The note by Aubrey, another founding Fellow of the Society, is to be found in his unpublished history of Wiltshire (written from 1685): 'M[emoran]D[u]M. This day (May 1691 the 18th being monday after Rogation Sunday) is a great Convention at St. Paul's-church of the Fraternity of the Accepted…Masons where Sr. Christopher Wren is to be adopted a Brother…there have been Kings, that have been of this – Sodalitie'.[152] Campbell points out that the lodge Wren joined was probably the one associated with St Paul's that met at the Goose and Gridiron alehouse, in the Cathedral churchyard.[153] The influence of Freemasonry on Wren's interest in the Eastern origins of the arts and sciences, and of Gothic in particular, is difficult to establish for certain, especially given the formative stage of the fraternity. But it is at least suggested by these shared interests and his eventually becoming a Freemason. Incidentally in the account by Wren's son of his father's opinions as to the origins of Gothic, its transmitters from the East were identified as a 'Fraternity of Architects' who 'stiled themselves Freemasons'.[154]

In this way there were three inter-related aspects to Wren's acceptance of Gothic in practice. Firstly, his aim, expressed to his clerical patrons, of avoiding stylistic mixtures and respecting the existing medieval context, which was invariably ecclesiastical. Secondly, the fact that Gothic relied on the use of geometric forms that, drawing on his and Locke's theories of perception, gave pleasure to the observer. And thirdly, stemming from the venerable nature of the context and of the proposed work itself, his development of a suitably virtuous origin for Gothic, as a style no longer advanced by the heathen and uncouth Goths but one now originating in the Holy Land and 'refined by the Christians'. In explaining the birth of Gothic, Wren favoured imaginary stone arches standing in the Arabian desert over the bent branches of the German forest suggested in the Renaissance. His search for Gothic prototypes thus matched his rationalist desire to trace the origin of the Orders. In both instances, Wren looked east.

CHAPTER THREE

GREEK CROSSES AND DOMES

'The eastern Way of Vaulting by Hemispheres'

Domes were a consistent feature in Wren's work. All his St Paul's Cathedral designs had one, from the repair of the old building proposed in 1666 just before the Great Fire to the various projects for the new one after it (figs 75 and 76). His first schemes for Trinity College library in Cambridge and palaces at Winchester and Whitehall had them, Tom Tower in Oxford had one and a pair of domes dominates the skyline at Greenwich Hospital (see figs 61, 68, 102, 156). Of the London churches, six had domed interiors, namely St Mary-at-Hill (1670–4; see fig. 135), St Benet Fink (1670–5, demolished in 1846), St Swithin London Stone (1677–83, destroyed in 1941), St Antholin Budge Row (1678–86, demolished in 1874), St Mary Abchurch (1681–6; fig. 77) and St Mildred Bread Street (1681–7, destroyed in 1941).[1] The dome at St Stephen Walbrook (1672–9) was expressed on the exterior, and Wren's proposals for St Mary's in Lincoln's Inn Fields of around 1695 also had an external dome (fig. 78; see figs 138–9).[2] These buildings resembled no preceding English church, or any other building in England for that matter. Inigo Jones had never built a dome other than on stage, in the form of 'Oberon's Palace' inspired by Bramante's Tempietto in Rome as illustrated in Serlio's third book.[3] Even his and John Webb's unbuilt schemes for Whitehall Palace, where a full-scale dome might have been expected, had only relatively small cupolas above towers in the Elizabethan manner.[4] This was despite Jones having witnessed ancient and modern examples on his travels in Italy in 1614. These domes had been known of in England since Elizabethan times. Images of the mightiest of antique pagan domes – at the Pantheon in Rome, as well as of smaller ones including those at the Temple of Vesta in Tivoli and early Christian mausoleums in Rome such as that of Constantine's daughters Costanza and Elena (Santa Costanza) – had also appeared in Serlio (fig. 79).[5] As too had Bramante's design for the largest modern dome, at St Peter's in Rome.[6] Evelyn had witnessed examples on his visits to Paris, Rome and Venice between 1643 and 1646. In particular, the Venetian domes at St Mark's caught his attention. He noted with some wonder in his Diary in June 1645: 'in the midst of this rich *Volto*, rises 5 *Cupolas*, the middle very large, and sustayn'd by 36 marble Columns, 8 of which are of precious Marbles.'[7] Thus if Wren's classical church lanterns and steeples, together with his triumphal column and colonnades, were all novel architectural structures in England when they were built, so the dome too lacked any large-scale native precedents. Hence Evelyn, when again writing in his Diary, this time in August 1666 concerning the proposed repair of old St Paul's, noted his and Wren's plan 'to build it with a noble *Cupola*, a forme of church building, not as yet knowne in England, but of wonderfull grace' (see fig. 76).[8]

75   The dome at St Paul's Cathedral, London

Wren echoed these words in his report to the Commissioners examining the repair of the old building, in attempting to explain the unfamiliar visual effect of this pioneering dome when seen from a distance: 'the outward Appearance of the Church will seem to swell in the Middle by Degrees, from a large Basis rising into a Rotundo bearing a *Cupola*, and then ending in a Lantern: and this with incomparable more Grace in the remoter Aspect, than it is possible for the lean Shaft of a Steeple to afford.'[9] Although Wren had not seen any Italian domed buildings at first hand, he would, like Evelyn, have witnessed

OPPOSITE 76 East–west section of old St Paul's Cathedral with dome, drawn by Wren, London (1666). All Souls College, Oxford

ABOVE 77 The interior of St Mary Abchurch, London (1681–6)

modern Roman Catholic examples in Paris while there in 1665. There the two main domed churches were Jacques Lemercier's Church of the Sorbonne and the Val-de-Grâce, the latter begun to the designs of François Mansart and completed to those of Lemercier. These are sometimes cited as Wren's inspiration for the form.[10] No doubt his own appreciation of the dome's 'wonderful grace' and its effect on the onlooker can be traced to experiencing these French examples, following Evelyn who was much influenced by all things French. And the domed churches of Rome, such as Santa Maria di Loreto and the greatest of them all, St Peter's, provided equally immediate, albeit Roman Catholic, models.[11] Moreover, as the Preface noted, when it came to the use of pendentives to support domes, there were modern examples in Europe in St Mark's in Venice, the medieval baptistery in Padua, Filippo Brunelleschi's Pazzi chapel in Florence and the early Baroque churches in Paris. But as this chapter will show,

GREEK CROSSES AND DOMES   71

Wren also looked further east, notably to the churches turned mosques and palaces of Constantinople, for the origins of the dome in Christian architecture, as too for inspiration concerning its structural possibilities and the plan-forms it determined. As with the Orders and the pointed arch, here again he searched for the origin of an architectural form in the East. This was in line with those contemporary Anglican theologians who sought to bypass Roman Catholic churches and propose earlier, Byzantine ones, particularly formed of a Greek cross with a dome, as meaningful models for new churches in England.

'AN ORNAMENT TO THE CHURCH OF ENGLAND': THE DOME AND THE EARLY CHRISTIAN CHURCH

Clearly, the dome's form perfectly reflected Wren's preference for 'natural' beauty, based as this principle was on pure geometric figures; indeed, he recommended in Tract one that, 'no Roof can have Dignity enough to appear above a Cornice, but the circular'.[12] Architectural forms could also, however, convey a symbolic meaning according to Wren. For example, he thought that the form of antique temples had expressed the characteristics of their dedication. He explained that 'each Deity had a peculiar Gesture, Face, and Dress hieroglyphically proper to it', adding that 'not only their Altars and Sacrifices were mystical, but the very Forms of their Temples'.[13] Temple forms could, for example, evoke opposing ideas. The expansive and light-filled form of the Temple of Peace in Rome (the Basilica of Maxentius and Constantine used as a hall of justice), with its 'humble Front, but embracing wide', and aspect 'contrived in

LEFT 78 Proposal for St Mary's in Lincoln's Inn Fields, London, drawing attributed to Wren (c.1695). Westminster City Archives, London

RIGHT 79 Santa Costanza, Rome (c.AD 354), from Sebastiano Serlio, *Il terzo libro di Sebastiano Serlio Bolognese* (1540), p. XX

Allusion to Peace and its Attributes', was contrasted in Tract four with the 'strong and stately' form of the Temple of Mars Ultor, also in Rome, with its 'terrible Front' (Palladio had illustrated both temples, one after the other in this order in his fourth book; figs 80 and 81).[14] The forms of both temples were thus seen as representing – 'hieroglyphically', as it were – the opposing functions and gods to which they had been dedicated. And he observed on the Greek Temple of Diana (Artemis) at Ephesus in Turkey that 'the nineteen Pillars in the Ailes represented her Period; the seven Pillars of the Chapel in the Middle of the *Cella*, the Quarter of her menstrual Course' (see fig. 28).[15] Wren may well have seen Eusebius's description of the interior of the rotunda of the Holy Sepulchre in Jerusalem, with its 'hemisphere attached to the highest part of the royal house, ringed with twelve columns to match the number of the Apostles'.[16] This expressive understanding of architectural form was in part a reflection of the Vitruvian principle of decorum, which not only required the decorative sensitivity to context discussed in the previous chapter, but also dictated that the ornamental style of a building should match (or be 'proper' to) its function or dedication (male or female, peacemaker or warrior, and so on).[17] However, the understanding was equally indebted to the tradition of Renaissance emblematics, in which moral virtues and vices were represented by pictures, often of a character with, as Wren put it, a particular 'gesture, face, and dress hieroglyphically proper to it'.[18] The potency of architectural forms for Wren, together with the fact that his use of the dome, or proposed use, was at Anglican foundations (colleges, palaces, churches, hospital and cathedral), suggests that it needed a justification in terms other than its visual effect. In other words, the dome needed to express a meaning not to do with any pagan or Catholic models but of relevance to Anglicans.

Indeed, as Wren was all too aware, it was the expressive nature of forms that had led some of the clergy at St Paul's to favour the Latin cross over the Greek one used in a scheme of 1670–2 and adapted in the Great Model of 1673 (see figs 52 and 141). The Latin cross was preferred as more expressive of the customary English (Gothic) cathedral type or, as Wren's son explained, 'the Chapter, and some others of the Clergy thought the Model not enough of a Cathedral-fashion; to instance particularly, in that, the Quire was design'd Circular, &c.' As a result, 'the Surveyor then turn'd his Thoughts to a Cathedral-form (as they call'd it) but so rectified, as to reconcile, as near as possible, the Gothick to a better Manner of Architecture; with a Cupola, and above that, instead of a Lantern, a lofty Spire, and large Porticoes' (this described the 'Warrant' design; see fig. 46).[19] Wren's son also acknowledged the role that such familiar associations had played in the design of this dome: 'nor could the Surveyor do otherwise than gratify the general Taste of the Age, which had been so used to Steeples, that these round Designs were hardly digested, unless raised to a remarkable Height'.[20] This proposal to use a dome in the new Cathedral followed Wren's scheme of 1666 for the repair of the old one (see fig. 76). Given that the dome was a form unprecedented

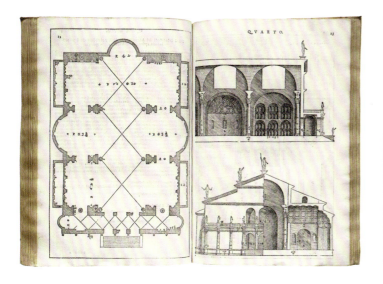

80 The Temple of Peace (the Basilica of Maxentius and Constantine), Rome, from Andrea Palladio, *I quattro libri dell'architettura* (1570), Book IV, ch. VI, pp. 12–13

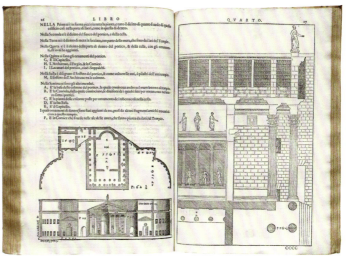

81 The Temple of Mars Ultor, Rome, from Palladio, *I quattro libri* (1570), Book IV, ch. VII, pp. 16–17

in church architecture in England (and as such at a disadvantage to what he called 'lofty spires'), and one that had pagan associations to boot (most obviously via the Pantheon), some explanation seems to have been needed for the Commissioners as to how it too was 'proper' for an English cathedral. For Wren emphasised that this dome could play an expressive role, since it would 'become an Ornament to his Majesty's most excellent Reign, to the Church of *England*, and to this great City'.[21] Wren clearly hoped that the dome on St Paul's, although unfamiliar, would over time become recognised as a national 'ornament' to, and even a symbol of, the tripartite unity of King, Church and City. Such a unity was of some pertinence after the recent turmoil of the Civil War.

The dome's legitimacy as a form symbolising the new-found national unity between Church and Crown would have been helped by its early use in the Christian architecture of the East, most notably for a similar purpose in Constantinople and Jerusalem. That most legendary of buildings, the Temple of Solomon, had been represented from the Renaissance onwards as a domed, or many-domed, building.[22] It featured as such on the title-page of James Ussher's *The Annals of the World* (1658 edition), the first, 1650, edition of which was in Wren's collection (Lot 99; fig. 82).[23] And it was noted that the Dome of the Rock was identified as the Temple in early views of Jerusalem (see fig. 64). Wren's contemporaries were well aware of the dome's Eastern roots. Writing in the 1664 version of his 'Account of Architects and Architecture', Evelyn credited the origins of the dome in its purest form, that is without the lantern 'much in vogue yet in *Italy*, especially at *Rome* and *Florence*', to Byzantine churches in the East. He cited the dome at Hagia Sophia in Constantinople, as well as that at the Holy Sepulchre in Jerusalem which had been sponsored by Empress Helena, the mother of Constantine, during her pilgrimage to the Holy Land in 326–7.[24] Whereas the lantern was needed to admit light in darker European climates, according to Evelyn, it was unnecessary in Eastern locations: he praised the solemnness of such ancient domes in their pure form,

> which yet are happily better to be endur'd in the more *Eastern Countries* where the Weather is constant; as we see it practis'd in what the Pious *Helena* erected in the *Holy-Land*, and her Son *Constantine the Great*, on that his magnificent Structure of *Santa Sophia* yet remaining at *Constantinople*,[25] and to this day imitated by the *Turks* for the Covering of their *Mosques*; and that it [the dome] was an *Oriental* Covering and

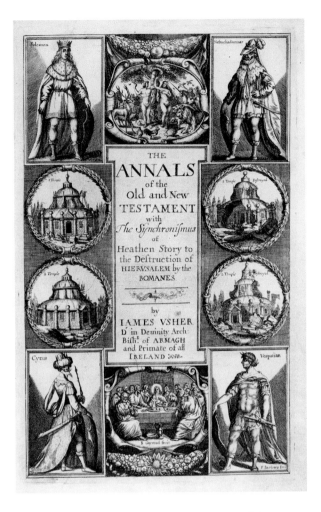

82 The title-page of James Ussher, *The Annals of the World* (1658 edition)

> invention, the [Tholos] of the *Greeks* was doubtless deriv'd from the *Hebrew* [script] *Thala* signifying to *Suspend* or hang as it were in the *Ayr*.[26]

Roger North also highlighted the early Christian origins of the dome and was well aware of later Turkish examples no doubt through his brother, Dudley ('Turkey') North. Writing on various architectural forms in his unpublished 'Of Building' of around 1696 he noted: 'that which wee call the cuppolo, dome or tower in the middle, with the cross iles, and east end, those were introduc't in the forme of a cross by the Christians and are peculiar to their churches'. Rather than use a central church tower, 'there was a way of volting this middle introduc't wherof the Santa Sofia in Constantinople is a glorious example. And these were the use if not the invention of that time, for I do not find in the wrighters of Antiquitys any arches made like half sphears or half ovals, as ye use then, and since has bin.'

Indeed, North added that the dome was, 'in my judgment a greater perfection in architecture than the ancients knew or made use of'. He concluded:

> But volts of this magnitude, as those Greek [i.e., Byzantine] fabriks, and Roman now, particularly St. Peter's at Rome and as I hope to see in St. Paul's London, are types of art, never enough to be admired and encouraged. And even ye barbarous Turks are in this glorious, who cover stupendous fabricks with hemisphere volts and open ye four sides, as well as abutt ye whole with 4 quarter spheres, which is a figure of so great perfection, I wonder it is not introduc't with us, who so much love room, and lofty coverings. A rude outline of this figure is in ye margin, than nature scarce admits a more perfect for churches.[27]

The margin has a sketch of a plan with four apses arranged in the form of a Greek cross (fig. 83). As far as North was concerned, the soon to be realised dome at St Paul's clearly stood in the tradition of the Byzantine examples.

This interest in the domed buildings of the early Christians reflected the wider concern of some Church of England theologians with the Eastern Church.[28] Anglicans looked to the Greek Church as an unbroken link to the early, or 'primitive', Christians. The Stuart cleric Samuel Purchas had identified in Greek Orthodoxy the legacy of the Roman emperor Constantine's early Church and its 'primitive' Christianity. He reported in his *Hakluytus Posthumus, Purchas, his Pilgrimage* (1625, a worked owned

83 Roger North's sketch of a church plan with four apses arranged in the form of a Greek cross, in 'Cursory Notes of Building occasioned by the Repair, or rather Metamorfosis, of an old house in the Country' (c.1696), fol. 36v. British Library, London, Add. MS 32540

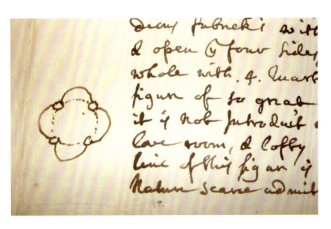

by Hooke) that the Turks called 'those of the Greekish Religion Romaeans, of their chiefe Citie Constantinople, otherwise named New Rome'.[29] Consequently, Anglicans sought to make links with the Greek Church. Epigram Pagitt had argued in 1630 that there were numerous points of 'Agreement' between the Eastern Christians and Protestants, particularly in denying 'the Popes Supremacie'.[30] A Greek Orthodox church was even briefly established in London in the 1670s, with the support of the king and the Bishop of London (Henry Compton), to accommodate Greek Christians fleeing the Ottoman empire under the dictatorial Köprülü viziers.[31] The first chapter noted that George Wheler looked to the Greek Orthodox Church and its Byzantine buildings as a pure model, free of Catholic corruption, for the liturgical and architectural practices of the English Church.[32] Following the accounts by Spon and Wheler of their travels in Greece and the Levant during 1675–6, published in 1678 and 1682 respectively (Lots 114 and 318), in 1689 Wheler published *An Account of the Churches, or Places of Assembly, of the Primitive Christians…with a Seasonable Application*. Here he focused on Byzantine churches as explicit models for the Anglican ones of his own day, as the title makes perfectly clear, and in so doing drew particular attention to their domes. For example, drawing on Eusebius's *De vita Constantini* and Procopius's *De aedificiis*, Wheler described and illustrated the plan of the Church of the Holy Apostles at Constantinople that had been destroyed in 1461, with its 'circular *Chancel* or *Cupolo*', or, more emphatically, its 'Great *Cupolo*' (see fig. 129).[33] Wheler also discussed the rotunda and dome of the Holy Sepulchre in Jerusalem. He quoted Eusebius's report that the dome was 'the Chief of the whole Work, raised up to the highest part of the Church' (fig. 84).[34]

The form of this and other early Christian domed churches in Jerusalem had already been described and illustrated by a number of English theologians and travellers. Based on the pilgrimage of Arculfus in the seventh century, Bede had described the Holy Sepulchre.[35] In recounting his travels in 1615, George Sandys included, as his subtitle put it, *A description of the Holy-Land of the Jews, and several sects of Christians living there; Of Jerusalem, sepulchre of Christ, Temple of Solomon, and what else either of antiquity, or worth observation*.[36] As well as the Sepulchre (figs 85–7), other domed churches were certainly among those antiquities deemed 'worth observation'. For he illustrated small views of the Chapel of the Ascension on the Mount of Olives (c.392), as rebuilt by Crusaders in the twelfth century although the dome was in fact a Muslim addition, and the Church of St John the Baptist

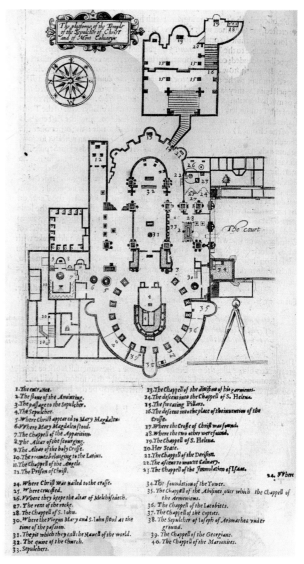

ABOVE LEFT 84 The Church of the Holy Sepulchre, Jerusalem (as rebuilt in 1027–48), photographed in 1862 by Francis Bedford. Royal Collection, London

ABOVE RIGHT 85 Plan of the Church of the Holy Sepulchre, from George Sandys, *A relation of a Journey begun an: Dom: 1610. Foure bookes. Containing a description of the Turkish Empire, of Ægypt, of the Holy Land* (1615), Book III, p. 162

LEFT 86 Section through the dome of the Church of the Holy Sepulchre, from Sandys, *Journey* (1615), Book III, p. 160

OPPOSITE ABOVE 87 Elevation of the Church of the Holy Sepulchre, from Sandys, *Journey* (1615), Book III, p. 165

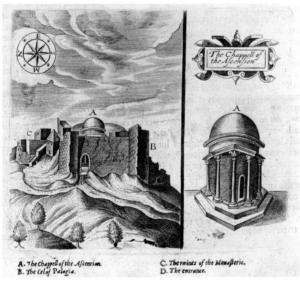

88 The Chapel of the Ascension, Jerusalem (as rebuilt by Crusaders in the 12th century), from Sandys, *Journey* (1615), Book III, p. 199

89 The Church of St John the Baptist, Jerusalem (c.324), from Sandys, *Journey* (1615), Book III, p. 184

(*c.*324; figs 88 and 89). Sandys followed in the footsteps of the Franciscan friars Bernardino Amico, with his albeit more detailed and accurate etchings, and Niccolò da Poggibonsi, with his woodcuts (see fig. 7).[37] As a rare early pilgrim from England, Faynes Moryson illustrated the Sepulchre's plan in his *Itinerary* of 1617 (fig. 90). He observed concerning its domes, or 'globes' as he called them: 'Above the roofe of the Church on the outside, are two faire Globes, whereof the greater covered with leade, lies over the Sepulcher, and the lesse, all made of stone, is over the Chauncell. And this greater Globe, on the inside of the Church is beautified with engraven Cedar trees.'[38] The Sepulchre was also represented on the title-page of Thomas Fuller's *The Historie of the Holy Warre* (1639) in a view clearly based on that by Sandys rather than the more accurate one by Amico (Fuller also showed a Saracen in the form of Saladin, who was the Sultan of Egypt and Syria, opposite a Christian knight; fig. 91). Fuller's work was in Hooke's collection.[39]

It was noted that Wren owned the sixth, 1670 edition of Sandys's popular work (Lot 109), so he could easily have studied these early Christian and Byzantine domed churches in Jerusalem: Hooke too had a copy, his the earlier, 1627 edition.[40] As the previous chapter pointed out, Wren understood the importance of the Holy Sepulchre not least through his work on the Temple Church in London (see fig. 69). Moreover, he highlighted its significance at the very beginning of his first Tract when observing that 'Modern *Rome* subsists still, by the Ruins and Imitations of the *old*; as does *Jerusalem*, by the Temple of the Sepulchre, and other Remains of *Helena's* Zeal'.[41] Then in the fourth Tract he singled it out again,

90 Plan of the Holy Sepulchre, from Faynes Moryson, *An Itinerary…containing his ten yeeres travel* (1617), chapter 2, p. 229

91 The title-page of Thomas Fuller, *The Historie of the Holy Warre* (1639)

LEFT 92 Model of the Church of the Holy Sepulchre, Jerusalem (late 17th century). Olive wood inlaid with mother-of-pearl and bone, 29.5 x 49 x 58 cm. Museum of Fine Arts, Boston

BELOW 93 Hagia Sophia, Constantinople (AD 537)

this time reporting that 'at this Day, small Models of Wood, garnished with Mother of Pearl, of the holy Sepulchre at *Jerusalem*, are usually made for Sale to Pilgrims and Foreigners'.[42] Wren would have seen such a model deposited at the Royal Society on 29 March 1677 by Thomas Povey, who was a Fellow but who had not himself visited the Holy Land. The Society's minutes recorded: 'Mr. Povey produced a model of the sepulchre of our Saviour at Jerusalem, said to have been made upon the place by the Maronites.'[43] Some of these models survive, complete with their cupolas and pointed arches, having been imported into Europe in the seventeenth century (fig. 92).[44] Wren could have been made aware of the domed Sepulchre's enduring importance to pilgrims by the travellers to Jerusalem (or by those, like Povey, who had talked to them) to whom he referred regarding the tomb of Absalom, as discussed in Chapter One. This interest in the Sepulchre and ownership of a 1670 edition of Sandys's work are important since they coincided with Wren's own designs for domed churches and cathedral, and his consequent need to justify the domed form in

GREEK CROSSES AND DOMES 79

Christian terms to the Anglican clergy (in much the same way he would the pointed arch).

Thus through the agency of the Royal Society Fellows Evelyn, Povey and later Wheler (not to mention the North brothers), the origins of the dome in early Christian and Byzantine church architecture cannot have escaped Wren's attention. Indeed, there were ample first-hand accounts, such as those of Sandys and Amico, illustrating the dome as a fundamentally Christian form. This understanding could only have given potency to Wren's own novel use of the dome on Anglican churches and cathedral, as also to his identification of it as an appropriate symbol for church unity and civic harmony at old St Paul's. A dome had after all been soused by Emperor Justinian on no lesser structure than the (originally) Christian Cathedral of Hagia Sophia in Constantinople (figs 93 and 94). Wren's particular interest in this dome has only relatively recently been recognised, by Lydia Soo and Pierre de la Ruffinière du Prey.[45] But Wren was fascinated by its construction, especially in the context of his work on the dome of the new St Paul's.

'IN THE LATER EASTERN EMPIRE, AS APPEARS AT ST. SOPHIA': THE DOMES OF HAGIA SOPHIA AND ST PAUL'S CATHEDRAL

When Wheler visited Constantinople in 1675 it had grown to become the largest city in Europe. This was in no small part due to its enviable position straddling two continents, for, as Henry Blount had put it in 1636, 'it stands almost in the middle of the World'.[46] The city's domed skyline had caught the imagination of engravers and artists, and been the subject of many early modern printed views. Woodcuts in Hartmann Schedel's *Liber Chronicarum* (the 'Nuremberg Chronicle'), published in 1493, showed the city and damage by lightning of the Nea Ekklesia ('New Church') in 1490 (fig. 95). Another, by the Flemish artist Pieter van Aelst, showed a procession of Suleiman the Magnificent through the Hippodrome: this formed a panel published in 1553 in 'Moeurs et fachons de faire de Turcz' (Customs and Fashions of the Turks; fig. 96).[47] Melchior Lorck (Lorichs) drew a panorama of Constantinople in 1559 and published an accurate woodcut of the Suleimaniye mosque in 1570 that was republished in 1626 in his posthumous *Wolgerissene und Geschnittenes Figuren zu Ross und Fus* ('Well-engraved and cut figures on horse and foot', with further editions in 1641 and 1646).[48] The mosque had only recently been built, in 1550–7, by the most famous Ottoman architect,

Sinan. A number of Lorck's drawings of Turkish figures with buildings in the background, including a mosque, were in the collection of Evelyn.[49] The cartographers Braun and Hogenberg published a bird's-eye view of Constantinople in the first volume of their series of such views of the cities of the known world, which appeared as *Civitates Orbis Terrarum* in 1572 (see fig. 4). A panorama of 1616 engraved by Pieter van den Keere (Petrus Kaerius) showed the city's mosques, monuments

OPPOSITE 94   Hagia Sophia, Constantinople

ABOVE 95   The Nea Ekklesia ('New Church'), Constantinople, being damaged by lightning, with a partial view of the Topkapi Palace next to the Hippodrome and Hagia Sophia. Woodcut from Hartmann Schedel, *Liber Chronicarum* (the 'Nuremberg Chronicle'; 1493), p. 257

and other landmarks, as did one by Mattheus Merian of 1635 (see fig. 145).⁵⁰ And collections of drawings by travellers included views of the city, such as that in the Dryden Album of about 1580–90 given to Trinity College in Cambridge by Jonathan Dryden, a Fellow, in 1663.⁵¹ All these views were made before the fire of 1660 that engulfed two thirds of Constantinople and which thereby prefigured London's own conflagration.⁵²

If views of the city were common enough in Wren's day, they were complemented by the many accounts made by early Christian chroniclers, medieval pilgrims en route to the shrines of the Holy Land and by later merchants.⁵³ Vivid descriptions of Constantinople's monuments, including famously of Hagia Sophia, had been given by Procopius in the mid-first century and then by George Cordinus (Kodinos) in the fourteenth. An early traveller was Pierre Gilles (Petrus Gyllius or Gillius), whose *De Topographia Constantinopoleos et de illius antiquitatibus, libri IV* was published in London in 1561 and was probably known to Wren since it was referred to in a draft for the inscription for the London Monument studied in Chapter Four. A series of descriptions of the city by English travellers followed. William Harborne lived there between 1583 and 1588, serving as the first

96 Procession of Suleiman the Magnificent through the Hippodrome in front of a panorama of Constantinople (detail). Woodcut after Pieter van Aelst, 'Moeurs et fachons de faire de Turcz' (Customs and Fashions of the Turks; 1553)

ambassador to the Ottoman court, whose account of his travels featured in Richard Hakluyt's *Voyages* (in the 1599 edition owned by Hooke).⁵⁴ This was followed by the visit of Henry Cavendish during the summer of 1589 that was recorded in a journal, as well as that by Richard Wragge in 1594.⁵⁵ Then there were the notable observations of John Sanderson and Thomas Coryat (who described the city in 1594 and 1613 respectively), in works published in 1625 by Purchas.⁵⁶ The visits to Constantinople recorded by William Biddulph in 1609 took place between 1601 and 1607.⁵⁷ Later still, Sandys published his account of the city in 1615, while Moryson published a description in 1617 that included the Seraglio and Hagia Sophia (inaccurately described, along with other mosques at this time, as 'round').⁵⁸ Blount followed suit in 1636 (in a work also owned, as the Introduction noted, by Hooke).⁵⁹ Wheler too included an account of the city in the second chapter of his popular work of 1682 on his journey in the Levant that Wren owned (Lot 114). This had a striking engraving of Ahmed's mosque that was described as 'a Magnificent square Building, covered with a great Cuppalo in the Middle, sustained by Four white Marble Pillars' (the 'Blue Mosque'; fig. 97). This was the same cross-in-square form that Wheler had admired in the early Christian churches at Tyre and Constantinople (see figs 33 and 129). Hence there were quite a few sources of information on Constantinople's urban form and architecture by the time Wren and Hooke were building up their libraries and designing their domes.

Wheler's description of Hagia Sophia reflected that by Procopius in emphasising the building's form, another cross-in-square, and in catching something of its splendour: 'It is a very great Length, and is crowned towards the East End, with a vast Cuppalo, sustained by four massy Pillars, encrusted as are all the Walls, with a whitish Marble. The great Cuppalo is encompassed by small ones somewhat lower. St. *Peters* at *Rome* may excel this Cuppalo in height, but not in Breadth nor Beauty.'[60] Sandys had gone even further and observed that the building 'exceedeth...all other fabrickes whatsoever throughout the whole Universe'.[61] Part of this wonder no doubt came from seeing a magnificent ancient sacred structure that for once was not a pagan temple or Muslim mosque but was Christian. Hagia Sophia seemed to answer the thorny question, posed by Anglicans since Laudian times, as to what an ancient, early Christian structure on the scale not of a church but of a cathedral might have looked like.[62] While it had featured in descriptions by these desk-bound clerics of the forms of early Christian churches, it was presented as a circular structure built by Constantine.[63] In fact it had been built by Justinian as the Roman empire's first Christian cathedral in 537, the earliest church on the site having been constructed by Constantine. Legend has it that at Hagia Sophia's consecration Justinian had exclaimed 'Solomon, I have outdone thee!'.[64] Until 1453 it served as a Greek Orthodox cathedral and seat of the Patriarch of Constantinople (except from 1204 to 1261, when it was converted to a Roman Catholic cathedral under the Latin empire). Only after 1453 had it become a mosque. Whether the report of Justinian's boast is true or false, the building's structure, with its great dome and four huge pillars, perfectly embodied the emperor's civic ambitions for unity and order. As such it became a primary model for domed churches throughout Christendom. Wren, it will be remembered, saw the symbolic purpose of his proposed dome at old St Paul's in just these terms.

Although information on Hagia Sophia was sketchy during the 1670s, and only became more detailed during the next decade, perhaps not surprisingly it nonetheless influenced the design and construction of St Paul's. The Justinian building was identified by Wren's son, possibly echoing the views of his father, as something of a precedent for a cathedral with an elevated dome (on pendentives) such as at St Paul's. For,

> Among all the Composures of the Ancients, we find no Cupolas raised above the necessary Loading of the Hemisphere, as is seen particularly in the Pantheon. In after Ages the Dome of Florence, and of the great Church of Venice, was raised higher. The Saracens mightily affected it, in imitation of the first most eminent Pattern, given to Justinian, in his Temple of Sancta Sophia, at Constantinople.[65]

The development of the elevated dome was thus traced back by Wren's son through the notable Italian examples of Brunelleschi's early fifteenth-century masterpiece in Florence and the eleventh-century St Mark's in Venice, to Hagia Sophia fully recognised here as a model Christian (and royal) building. Indeed, he followed Evelyn in emphasising that Hagia Sophia's dome had furnished the 'Saracens', or in this case principally the Turks, with a model when building their mosques, and therefore that the dome in the East was first and foremost a Christian (and not a Muslim) form. The clear implication from this, albeit indirect, report is that Hagia Sophia, rather than the pagan Pantheon, was also an inspiration for the form of elevated dome used at St Paul's, and this had risen in emulation of that at the great cathedral in Constantinople.

Hagia Sophia fascinated Wren, despite the fact that he had never seen it, and he went to great lengths to study its structure. Attributed to him, although possibly in Hawksmoor's hand, are two plans of the building's ritual south-east corner and one cross-section, which are without date or obvious source (figs 98 and 99).[66] Curiously enough, these drawings were found at St Paul's among preliminary studies for the Cathedral, a fact that strongly suggests their influence there.[67] The plans differ

97 Ahmed's mosque, the Blue Mosque, Constantinople, from George Wheler, *A Journey into Greece by George Wheler, Esq., in Company of Dr Spon of Lyons in Six Books* (1682), Book II, p. 186

in terms of the projection or otherwise of the apse, and may well have been drawn to inform the south-east corner arrangement at St Paul's with its similar staircase within the walls (fig. 100). A month after talking about the tomb of Porsenna, in November 1677 Wren discussed Hagia Sophia with Hooke, who recorded in his Diary: 'To Sir Chr Wrens, at Mans with him and Mr. Smith, a description of Star Sophia'.[68] The Diary text surrounds a small, diagrammatic sketch of the building's plan: Hagia Sophia's rectangular form is 'perfected' into a square within a square, with a non-existent double row of internal columns and a portico as the narthex, while the apse is shown correctly (fig. 101). Man's coffee house was, incidentally, a fitting setting for this conversation given the popular associations between such coffee houses and their Ottoman origins.[69]

Wren's companion and source for the plan, Thomas Smith, was a Fellow of the Royal Society and an Oxford divine who had lived in Constantinople for three years from 1668 while acting as the chaplain to the Levant

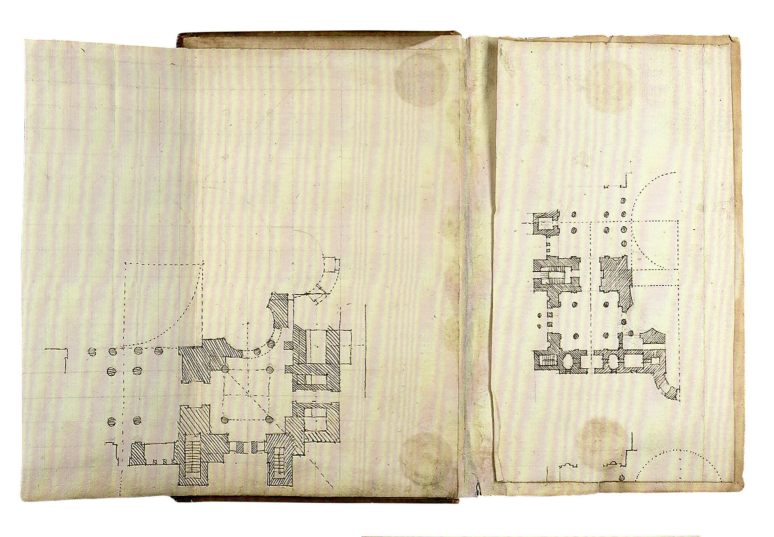

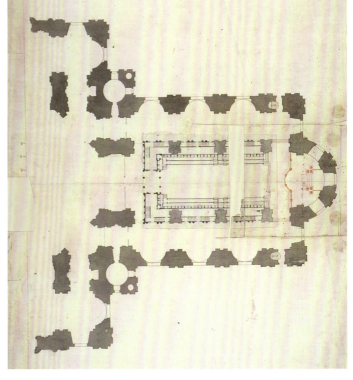

OPPOSITE 98   Section of Hagia Sophia, attributed to Wren (or perhaps drawn by Hawksmoor). Queen's University at Kingston, Ontario

ABOVE 99   Plans of Hagia Sophia, attributed to Wren (or perhaps drawn by Hawksmoor). Queen's University at Kingston, Ontario

RIGHT 100   Plan of the choir of St Paul's Cathedral, showing staircases within the walls, drawn by Hawksmoor (c.1693). All Souls College, Oxford

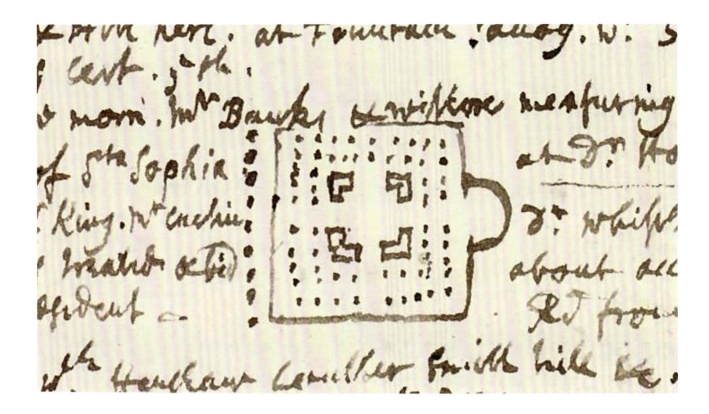

Company under their ambassador Daniel Harvey.[70] He came back to England in 1671. Before his visit Smith had turned to the Koran and to Arab histories in search of information regarding the origin of the Druids, making links between Britain and the East that Wren might have found interesting.[71] Smith too proposed a rapprochement with the Greek Orthodox Church. His account of Hagia Sophia had been published in *Epistolae Duae, quarum altera de moeibus ac institutis Turcarum agit* (1672) and was republished in English as *Remarks upon the Manners, Religion and Government of the Turks. Together with a Survey of the Seven Churches of Asia as they now lye in their Ruines: and a Brief Description of Constantinople* (1678). It also appeared in the Society's *Transactions* (on 20 October 1683 and 20 January 1684).[72] Wren owned a copy of Smith's *An Account of the Greek Church as to its doctrine and rites of worship* (1680; Lot 59), on the subject of the Orthodox Church under 'Turkish Tyranny' that had a further description of Hagia Sophia.[73] Hooke had the earlier, 1678, Latin edition published in London, which he mentioned in his Diary in November of that year.[74] He evidently knew Smith well, adding in the same entry that he had been drinking with 'Aubrey and Smith at Sun. half a glass of wine agreed well'.

Wren had contact with other English travellers to Constantinople, as well as former diplomats, who therefore also had knowledge of Hagia Sophia.[75] He was a friend of Isaac Barrow, the Master of Trinity College in Cambridge, who, just before his death in 1677, had appointed Wren to design the college library (built from 1676 to 1695): Barrow had spent four years, in 1655–9, travelling through Europe and then on to Turkey, staying seven months in Smyrna and eighteen in Constantinople with the English ambassador, Thomas Bendish. While there Barrow spent much time studying divinity and in particular the Greek Orthodox Church.[76] He was ordained on his return and in 1662 made Professor of Geometry at Gresham College, lauding Wren in his Latin oration as 'Once the child prodigy, now a miracle man'.[77] Barrow would have had ample opportunity to discuss the geometry of Hagia Sophia, and Ottoman domes more generally, with Wren and Hooke, not least at the Royal Society of which he was a Fellow.[78] And although an infrequent visitor to Cambridge, Wren certainly went there in October 1676 probably in connection with Barrow's library.[79] His first design, of around 1675, was for a building with a dome that in this case was raised on a drum (with semicircular windows; fig. 102).[80] As will be seen in a moment, Wren praised this dome and drum combination that he wrongly

101 Plan of Hagia Sophia sketched by Robert Hooke in his Diary (17 November 1677). London Metropolitan Archives, MS 01758

102 First scheme for the library at Trinity College, Cambridge, east elevation drawn by Wren (c.1675). All Souls College, Oxford

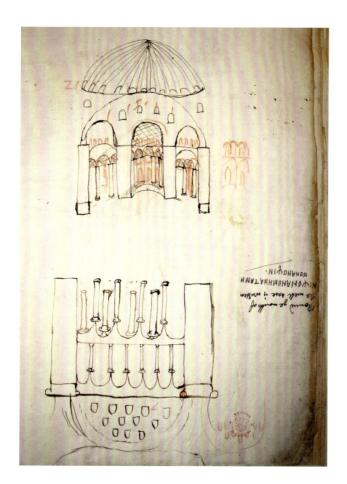

104   Dome of Hagia Sophia, from Covel's 'Autograph Journal' (1670–8), fol. 120r. British Library, London, Add. MS 22912

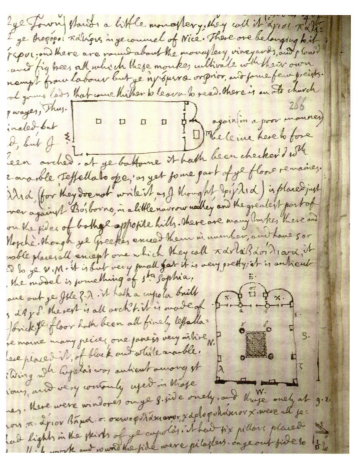

105   Plan of the Pantobasilissa (Kemerli Kilise) in Trillia, from Covel's 'Autograph Journal' (1670–8), fol. 266r. British Library, London, Add. MS 22912

identified with Hagia Sophia in his Tracts (it does not have a drum). Surely Barrow must have recalled his Ottoman experiences on seeing this novel dome design for Cambridge.

Cambridge also became the home of John Covel, 'the greate oriental Traveler' as Evelyn described him after a meeting in 1695.[81] As the Introduction noted, Covel was the chaplain to the Levant Company in Constantinople between 1670 and 1677 when he befriended Dudley North as well as the French travel writer and artist Guillaume-Joseph Grelot. He took a keen interest in the Greek Church, as well as the Arabic and Turkish languages.[82] Covel returned in early 1679, eventually becoming Master of Christ's College in July 1688 and

OPPOSITE   103   The Yeni Camii in Constantinople, from John Covel's 'Autograph Journal of Dr John Covel during his travels in Asia and Italy' (1670–8), fol. 118r. British Library, London, Add. MS 22912

the University's Vice Chancellor shortly thereafter. During his time in Turkey he had kept a journal, as the Introduction also noted, with sketches of Ottoman festivities as well as external views of mosques including the Yeni Camii in Constantinople (fig. 103) and the Selimiye in Adrianople (Edirne), sketches that, given Covel's fame, Wren might well have seen.[83] Concerning the Sultan's palace at Adrianople, Covel recorded: 'Here are adornments in building very costly and comely, utterly unknown in our parts of the world.'[84] A year before Wheler, in 1674 Covel and North had gained rare access, as non-Muslims, to measure the interior of Hagia Sophia, and his journal has five sheets with rough sketches of its plan and dome (fig. 104; much as Grelot later illustrated, with more sophistication, in 1680; see figs 106–8).[85] In December 1676 Covel visited Trillia and saw Byzantine churches including the Pantobasilissa (Kemerli Kilise), which was of a domed, cross-in-square form that he described and sketched in plan (fig. 105).[86]

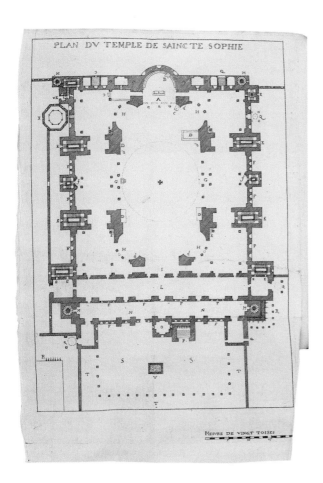

Covel maintained his interest in Constantinople while in Cambridge, as Roger North recorded when commenting on his brother's time in Turkey:

> Our merchant had then residing with him a virtuoso, who was a good mathematician and draughtsman; and they together concerted a design of making an exact plan of the city of Constantinople, and carried it on till it came very near being completed. They took the liberty of measuring in the street a distance between two stations, which were two of their mosque towers, from which their priests cry to prayers.... But this work lying a little neglected, it hath so happened, that as well the proof papers, as the map itself, were all taken away; and the merchant hath much lamented the loss, but never could recover them. And I have heard since, that the chief of them are in England, and kept as great curiosities by Dr. C—l [Covel], master of C—t's [Christ's] coll. in Cambridge.[87]

The mathematician in question was a Signor Bani or Bauni (from Livorno): Covel's journal included a sketch plan of Constantinople that was based on North and Bauni's plan.[88] On occasional visits to Cambridge Wren could easily have discussed the measurements and dome of Hagia Sophia with Covel, as he had with Smith in London, as well as viewed the 'great oriental traveller's' journal and even this 'great curiosity' of a plan. Moreover, as noted in the previous chapter, Wren must have known the Turkish scholar Paul Rycaut, who had been employed as the private secretary to Heneage Finch, the Levant Company's ambassador to Constantinople between 1661 and 1667.[89] As the Introduction discussed, Rycaut had gone on to become the consul at Smyrna, serving there until 1677.[90] He travelled home twice during this time in Turkey, being elected a Fellow of the Royal Society on 12 December 1666 when he could easily have met (or re-met) Wren;[91] as was also noted, Hooke collected Rycaut's works on Turkey and the Greek Church to which Wren would have had equally easy access.[92]

Travelling fellows of the Royal Society and Cambridge academics were not the only eye-witness sources on Hagia Sophia and its magnificent dome available to Wren and Hooke. Both men would have seen the Cathedral described in some detail, and handsomely illustrated for the first time both inside and out, in Grelot's *Relation Nouvelle d'un Voyage de Constantinople enrichie de plans levés par l'auteur sur les lieux* (1680; figs 106–8). Grelot's thirteen engraved plates included the Yeni Camii ('New Mosque'), Ahmed's mosque, the Suleimaniye, as well as panoramas of the city, and had been based on drawings done on the spot, as his title made clear (*par l'auteur sur les lieux*; figs 109–12). He too emphasised that Ottoman domes inevitably led back to the great Christian domes of late antiquity for, when the Turks had occasion to build mosques, 'they took their Models from those of the Christians' and 'this is the reason that all the Mosques in Constantinople are but very imperfect copies of the beautiful church of Saint Sophia'.[93] Wren owned two editions, a French one of 1689 (Lot 367, identical to the first edition) and an earlier English translation of 1683 (Lot 207), which Evelyn also had.[94] Hooke had an earlier, French one of 1681.[95] Grelot's plates were the first of their kind to reach European eyes. They surely had a profound effect on Wren at a time when he was designing St Paul's. Indeed, his assistant at the Cathedral, Hawksmoor, is thought to have adopted the square plan of the Suleimaniye as illustrated by Grelot in a preliminary design for the Radcliffe library in Oxford, of about 1712 (figs 113 and 114).[96] However, neither of the two plans of Hagia Sophia drawn by Wren (or Hawksmoor working for him; see fig. 99) reproduced exactly that published by Grelot in terms of the dimensions of walls and positioning of staircases, which suggests the influence of a further sketch plan by Grelot in Chardin's possession.[97]

As the Introduction noted, Grelot's studies had been carried out between 1665 and 1671 under the auspices of Chardin.[98] It was pointed out that Wren owned a copy of Chardin's *Journal du Voyage du Chevalier Chardin*, first published in London in 1686 with eighteen engravings again by Grelot (Lot 145). Hooke had two editions, this in French and one in English issued in the same year: and they must have impressed him since he mentioned Chardin's volume in his Diary three times in December 1688.[99] It will be remembered that Chardin had arrived in England in 1680 and had met Hooke in July that year.[100] And that a month later Evelyn and Wren, serving as

OPPOSITE

ABOVE LEFT 106 Plan of Hagia Sophia, from Guillaume-Joseph Grelot, *Relation Nouvelle d'un Voyage de Constantinople enrichie de plans levés par l'auteur sur les lieux* (1680), between pp. 108 and 109

ABOVE RIGHT 107 Interior view of Hagia Sophia facing the main apse, from Grelot, *Voyage de Constantinople* (1680), between pp. 146 and 147

BELOW 108 Hagia Sophia, from Grelot, *Voyage de Constantinople* (1680), between pp. 42 and 43

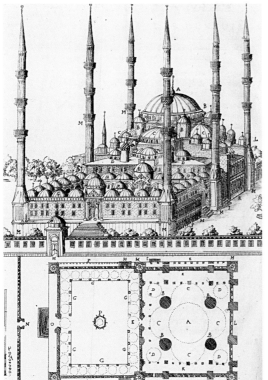

ABOVE 109 The Yeni Camii (originally named the Valide Sultan Camii as indicated here), from Grelot, *Voyage de Constantinople* (1680), between pp. 282 and 283

LEFT 110 Ahmed's mosque, from Grelot, *Voyage de Constantinople* (1680), between pp. 270 and 271

OPPOSITE

ABOVE 111 The Suleimaniye, from Grelot's *Voyage de Constantinople* (1680), between pp. 276 and 277

BELOW 112 Panorama of Constantinople, from Grelot, *Voyage de Constantinople* (1680), between pp. 74 and 75

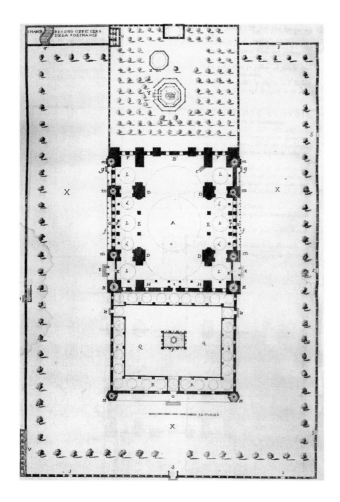

113 Plan of the Suleimaniye, from Grelot, *Voyage de Constantinople* (1680), between pp. 278 and 279

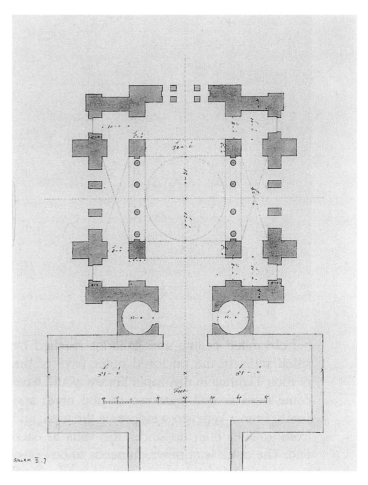

114 Hawksmoor's design (Project II) for the Radcliffe library, Oxford, *c.*1712. Ashmolean Museum, Oxford

delegates of the Royal Society, also visited Chardin, who was 'in Eastern habite' and talked about the antiquities witnessed on his travels. Wren eventually saw at least some of Grelot's drawings made for Chardin, denied on that visit, for he wrote in August 1681 with disappointment that from views of cities in Georgia and Persia he 'received noe other instruction but that they build as the Turkes doe, the Cypresses overtop the Low Houses [and] the cupp[o]les of the Mosques [overtop] the Cypresses'. Wren added that, concerning an album of drawings of Kilmanoor in India, the Frenchman 'was in too much haste to be able to open it without great inconvenience'.[101] Chardin had visited India in 1664 or 1665 and again from 1667 to 1669 and in 1677–8 in search of precious stones; on 8 July 1680 Hooke recorded in the Royal Society minutes 'that Mor. Chardin was Returnd from India and brought wth him a book'.[102] Despite Wren's frustration, Chardin could offer a rare, eye-witness account of Byzantine buildings in Turkey and of mosques in Persia, not least their domes referred to here, to keen students such as Wren and Hooke. Wren might have been especially interested in Chardin's plates of the domed royal funerary chambers at Qom, published in 1686 but possibly seen earlier, given his design of the domed crypt at St Paul's (figs 115 and 116; see fig. 19).

Contact with Chardin could help explain a further important record of Wren's knowledge of Hagia Sophia's central and abutting domes, and of mosques more generally, found in Tract two. This includes a passing reference to the wandering dervishes who were members of the Muslim order housed in the *tabhane*, a hospice for travellers located among the mosques' many domed courtyards. He noted that in contrast to the Gothic fan vault,

> Another Way, (which I cannot find used by the Ancients, but in the later eastern Empire, as appears at *St. Sophia*, and by that Example, in all the Mosques and Cloysters of the *Dervises*, and every where

94 CHRISTOPHER WREN

at present in the *East*) and of all others the most geometrical, is composed of Hemispheres, and their Sections only: and whereas a Sphere may be cut all manner of Ways, and that still into Circles, it may be accommodated to lie upon all Positions of the Pillars.[103]

Wren was describing a dome on pendentives, recognised by him to be of Eastern origin. He continued: 'Cut the Hemisphere again horizontally, the Section will be an entire Circle' and 'if the horizontal Circle be taken away, you may build upon that Circle an upright Wall, which may bear a Cupola again above, as is done at *St. Sophia* and *St. Peter's*'.[104] In fact, the dome at Hagia Sophia rests directly on pendentives (see fig. 94), not on an intermediary 'upright' or drum in the manner found at St Peter's. However, externally its base is buttressed by a clerestory that has the appearance of a drum. And Procopius had implied the presence of a drum, in the form of a clerestory containing windows, when writing in his *De aedificiis* that: 'Upon the crowns of the arches rests a circular structure, cylindrical in shape; it is through this that the light of day always first smiles.'[105] He went on to note that at the Church of the Holy Apostles in Constantinople,

> That portion of the roof which is above the sanctuary, as it is called, is built, in the centre at least, on a plan resembling that of the Church of Sophia, except that it is inferior to it in size. The arches, four in number, rise aloft and are bound together in the same manner, and the circular drum which stands upon them is pierced by the windows, and the dome which arches above this seems to float in the air and not to rest upon solid masonry, though actually it is well supported.[106]

Clearly, the relationship between pendentives and dome at Hagia Sophia was better understood by Wren (or Hawksmoor) when it came to drawing the section found among studies for St Paul's (see fig. 98). The source for the section at least was almost certainly the plates of Grelot, possibly once again using additional drawings in the possession of Chardin.[107] From Wren's following remarks in this Tract on what he called the 'eastern Way of Vaulting by Hemispheres' there can be no doubt that he saw Hagia Sophia as a model for the vaulting of his own great Cathedral. For he recorded that the ancient building informed the modern one in direct, structural terms:

> I question not but those at *Constantinople* had it [i.e., dome on pendentives] from the *Greeks* [i.e., Byzantines] before them, it is so natural, and is yet

found in the present Seraglio, which was the episcopal Palace of old; the imperial Palace, whose Ruins still appear, being further eastward. Now, because I have for just Reasons followed this way in the [domical] vaulting of the Church of *St. Paul's*, I think it proper to shew, that it is the lightest Manner, and requires less Butment than the Cross-vaulting, as well as that it is of an agreeable View.[108]

ABOVE 115 Funerary chamber of Abbas II at the Fatima Masumeh Shrine at Qom, Persia, from John Chardin, *Travels into Persia and the East Indies, with Figures* (1686), between pp. 398 and 399

BELOW 116 Crypt at St Paul's Cathedral (with the tomb of Nelson installed in 1806)

Wren's source for the domes of the Topkapi Palace (the Seraglio) is unclear, since access was generally forbidden: Grelot for example drew only what he could see from outside (the entrance gate and a distant view; figs 117 and 118). But some spaces covered by domes were accessible to dignitaries and ambassadors, including the Council Chamber or Hall of the Divan, the Chancery, and the Archives.[109] Wren might have got information about the palace from his 1670 edition of Sandys's *Travels* that contained, as the title-page put it, *a description of Constantinople, the Grand Signior's seraglio, and his manner of living*. The 1673 edition included a fold-out 'Prospect of the Grand Signiors Seraglio from Galata' with a view of Hagia Sophia. Details were also to be found in Ottaviano Bon's *A Description of the grand Signor's Seraglio, or Turkish Emperours Court* (written around 1604 and first published by John Greaves in 1650), which was in Hooke's collection, as well as in Tavernier's *Nouvelle Relation de l'intéreur du Sérail du Grand Seigneur* (1675).[110] These sources could have been supplemented by accounts from the likes of Dudley North, who also drew the palace from a distance.[111]

Wren's reference to the vaulting of St Paul's indicates that this passage in Tract two is likely to date from the end of the 1680s, given the progress of design and

OPPOSITE ABOVE 117   The entrance gate to the Topkapi Palace (the Seraglio), from Grelot, *Voyage de Constantinople* (1680), between pp. 94 and 95

OPPOSITE BELOW 118   View of the Topkapi Palace (detail), from Grelot, *Voyage de Constantinople* (1680), between pp. 86 and 87

ABOVE 119   Saucer domes in the nave of St Paul's Cathedral

GREEK CROSSES AND DOMES

construction there, and further suggests that the Tracts were worked on over a period of time.[112] As he mentions, his saucer domes sitting on pendentives covering the nave and chancel at the Cathedral had the advantages over Gothic cross-vaults of needing less abutment and being 'of an agreeable View' (fig. 119).[113] These domes are not visible on the exterior of St Paul's. In structural terms, Hagia Sophia influenced the design of these saucer domes more than it did that of the main dome, whose inner structure is conical and owed its external appearance to Serlio's illustration of Bramante's design for St Peter's.[114] Double domes of the type used at St Paul's were, however, a feature of Persian and Indian architecture (the Shah mosque in Isfahan begun in 1611, for example). As might be expected, Wren was interested in Eastern construction methods when designing the Cathedral dome. For he consulted Dudley North to find out how the Ottomans covered their domes. In recalling his brother's time in Turkey, Roger later recorded that

> our merchant was a builder himself; and no foreigner ever looked more strictly into the manner of the Turkish buildings than he had done. But he could not give Sir Christopher Wren satisfaction about covering their vaults with lead. For, when he had the covering of the great dome of St Paul's in deliberation, he was pleased to inquire of that matter. The merchant informed him so far, as to assure him, the Turks never laid lead upon wood, but upon loam, or mere clay only: but how they fastened it he could not tell. Sir Christopher was not satisfied, that the lead would hang upon loam, and not slip, without some fastening.

Roger North added: 'Our merchant told us, that the ordinary coverings of porticoes were half-sweep vaults, which stood like mole-hills in a row; and all public buildings whatsoever were covered with vaults, and leaded upon loam.'[115] As Chapter One pointed out, Wren knew the North brothers quite well. Hooke noted in his Diary their discussion of Turkish buildings in December 1688: 'With Sr Ch. Wren, Sir Dly North and his Bro. at Child', a coffee-house in St Paul's churchyard where, appropriately, they talked 'of Turky building, Pottery, Humhums [hamams] etc'.[116] Perhaps these enquiries by Wren about the covering of Turkish domes were at his Saturday meetings with the Norths on site at St Paul's, which according to Roger's report was by 'then well advanced'.[117] The main and side domes at Hagia Sophia, and on mosques more generally, thus served as a source not only for the construction of domes at St Paul's but, more importantly given the tendency of its clergy to favour tradition, for the suitability of the form to Christian architecture.

'A CUPOLO RAISED IN THE MIDDLE': GREEK CROSSES AND DOMES AT ST STEPHEN WALBROOK AND THE GREAT MODEL OF ST PAUL'S CATHEDRAL

Interest in the form of Byzantine churches was greatly stimulated in Wren's day by the movement advanced by Wheler, Beveridge, Rycaut, Smith and others to bring the Church of England into greater unity with Eastern Orthodoxy; this was in order to bypass Roman Catholicism and reconnect with Anglicanism's own supposedly 'primitive' past. Wren seems to have taken a keen interest in the form of the churches of these early, or 'primitive', Christians. His son recorded in *Parentalia* that the Norman cathedral on the site of old St Paul's 'had originally, as the *Surveyor* believ'd, a semicircular *Presbyterium* or Chancel, after the usual *Mode* of the *Primitive Churches*'.[118] An example of such a chancel is to be found at the Basilica of the Nativity at Bethlehem illustrated by Sandys in 1615 and Amico in 1620, where the sanctuary is in the form of an apse enclosing the altar (fig. 120). The semi-circular chancel featured in three 'ideal' Byzantine church plans published by Leone Allatius (or Allacci) in his *De templis Graecorum recentioribus* of 1645 (fig. 121): and it was developed by Beveridge in his *Synodikon* of 1672 that relied on Allatius (see fig. 126).[119] This long-destroyed Norman chancel at St Paul's may have influenced the small plan for a new cathedral on Wren's post-Fire plan for the City of 1666 (fig. 122; see fig. 149).[120] The Cathedral plan was novel in not following the medieval Latin cross form. Reflecting Wren's reputed understanding of the early Christian plan of its Norman predecessor, it comprises a large circular chancel, almost certainly domed, that is attached to a rectangular nave with its narthex.[121] The narthex (porch or vestibule) was an equally typical element of early Christian and Byzantine churches, as for example with S. Croce in Gerusalemme built in Rome by Helena, the mother of Constantine, in 326–8 (which had been engraved by Antonio Lafréry in 1575).[122] It was described by Allatius as part of his 'ideal' plans (here serving more as a nave than a vestibule) and later by the clergyman William Cave in his *Primitive Christianity* of 1672 (who partly relied on 'the learned *Leo Allatius*').[123] A narthex was a prominent feature of an imaginary or 'ideal' early Christian church

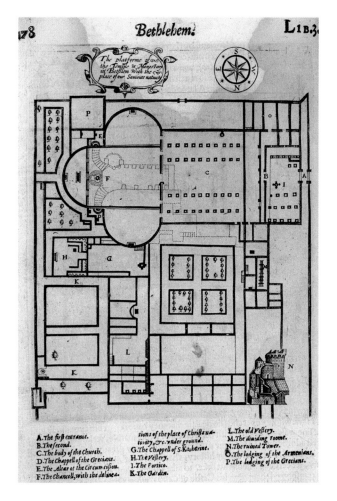

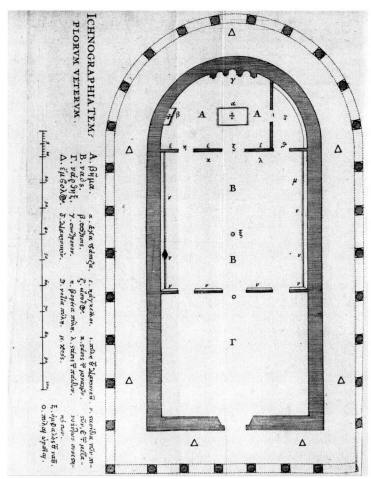

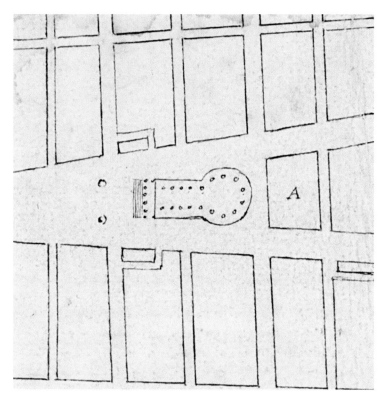

ABOVE LEFT 120   Plan of the Basilica of the Nativity at Bethlehem, from George Sandys, *A relation of a Journey begun an: Dom: 1610. Foure bookes. Containing a description of the Turkish Empire, of Ægypt, of the Holy Land* (1615), Book III, p. 178

ABOVE RIGHT 121   An 'ideal' Byzantine church plan, from Leone Allatius, *De templis Graecorum recentioribus* (1645), facing Letter One on p. 1

RIGHT 122   St Paul's Cathedral on Wren's post-Fire plan for the City, 1666 (see fig. 149)

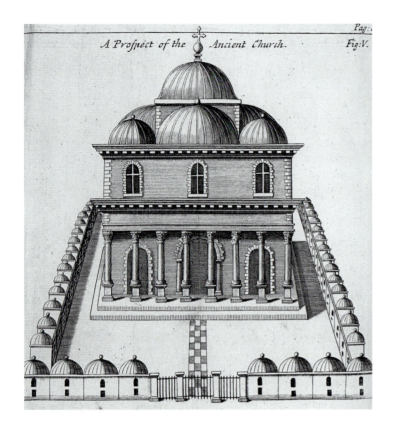
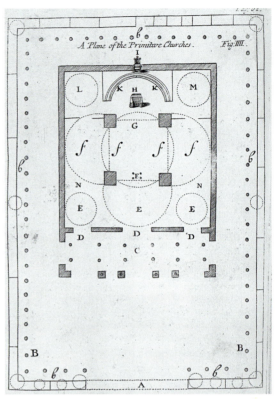

ABOVE LEFT 123 An 'ideal' early Christian church, from George Wheler, *An Account of the Churches, or Places of Assembly, of the Primitive Christians from the churches of Tyre, Jerusalem, and Constantinople described by Eusebius...with a Seasonable Application* (1689), between pp. 62 and 63

ABOVE RIGHT 124 Plan of an 'ideal' early Christian church, from Wheler, *Account* (1689), between pp. 62 and 63

LEFT 125 Wren's model of the nave of his early scheme for St Paul's Cathedral, from the south-east (1669). St Paul's Cathedral, London

described and illustrated by Wheler in his *Account* of 1689 (figs 123 and 124). The form of the Cathedral represented in the tiny plan went on to inform Wren's early scheme for St Paul's of 1669. This comprised a barrel-vaulted nave and chancel, flanked externally by ground-floor loggias: its west end was joined to a building with a dome, which was possibly a rotunda that in this scheme served as a vestibule.[124] It is known through a partial model of the nave, and a description in *Parentalia* that recorded it had 'a convenient Quire, with a Vestibule, and Porticoes, and a Dome conspicuous above the Houses': the description re-emphasised that 'it had Porticoes on the Outside, which might prevent Disturbance within' (fig. 125).[125] The arrangement of a rotunda joined to a rectangular nave reflected that of the Temple Church and, in turn, the Holy Sepulchre. In addition, the unusual 'porticoes' or loggias on the exterior and the internal barrel-vault once again found a ready source in Allatius (see fig. 121). A further preliminary design for St Paul's, this time between 1670–5 for a circular cathedral with four apses (like fig. 83) and an internal ring of columns, was partially based on another early Christian church in Rome.[126] This was Santa Costanza, built around AD 320 as the mausoleum for Constantine's daughters. As was

100 CHRISTOPHER WREN

noted, Serlio's third book illustrated this mausoleum-cum-church, although it incorrectly showed the internal dome as expressed on the exterior, and Palladio's fourth book had a plan and elevation:[127] both treatises were in Wren's collection (Lots 529, 540 and 548; see fig. 79). A domed early Christian church thus proved the starting point for one of his earliest Cathedral designs (and a subsequent one explored the use of the Pantheon as a model).[128]

Allatius's book on Byzantine churches, or 'later Greek temples' as his title put it, was available well before the 1670s in important English collections, and at some point Evelyn acquired a copy (as also one of Cave).[129] The essential elements of his three plans were a western entrance, three parts (narthex, naos or choir and bema or sanctuary in the form of an apse), barrel-vaulted ceilings and galleries for women.[130] As noted, his plans influenced the English clergymen Cave and Beveridge in their publications of 1672 around the time of Wren's earliest churches (fig. 126).[131] Indeed, further influences of Allatius and his followers on Wren can be detected, this time on his designs for these churches. The arrangement of St Clement Danes has some of the key features of Allatius's and Beveridge's churches, for example (fig 127; see fig. 121). Wren regularised the plan of the destroyed medieval church on the site, from about 1679, into a symmetrical design with a semi-circular chancel apse (covered by a half-dome) and a nave with a barrel-vault (that sits on arches); the nave is entered through a small porch and is surrounded by a gallery (fig. 128).[132] Wren's interest in early Christian church plans also informed his reorganisation of the layout, and the centrally placed pulpit in particular, of the Temple Church from 1682.[133] Here the 'Round' (with its internal pendentive dome) made a natural narthex while, as Robin Griffith-Jones has pointed out, 'Wren's own screen ensured that three doors led from the narthex into the nave', in following early Christian churches such as that at Tyre described by Eusebius.[134] Griffith-Jones concluded: 'Wren used the space and traditions of the Temple Church to re-create the character of an early Christian church.'[135] Cave's vision of the early church under Constantine influenced the addition of chancel screens in St Peter Cornhill, whose rector was Beveridge, and slightly later at All Hallows the Great, whose rector was Cave himself.[136] Once again, these screens reflected the text of Allatius, who had emphasised the importance to the Byzantine church plan and liturgy of the 'bema screen' and its central 'beautiful gate'.[137] Moreover, Cave's observation that the earliest Christians had been 'careful to keep a decent mean between a sordid *slovenliness*, and a too curious and over-nice *superstition*' in the adornment of their churches, and that these were 'built and beautified so far as consisted with the ability and simplicity of those days', might aptly describe the exterior of Wren's churches.[138] This is also true of Wheler's comments slightly later concerning the 'Beauteous Symetry' and 'Grave, and yet Magnificent' appearance of the ancient churches, which matched the 'useful Plainness' of their ritual.[139] In comments made in 1711 to the Commission for building the Queen Anne churches, Wren himself recommended that when it came to 'inriching the outward Walls', then 'Plainness and Duration ought principally, if not wholly, to be studied'.[140] After all, as far as he was concerned the greatest temple of them all, in Jerusalem, had been a plain and monolithic Tyrian edifice, rather than the Corinthian one imagined by the Jesuit Villalpando.

Wren's references to these early Christian and Byzantine buildings in his work thus coincided with Evelyn's and Roger North's interest in their domes. As has been seen, North observed that the plan in the form of a cross with a dome or tower in the middle had been introduced by the Christians and was peculiar to their churches. Wheler too had observed in his *Account* of 1689 that the plans of the early Christian and Byzantine churches he had seen were remarkably alike. In the case of the destroyed church at Tyre, for example, he concluded that its square plan contained four columns defining a Greek cross with a central dome (which he also illustrated; see fig. 33).[141] He accurately observed that Hagia Sophia's plan is similarly subdivided into nine rectangles by four central columns (it will be remembered that the building's plan had been duly 'corrected' into a perfect square by Hooke in his Diary sketch of 1677 following discussions with Wren and Smith; see fig. 101). By the time Wheler described Hagia Sophia's form, he would have had Grelot's plan, published in 1680, to assist him (while Grelot also made the interior closer to a square than it is; see fig. 106). Also available was the earliest description of the building's mighty central piers and dome, by Procopius:

> And in the centre of the church stand four man-made eminences, which they call piers…From these spring four arches which rise over the four sides of a square …And since the arches where they are joined together are so constructed as to form a four-cornered plan, the stonework between the arches produces four triangles [pendentives]…And while each supporting end of a triangle, having been contracted to a point by the coming together of each pair of arches, makes the

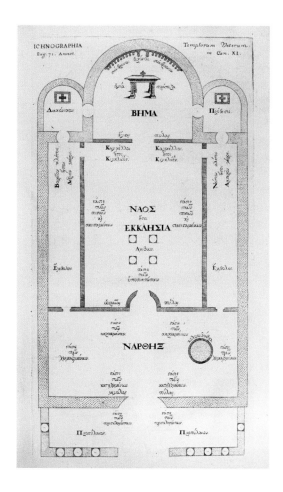
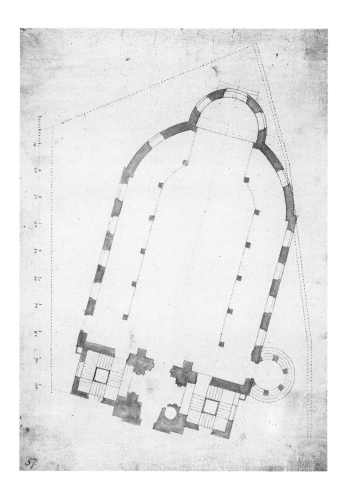

lower point an acute angle, yet as the triangle rises and its width is extended by the intermediate surface, it ends in the segment of a circle which it supports, and forms the remaining angles at that level. And upon this circle rests the huge spherical dome which makes the structure exceptionally beautiful. Yet it seems not to rest upon solid masonry, but to cover the space with its golden dome suspended from Heaven.[142]

Wheler drew on Procopius and Eusebius, whom he verified by direct observation on a visit to the site, when describing the destroyed Church of the Holy Apostles at Constantinople. This also not only had a dome, as noted earlier, but a square perimeter containing four columns defining a Greek cross (fig. 129): for that church

> is, I suppose, Square without, and Divided within into four Parts, in Form of a Cross; as most of the Ancient Churches I have seen in *Greece*, and now extant, remain to this day: As that of *Sancta Sophia*, at *Constantinople*; *Jovianus* at *Corfu*; of *Romanus* at *S. Luke*'s Convent under the *Helicon*; that at *Heraclea*, &c. Which have a *Cupolo* raised in the middle; with half *Cupolo*'s joyned to the East, West, North and South; and small *Cupolo*'s filling up each Corner.[143]

The emphasis on the centre in this form of plan facilitated the liturgical practices of Greek Orthodoxy, in allowing the clergy to be positioned under the dome and the congregation to occupy the side aisles. An ambo projected into the centre for readings, while the altar was placed in the east. A centralised space such as this suited preaching, at the heart of Protestant liturgy, in contrast to the long nave and aisles that facilitated the processions of Roman

LEFT 126 An 'ideal' early Christian church, from William Beveridge's *Synodikon sive Pandectae Canonum SS. Apostolorum, et Conciliorum ab Ecclesia Graeca receptorum*, vol. 2 (1672), facing p. 71

RIGHT 127 Plan of St Clement Danes, London, drawn by Thomas Laine (c.1680). All Souls College, Oxford

OPPOSITE 128 St Clement Danes, London

102 CHRISTOPHER WREN

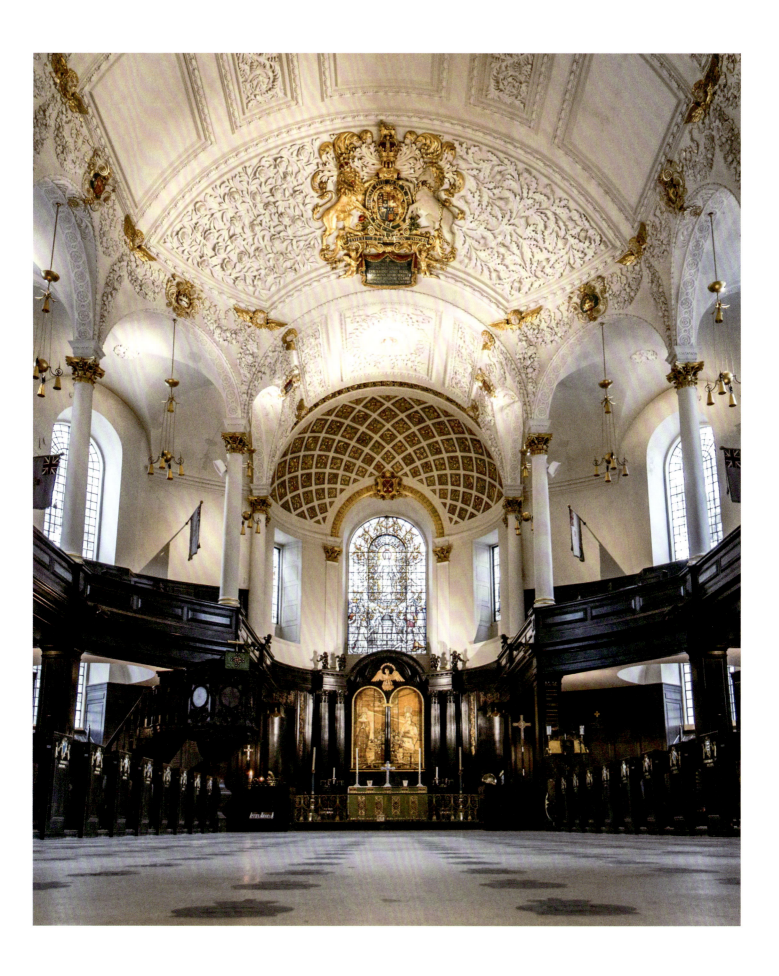

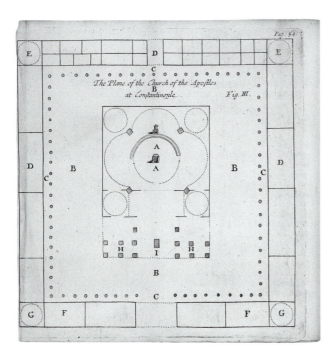

129 Plan of the Church of the Holy Apostles, Constantinople (destroyed), from Wheler, *Account* (1689), between pp. 54 and 55

130 The Katholikon monastery of Hosios Loukas, Mount Helicon, Greece

Catholic ritual.[144] Hardly surprisingly, therefore, it was the arrangement of these churches that Wheler used to inform his description and illustration of the 'ideal' early Christian church concluding his book (see figs 123 and 124). Wheler's plan thus united Anglican requirements and Eastern precedent. This fit was perhaps why North and he had not emphasised the basilica as an equally dominant early Christian form and one that had been hugely influential in Renaissance church design.[145]

Nevertheless, when justifying his 'ideal' church plan Wheler was certainly correct that Byzantine churches in and around Greece and Turkey were frequently square in plan or almost so, with four central columns and a dome rising on pendentives (to transition from square to circle).[146] The resulting cross-in-square pattern resembles the five dots on a dice and is known in Byzantine architecture as a quincunx, or 'five-pointed'. Sometimes these churches had barrel-vaulted extensions or small domes at the sides of the central one to emphasise internally the Greek cross. Wheler cited the example of the monastery of Hosios Loukas, situated on the slopes of Mount Helicon in Greece (fig. 130). Further variants in Athens include the Kapnikarea, the Holy Apostles of Solaki and Saint Assomati; a prominent example in

Corfu is the church of Saints Jason and Sosipater; while in Constantinople there is the church of the Myrelaion monastery (fig. 131) and that of St John, not to mention on a larger scale Hagia Sophia and later mosques like Ahmed's, illustrated by Grelot in 1680 and Wheler in 1682 (see figs 97 and 110). In his 1620 edition, Amico had illustrated two examples in Jerusalem of this form of plan with its dome: one was the twelfth-century Armenian Cathedral of St James and the other was a reconstruction of the ruined Byzantine church of St Anne (figs 132 and 133). Much later, in 1686 Chardin illustrated the plan of the Byzantine Cathedral of Echmiadzin in Armenia that Wren would have seen (see fig. 18). Indeed, his awareness of Byzantine churches is evident from the Tracts. His observation quoted earlier concerning the 'Greek' origins of the dome on pendentives ('I question not but those at *Constantinople* had it from the *Greeks* before them, it is so natural') was not in reference to Greek antiquity, as some have concluded.[147] Rather, it was these Byzantine buildings in Greece and the Levant that made such strong impressions on Wheler.

Wheler intended the 'ideal' church of his *Account*, with its cross-in-square arrangement and dome, as an example of what his title had promised was a 'seasonable application' of Byzantine church principles and that this church would in turn be useful as a model for the Anglican churches of his own day. While no English church up to Wren's time had a 'Byzantine' cross-in-square plan, let alone boasted a dome, it was the basis for a number of his churches in the City of London (fig. 134).[148] Wren's earliest use of a version of this arrangement was at St Mary-at-Hill, designed with Hooke in 1670–4. This has an almost square plan with four central columns and four short, barrel-vaulted arms (defining a Greek cross) that meet in the centre at a shallow, coffered saucer dome: the joins between barrel-vaults and dome elegantly define four pendentives (fig. 135). Equally of note are St Anne and St Agnes (1677–80) and St Martin Ludgate (1677–82), again designed with Hooke, both of which have square plans with Greek crosses defined by four columns supporting

131 The church of the Myrelaion monastery (now the Bodrum mosque), Constantinople

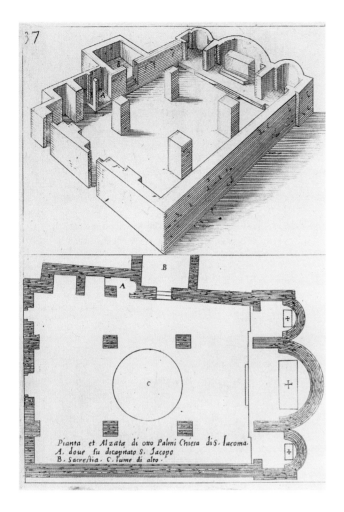
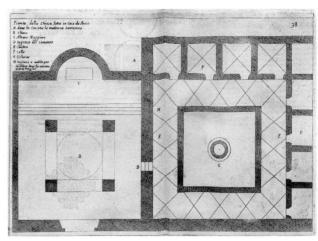

LEFT 132 Plan of the Armenian Cathedral of St James, Jerusalem (12th century), from Bernardino Amico, *Trattato delle piante et imagini de sacri edificii di Terra Santa, disegnate in Gierusalemme secondo le regole della prospettiua, & vera misura della lor grandezza, etc.* (1620 edn), fig. 37

ABOVE 133 Reconstruction of the ruined Byzantine church of St Anne, Jerusalem, from Amico, *Trattato* (1620 edn), fig. 38

OPPOSITE 134 Plans of (A) St Mary-at-Hill, (B) St Anne and St Agnes, (C) St Martin Ludgate, (D) St Stephen Walbrook, London

side barrel-vaults that meet in the centre (figs 136 and 137).[149] Two unbuilt designs by Wren also had cross-in-square plans, namely the French Protestant church in the Savoy (*c*.1685) and St Mary's in Lincoln's Inn Fields (*c*.1695).[150] St Mary's in particular followed the Byzantine 'type' in having a central dome, this time expressed on the exterior, that must have rested on pendentives (see fig. 78). Paul Jeffery described it as 'a true quincunx design, with domes over the corners': these were also a feature of Wheler's ideal church (see fig. 123).[151]

Wren's knowledge of Byzantine architecture in the early 1670s is, however, most strongly suggested by St Stephen Walbrook (also designed with Hooke, between 1672 and 1679).[152] The church's arrangement, best described as conforming to the Byzantine type developed from the cross-in-square and known as a 'Greek-cross-domed-octagon',[153] is sometimes recognised as betraying an Eastern influence (figs 138 and 139).[154] Lydia Soo, for example, observed that 'a remarkable similarity can be found in the layering of geometries, the handling of illumination, and the lightness and buoyancy of the structure found at both Wren's St Stephen Walbrook (from 1672) and Sinan's Selimiye (1568–75)'.[155] Within a rectangular outline is nested a square space defined by twelve columns, eight of which support arches and, between these, pendentives. These pendentives in turn support a large dome, fully expressed on the exterior, below which are barrel-vaults on the axes that define an almost regular Greek cross (this cross is equally apparent at roof level). The eight arches cut across the remaining outer four corner columns (defining the square) in the manner of the Byzantine 'squinch' (as found in the Selimiye). As well as the central dome and Greek-cross-domed-octagon arrangement, the use of 'Diocletian' (or 'thermal') windows in this church reflected any number of Byzantine church and mosque examples (such as St Theodore in Constantinople). Such references would have been particularly fitting here given that St Stephen was one of the first deacons, and the first Christian martyr, of Jerusalem. Elsewhere, the domed-octagon type with eight pendentives was adapted by Wren at St Mary Abchurch and in a further variation at St Antholin (see fig. 77).[156]

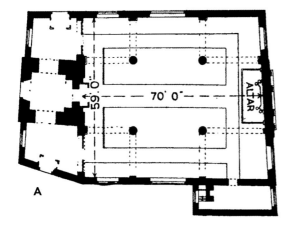
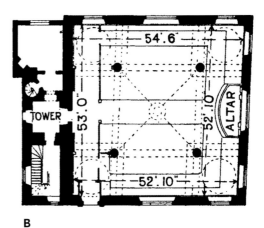
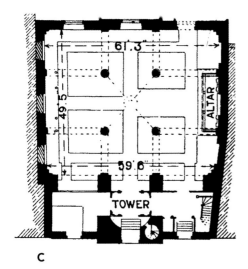
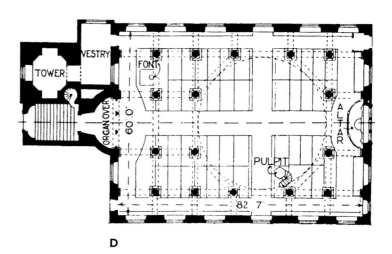

The audacious dome at St Mary Abchurch, spanning from wall to wall, demonstrates that the arrangement of cross vaults on four columns at St Martin Ludgate, for example, was more a matter of choice than necessity. For any contemporary visitor to Wren's churches with Wheler's book in their hands, such as Evelyn with his copy,[157] the similarities between the centralised form of the 'ideal' church and these churches would have been unmistakable.

That these cross-in-square and Greek-cross-domed-octagon churches formed a distinct group in Wren and Hooke's work has often been recognised, but their centralised plan is commonly linked with Dutch, and sometimes French, examples. In 1971 Margaret Whinney commented that they 'seem to have direct links with Holland', cautioning, 'though it is not possible to say how Wren knew of the pattern'.[158] In 1996 Jeffery pointed to Wren's experience of centralised churches with domes in Paris.[159] In 2004 Kerry Downes too commented that some of the church forms 'derive from a Byzantine type known to Wren by repute and used in the Protestant Netherlands; in this, the arms of a Greek cross are defined within a square by four large columns (as in St Martin Ludgate)'.[160] A year later Sergey Kravtsov also suggested Dutch churches as Wren's source, although he pointed out the chronological difficulties; both groups were understood as ultimately modelled on Villalpando's cross-in-square plan of Solomon's Temple (even though Wren was sceptical of Villalpando).[161] There is in fact no evidence that either Wren or Hooke had any specific knowledge of Dutch examples of this form of church before the early 1670s or even that they visited Holland.[162] But of much more importance than which modern examples of this arrangement Wren may have seen in Europe is whether, by the early 1670s, he knew (clearly by repute) that its origins lay in early Christian and Byzantine churches.

OPPOSITE 135 St Mary-at-Hill, London (1670–4)

ABOVE 136 St Anne and St Agnes, London (1677–80)

BELOW 137 St Martin Ludgate, London (1677–82)

For such knowledge would throw light on his intention to reflect Anglican admiration for 'primitive' Christianity in the East through the use of both it and the dome, as well as the other forms associated with Eastern churches discussed earlier.

While the first use of the distinctive cross-in-square arrangement, at St Mary-at-Hill from 1670, predates Wheler's publications, Wren and Hooke could easily have known before then of its Byzantine origins. There can be no doubt that at some point Wren studied Byzantine domed structures, as has been seen: to recapitulate, at the opening of the first Tract he stressed the importance of the domed Holy Sepulchre as a prototype in modern Jerusalem, and in the second he mentioned 'Greek', that is Byzantine, domes on pendentives and the example of Hagia Sophia. Indeed, according to his son, Wren knew the 'usual mode' of 'primitive' churches that must have included the cross-in-square form. The earliest listed source for this form in the catalogue of Wren's library made at the time of its sale is an engraving by Lafréry. This shows the plan and section of the by-then destroyed fifth-century Oratory of the Holy Cross at the Constantinian St John Lateran in Rome (Lot 560): it is dated 1568 and was published by Labacco in 1572.[163] Here the central space was in the form of a Greek cross

OPPOSITE 138   St Stephen Walbrook, London (1672–9)

ABOVE 139   St Stephen Walbrook, south side

GREEK CROSSES AND DOMES   111

140 Oratory of the Holy Cross at the Constantinian St John Lateran, Rome (5th century), engraving by Antonio Lafréry, from Antonio Labacco, *Libro d'Antonio Labacco appartenente a l'architettura nel qual si figurano alcune notabili antiquita di Roma* (1572 edn), pl. IV

with a faceted dome, and the addition of spaces in the four corners completed a square outline (fig. 140). The catalogue is incomplete, however, and Wren might well have owned unrecorded sources before 1670. It will be recalled that Amico had illustrated Jerusalem churches of this form in his *Trattato* of 1620 that Wren could easily have seen (see figs 132 and 133). Like Allatius's work, Amico's fuller second edition of 1620 was available by the 1670s in important English collections including that at Covel's college in Cambridge, Christ's.[164] References to the cross-in-square planning of early Christian and later Byzantine churches were equally easy to find, not only in ancient sources such as Eusebius and Procopius but in modern ones too. After discussing the liturgical planning of Byzantine churches in 1645, Allatius went on in the second part of his work to categorise their vault and plan types: he included those that were domed as well as ones 'in the form of a cross' and in so doing mentioned Hagia Sophia.[165] And with reference to Allatius, Cave discussed the layout of the early Christian church in his *Primitive Christianity* of 1672: he too cited the church at Tyre and the Church of the Holy Apostles as described by Eusebius.

Quite a few of Hooke's and Wren's contemporaries could have confirmed from first-hand experience that the cross-in-square form with its dome, unique in English churches, was far from novel in Byzantine ones. One possible eye-witness source was Dudley North (especially so given his brother's evident knowledge of what he terms 'Greek fabriks'). Basire, Smith, Barrow, Rycaut and Heneage Finch were all in Turkey in the late 1650s or during the 1660s and all, bar Basire and Finch, were Fellows of the Royal Society.[166] As Chapter One noted, Basire had also visited Jerusalem in 1652 and was therefore in a position to report on the domed cross-in-square churches illustrated by Amico. Basire, Smith and Rycaut held a common motivation for their Eastern studies through their advocacy of greater unity between Anglicanism and Greek Orthodoxy (Rycaut wrote a book on the state of the Greek churches in Turkey, published in 1679, which Hooke owned).[167] In the case of Smith and North we know for certain that they discussed Byzantine architecture with Wren and Hooke. Others associated with the Levant Company would also have been in a position to provide both architects with eye-witness accounts of Eastern churches. These included the merchants Jerome Salter and Jacob Turner (in Smyrna from 1663 and a friend of Covel's), and the chaplain John Luke (in Smyrna from 1664 to 1669 and 1674 to 1683, after which he was appointed to the chair of Arabic at Cambridge); Luke had a special interest in the Byzantine pilgrimage churches in Chonai (Colossae) in southern Turkey and his notes (dated to 1669) informed Rycaut's book on the subject.[168] Through their work in Constantinople and Smyrna, Smith and Luke helped promote interest among theologians in the physical remains of the 'Seven Churches of Asia Minor' which were centres of early Christianity – Ephesus, Smyrna, Pergamum, Thyatira, Sardis, Philadelphia and Laodicea mentioned in Revelation.[169]

Another likely source for information on early Christian and Byzantine church forms was Blount, who had visited Constantinople in the 1630s. He was made a

Royal Society Fellow in 1661 and lived until 1682. Blount was a well-known expert on the East: Evelyn described him as 'the famous Travellor' after their meeting in August 1659, while Pepys recorded in September 1664 that he had 'called at the Coffee-house, and there had very good discourse with Sir Blunt and Dr. Whistler about Egypt'.[170] Hooke too recorded a meeting with the traveller in December 1675, this time at Garraway's coffee house, and referred to his 1669 edition of Blount's *Voyage* in December 1688 and January 1689.[171] Blount was certainly fascinated by the forms of religious buildings he encountered. For example, he gave a vivid description, using church terminology, of the minarets, square form and dome of the Selimiye in Adrianople (which Covel sketched in 1675). Of the town's three hills, Blount told his readers such as Hooke,

> the middest is the highest, and largest, upon the top whereof, as the crowne, and glory of the other buildings, stands a stately *Mescheeto* [mosque] built by *Sultan Solyman* the Second, with foure high, and curious *Spyres*, at each corner one, as the manner of *Turky* is; not upon the *Church* like our *Steeples*, but from the *Ground*; each of them hath three rounds [balconies] on the outside, for the *Priests* walke, and at the top a great *Globe*, and *halfe-moone* of Gold: The Body of the *Meskeeto* like those of *Constantinople* (though farre more curious) is at the bottom quadrangular [square], having foure Stories in heighth; the two uppermost so contracted, as that division which quarters the two lowest into foure *angles* a peece [squinches], casts each of them into eight; at either *angle* of the upper story is a great round *Pyramide* [pendentive]: they support the roofe, in forme round [dome], and eminent, all covered with Lead, upon the top whereof is set a *globe of Gold*, whereon stands a golden pillar, and a *halfe moone*.[172]

A later source in the Royal Society for information on Eastern churches was Wheler. He had returned to England in November 1676, thereby coinciding with or just before the design of most of Wren's cross-in-square churches, and was elected a Fellow of the Society the following year. Wheler would surely have pursued his timely (or 'seasonable' as he put it) project to advance the pure forms of Eastern Christianity, which his 'ideal' church of 1689 embodied, as soon as possible on his return and especially after ordination in 1683. He certainly approved of Wren's churches: when writing around 1692 to Thomas Seymour, a goldsmith proposing a new church in Spitalfields, he observed that 'Sir Christopher Wren is ye most proper person to be consulted on this matter, both because he is the most intelligent and learned man in England in such matters and likewise because he hath been most concerned in contriving the most beautiful churches in London.'[173]

It is clear that the geometric qualities of the centralised arrangement would have appealed to Wren's sense of 'natural' beauty. Yet it seems difficult to believe that he was not also well aware of its Byzantine origins, as too that of the dome as a Christian form, given his evident interest in the forms of earliest Christian churches. And if so, both forms when used on his own churches would surely have been seen as recalling their origins in the East in the cradle of Christianity, as they did to some Anglicans, rather than to have no meaning at all – or worse still, in the case of the dome, to have associations with pagan and Roman Catholic architecture. After all, in much the same way, the links between the Temple of Solomon and the 'Tyrian' Order had given the apparently pagan Orders a firm biblical foundation in Wren's mind. It should not be forgotten that Wren was a Christian from a prominent Church family.[174] He certainly recognised the symbolic potential of architectural forms, giving the example of ancient temples; and in the tradition of Justinian's dome at Hagia Sophia, he thought that his proposed dome at old St Paul's, in particular, would signify the unity of the Church, the City and the Crown. Indeed, while Wren had argued that the Saracens disliked 'the *Christian* Form of a Cross', as the previous chapter noted, his son later added that they had built mosques 'of a round Form, because they would not imitate the christian Figure of a Cross; nor the old Greek Manner, which they thought to be idolatrous'.[175] By the 'old Greek Manner' he meant the Greek cross, here acknowledging its (idolatrous) potential as an Early Christian symbol. Wren's awareness of Byzantine churches could also help explain his enthusiasm for the use of a centralised plan in the form of a Greek cross, together with a dome, in his Cathedral scheme of 1670–2 and as adapted in the Great Model of 1673 (fig. 141; see fig. 52).[176] According to Wren's son, 'the Surveyor in private Conversation, always seem'd to set a higher Value on this Design, than any he made before or since'.[177] The sources commonly suggested for this design are French examples of Greek cross churches, but with no mention of Eastern originals.[178] In the end, custom triumphed over idealism at St Paul's, while many of the London churches were elongated to fit old foundations and site prerequisites. But, as with other aspects of architectural history, Wren's interest in the churches of the early Christians went on

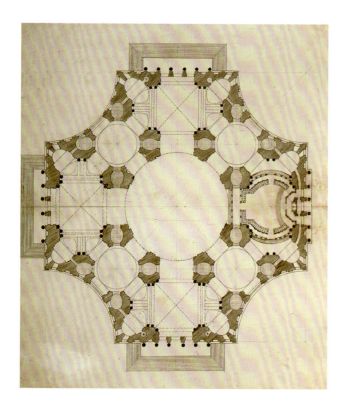

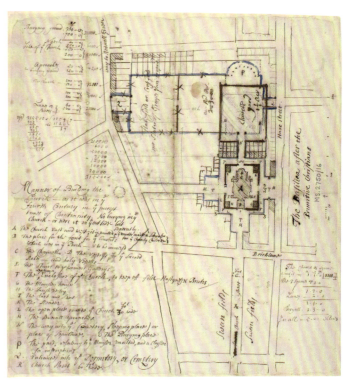

141 Plan of Wren's Greek cross design for St Paul's Cathedral (c.1670–2), drawn by Edward Woodroofe. All Souls College, Oxford

142 Hawksmoor's plan for an ideal 'Basilica after the Primitive Christians' (1711–12). Lambeth Palace Library, London, MS 2750/16

to stimulate Hawksmoor and, in this case, his plan for an ideal 'Basilica after the Primitive Christians' drawn in 1711–12 to inform his own church plans (fig. 142).[179]

'BUILT AFTER THE TURKISH MODEL': TURKISH DOMES AT THE ROYAL BAGNIO IN LONDON

By the end of the 1680s there was a further group of buildings in London that would have helped Wren and his contemporaries associate the dome with the East. This group comprised the Ottoman-inspired public baths (or 'bagnios', described in Turkish as a *hamam*), the first of which, with its distinct Turkish character, was called the Royal Bagnio and opened in 1679 in Newgate Street (subsequently 'Bath Street', the baths demolished in 1876).[180] In the absence of a record of its architect, the building has sometimes even been attributed to Wren, possibly on the basis of its implied connections with Charles II.[181] Edward Hatton's *A New View of London* of 1708 (Lot 484) recorded that it was 'the only true Bagnio built after the *Turkish* Model', an identification made through its dome, marble slabs and a lion's-head water spout.[182] According to Aubrey, these particular baths had been built by 'Turkish merchants', probably meaning merchants of the Levant or 'Turkey' Company.[183] To such merchants and travellers, Ottoman bathing under domes was a fairly familiar experience. Evelyn recorded a visit to a Turkish bath when in Venice in June 1645: 'The next morning finding my-selfe extreamly weary, & beaten with my Journey, I went to one of their *Bagnias*, which are made, & treate after the Eastern manner.'[184] Wheler reported in his *Journey* of 1682 that the baths of Constantinople 'have a Room without, with a Sopha round it, to undress themselves; and a large square Room beyond that, covered with a Cuppalo, through which the Light is let by Bell-glasses; and about it are many little Appartments, covered with small Cuppalo's, much resembling that built in *London*'.[185]

It will be remembered that in December 1688 Wren and Hooke discussed Turkish baths with the North brothers in a coffee house, and knowledge of the Eastern origins of domed baths such as the Royal Bagnio was common enough in London. For example, Samuel Haworth, in his *Description of the Duke's Bagnio, and of the*

114 CHRISTOPHER WREN

Mineral Bath, and New Spaw thereunto belonging (1683), left his readers in no doubt on the subject:

> the present Practice of the *Turks* obviously presents it self to our Consideration; the Wisdom of whose Governours hath thought fit to provide such Accommodations in all the principal Places of that vast Empire, and endow them with large Revenues… It's rare to see any there afflicted either with *Gout, Dropsie*, or *Rheumatisms*; the Reason of which can be ascribed to nothing so much as this wholesom Custom of using *Bagnios*.[186]

An anonymous pamphlet entitled *A True Account of the Royal Bagnio, with a Discourse of its Virtues* (1680) asserted: 'To those who have been in the *Ottoman* Empire, this paper is insignificant, they knowing already the mighty perfections and wonderful Operations which these *Bagnios* have effected, and still continue so to do.'[187] The author went on to point out that the Turks' 'Noble Edifices are like unto Great Palaces' and noted that any 'description of that erected lately at *London*, especially of the outward building' was superfluous, 'every man having the liberty to be themselves ocular witnesses of it, for 'tis as near the *Turkish* Fashion as may be'.[188] Clearly, the Royal Bagnio was assumed to be fully recognisable as Ottoman in character to Wren's contemporaries. Even Turkish rituals were to be replicated, since 'near unto the Bagnio there is a Coffee House, for the conveniency of those that go to the Bagnio, for according to the Opinion of many there is no Liquor more convenient after one has been in than Coffee, and so 'tis esteemed by the *Turks*, who constantly use it'.[189]

The practice of Turkish bathing became well-established in London in the second half of the seventeenth century. Besides the Royal Bagnio, Hatton mentioned the Queen's Bagnio, situated in Long Acre and kept by a surgeon called Mr Ayme; the Castle Yard Bagnio called Trimnel's; Pierault's Bagnio, situated in St James's Street and opened in 1699; and Hummums in Covent Garden.[190] Also on Long Acre was the King's Bagnio, which an advertisement of 1686 showed with its dome supported by a colonnade, and the Duke of York's Bagnio of 1683 that had a similar dome (fig. 143).[191] Haworth described in some detail the way in which the visitor moved through Duke's:

> the first Room we enter to go into the *Bagnio*, is a large Hal, where the Porter stands to receive the Money. Hence we pass thorow an Entry into another Room, where hangs a Pair of Scales, to weigh such as

143 An advertisement of March 1686 for the King's Bagnio, London, by William Jennens. Yale Center for British Art, New Haven, Connecticut

> our of Curiosity would know how much they lose in Weigh while they are in the *Bagnio*. Thorow this Room we pass into a large Room, called the *Dressing-room*: This Room hath on each side several private Boxes, for Persons to undress and dress themselves in: The middle Walk, between the Rows of Boxes, is paved with Black and White Marble.[192]

The most important space was clearly the bath itself, which as at other 'bagnios' was covered by a dome supported on columns:

> At the farther end of this Room is an Entry, which is somewhat warmer; in this Entry the Rubbers [masseurs] stand and wait, when they are not employ'd. On the farther side of this Entry is a Door or Passage into the *Bagnio* it self, which is a stately Edifice, of

GREEK CROSSES AND DOMES

144 An admission token of c.1680 for the Duke of York's Bagnio, Long Acre, London. British Museum, London

an Oval Figure, in length 45 Foot, and in breadth 35. 'Tis covered at the top with a high and large *Cupola*, in which there are several round Glasses fixt, to let in Light, which are much larger, and so fewer in number, than those at the *Royal Bagnio*. This *Cupola* is supported by eight Cylindrical Columns of white Stone Pillars, each of which are 20 Inches Diameter, and 16 Foot high. Between these Pillars and the Sides of the *Bagnio* is a sumptuous Walk, about 7 Foot and a half broad, quite round the *Bagnio*.[193]

An illustration of this dome has also survived, this time on an admission token of about 1680 (fig. 144).[194] The Ottoman feel of Duke's was once again enhanced by 'a Coffee-house fronting the Street'.[195] Well aware of their originals as Wren was, these buildings were the closest thing to Ottoman architecture that he would have actually seen. But at least the experience of the coffee houses and domes of Constantinople might be had closer to home.

'YOU ARE A SECOND CONSTANTINE': LONDON AS THE NEW CONSTANTINOPLE

The influence of the churches in the East on those being built by Wren in London, and of Hagia Sophia on St Paul's, would have helped confirm the enduring idea of the city as a 'New Constantinople' projected by the first Stuarts.[196] The theological argument for London's identification with Constantinople claimed that just as Constantine had refounded the capital of his newly established Christian empire in the East, so the Stuarts were refounding London as an imperial capital of the Protestant Church and of wider Christendom, in the West. Thus Laud likened foundation ceremonies such as that for Jones's work at old St Paul's to the re-consecration of pagan temples under Constantine: indeed, such a ceremony was used to found Wren's new Cathedral.[197] This identification was helped by the fact that according to James Howell in his *Londonopolis…The Imperial Chamber, and Chief Emporium of Great Britain* (1657), much of London lay over an ancient walled enclosure built by '*Constantine* the Great, at the instance of his Mother *Helena*', which 'took up in compasse, above three miles, so that it inclosed the Model of the City almost four-square'.[198] Wren may well have considered that the Cathedral too stood on the site of an ancient church consecrated under Constantine's rule. As his son reported in *Parentalia*, 'the Time of the Persecution was short, for under Constantine, the Church flourish'd again; the Churches in Rome, and other Parts of the Empire were soon rebuilt, and most likely ours among the first…as the Surveyor conceiv'd, upon the old Foundations left by the Persecutors'.[199] Such a Constantinian antiquity could only have served to further justify in Wren's mind his reference to early Christian and Byzantine models (in particular to the structure of Hagia Sophia) in the various designs for a new Cathedral on the site.

This Stuart conception of London as a New Constantinople – in theological, if not quite yet in architectural, terms – also found support through legendary British links with Constantine himself. Conveniently, Geoffrey of Monmouth had reported the birth of Constantine in Britain, the son of Helena who he claimed was a daughter of the King of Britain, Cole of Colchester.[200] Constantine had supposedly then spread his Christian empire from Britain, firstly to Rome and then to the East. This legend enjoyed much currency under the Stuarts, in their quest to find a pure or uncorrupted (that is, non-Catholic) ancestry for the English Church, a quest that was the theological forerunner of Wheler's identification of Anglicanism with the surviving forms of the early Church in the East. It helped justify the frequent presentation in court propaganda of James I as the 'new Constantine', a conceit that was made manifest through a number of references in civic and royal structures built during the reigns of Charles I and II to the Arch of Constantine in Rome.[201] In the same vein Henry Stubbe presented Charles II as Constantine 'reborn' in the course of his quest for Protestantism's theological origins in the East.[202] Geoffrey's legend was itself still cultivated in Wren's time. Evelyn, for example, referred to Helena as 'our Country-Woman' and King Cole as 'father of *Helena* mother of *Constantine* the *Greate*'.[203] Edward Stillingfleet's *Origines Britannicae: or the Antiquities of the British Churches* (1685, of which Wren had two copies, Lots 100 and 276) repeated the legend with reference to

the early Church in Britain as mentioned in Eusebius's *De vita Constantini*.²⁰⁴ The Constantinian Church embodied a balanced relationship between the State and its divinely appointed ruler that appealed to widely differing factions of the Church of England after the Restoration, and offered a model of kingship to which they encouraged Charles II to aspire.²⁰⁵ Hence Carew Reynell reminded the king: 'you are a second Constantine to stay / Our Holy Church from falling to decay!'²⁰⁶ This cultivation of a direct link between the British monarchy and the Christian Church under Constantine provided a further context for interest in its architecture among Wren and his contemporaries.

ABOVE 145 Panorama of Constantinople in 1635, engraved by Mattheus Merian, published in Frankfurt

BELOW 146 Panorama of London in c.1705, engraved by Johann Baptist Homann, published in Nuremberg

Even before the Great Fire and Wren's work in the City, Evelyn had compared the panoramas of London and Constantinople: for he wrote in June 1653 that he had considered 'the Prospect' of London, 'which (after *Constantinople*) is doubtlesse for Citty, river, Ships, Meadows, hill, Woods, & all other distinguishable amenities, the most noble the whole World has to shew'.²⁰⁷ Evelyn must have based his observation on recent views of Constantinople such as that by Merian of 1635 (fig. 145). The foreground shows a city located in meadows and woods, the centre ships and trade, while the skyline is dominated by the fabric of religion in the form of domes and minarets: as such Constantinople set the pattern for other cities in Christendom, as Evelyn suggested. As Johann Baptist Homann's panorama of London of about 1705 illustrates (fig. 146), Wren and Hooke had gone on after the Fire to make Evelyn's comparison closer still through their church towers and cupolas and, most magnificently of all, their domed Cathedral.

GREEK CROSSES AND DOMES 117

CHAPTER FOUR

MONUMENTAL COLUMNS AND COLONNADES

'Long Porticoes were the general Method of building Cities in the hot Climates'

Wren began his 'Discourse' on the origins of classical architecture – what he called his 'larger Idea of the whole Art' – not with an individual building or primitive hut, as Vitruvius had done, but with the first city that had been located in the East. He observed, once again following Josephus, that 'the Project of Building is as natural to Mankind as to Birds, and was practis'd before the Floud. By Josephus we learn that Cain built the first City *Enos*, and enclos'd it with Walls and Rampires.'[1] Enos (or Enoch) was thought to have been situated at the foot of the mountain of Libanus in Syria or, rather, in what was then Phoenicia not far from the site of Jerusalem.[2] For Wren it was the Eastern city, thus enclosed by its walls, which was the principal expression of architectural magnificence and source of national well-being in the ancient world. Having commented in Tract one that 'the Emulation of the Cities of *Greece* was the true Cause of their Greatness',[3] he continued in the 'Discourse' with reference to Herodotus by enthusiastically pointing out that 'the Walls of Babylon were most stupendious Works built with Brick and cemented with Bitumen: the Height of them, according to Herodotus, was Two hundred Royal Cubits, and the Breadth Fifty'. The city was illustrated in his 1592 edition of Herodotus (Lot 122; fig. 148). He noted that in these walls were 'one hundred Gates of Brass, with Ornaments in Architecture of the same Metal' and that 'the Extent of the City must add to the Surprise, which being a Square contain'd a Front on every Side of One hundred and Twenty Stadia, that is, Fifteen of our Miles, and makes up in the whole Threescore miles'.[4] Much like Oldenburg in 1671, Wren's admiration and 'surprise' at the 'stupendious works' of the ancient city is clear. But as far as actual remains of them were concerned, he had little to go on. Chapter Two noted that he observed in his second Tract that 'among the *Greeks* little was then remaining'.[5] In his day the ruins of ancient cities in Greece such as Sparta and Thebes were still largely unexplored, and hardly any physical evidence of Roman town planning had been unearthed. The cities of Herculaneum and Pompeii were yet to be excavated (the former in 1738 and the latter in 1748), while the large suburban villa of Hadrian at Tivoli was known about but not fully explored and mapped until the second half of the eighteenth century (notably by Giovanni Battista Piranesi). Evelyn described the villa as 'now onely an heape of ruines' when he saw it from a distance in May 1645.[6] With its mass of often half-buried antique ruins and medieval additions, Rome too offered few guidelines. In trying to understand the principles of

147 The colonnade at Greenwich Hospital by Wren (1696–8)

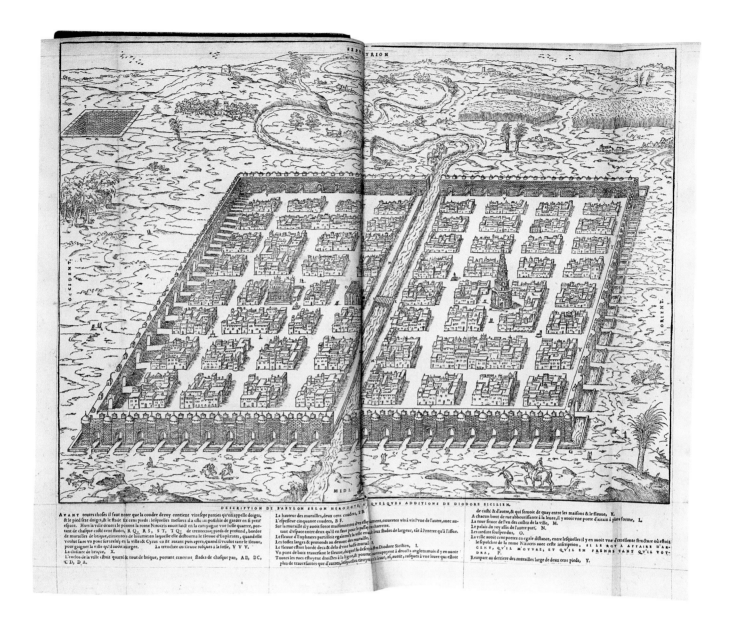

ancient city planning in order to inform his own urban and palace layouts, in the City of London and later at Chelsea and Greenwich, Wren had to rely at first on textual descriptions. Vitruvius and Polybius described 'ideal' plans for cities, for example, and Strabo the lost Eastern cities of Alexandria, Tarsus and Anchiale. Then from the early 1680s, reports and illustrations by travellers such as Chardin started to appear of the ruined ancient cities in Syria and Persia, which Wren used in the Tracts to confirm these ancient sources on the planning of lost cities.

148   Reconstruction of the city of Babylon, from *Herodoti Halicarnassei Historiarum lib. IX… Ejusdem narratio de vita Homeri… Ctesiae quaedam de rebus Persarum et Indiarum* (1592), between prefatory material and Book 1, p. 1

Wren's admiration for the ancient cities of the East arose from their magnificent scale, regular form and enclosing walls. The first part of this chapter will examine his own plan for a city, made for the City of London after the Fire in 1666, and its reliance on two ancient plans for walled cities that were used in order to imbue it with the same magnificent quality. Wren's understanding as to the development of the ancient cities of Greece and further east is seen as justifying his use in this plan of another novel form in England, the colonnade (fig. 147). With its riverside colonnade and wide streets, his plan is also interpreted in the contemporary context of the promotion of health and trade by the Royal Society. The chapter will conclude by examining a further design by Wren and Hooke in the City prompted by the Fire, the Monument. This celebrated the city's recovery by taking the form of a triumphal column modelled not just on those found in Rome, which had the most obvious pagan examples, but also on the Christian ones in Constantinople. The chapter will show how the Monument's decoration conveyed the message of London revived as the New Jerusalem based on ideas concerning emblems and hieroglyphs traced back to the East.

'COMMODIOUS FOR HEALTH': IDEAL ANCIENT CITIES AND THE PLAN FOR LONDON

Much of the architectural work undertaken by Wren and Hooke arose because of a single disaster, the Fire of London in 1666. This was the stimulus for the City churches, the Cathedral and the Monument to the recovery from the Fire itself. Fire had broken out on Sunday 2 September, in the shop of the baker Thomas Farynor at 25 Pudding Lane. It was not extinguished until five days later, by which time five-sixths of the City's square mile had been reduced to rubble.[7] The smouldering ashes were still igniting six months later. Most notably, old St Paul's was largely ruined. Evelyn observed at first hand the destruction of 'the Churches, Publique Halls, Exchange, Hospitals, Monuments, & ornaments' and how the fire went 'leaping after a prodigious manner from house to house & streete to streete'.[8] Explanations ranged from the practical – a faulty oven – to the apocalyptic. The coincidence of 1666 with the number 666, identified as the sign of the Beast in Revelation (13:18), seemed particularly ominous to some Protestants as the possible harbinger of a Messianic age.[9] William Bedloe in *A Narrative and Impartial Discovery of the Horrid Popish Plot: Carried on for the Burning and Destroying of the Cities of London and Westminster* (1679) 'impartially' accused the Papists of copying the Gunpowder plot. A new plan for London was thus urgently needed, not only from a practical point of view but also to provide a sense of stability and of national well-being (even 'greatness', to quote Wren on the Greek city) in this climate of religious anxiety. Hence in the following years, images in Wren's mind of Solomon's Temple and of other ancient Tyrian 'Wonders' of the East, as well as of a rebuilt London conceived in succession to Jerusalem and Constantinople, would have answered this need for stability and sense of permanence.

In the decades before the Fire, the Stuart monarchy had tried to bring a degree of order to the medieval fabric of London. As previous chapters have noted, Court mythology had idealised the city in Christian terms as a New Jerusalem and Constantinople, and Jones's buildings had attempted to reflect this ambition through imposing a classical order onto the urban fabric.[10] Nevertheless his work involved single buildings and two squares, at Covent Garden and Lincoln's Inn, not a coherent new plan. The opportunity to produce a plan for a city, that is one to be built entirely from scratch, was uncommon in Europe and unprecedented in Britain since Roman times. Palmanova, established in north-eastern Italy by Venice from 1593, was a rare example. But Wren had that very chance in the immediate aftermath of the Fire. His plan for the City survives in two drawings whose details differ slightly (fig. 149).[11] With the flames barely extinguished, it was presented to the king by 11 September 1666.[12] In attempting to give the new City order and magnificence, which were qualities he admired in the ancient cities of the East, Wren drew on a number of precedents, both ancient and modern. Streets were to be laid out in a rectangular grid and in a radial pattern centred on nodes, resembling a spider's web. The latter is often interpreted in the context of the nearly contemporary examples of Baroque planning in Rome and Paris, notably the long streets radiating from the Piazza del Popolo in Rome laid out under Sixtus V around 1588 and the scheme for the Place de France in Paris promoted by Henri IV.[13] Following the model of Sixtus V's plan, the nodes in Wren's scheme were located on existing sites of public buildings, namely the Cathedral, Royal Exchange, Custom House and Tower (which had survived the fire).[14]

However, less well recognised is Wren's reliance on descriptions of ancient urban planning. In the area of the plan to the west of the (now subterranean) river Fleet, eight streets radiated from a piazza and formed an octagon that was more or less aligned with the cardinal points. The same pattern reappears, in a more fragmentary form, on the east of the City. This pattern reflected Vitruvius's description of an octagonal gated city (I.vi.7) that had been illustrated by Cesariano in his Italian edition of the Roman's work of 1521 (fig. 150).[15] His account was of an ideal city, not of any actual one built by the Greeks or Romans. The city was laid out radially in accordance with the eight winds, taking its form from the octagonal Tower of the Winds in Athens (I.vi.4; see fig. 47). Vitruvius made clear that his layout regulated the weather to facilitate public health, noting that by 'this division, troublesome winds will be excluded from the dwellings and the streets'.[16] This was also a major concern of Wren's; he had pointed out in his 1657 lecture at Gresham that London 'doth yet enjoy so healthy an Air', while his plan was described in *Parentalia* as 'commodious for Health'.[17]

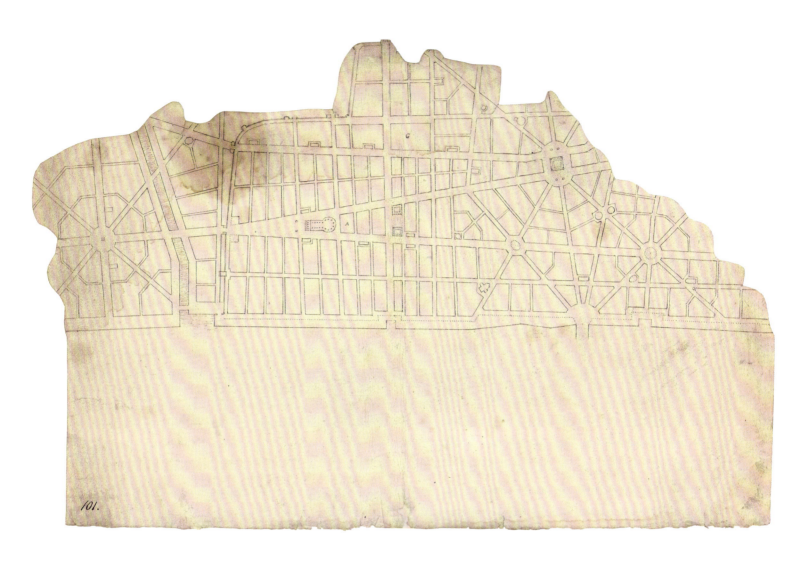

The promotion of public health became a particular interest of Royal Society Fellows, notably Robert Boyle, following the Plague.[18]

This was not, however, the only ancient precedent that Wren drew on when reforming the City's medieval street pattern of unhealthy lanes and alleyways. Vitruvius went on to mention, briefly, the nomadic Roman Praetorian camp, or military city (I.v.2).[19] This was square, was enclosed by a wall with gates and was laid out in a grid pattern: as such it had some of the same qualities that Wren admired in the ancient city of Babylon (see fig. 148). The Greek historian Polybius described this camp in greater detail when chronicling the Roman conquest of the Greeks between 200 and 167 BC.[20] His description of the camp had been closely studied by Renaissance architects, most notably Serlio, who produced drawings of its layout, and Palladio, who published views in his *Commentari di Giulio Cesare* (1575; fig. 151).[21] Editions of Polybius such as Edward Grimeston's *The history of Polybius the Megalopolitan* (1633) also illustrated the camp and his version was used by Aubrey in the second part of his 'Monumenta Britannica' (1663–93) on the camp. Polybius's description offered an important clue as to the layout of actual Roman towns, having formed the basis of permanent urban settlements beyond Italy, including the palace of Diocletian in Split and as far afield as the cities of Dura-Europos in Syria and Masada in Israel.[22] It influenced early modern ideal cities such as Simon Stevin's plan published posthumously in *Materiae Politicae* (1650). Wren's interest in the Roman camp is attested by his ownership of Flavius Renatus Vegetius's *De Re Militari* (1670 edition, Lot 307), with its description of the camp in book one. The camp directly informed an untitled plan for a barracks, probably for Hyde Park, drawn by Wren in the 1670s (fig. 152).[23] And in his City plan, the ordinary houses north and south of the Cathedral were organised in a rectangular grid, in a similar fashion to the barracks in the camp.[24] The camp was not the only source for such grid planning, which had been especially popular in the Low Countries, although examples there also took

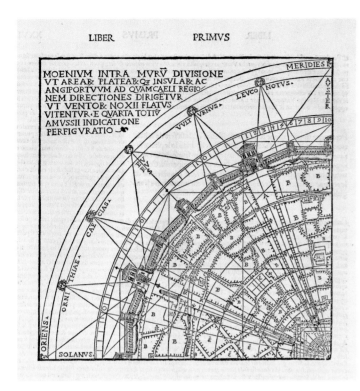

OPPOSITE 149 Plan for London, first version drawn by Wren, 1666. All Souls College, Oxford

LEFT 150 Two of the eight gates in one quadrant of an octagonal city, illustrated by Cesare Cesariano, from Vitruvius, *Di Lucio Vitruvio Pollione De architectura libri dece traducti de latino in vulgare* (1521), fol. XXVIv

BELOW 151 Roman camp in the march against the Bellovaci, from Andrea Palladio, *Commentari di Giulio Cesare* (1575), pl. 28

their cue from the ancient camp.[25] Direct reference to the Roman camp and its grid plan in this particular part of the City may have been justified in Wren's mind by his understanding of ancient London, if a second-hand report can be believed. An essay by Wren's son entitled 'Of *London* in ancient Times, and the Boundary of the *Roman* Colony, discern'd by the *Surveyor*, after the *great Fire*', noted that 'on the West-side was situated the *Praetorian Camp*, which was also wall'd in to *Ludgate*'.[26]

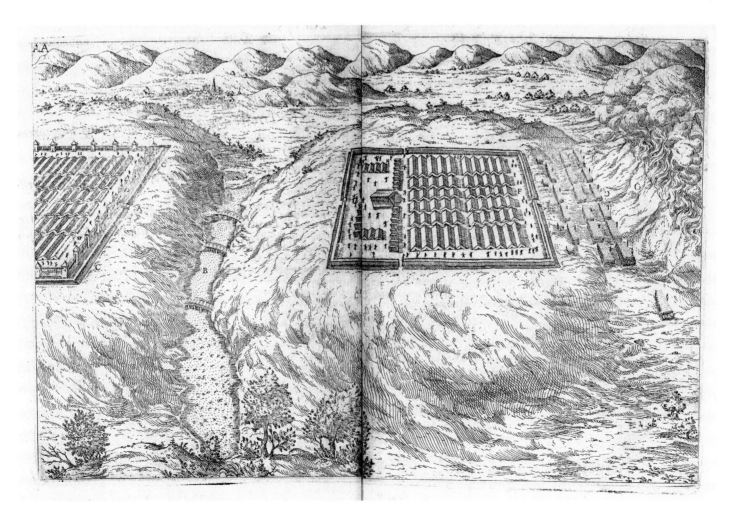

MONUMENTAL COLUMNS AND COLONNADES

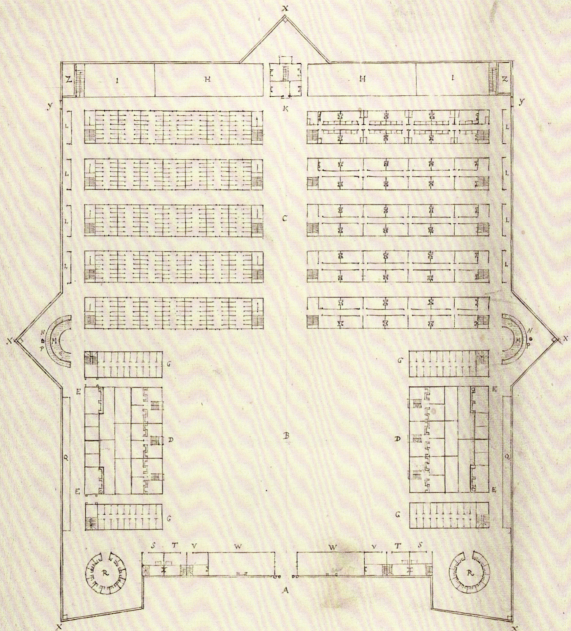

A. The Port.
B. The Parade 275 f. long, 240 broad.
C. The Street 50 f. broad, between 10 Rowes of Stables, each Rowe containing 100 Horse, & 100 Beds above, by 4 Beds to a Chamber in the 2d floor, & 3 in ye Garrets, each Roome being 25 f long & 14 broad.
D. 6 litle houses for Officers Lodging
E. 4 Sutlers Houses
G. 4 Eating roomes, each for 200 men.
H. 2 Hay-Barnes, proportioned for one Month's Hay for 1000 Horse
I. 2 Granaries.
K. The Commissaries Office & House.
L. Dunghills enclosed with lowe Walls.
M. 2 Washing pooles.
N. 2 Cisternes soe contrived that 20 Horse may drinke at once.
P. The pumpes or Cocks.
Q. Sheds for Fewell.
R. Two Necessary-Places being litle Cabbins built about a round Court.
S. 2 Farriers Shops & Lodgings.
T. 2 Armorers.
V. 2 Sadlers.
W. The Courts of Guard.
X. The Brickwall enclosing the Ground with Sentry-Boxes at the angles.
Y. 2 Posternes. Z. 2 litle Magazins.

'THUS WERE CITIES SUDDENLY RAISED, AND THUS WAS TADMOR BUILT': EASTERN COLONNADES IN LONDON

An equally important aim of the Royal Society was the promotion of trade. A few years before the Great Fire, Wren had presented London as one of the world's leading capitals through its commerce and mathematical arts. In his inaugural lecture at Gresham College in 1657, he presented the city as standing in succession not to Rome but, further east, to Tyre, Rhodes and Alexandria:

> And now since Navigation brings with it both Wealth, Splendor, Politeness and Learning, what greater Happiness can I wish to the *Londoners*? Than that they may continually deserve to be deem'd as formerly, the great Navigators of the World; that they always may be, what the *Tyrians* first, and then the *Rhodians* were call'd, '*The Masters of the Sea*;' and that *London* may be an *Alexandria*, the establish'd Residence of Mathematical Arts.[27]

This desire for Londoners to emulate the Tyrians as 'Masters of the Sea' eventually found expression at Wren's Greenwich Hospital, built for seamen of the Royal Navy, through the decorative combination of lion and unicorn with the trade winds and Neptune's trident on the west façade of the Painted Hall (fig. 153). Contemporary trade with the Levant region via the Turkey Company gave potency to this idea of London as a modern Tyre and Rhodes, much as Gresham's encouragement of geometry and mathematics would have helped confirm the city to Wren as a modern Alexandria. For just as Alexandria had been the home of the geometrical studies of Euclid and the astronomical ones of Ptolemy, so the college at Gresham was hosting such luminaries as Isaac Barrow and Robert Boyle. The Introduction noted that Thomas Sprat sought to link the modern projects of the Royal Society with the ancient ones of the Syrians, Egyptians and Chaldeans.[28] And one of the Society's central concerns in promoting astronomy and optics was the improvement of navigation in order to assist trade, not least with the growing markets in the East.[29]

OPPOSITE 152 Plan of a barracks drawn by Wren, probably for Hyde Park, c.1670s. All Souls College, Oxford

RIGHT 153 The lion and unicorn with the trade winds and Neptune's trident on the west façade of the Painted Hall, Greenwich Hospital

Wren's mercantile vision for London, as a kind of latter-day Tyre, went on to inform his plan for the City after the Fire. His Custom House, shown in the revised version of the plan on the riverside site of its destroyed predecessor and constructed three years after the fire (in 1669), had two wings elevated on columns creating an open area for the purpose of facilitating trade. Later itself destroyed, the building was briefly described in *Parentalia*: it was 'adorned with an upper and lower Order of Architecture: In the latter are Stone Columns, and Entablement of the Tuscan Order; in the former are Pilasters, Entablature, and five Pediments of the Ionick Order. The West-end is elevated on Columns, forming a Piazza.'[30] Together with Wren's church steeples and Cathedral dome, the Custom House was shown as a backdrop to the bustling trade route of the Thames in Homann's panorama of London of about 1705 (see fig. 146, no. 60). Wren's scheme for the other great centre of trade, the Royal Exchange (eventually built to Edward Jerman's design in 1669), also utilised porticoes.[31] This building was shown in both versions of the City plan as a square block positioned on the site of its predecessor, like the Custom House, and at the centre of radial streets to emphasise its importance. Although the destroyed Exchange (which had been opened in 1571) had had an arcade round a courtyard for doing business, Wren's design was more directly modelled on ancient forums, in the form of a courtyard enclosed by double porticoes. In both versions of the city plan, these porticoes were indicated by a double row of dots. The description in *Parentalia* by Wren's son made all this clear: 'The Exchange to stand free in the Middle of a Piazza' and 'be

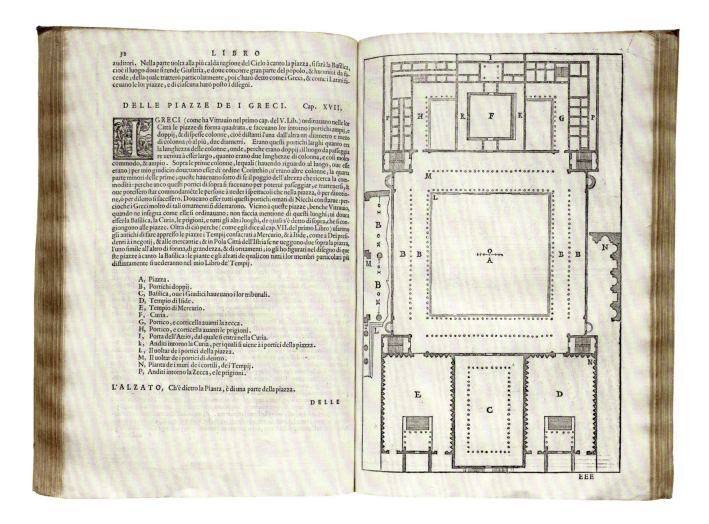

contriv'd after the Form of the Roman Forum, with double Porticos'.³² In fact, as a square, Wren's Exchange more closely resembled the Greek forum after Vitruvius (V.i.1–3), the Roman being rectangular. He would have seen a plan of both Greek and Roman forums in his copy of Palladio's *I quattro libri dell'architettura* (1570; Lot 529; fig. 154). Palladio had followed Vitruvius, who recorded that 'the Greeks plan the forum on the square with most ample double colonnades and close-set columns; they ornament them with stone or marble architraves, and above they make promenades on the boarded floors'.³³ Palladio illustrated what he called the 'wide, double porticoes' provided 'for people to walk in, do business and comfortably watch the events organized in the square'.³⁴ And he included four staircases in the corners of the forum, which would explain the small square boxes shown in each corner of Wren's Exchange plan (see fig. 149).

In order to encourage trade, Wren's plan envisaged a free-standing double portico, or colonnade, by the Thames. The earlier of the two versions has a line of dots on the riverbank, which almost certainly indicated a continuous colonnade; on the subsequent plan, in one of the few changes, this has become a series of rectangular blocks that probably indicate covered porticoes (after the Greek stoa).³⁵ According to Wren's son in *Parentalia*, the plan would have improved the City, 'by making a commodious Key on the whole Bank of the River, from Blackfriars to the Tower' that was 'spacious & convenient, without any Interruptions'.³⁶ Whereas the land running down to the river before the Fire had been private, Wren's colonnaded quay opened up a major public promenade.³⁷ The riverfront was even shown straightened on his plan, better to accommodate the quay. Just the previous year to this plan Wren had confessed to Dr Edward Browne, his travelling companion in Paris, that, as Browne recorded,

ABOVE 154 'Greek Forum', from Andrea Palladio, *I quattro libri dell'architettura* (1570), Book III, ch. XVII, pp. 32–3

OPPOSITE 155 The colonnade at Chelsea Hospital by Wren (1682–5)

'the greatest work about Paris' was 'the Quay, or Key upon the river side' being built 'with so vast expence and such great quantity of materialls, that it exceeded all manner of ways the buildings of the two greatest Pyramids in Ægypt'.[38] These wonders of the East were never far from Wren's thoughts, it seems. The colonnade on his London quay formed an ordered front to the buildings behind, indicated as blocks on the plan but identified in *Parentalia* as warehouses and buildings of the City Companies.[39] Open yet covered, this colonnade too was a way to help satisfy the Royal Society's ambition for the new city to be healthy and profitable.

Thirty years after his London plan, Wren returned to the idea of a riverside colonnade: a list in *Parentalia* of unexecuted designs for a new Whitehall Palace, following the fire in 1697, included a 'General Plan of the Palace, a Gallery of Communication with the Parliament-house, consisting of a long Portico of Dorick Columns on the Bank of the Thames, extending from Whitehall to Westminster'.[40] He also used colonnades at Chelsea Hospital as an attached element (1682–5), and at Greenwich Hospital as a partly attached, partly free-standing form that fronts a series of open courtyards and buildings (as envisaged from the first plan of 1694; figs

155 and 156; see fig. 147). These particular colonnades were not intended to promote commerce but, rather, health. There were many examples, both at home and abroad, of the elevation of buildings on columns to form courtyard arcades and walkways. The arrangement was a college type, much used at Oxford and Cambridge, and was found, as noted, at the Elizabethan Exchange in London. Wren would certainly have been familiar with the arcades in Jones's piazza at Covent Garden and possibly with those at Vigevano and Venice, as well as in the medieval streets of Bologna. But these are all composed of arches and are arcades rather than free-standing colonnades or porticoes. Instead, when tracing in the Tracts the origins of the type of classical colonnade used at Chelsea and Greenwich, Wren looked to more ancient urban practices in Greece and further east.

In the first of his Tracts Wren reflected on the Greek 'Stoa', or free-standing portico: 'when Men first cohabited in civil Commerce, there was Necessity of Forums and publick Places of Meeting' and so, 'in hot Countries, where Civility first began, they desired to exclude the Sun only, and admit all possible Air for Coolness and Health: this brought in naturally the Use of Porticoes, or Roofs for Shade, set upon Pillars'.[41] Bearing in mind this

OPPOSITE ABOVE 156 *The colonnade at Greenwich Hospital by Wren (1696–8)*

OPPOSITE BELOW 157 *The colonnade at Trinity College, Cambridge, by Wren (1676–7)*

RIGHT 158 Proposed colonnade round St Paul's Cathedral (c.1696–7), drawing in Hawksmoor's hand. St Paul's Cathedral, London

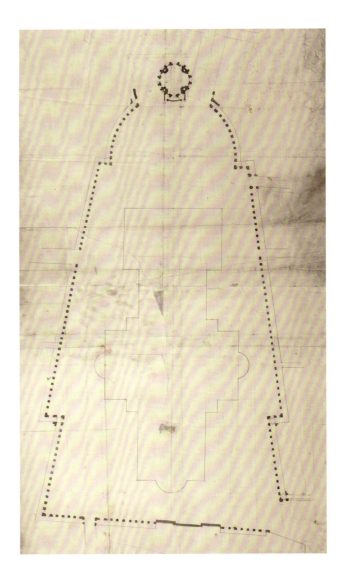

function of ancient porticoes, appropriately enough at Greenwich Hospital, *Parentalia* recorded, 'these Porticos are intended for Communication from the Hall & Chapel to the Wards and Dormitories; and to protect the Men from the Inclemency of Weather, and give them Air, at anytime, without incommoding them'.[42] Wren continued in his second Tract: 'people could not assemble and converse, but under shade in hot Countries; therefore, the *Forum* of every City was also at first planted round with Walkes of Trees' and added that 'these Avenues were afterwards, as Cities grew more wealthy, reformed into Porticoes of Marble'.[43] When writing to Barrow around 1675, Wren explained that his proposed Doric 'double portico' elevating the library at Trinity College was 'according to the manner of the ancients who made double walks (with three rowes of pillars, or two rowes and a wall), about the forum' (fig. 157).[44] A double portico was particularly appropriate for a place of learning: the first setting for the teaching of Stoicism was the Stoa Poikile in Athens (after which the philosophy was named), a fact Wren might be expected to have known as one of its followers.[45] His understanding as to the civic function of ancient porticoes here again reflected ideas current in the Royal Society. Sprat had observed in 1667 in his *History of the Royal Society* that 'The *Greeks*, being of a vigorous, and active humour, establish't their Philosophy, in the *Walks*, and *Porches*, and *Gardens*, and such publick places about their Cities: whereas the Graver, and more reserv'd *Aegyptians*, had confin'd it to their *Temples*.'[46] Wren, who owned a copy of Sprat's work (Lot 365), considered that the Stoa's progression from timber to stone was mirrored in the development of temple precincts. At first these were surrounded by trees, or sacred groves, to provide shade but 'when the Temples were brought into Cities, the like Walks were represented with Stone Pillars, supporting the more durable Shade of a Roof'; he concluded: 'this, I am apt to think, was the true Original of Colonades environing the Temples in single or double Ailes'.[47] This might help explain the proposal of about 1696–7, in Hawksmoor's hand, to enclose the precinct at St Paul's with a single colonnade (fig. 158).[48]

Wren came to understand long colonnades as the founding, or ordering, form of the ancient city itself. In this he drew on examples of colonnades in the East, in the absence of more immediate ones in Rome.[49] This idea of urban form was developed in the third Tract, where Wren asserted that 'these long Porticoes were the general Method of building Cities in the hot Climates'. He continued with a Greek example from Egypt:

When *Alexander* had determined to build *Alexandria*, and had settled the Place, he left *Dinocrates* his Architect to compleat the same, who drew a long Street with Porticoes on both Sides, from the Lake *Maeotis* to the Sea, and another cross it, that lead to *Pelusium*; then built Walls and large Towers, each capable to quarter five hundred Men; the noble Ruins of which remain at this Day; (a) then giving great Privileges to *Egyptians* and *Jews*, they soon filled the Quarters between the Porticoes with private and publick Buildings. Thus were Cities suddenly raised.[50]

The two main streets of ancient Alexandria had been lined with colonnades that intersected in the centre of the city close to Alexander's mausoleum.[51] Wren's awareness of this seems to have been based in part on contemporary report ('the noble Ruins of which remain at this Day') and in part on antique sources. Prominent English visitors to Alexandria included Blount. His *Voyage into the Levant... by way of...Egypt, unto Gran Cairo*, first published in 1636, mentioned its 'Pillars in great number' and that it 'bears yet the Monuments of its ancient glory' (Hooke, as noted, owned the 1669 edition).[52] But the city was also home to English factors and consuls who engaged in trade on behalf of the Levant Company.[53] Wren's interest in the Nile and his observation in the 'Discourse' that 'the Turks neglected all the upper Canales, except one which still supply's Alexandria' further suggests his contact with such recent visitors or their books (fig. 159).[54] Concerning the city's ancient history, he could have drawn on a wide variety of sources: these included Vitruvius (II.preface.4), Diodorus Siculus (*Library of History*, 17.52.1–3), Josephus (*The Wars of the Jews*, 2.487–8) and Strabo (*Geography*, 17.1.8–10, Lot 131).[55] Incidentally, the '(a)' used here in Wren's text referred to a footnote, probably added for publication in *Parentalia*, that reads: 'Near this City stands a Pillar, erected by one of the *Ptolomys*, (but vulgarly called *Pompey's* Pillar) the Shaft of which consists of one solid Stone of Granate 90 Feet high, and 38 in Compass. [Le Bruyn's *Voyage*, p. 171].'[56] This is Cornelis de Bruyn's *Voyage to the Levant* (1698, of which, as noted, Wren owned the 1702 English edition, Lot 140). The pillar in question was in fact erected for Diocletian in 293 and is still standing.

Wren gave further examples of the use of colonnaded streets to generate urban form in Tract three. Here, in the spirit of providing rational explanations for the problems posed by the construction – and sometimes destruction – of legendary antique buildings, he asked:

> Now, how was *Tarsus* and *Anchiala* built in a Day? that is, I suppose, the Walls and Gates were set out in a Day; and this Way of setting out the principal Streets by Porticoes, occasioned that hundreds of Pillars, of all sorts, were to be bought at the Quarries ready made, where great Numbers of Artizans wrought for Sale of what they raised.[57]

Tarsus was a city in the Roman province of Ciliciea in modern-day Turkey, and Anchiale (or Anchialos) was an Assyrian city on the coast of the Black Sea now also in Turkey. Wren's source was once again Strabo, who reported that in Anchiale there was 'the following inscription in Assyrian letters: "Sardanapallus, the sun of Anacyndaraxes, built Anchiale and Tarsus in one day"'.[58] Here Wren's understanding of the urban role of colonnades was given credibility, since they provided a neat answer to the logical question of how these cities could have been erected so quickly. Moreover, the conception of the ancient colonnade as a screen to public buildings behind is identical to the way that colonnades were used in Wren's plan for London and at his two hospitals. His colonnades, especially those at Greenwich, are first and foremost space-defining rather than ornamental, in much the same way that he envisaged the ancient ones. They front and help define courtyards, while linking the various buildings of the hospital to form a coherent whole, just as he envisaged the ancient colonnades fronted the private and public buildings of the city.

Colonnaded streets were a prominent and distinctive feature of Roman cities in their Eastern empire. Ross Burns has shown that colonnaded axes define the visitor's experience of many of the great cities there:

159 Alexandria and its waterways, from Henry de Beauvau, *Relation journalière du voyage du Levant* (1615), p. 168

in the course of little more than a hundred years from the second century AD, the street was transformed in those provinces from a mundane passageway 'into a monumental landscape able in one sweeping vision to encompass the entire city'.[59] Such colonnaded streets are found, for example, at Tyre in Lebanon and at Apamea and Palmyra in Syria (figs 160 and 161).[60] Palmyra was an ancient Semitic city identified by Josephus with the biblical city of Tadmor built by Solomon, part of whose site had a square-grid layout similar to the Roman camp.[61] Its two colonnaded streets (the *via praetoria* and the *via principalis*) formed part of the Roman camp of Diocletian within the city. Ever keen to find physical evidence of Solomonic antiquity, the Royal Society took a special interest in Palmyra. Evelyn noted with some wonder in November 1695: 'At Gressam Colledge was brought the prospect of the Ruines of Palmira, far exceeding any of the Roman extant, the history will be in The Transactions.'[62] The site featured in three separate studies published in

160   Colonnade at Apamea in Syria, northern monumental street

the *Transactions* at the end of 1695.[63] William Halifax, the chaplain of the Levant Company (preceding Maundrell), had visited the ruined city in 1691 with measuring rod in hand and he reported in one of these studies:

> Proceeding forward, directly from the *Obelisk*, about 100 Paces, you come to a Magnificent *Entrance*... This *Entrance* leads you into a Noble Piazza of more than half a Mile long, 930 Yards according to our Measuring, and 40 Foot in breadth, enclosed with two rows of stately *Marble Pillars*, 26 Foot high, and 8 or 9 about. Of these remain standing and intire 129. but by a moderate Calculation, there could not have been less at first than 560. Covering there is none remaining, nor any Pavement at the bottom, unless it be buried under the Rubbish.[64]

On the basis of Halifax and his party's report of ancient inscriptions, Edmund Halley was happy to conclude that the ruins of Palmyra were indeed those of Tadmor and reported to the Royal Society that it 'Seems very well to be proved to be the same City which *Solomon* the Great King of *Israel* is said to have founded under that Name in the

161 Colonnade at Palmyra in Syria

Desart'.⁶⁵ In this regard at least, architectural discoveries in the East were serving to confirm biblical narratives rather than undermine them in Royal Society quarters.⁶⁶ Others had visited Palmyra before Halifax. Jacob Spon stopped at the site on his travels in the Levant in 1675–6, and in 1679 he published illustrations of its inscriptions in his *Miscellanea Eruditae Antiquitatis* (of which Wren owned a 1685 edition, Lot 246).⁶⁷ Robert Huntington made a brief visit in 1678, noting in his letter on Egypt to the Royal Society in 1684: 'those 4 tall square Pillars at *Tadmore* (in its middle age *Palmyra*) which are each of them but of, I think, one piece; while all the rest, exceeding many, of another stone, are of several pieces and round'.⁶⁸

Wren certainly knew of Palmyra, the reports of surviving colonnades at which agreed with his understanding of ancient city planning as gleaned from antique texts. Having determined in Tract three that after the space behind colonnades had been in-filled with private and public buildings, 'thus were Cities suddenly raised', he added: 'and thus was *Tadmor* built, the Ruins of which shew nothing at present to Travellers, but incredible Numbers of Pillars of the *Dorick* Order, some yet standing, more broken, which were certainly the Remains of long Porticoes to shade the Streets'.⁶⁹ Wren's use of the biblical name for the city indicates that he too identified the ruined pillars with Solomon's desert city. In fact, Palmyra's colonnades are an un-Solomonic Corinthian (see fig. 161). His description of them as Doric must predate the first panoramic view of the ruined city that Evelyn saw in 1695 (in which the columns were clearly shown as Corinthian; fig. 162). That was published following Halifax's report in the *Transactions* at the end of 1695 and republished a year later by Abednego Seller in *The Antiquities of Palmyra* (and subsequently copied by de Bruyn). These Royal Society explorers cannot have been the 'Travellers' who appear to have supplied Wren with his inaccurate report in the Tracts. Possible candidates were Huntington or Spon (or

more likely Spon via Wheler). Conveniently enough, the misidentification of the colonnades as Doric reflected Wren's understanding in Tract one of the first examples that had been built in cities to imitate avenues of trees: here he observed that 'a Walk of Trees is more beautiful than the most artificial Portico; but these not being easily preserved in Market-places', the ancients 'made the more durable Shades of Porticoes; in which we see they imitated Nature, most Trees in their Prime'; these trees 'observe near the Proportion of *Dorick* Pillars in the Length of their Bole, before they part into Branches'. He concluded on porticoes that 'the longer the more beautiful in *infinitum*'.[70] A stoa's outer columns were usually Doric, as also the colonnades adjoining the ancient theatre, as Vitruvius recorded (V.ix.1). The Doric had the additional virtue as far as Wren was concerned of representing a refined version of the original Tyrian Order, also fashioned in long timber porticoes, and thus the origin of the Orders and that of the ancient city went hand in hand.

Wren's conception of the wider urban role of the colonnaded streets at Alexandria, Tarsus, Anchiale and eventually at Palmyra thus clearly informed his own attempt to make public spaces through the arrangement of institutional buildings linked and supported by colonnades. And when designing these colonnades in London and Cambridge, he followed what he saw as ancient Eastern precedent and preferred the Doric. For this was the Order that was used on colonnades at Trinity College library, at Chelsea and Greenwich Hospitals in a plain form and as proposed in 1697 for the bank of the Thames from Whitehall to Westminster (see figs 147, 155–7). Although Wren's earliest proposal for a colonnade,

162 A view of Palmyra on the southern side, unattributed engraving, from the Royal Society's *Philosophical Transactions*, 19 no. 218 (1695), before p. 125

in his plan for London of 1666, predates the Tracts, the feature served the same urban function – of walkway and screen to the buildings behind – as the ancient examples outlined in them. His understanding of the role of the colonnades at Alexandria and Tarsus could easily have been formulated at any time, based as it was on ancient sources (his Strabo edition was of 1620, for example). Wren started his historical studies much earlier than when the Tracts are thought to have been written (from the mid-1670s), for these studies would have formed part of his classical education. His early knowledge of Vitruvius and Herodotus is shown by his reference to them in his Gresham lecture of 1657, his reliance on Vitruvius and Polybius in his City plan of 1666 and his use of the Halicarnassus mausoleum as described by Pliny as the basis of a lantern in the Great Model for St Paul's of 1673 (see fig. 52). He had studied the Greek stoa by 1675, the year of his letter to Barrow. And while it remains unclear as to when Wren became aware through travellers of the actual remains of such colonnades at Alexandria and Palmyra, it could easily have been before his own version at Chelsea in 1682: Blount had visited Alexandria many years previously, in 1634, and Huntington had returned to Oxford in 1681.

In providing evidence as to the planning of the ancient city, especially as to how it might have been set out quickly, the ruins of Rome's Eastern empire were more informative than those of ancient Rome itself. Here again, this interest in the architecture of the East represented something of a shift away from the models illustrated by Serlio and Palladio that had been cultivated by the previous generation of English architects. If the emulation by the Greeks of their ancient cities had been the 'true Cause of their Greatness', as Wren put it in his first Tract, his own emulation of one of their basic urban forms can only have had the same intention.

 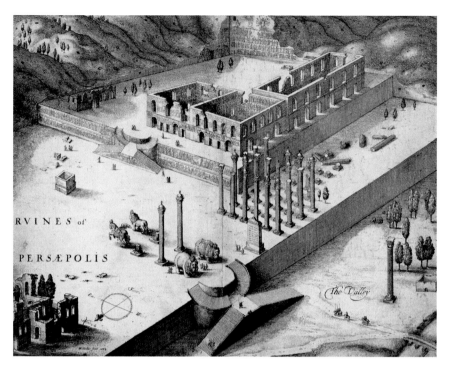

Wren could have drawn on another ancient example of free-standing columns in his design of colonnades. As Chapter One discussed, his awareness of Eastern cities included Persepolis in Persia, which had many such columns arranged in rows. The Italian explorer and pilgrim Pietro della Valle had visited Persepolis in October 1621 and his account of the ruins eventually appeared in 1658.[71] Meanwhile Thomas Herbert had described the city at length in his popular *Relation of Some Yeares Travaile* of 1634 and illustrated it with a view of some of these columns (what was left of an audience hall of a hundred pillars): this was engraved by William Marshall, and reappeared in the expanded, 1638 edition (together with views of Isfahan and a caravanserai; fig. 163). Marshall's view was replaced in the even fuller 1665 edition by a much more complete one of the site by Wenceslaus Hollar (fig. 164), which was used again by Herbert in the 1667 edition owned by Hooke.[72]

Neither of the views had been drawn on site, so in the same year the Royal Society enquired if someone 'might be engaged to make a Draught of the Place'.[73] The columns featured prominently in Herbert's description, some of which were 'ranked in perfect order or rows, such as we see in Cathedrals, or in the Halls of Illustrious Princes'; he continued: 'it is evident there were in all an hundred Pillars when the place was in perfection: as appears by the vacant spaces and also by the bases or foundations of several rows of Columns which are yet visible'.[74]

Persepolis was of continual fascination to Wren and his Royal Society colleagues. At Wren's home in

LEFT 163 Audience Hall at Persepolis, Persia, engraved by William Marshall, from Thomas Herbert, *A Relation of Some Yeares Travaile* (1634 edn), p. 58

RIGHT 164 The Royal Palace of Darius at Persepolis, engraved by Wenceslaus Hollar, from Thomas Herbert, *A Relation of Some Yeares Travaile* (1665 edn), p. 152

OPPOSITE

ABOVE 165 Persepolis, from John Chardin, *Voyages de Monsieur le Chevalier Chardin en Perse et autres lieux de l'Orient*, vol. 3 (1711), no. 52

BELOW LEFT 166 Tomb near Persepolis, from John Chardin, *Voyages de Monsieur le Chevalier Chardin*, vol. 3 (1711), no. 67

BELOW RIGHT 167 View of Persepolis, unattributed engraving but based on a drawing by Engelbert Kämpfer, first published in the Royal Society's *Philosophical Transactions*, 18 no. 210 (1694), and republished in John Lowthorp, *The Philosophical Transactions and Collections*, vol. 3 (1705), p. 527, pl. 6

October 1677 he and Hooke not only discussed the Tyrian tomb of Porsenna, as was noted in the first chapter, but 'Discoursed also of hersepolis' (Persepolis).[75] This discussion was surely 'informed' by Hooke's copy of Herbert's account. As has been seen, Hooke visited Chardin in July 1680 to hear about the city, while a month later Wren and Evelyn went to hear the renowned traveller's report (but not yet see his drawings) of the columns and ruins there: Chapter One discussed Evelyn's Diary record of the meeting, and Chardin's description of, 'the remainders of the *Palace* which *Alexander* burnt in his frolique at *Persepolis*, with divers Temples, Columns, Relievos, & statues, yet extant, which he affirm'd were Sculptures far exceeding, any thing he had observ'd either at *Rome*, Greece or any other part of the World,

where Magnificence was in estimation'.[76] Evelyn later helped Chardin with the publication of his illustrations, specifically mentioning in his Diary those of Persepolis that eventually appeared in the third volume of the Frenchman's *Voyage* published in 1711 in Amsterdam (figs 165 and 166).[77] As Evelyn noted in February 1684:

> I went to Sir John *Chardins*, who desired my Assistance for the ingraving of the plates, the translation & Printing of his historie of that wonderfull *Persian* monument neare *Persepolis*, & other rare Antiquities, which he had Caus'd to be drawne from the originals, at his 2d journey into *Persia*: which we now concluded upon: And afterwards I went to Dr. *Tenison* (with Sir *Chr:Wren*).[78]

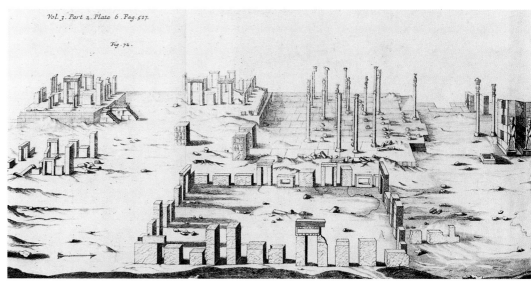

MONUMENTAL COLUMNS AND COLONNADES 135

Whether Wren accompanied Evelyn on his visit to Chardin or just to see Thomas Tenison (later Archbishop of Canterbury) is not clear, but they cannot have failed to talk about Persepolis on their way to Tenison. In any case, it will be remembered from Chapter Three that Wren had seen the drawings for Chardin's plates by August 1681. A further panorama of Persepolis, unattributed but supplied by Nicholaes Witsen, was published in the Royal Society's *Transactions* in May 1694, by which time the ruins were being described as 'Famous' (fig. 167).[79] As with Hollar's view, both Chardin's and Witsen's panoramas showed clearly the partly ruined, free-standing columns. These columns would surely have especially interested Wren when discussing Persepolis, given their non-Vitruvian forms and his understanding of the use of such columns in ancient cities to order urban space.

'THAT AT CONSTANTINOPLE': EASTERN COLUMNS IN LONDON

If Wren's classical colonnades were a novel sight in England, so too was his and Hooke's giant column celebrating the City's recovery from the Fire (fig. 169). This column, called the Monument, was built between 1671 and 1677 near Pudding Lane. The way in which it was set within the city fabric reflected a key concept of Wren's plan for London where, as has been seen, important buildings were placed on main junctions and given space around them (see fig. 149). The Monument was built on the border of an existing main road, New Fish Street, which led directly from the main artery of London Bridge (the only bridge in the City at that time), while on the giant column's other side was a newly formed square adjacent to one that had featured in Wren's plan (fig. 168). This area around the Monument was much larger than it is today. The new square was significant because it was the first major urban space in the city since Jones's Covent Garden and Lincoln's Inn Fields were designed within the medieval fabric under the first Stuarts.

Wren played a prominent role in the design of the Monument, working closely with Hooke.[80] Evelyn credited Wren with its design, noting in his Diary in May 1681 that Wren was building St Paul's, the City churches and the column 'in memorie of the Citties Conflagration'.[81] However, the overall design probably had more to do with Hooke than Wren. The first version was undoubtedly by Hooke. It is recorded in a drawing in his hand of 1671, marked as approved by Wren on behalf of the king (fig. 170).[82] Wren was nevertheless heavily involved at key stages. Both men seem to have acted in their professional capacities, rather than as informal collaborators, Wren as the Royal Surveyor (since 1669) liaising with the king and Hooke as the City Surveyor (since 1667) reporting to the Court of Aldermen and their City Lands Committee.

The Monument's primary models in Rome were the pagan columns of Trajan and Marcus Aurelius, which had been turned into papal memorials by Sixtus V in 1588 through the addition of statues of saints. These pillars were, unsurprisingly, cited in a draft for the Latin inscription on the pedestal of the Monument that explained its purpose and which was published in *Parentalia*.[83] The title of the draft stated that it was 'according to the first conception of Sir C.W.', although the final version of the inscription had major input from Thomas Gale, Master of St Paul's School.[84] More curiously, a note again in Latin at the end of the draft, which was probably also by Wren or approved by him but was not included on the inscription

BELOW 168 View of the Monument and surrounding square, off Fish Street Hill, London (c.1728), engraving by Sutton Nicholls

OPPOSITE 169 The Monument, London (1671–7)

as carved, referred to the less well-known triumphal columns at Constantinople.[85] In fact, the note to the draft appears to conflate the Constantinople columns: 'N.B. Palmus Romanus architectonicus continet IX. Pollices Anglicanos. Columna, dicta Historica, Constantinopoli, sive Imp. Theodosii, sive Arcadii, alta est CXLVII. Pedes. Secundum computum Petri Gylii.' This can be translated as 'N.B. The Roman architectural palm contains 9 English inches. Column, called Historic Column or Column of Constantinople, or Column of Emp.[eror] Theodosius or Column of Arcadius. It is 147 feet tall according to the calculation of Petrus Gyllius.' Referred to here were the column of Constantine (which is still standing; see fig. 180), of Theodosius I (which by then had been destroyed) and of his son, Arcadius (the 'Historical column', so-called because of its bas-relief sculpture, which was then still standing but was later destroyed).[86] The column of Theodosius had been modelled on that of Trajan in Rome. To quote Evelyn's translation of Fréart's *Parallèle de l'Architecture antique et de la moderne* (1650), Trajan's column 'has since become a *Rule*, and been follow'd on sundry Occasions'; he continued: 'Two most renowned *Examples* of this are yet remaining; the *Column* of *Antoninus* at *Rome* also, and that at *Constantinople*, erected to the *Emperour Theodosius* after his Victory against the *Scythians*.'[87] Given that the role of the inscription on the Monument was to explain it, the purpose of this note, if intended for carving, seems to have been to direct the observer's attention eastwards to the example of the columns of the Christian emperors of Constantinople.

This Latin note's concluding reference is to Pierre Gilles's *De Bosporo Thracio libri III* and *De Topographia Constantinopoleos*, both first published in London in 1561 and, it was pointed out, among the earliest books to describe Constantinople. A later edition of the *De Topographia* (of 1632) came to illustrate the Column of Arcadius on its title page. The triumphal columns were also prominent features in views of the city, such as those of 1493 by Schedel (see fig. 95) and 1559 by Lorck. They were discussed and illustrated in many subsequent English works published during Wren's lifetime and as such became the city's most accurately represented antiquities. For example, his copy of the 1670 edition of Sandys's *Travels* (Lot 109) included a full-page illustration of the Column of Arcadius (fig. 171). This edition appeared about the same time, or just before, the column in London was being designed. Arcadius's column was sketched by Covel in his journal of around 1675 and featured in Charles du Fresne du Cange's *Historia Byzantina duplici commentario illustrata* of 1680 and in Wheler's *Journey* of 1682 (Lot 114; fig. 172). Wheler reported:

From the Hippodrome we walked a good way Southwards, to see another Pillar of white Marble; which, because it is carved from top to bottom, with a Basso-relievo, expressing some War-like Actions of the Emperour *Arcadius*, is therefore called the Historical Pillar…It is very like those at Rome, of the Emperours *Trajan* and *Antonine*…Three sides of the Basis are carved with Trophies; and, on the Northern side, I suppose, was an Inscription; but quite eaten away by that penetrating Wind. On the South-side, on the

OPPOSITE 170 The first scheme for the Monument, drawn by Robert Hooke (1671). All Souls College, Oxford

RIGHT 171 The Column of Arcadius, Constantinople, from George Sandys, *Travels: containing an history of the original and present state of the Turkish Empire… a description of Constantinople, the Grand Signior's seraglio, and his manner of living* (1670), Book I, p. 35

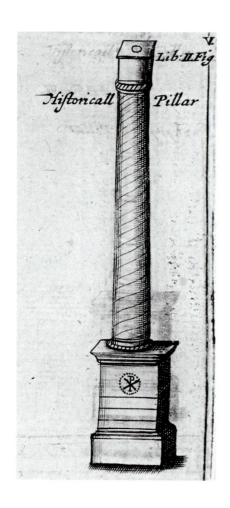 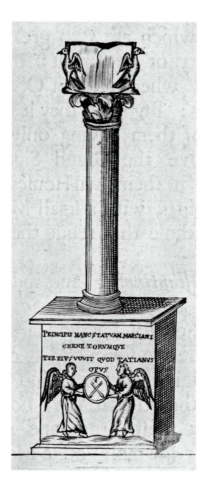 

highest part of the Basis, in a Wreath, sustained by two Victories, is the *Labarum*; which is a Knot...which the Christian Emperours, from *Constantine*, placed in their Banners, instead of the *Roman* Eagle.[88]

Wheler thus explained how to recognise the difference between this Christian column and the pagan versions with their Roman eagles. On the following pages Wren would have seen the illustrations of the Column of Constantine and that of Marcian (also still standing today, with its Christian Victories or angels; figs 173 and 174). Published just after the Monument was erected, these books provided an explanation of its ancient prototypes not in Rome but in Constantinople, especially to contemporaries unable to witness them at first hand (such as Wren himself). Irrespective of whether the note to the draft inscription, as published in *Parentalia*, was ever intended for carving, its reference to these columns of the Christian emperors at least suggests that Wren and Hooke had them in mind too, alongside their better-known pagan cousins in Rome. For the triumphal columns formed part of the emerging image of Constantinople as an early Christian capital and therefore a prerequisite for a city projected as its replacement.

Nevertheless, a free-standing monumental column must have been a strange sight to many Londoners. Such a structure was without precedent in England and few would have seen or read about the antique examples in Rome or Constantinople. In fact, the only actual classical columns most people would have seen up to this time were either pilasters attached to façades, such as at Jones's Banqueting House, or in rows composing porticoes, such as at his old St Paul's. And so, in order to make the

LEFT 172 The Column of Arcadius, with its early Christian emblem, from George Wheler, *A Journey into Greece by George Wheler, Esq., in Company of Dr Spon of Lyons in Six Books* (1682), Book II, p. 189

CENTRE 173 The Column of Marcian, Constantinople, with its early Christian emblem, from Wheler, *Journey* (1682), Book II, p. 191

RIGHT 174 The Column of Marcian (AD 450)

structure legible as a Christian monument, Wren and Hooke used imagery more familiar to native viewers, such as heraldry and bas-relief carving that both architects identified with Eastern emblematics.[89]

'HIEROGLYPHICALLY PROPER TO IT': THE MONUMENT AND CESARE RIPA'S EGYPTIAN HIEROGLYPHICS

According to Josephus, a free-standing column had stood in his day in the exotic Eastern land of 'Seiris' and had served as the repository of the secrets of nature; these were represented in pictures, or possibly in hieroglyphs, inscribed on the shaft for preservation from calamities such as fire.[90] Wren was well aware of this legend, having consulted his editions of the Jewish historian (Lot 255).[91] In the 'Discourse' he noted: 'the Sons of Seth, the other son of Adam, erected two Columns of Brick and Stone to preserve their Mathematical Science to Posterity, so well built that though the one of Brick was destroy'd by the Deluge, the other of Stone was standing in the time of Josephus.'[92] These twin columns became significant in the medieval lore of alchemy and of masonry (and, eventually, Freemasonry), as arcane symbols of lost wisdom. The Royal Society's quest for the original, or Universal, language spoken before the Fall naturally led them east to these columns and the hieroglyphs of Egypt. More importantly, legends concerning the importance of monumental stone columns in times of disaster must have had a particular potency for Wren and Hooke given the recent destruction and the choice of a column to commemorate it.

This and other ancient legends of arcane pictures representing the secrets of nature, particularly identified with (as yet un-deciphered) Egyptian hieroglyphics, had spawned a vast quantity of hieroglyphic, or moral emblem, books in the Renaissance. Most notable were Piero Valeriano's *Hieroglyphica*, first published in 1556, and Cesare Ripa's *Iconologia* of 1593. In fusing pseudo-Egyptian sources with Chaldean and Eastern mysticism, medieval heraldry and various branches of early Renaissance Neo-platonism, these emblem books had an enormous influence on every aspect of Renaissance art. Jones used them in his Stuart masque designs, as but one example.[93] The picture-arts of heraldry and, when combined with a motto, *imprese* shields and devices were considered by Renaissance commentators to be a branch of emblematics and to have also originated in the East. An anonymous letter of commendation in Samuel Daniel's 1585 translation of Paolo Giovio's *Dialogo dell'imprese militare et amorose* (1559) observed:

> concerning the arte of *Imprese*, I need not draw the petigree of it, sith it is knowne that it descended from the aunciant *Aegiptians*, and *Chaldeans*, in the Schoole of *Memphis*…by the picture of a Stork they signified …[family devotion]. By a Serpent pollicie…From hence were derived by succession of pregnant wittes *Stemmata* Coates of Armes, *Insignia* Ensignes, and the olde Images which the *Romaines* used as witnesses of their Auncestors, *Emblemes* and *Devises*.[94]

Wren's understanding of how such emblems functioned is amply demonstrated by his comment in the fourth Tract, quoted in the previous chapter, that, in the case of the dedication of antique temples, 'each Deity had a peculiar Gesture, Face, and Dress hieroglyphically proper to it; as their Stories were but Morals involved'.[95] His interest in ancient Egyptian signs and symbols is attested by his ownership of Johann Georg Herwarth von Hohenburg's *Thesaurus Hieroglyphicorum* (1610; Lot 261) and Claud du Molinet's *Le cabinet de la Bibliotheque de Sainte Genevieve: divisé en deux parties: contenant les antiquitez de la réligion des chrétiens, des Egyptiens, & des Romains* (1692; Lot 546). He also owned Otto van Veen's work on emblematics entitled *Quinti Horatii Flacci emblemata Imaginibus in oes incisis, notisq[ue], illustrata* (1682 edition; Lot 370). Hooke too was a keen student of these books of emblems and hieroglyphs, including Michael Maier's *Arcana Arcanissima hoc est Hieroglyphica Aegyptio-Graeca* (1613 but undated in his library catalogue), Valeriano's *Hieroglyphica* (a 1567 edition), Nicolas Caussin's *Symbolica Aegyptiae Sapientia* (1647) and Kircher's *Prodromus Coptus sive Aegyptianus* (1636).[96] Actual examples of hieroglyphics were also studied by members of the Royal Society. When in Venice in August 1645, Evelyn had been presented with an Egyptian stela decorated with hieroglyphics, which broke on its journey to England and a drawing of which he sent to Kircher.[97]

Although hieroglyphics remained largely unintelligible, Wren's contemporaries understood that, much like the ancient picture language of heraldry, it signified particular human characteristics and moral virtues, akin to nature's underlying laws. Sprat, writing to Wren in 1663, observed that the art of communication of the Egyptians consisted 'in giving things themselves, instead of Words, for Similitudes; in painting a Snake with its Tail in its Mouth, to signify the Year; a Lyon for Courage; the Sun, Moon and Stars, for a thousand Concepts'.[98] A snake in a circle,

called the Ouroboros, symbolised 'eternity' (*eternità*) in alchemical emblematics, of which a version could be found in Ripa's *Iconologia*, for example. Wren used it and other emblems from Ripa in a sketch of 1678 for the monument inside the proposed mausoleum for Charles I at Windsor Castle (fig. 175).[99] The moral emblems that comprised this sculpture were described in *Parentalia* as:

> Four Statues, Emblems of heroick Virtues, standing on a square Basis, or Plinth, & pressing underneath, Prostrate Figures of Rebellion, Heresy, Hypocrisy, Envy, &c. support a large Shield, on which is a Statue erect of the royal Martyr, in modern Armour; over his Head is a Group of Cherubims, bearing a Crown, Branches of Palm, and other Devices.[100]

175 Wren's design for a monument inside the proposed mausoleum for Charles I at Windsor Castle, 1678, unidentified draughtsman. All Souls College, Oxford

As one of these 'other devices', the snake of eternity can clearly be seen crowning the figural group. Cherubims with palm were a sign of the Jerusalem Temple and as such here signified Charles I as the new Solomon. Incidentally, Wren may well have based the mausoleum's plan on similar circular forms in the Baths of Constantine in Rome (specifically the tepidarium and the calidarium), in so doing signalling the king's parallel status as the new Constantine.[101] Despite his rational leanings, Wren's faith in the esoteric potency of such emblems to convey moral virtues clearly inspired his view that the form of certain ancient buildings had been designed to symbolise particular attributes and qualities. The previous chapter explored this understanding concerning the Greek Temple of Diana, and the Roman ones of peace and war (see figs 28, 80, 81). Wren's 'hieroglyphic' understanding of form and decoration broke new ground in not relying on Vitruvius for its authority.[102] Rather, it was influenced by the arcane heraldic and emblematic conventions of the Egyptian and Chaldean peoples, as interpreted in the Renaissance and studied by Royal Society colleagues such as Hooke and Sprat. As with Wren's acceptance of Chaldean astrology, in this influence too he was not an out and out 'Modern'.

The emblematic tradition informed the design of the Monument's ornament. Celebrating the rise of the new City from the ashes of the old required a symbolic programme and for this Hooke and Wren adopted imagery taken from the familiar, inter-related symbolism of heraldry and alchemy.[103] Heraldry emphasises continuity and lineage, and alchemy transformation and rebirth, all potent themes following a period of civil upheavals and fire. Hooke's earliest design proposed using the two mythical beasts most associated with the basic element of fire in alchemical emblematics, namely the dragon (at the base) and phoenix (at the top; see fig. 170).[104] In the event, the phoenix was replaced by a fire-ball, but a dragon sits at each corner of the column's pedestal, carved by Edward Pearce: those to the west are crouching and those to the east more upright (fig. 176). Their inspiration was the coat of arms of the City of London. But the cross on the dragons' wings also identified them with the heraldic emblem of the Order of the Garter, whose patron was St George, as Wren was well aware, and whose symbolic role was to protect London as the New Jerusalem.[105] Other aspects of the Monument's iconography draw on emblematic conventions more directly still. In April 1673 Hooke borrowed from the Royal Society library, which was then kept at Arundel House, a copy of Ripa's *Iconologia*: he eventually returned

it almost four years later, in January 1677 (around the time of the Monument's completion), going on to purchase in October a French edition of that year.[106] The iconography of the Monument's bas-relief panel carved by Caius Gabriel Cibber in the western face of the pedestal, which told the story of the fire and the virtues of reconstruction, closely depended on Ripa (fig. 177).[107] For example, the female figure guiding Charles II holds a compass and set-square. According to Ripa, the compass was one of the attributes of 'drawing' (*desegno*) and 'practice' (*pratica*), while the set-square and compass together were attributes of 'measure' (*misura*) and 'judgement' (*giudizio*; fig. 178) and as such became popular emblems of Freemasonry. Also among the emblematic figures on the pedestal are those of Time and the City of London, joined by the virtues of Providence, Liberty, Fortitude, Plenty and Peace.[108] In acknowledging the emblematic nature of these characters, the City's financial Accounts described them as

ABOVE 176 Dragons on the eastern side of the pedestal of the Monument, carved by Edward Pearce

BELOW LEFT 177 The bas-relief panel on the western side of the pedestal of the Monument, carved by Caius Gabriel Cibber

BELOW RIGHT 178 The emblem of 'judgement' (*giudizio*), with compass and set-square, from Cesare Ripa, *Iconologia* (1593), p. 244

MONUMENTAL COLUMNS AND COLONNADES

'Hieroglifick figures'; this reference to Egyptian antiquity was underlined by the fact that the giant pillar was itself sometimes referred to by contemporaries as an 'obelisk' or even a 'pyramid', thereby confirming a confusion as to the origins of its form.[109]

'A PILLAR IN FLAMES': SOLOMON'S PILLAR IN THE NEW JERUSALEM

The Rebuilding Act of 1667 called for the erection of what it referred to as 'a Pillar of Brase or Stone'.[110] Hooke's initial scheme had interpreted this with brass flames leaping from the column's shaft (see fig. 170) and was described in *Parentalia* thus: 'this Monument of the Conflagration, and Resurrection of the City of London, was represented by a Pillar in Flames'; the flames 'blazing from the Loop-holes of the Shaft' were 'figur'd in Brass-work gilt; and on the Top was a Phaenix rising from her Ashes, of Brass gilt likewise'.[111] The shaft, alight but undamaged by the flames, conveyed the idea of the Monument's immutability, in the tradition of the twin pillars described by Josephus, and in so doing complemented the dragons at the base and the reborn phoenix at the apex. A further legendary Eastern precedent for such an immutable, free-standing column could be found in the description of the entrance to the inner sanctuary of the Temple of Solomon (1 Kings 7.15–22). Here the Tyrian architect Hiram had built two columns, one of fire representing 'establishment' and called 'Jachin', the other of smoke representing 'strength' and called 'Boaz'.[112] These pillars, which Kings recorded had brass capitals, symbolised the flight of the Hebrews from Egypt: according to the account in Exodus (13.21–2), 'the Lord went before them by day in a pillar of cloud, to lead them the way; and by night in a pillar of fire, to give them light'. London's own 'fire pillar' was built in a city cast by Anglican theologians as the New Jerusalem. It too symbolised the establishment of a new, or rather 'reborn', nation. And again like its biblical counterpart, the building of London's pillar followed civil and religious upheaval and also plague, likened at the time to that visited on Egypt just before the Exodus.[113] Indeed, this biblical analogy was referred to in Cibber's bas-relief panel on the Monument, where the many-breasted Artemis of Ephesus was carved above a beehive (fig. 179). This emblem was in allusion to milk and honey, and was thus a rebus for the promised land of Israel, towards which the fire pillar had been a beacon.[114] The deliverance of the New Jerusalem in London was, by implication, pictured here on the Monument as through the act of rebuilding under the watchful eye of the new Solomon, Charles II.[115]

179 Detail of the Monument's bas-relief panel carved by Caius Gabriel Cibber (see fig. 177), showing the female figure representing 'judgement' and 'design' guiding Charles II, and the many-breasted Artemis/Diana of Ephesus above a beehive

CONCLUSION

EASTERN WONDERS AND NATIONAL IDENTITY

'The obstinate Valour of the Jews'

The principal work documenting Wren's life, compiled with his approval and finally published in 1750, was *Parentalia: Or, Memoirs of the Family of the Wrens*. The main body of its text concluded with a Latin epitaph that was probably composed by the editor of the work, Wren's son. Here, before the appendix comprising the Tracts, there is a curious and overlooked reference to the Eastern influences on Wren that have formed the topic of this book. The first verse of the epitaph can be translated as:

On the same: astronomer, and architect, founder of the Basilica of Saint Paul and of the City of London.
Wren, who built the church of St Paul with remarkable skill,
was deeply versed in the stars and heavens.
His hand restored the honours of the Temple of the Crossroads;
whether Mausolean or Babylonian work.
*Augusta was reborn grander from the flames,
the standing buildings could not show his skill.
[in the margin: *old name for London*][1]

180 The Column of Constantine, Constantinople (AD 330)

The second verse continued with a quotation from Martial's *Epigrams*, on Vulcan's burning of Troy and its refoundation in Rome (it has been seen that Wren had himself quoted Martial when describing the Mausoleum at Halicarnassus).[2] But Martial's reference to Rome was here replaced by one to London in yet another of its legendary guises, New Troy. The verse can be translated as:

On London restored after the fire.
As the flames renew the nest of the Assyrian phoenix, whenever one bird has lived ten centuries:
so *New Troy, renewed, has shed her old age,
and has assumed the looks of her guardian.
[*in the margin: *old name for London*][3]

The idea of London replacing Rome as the New Troy had been a popular conceit. It was seen in Chapter Three that long before Wren's time, Britain had been linked with the East through various legends recorded in Geoffrey of Monmouth and Bede.[4] Alongside the story of Constantine's British birth, a Trojan Prince called Brutus, or Brute, was said to have landed in the country from Troy and subsequently founded London and established the unified kingdom of 'Britain'. In reaction to the problem of legitimacy surrounding their rule, Stuart kings cultivated an identity not just as the new Constantine refounding

Constantinople but as the 'second' Brute. As a result, Stuart London was commonly projected as a new Troy or Troynovant (and as such was seen as older than Rome). This idea of London under the Stuarts reviving, as it were, the centres of Eastern civilisation and Christianity had lent legitimacy to the classical architecture of Jones and it continued to be celebrated in the mythology of the court and City Companies well into Wren's era. For example, the anonymous *Troia Redeviva, or, The Glories of London Surveyed: in an heroick Poem* (1674) celebrated the rebuilding of the city after the Great Fire in Trojan terms.[5] And a few years later John Banks's *The Destruction of Troy a Tragedy* (1679) used the story of Troynovant as a thinly disguised critique of, or commentary on, London at that time.[6] The changes to Martial's verse in *Parentalia* thus linked Wren's work directly to this legend of London reborn with Trojan virtues.

Martial's *Epigrams* had also been quoted a few pages earlier in *Parentalia*, this time as a footnote to a transcription of the actual Latin epitaph composed by Wren's son and carved above the architect's tomb in St Paul's. This footnote can be translated as: 'The marble you are reading, traveller, is small indeed, but will not yield to the stones of Mausolus and the pyramids.'[7] These hitherto unexplained comparisons of Wren's work to Mausolean, Egyptian and Babylonian antiquities, together with references to magical Syrian fire-birds and London rebuilt in the spirit of ancient Troy, take our gaze past Rome to the great civilisations of the East. It is true that this material formed part of the purpose of *Parentalia*, a project where Wren's family edited and selected records to construct an image of him, rather than a wholly accurate report of his own thoughts. Nevertheless, as far as Wren's son was concerned, this comparison evidently represented the last word on his father's achievements.

'WHERE GOD HIMSELFE DID PLACE HIS OWNE COMMONWEALTH': IN SEARCH OF THE ORIGINS OF ARCHITECTURE

This book began by asking why Wren's buildings look as distinctive as they do, with their domes and colonnades and their lanterns and Greek cross plans. Even by just glancing at them it becomes immediately apparent that Wren had studied the monuments of Roman antiquity which, when codified by Serlio and others, had formed the principal source for Renaissance architects. Wren drew on the ancient buildings of Rome – its theatres for the Sheldonian and basilicas for St Paul's – just as Inigo Jones had done. And he undoubtedly knew more modern, Renaissance examples of domes on pendentives and of arcaded streets. Certainly, these examples were the primary inspiration for much of his work, not least because they were far better illustrated in the many Renaissance treatises and pattern books at his disposal. But another, less studied, influence on him were buildings and cultures unknown to Jones and the previous generation of architects. As Fellows of the Royal Society were in the process of exploring, the Greek and Roman empires had extended south through Turkey and Syria into Egypt, leaving a legacy of classical ruins in these lands that were largely undocumented by Renaissance treatise writers. Added to these Graeco-Roman ruins were the buildings of civilisations like the Babylonian and Persian, as also the later Byzantine and Ottoman, whose monuments had classical forms with novel attributes (see figs 16, 164–6). Wren's growing awareness of these surviving and destroyed buildings can now be seen to have informed not only some of his designs but also, more fundamentally, his understanding of the origins and purpose of architecture itself. To his logical mind, the classical world of Greece and Rome must have had a precursor, and Eastern civilisations with their recently discovered antiquities seemed to fill the void. In particular, the Graeco-Roman column needed a backstory. The Vitruvian idea of the spontaneous appearance of the Doric Order in all its perfection was dismissed by Wren in fashioning the Tyrian column as its prototype. The fact that its inventors, the Phoenicians, had been great travellers made them plausible candidates as the originators of the classical tradition across the Mediterranean.

Wren would have read George Sandys's opening address to the future king, Charles I, in his *Journey* of 1615. Here the Holy Land was presented as once the seat of the 'most glorious and triumphant Empires' and

> where Arts and Sciences have bene invented, and perfected; where wisdome, virtue, policie, and civility have bene planted, have flourished: and lastly where God himselfe did place his owne Commonwealth, gave lawes and oracles, inspired his Prophets, sent Angels to converse with men; above all, where the Sonne of God descended to become man; where he honoured the earth with his beautifull steps.[8]

It was on these very terms, as the location of the invention of arts and sciences and cradle of Christianity, that the East held a special appeal to Wren and Hooke. Jerusalem and Constantinople were central to this fascination, in providing models not of pagan but of Christian (or Christianised) antiquity. Hence Wren sought information on Solomon's Temple, the tomb of Absalom and the Holy Sepulchre in one city, and Hagia Sophia and the smaller Byzantine churches, as also the triumphal columns (or so *Parentalia* suggested) in the other (fig. 180). The colonnades at Palmyra too were understood to be Solomon's work. In this regard at least, these buildings in the East, as far as Wren could visualise them, had an advantage as inspiration and models over their pagan and Roman Catholic counterparts in Rome and Paris further west. This did not stop Wren drawing on these and other Western models, both ancient and modern, which he did extensively. But it might be expected that his Christian faith, together with his understanding of the ancient principle of decorum – which emphasised the appropriate choice of models and ornament – would have directed him east in the search for the origins and meaning of forms.

Wren was equally aware that the East had been the birthplace of branches of natural philosophy well before the Greeks. He referred at Gresham College in 1657 to Babylonian medicine and Chaldaean astrology, as also to Alexandria as the home of the mathematical arts. The East was equally the source of skilful geometrical practices that he identified in the Tyrian-styled tombs, Saracen mosques and Byzantine churches-cum-mosques like Hagia Sophia. This idea that geometry, masonry and the esoteric arts had Eastern origins reflected the lore of contemporary Freemasonry. Just as the Phoenicians had invented the Orders, so to his mind the later Saracens had invented the pointed arch and the Byzantines the dome on pendentives. And just as he identified the Phoenicians as having spread the classical style in the Mediterranean, he seized on the Crusaders in order to account for the transmission to the West of the Gothic or what he terms the 'Saracen style'. This association between Christendom and Gothic, despite the style's Arab paternity, overcame its heathen reputation and licensed its use by him on Christian structures such as cathedrals, abbeys and colleges. Wren thus came to see both classical and Gothic styles as originating in the architecture of the Holy Land and the wider East.

This fascination with legendary Tyrian structures was both theoretical and practical. Wren saw them as the originals of the classical architecture of Greece and Rome, and as such appears to have attempted to understand their physical form through drawings and reconstructions and to use them on occasions as the basis of built forms. They were joined by surviving structures such as the colonnades at Alexandria and Palmyra (albeit understood more in the imagination than in actuality), as well as the domes of the church of the Holy Sepulchre and Hagia Sophia, in providing Wren with both inspiration and justification for forms without precedents in the recent classical buildings of England. In fact, in the case of colonnades and domes on pendentives with abutments, the principal surviving antique examples were to be found not in Rome or elsewhere in Italy but in the East: indeed, this is where both had originated. This can only have encouraged Wren's belief that other forms originated there too, most notably the Orders and the pointed arch. With practical help from Hooke and theoretical justification from his 'larger idea' of architecture's origins, Wren designed new forms of church lanterns and steeples, a triumphal column and long colonnades, as well as large domes and centralised churches that he introduced into English architecture. In this way he broadened the possibilities of designing with the classical language based on his Eastern studies and in so doing reinvented the very art of building, just as other great masters such as Alberti and Palladio had once done.

Many of Wren's preoccupations with Eastern antiquities influenced his assistants in the Office of Works. Hawksmoor went on to produce his idealised church plan in 1711–12, entitled 'The Basilica after the Primitive Christians', which embodied liturgical practices of the Eastern Orthodox Church (see fig. 142).[9] This plan formed a model for the proposed fifty new churches in London. It was a further product of the movement within the Church of England seeking greater unity with the Eastern Church, in order to bypass Roman Catholicism, to which some of Wren's London churches had equally given expression. Hawksmoor also followed Wren's obsession with the Tyrian mausoleums of Halicarnassus and Porsenna, as well as the Temple of Solomon and mosques of Constantinople (see figs 36, 113, 114).[10] Vanbrugh, too, followed in his master's footsteps. Wren's legitimisation, and use, of Gothic paved the way for Vanbrugh's hybrid Gothic and classical compositions such as Kimbolton Castle, through which he attempted to formulate a national architectural style.[11] Although Wren was much less captivated by the exotic quality of Eastern buildings than by their structural complexity and urban significance, his interest in Eastern wonders foreshadows the rise of Orientalism in the eighteenth century.[12]

In tracing the origins of the Orders to the great monuments of biblical and Tyrian antiquity, Wren gave his own use of the classical style in the service of Church and King as firm and universal a foundation as possible. The need for this can hardly be doubted, in the wake of the unrest of the Civil War and its aftermath and the catastrophic events of the Great Plague and Fire of London. National stability was achievable, as Wren observed in the opening lines of his first Tract, through public architecture since

> ARCHITECTURE has its political Use; publick Buildings being the Ornament of a Country; it establishes a Nation, draws People and Commerce; makes the People love their native Country, which Passion is the Original of all great Actions in a Common-wealth. The Emulation of the Cities of *Greece* was the true Cause of their Greatness. The obstinate Valour of the *Jews*, occasioned by the Love of their Temple, was a Cement that held together that People, for many Ages, through infinite Changes.... Modern *Rome* subsists still, by the Ruins and Imitations of the *old*; as does *Jerusalem*, by the Temple of the Sepulchre, and other Remains of *Helena's* Zeal.[13]

Wren's call to arms on behalf of classical architecture places modern Rome and Jerusalem, the Western and Eastern centres of Christendom, on an equal footing, and imagines that both were 'still' being constructed in imitation of their ancient buildings. The fact that Solomon's Temple and the Holy Sepulchre were singled out as examples in this process of national renewal underlines their importance as enduring biblical exemplars to Wren, following the lore of the Knights Templar. Wren's case that drawing on these buildings as inspiration ('Imitations of the old') formed a basis not just for architectural but also for national greatness should thus be understood in the wider context of the mission to 'establish a nation' in the wake of the Civil War and Restoration.[14] In this regard, when it came to expressing the grandeur of Church and Crown, Ottoman architecture with its mighty domes provided a particularly powerful example.[15]

Wren was clearly sensitive to the monarch's civic role as a patron of architecture, born as he was into a family of High Church Royalists and as a loyal Surveyor-General of the Royal Works.[16] His chosen models of Tyrian architecture were the tombs and temples of the legendary antique–biblical rulers, Mausolus and Absalom, Porsenna and Solomon. Discussing Solomon's Temple in his fourth Tract, he observed, no doubt with a nod to his own era, that 'Great Monarchs are ambitious to leave great Monuments behind them', and the Temple's successor, Justinian's Hagia Sophia, would have borne particular witness to this fact.[17] When conceiving such monuments for his own 'great monarch', Wren's understanding of the Eastern origins of classicism could surely only have met with enthusiasm from a king who identified with David and Solomon and dressed, according to Evelyn, in the 'Eastern fashion' after 'the Persian mode'.[18]

NOTES

PREFACE

1. J. Evelyn, *The Diary of John Evelyn*, ed. E. S. de Beer (1959), p. 339 (11 July 1654).
2. On occasions Wren's interests merged, as with the Monument (1671–7), one of whose projected functions was said to be to act as an observatory. See J. Noorthouck, *A New History of London Including Westminster and Southwark* (1773), Book 2, ch. 10, 'Bridge Ward within', pp. 560–6, in *British History Online*, www.british-history.ac.uk/no-series/new-history-london/pp560–566 (accessed 7 April 2019).
3. See M. Whinney, *Wren* (1971), pp. 19–21; but see also A. Geraghty, 'Wren's Preliminary Design for the Sheldonian Theatre', *Architectural History*, vol. 45 (2002), pp. 275–88; Geraghty, *The Sheldonian Theatre: Architecture and Learning in Seventeenth-Century Oxford* (2013).
4. See V. Hart, *Nicholas Hawksmoor: Rebuilding Ancient Wonders* (2002); Hart, *Sir John Vanbrugh: Storyteller in Stone* (2008).
5. L. Soo, *Wren's 'Tracts' on Architecture and Other Writings* (1998), p. 157; on this passage see M. F. Walker, *Architects and Intellectual Culture in Post-Restoration England* (2017), pp. 182–92.
6. See J. A. Bennett, 'Christopher Wren: The Natural Causes of Beauty', *Architectural History*, vol. 15 (1972), pp. 5–22; Soo 1998, pp. 141–9; C. van Eck, 'Understanding Roman Architecture from a Distance: Sir Christopher Wren on the Temples of Peace and of Mars the Avenger', in *The Companion to the History of Architecture*, vol. 1: *Renaissance and Baroque Architecture*, ed. A. Payne (2017), pp. 498–523.
7. See A. Grafton, *New Worlds, Ancient Texts: The Power of Tradition and the Shock of Discovery* (1992).
8. Soo 1998, Tract four, p. 172.
9. J. Aubrey, 'Monumenta Britannica', Bodleian Library, Oxford, MSS Top.Gen.c.24–25: see Aubrey, *Monumenta Britannica; or, A Miscellany of British antiquities*, ed. R. Legg et al., vol. 2 (1980–2), pp. 678–9.
10. On the Royal Society see D. Carey, 'Compiling Nature's History: Travellers and Travel Narratives in the Early Royal Society', *Annals of Science*, vol. 54 (1997), pp. 269–92.
11. Preface to Claude Perrault's French translation of Vitruvius of 1684, n.p [sig. ccux]: 'a envoyé dans l'Italie, dans l'Egypte, dans la Grece, dans la Syrie, dans la Perse, & enfin par tous les lieux où il reste des marques de la capacité & de la hardiesse des anciens Architectes'. Wren owned this translation (Lot 545): for Wren and his son's library as recorded in a sale catalogue of 1748 (whose lot numbers are cited throughout this book) see D. J. Watkin, ed., *Sale Catalogues of Libraries of Eminent Persons*, vol. 4: *Architects* (1972), pp. 135–91. See N. Dew, *Orientalism in Louis IV's France* (2009). On the French interest in the Levant from the 1620s, including François Blondel's visit to Constantinople in the 1650s, see J. Sweetman, *The Oriental Obsession: Islamic Inspiration in British and American Art and Architecture 1500–1920* (1988), pp. 44–6; L. Soo, 'The English in the Levant: Social Networks and the Study of Architecture', in O. Horsfall Turner, ed., *'The*

12 See J. Rykwert, *The First Moderns* (1980), ch. 3, 'The Marvelous and the Distant', esp. pp. 54–8.

13 C. Perrault, *Parrallèle des anciens et des modernes* (1697), Book Four, p. 274: 'en cas que l'on eût achevé le Louvre, de ne point faire à la françoise tout le grand nombre d'appartemens qu'il doit contenir, mais d'en faire à la mode de toutes les Nations du Monde: à l'Italienne, à l'Espagnolle, à l'Allemande, à la Turque, à la Persienne, à la maniere du Mongol, à la maniere de la Chine, non seulement par une exacte imitation de tous les ornemens dont ces Nations embellissent differemment les dedans de leurs Palais…en sorte que tous les Etrangers eussent le plaisir de retrouver chez Nous en quelque sorte leur proper Pays, & toute la magnificence du Monde refermée dans un seul Palais'.

14 See J. Bikker, 'Re-reading Wren's Mind in Light of the Bookish Evidence', in P. R. du Prey, ed., *Architects, Books and Libraries: A Collection of Essays published in conjunction with the Exhibition of the Same Name* (1995), pp. 16–23; J. M. Levine, *Between the Ancients and the Moderns: Baroque Culture in Restoration England* (1999), pp. 161–209 (on Wren).

15 J. Evelyn, 'An Account of Architects and Architecture', in *A Parallel of the Ancient Architecture with the Modern* (1707 edn), p. 46.

16 Domes and free-standing colonnades were absent in the work of Jones, whose arcades at Covent Garden were arched and not free-standing. Levine 1999, p. 176: 'As Evelyn and Pratt had noticed, England had then almost no classical architecture to offer, apart from a few buildings by Inigo Jones. Domes and colonnades were an exotic import in a thoroughly Gothic landscape.'

17 Wren's study of Roman architecture was limited to the Renaissance treatises viewed alongside the domestic architecture of Jones. This was supplemented with Fréart de Chambray's *Parallèle de l'Architecture antique et de la moderne* (1650, which Wren owned in Evelyn's 1664 and 1707 translation, Lot 567), the adaptation of the Vitruvian rules in Perrault's *Ordonnance des cinq espèces de colonnes selon la methode des Anciens* (1683) and in his translation of Vitruvius into French of 1684 (Lot 545). See Rykwert 1980, pp. 148–9; J. A. Bennett, *The Mathematical Sciences of Christopher Wren* (1982), pp. 122–3; E. Harris, *British Architectural Books and Writers 1556–1785* (1990), pp. 368–71, 505–6.

18 This book will use the terms the 'East' and the 'Levant' to encapsulate this eastern Mediterranean area, in preference to the 'Orient', which has come to signify China, the 'Near East', which is a nineteenth-century term (with imperialist connotations), and the 'Middle East' that has replaced it.

19 On Allacci's *De septem orbis spectaculis* (1640) see P. R. du Prey, *Hawksmoor's London Churches: Architecture and Theology* (2000), pp. 3–4, also 9–12, 14–16. On Pliny's ancient wonders see P. Fane-Saunders, *Pliny the Elder and the Emergence of Renaissance Architecture* (2016).

20 See Fane-Saunders 2016, pp. 120, 127.

21 F. Colonna, *Hypnerotomachia Poliphili* (1499), fols di*v*–dii*r*. See Fane-Saunders 2016, p. 135.

22 See Fane-Saunders 2016, pp. 173–94.

23 S. Serlio, *Il terzo libro di Sebastiano Serlio bolognese* (1540), pp. XCIIII–XCV, CLIIII–CLV; see Serlio, *Sebastiano Serlio on Architecture* [Books I–'VIII'], trans. V. Hart and P. Hicks, vol. 1 (1996), pp. 184–5, 244–6. These woodcuts would have been known to Wren through his 1663 edition (Lot 540); on Serlio's woodcut as a source for the dome of St Paul's see V. Hart, *St Paul's Cathedral: Sir Christopher Wren* (1995), pp. 22–3.

24 T. Fuller, *The Holy State and the Profane State* (1642), Book III, ch. 24, pp. 226–8.

25 Robert Hooke owned copies of Africanus and Fuller: Africanus, 'Libri Latini, &c. in Octavo', lot 31, p. 22, see www.hookesbooks.com/hookes-books-database/browse-bh-in-full (accessed 7 April 2019); Fuller, 'English Books in Folio', lot 121, p. 40, see ibid.

26 See Ch. Three.

27 See K. B. Moore, *The Architecture of the Christian Holy Land: Reception from Late Antiquity through the Renaissance* (2017), pp. 240–84.

28 See n. 11 above.

29 References in the so-called fifth Tract or 'Discourse on Architecture'; see Soo 1998, pp. 188–9.

30 'Libri Latini, &c. in Folio', lot 3, p. 1; see www.hookesbooks.com.

31 R. Hooke, *The Diary of Robert Hooke: 1672–1680*, ed. H. W. Robinson and W. Adams (1935), p. 225 (London Metropolitan Archives, MS 01758, henceforth Diary; see n. 61 below).

32 Wren noted 'In all the Editions of Pliny' in his 'Discourse', in Soo 1998, p. 195.

33 Hooke records a conversation with Edmond Halley concerning Pliny on 16 February 1689 and another on 23 April (with unknown); on 6 November he refers to a 'Manuscript *Pliny*' in reference to textual corrections identified by Halley and published in *Philosophical Transactions* the following year. On New Year's Day 1690 he noted that he had met 'Dr [Thomas] Gale and [William] Perry, then Hall[e]y, Waller, and [Alex] Pitfield…talked of place in Pliny': R. Hooke, 'Diary, 1688 to 1693', in R. T. Gunther, ed., 'Life and Work of Robert Hooke (Part IV)', in *Early Science in Oxford*, vol. 10 (1935), pp. 98, 116, 162, 176 (British Library, MS Sloane 4024, henceforth Diary 2). Like Wren, Hooke was a keen student of Pliny, noting on 18 February 1689: 'Examin'd Hardwine's [Jean Hardouin's] *Pliny*, English *Pliny* from the French: neither true', and

on the following day 'Perused *Pliny*'; Hooke, Diary 2, p. 99. Evelyn owned a 1635 edition; see Evelyn, *The Evelyn Library: Sold by Order of the Trustees of the Wills of J. H. C. Evelyn, deceased and Major Peter Evelyn, deceased*, vol. 3 (1977), no. 1193, p. 96.

34 Soo 1998, 'Discourse', pp. 189, 190.

35 On the Tracts and the 'Discourse' see ibid., pp. 119–95; Hart 1995; on the four Tracts see S. Wren, ed., *Parentalia: Or, Memoirs of the Family of the Wrens* (1750), pp. 236–59 (henceforth Wren 1750).

36 'Discourse' in the 'Heirloom' copy of *Parentalia* held at the Royal Institute of British Architects, London: see Soo 1998, 'Discourse', pp. 188–95.

37 The Tracts are dated from the beginning to the mid-1670s in Soo 1998, p. 153. On the dating of them to the later 1670s, see A. Tinniswood, *His Invention so Fertile: A Life of Christopher Wren* (2001), p. 404 n. 56. The second Tract must be post 1680 since there is a reliance on Guillaume-Joseph Grelot's *Relation Nouvelle d'un Voyage de Constantinople enrichie de plans levés par l'auteur sur les lieux* published that year; see du Prey 2000, p. 154 n. 86. See also Ch. One pp. 31–2 and Ch. Three n. 112 below.

38 Soo 1998, Tract two, p. 158.

39 See J. A. Bennett and S. Mandelbrote, eds, *The Garden, the Ark, the Tower, the Temple: Biblical Metaphors of Knowledge in Early Modern Europe* (1998), pp. 103–22.

40 Soo 1998, 'Discourse', p. 188.

41 See Van Eck 2017, pp. 498–523.

42 See R. Krautheimer, *Early Christian and Byzantine Architecture* (1986 edn).

43 Royal Society, GB 117, 'Journal Book of the Royal Society', vol. 11 (1702–14), 25 June 1712. See Soo 1998, p. 122.

44 See A. Wragge-Morley, 'Restitution, Description and Knowledge in English Architecture and Natural Philosophy, 1650–1750', *Architectural Research Quarterly*, vol. 14 (2010), pp. 247–54. On Hagia Sophia see Ch. Three.

45 Even such irrational events as miracles were subject to the same method of rational enquiry. During his inaugural lecture at Gresham College in 1657 Wren had asserted: 'Neither need we fear to diminish a Miracle by explaining it'; Wren 1750, p. 27; and as he put it in Tract four (in reference to Cicero), 'Reason is the best Art of Divination'; Soo 1998, p. 182.

46 Soo 1998, 'Discourse', p. 192.

47 Ibid., pp. 189–90. See K. J. Williams, *The Antiquary: John Aubrey's Historical Scholarship* (2016), p. 90.

48 Kircher's explanation was along the lines earlier proposed by the Royal Society Fellow John Wilkins, in his *An Essay Towards a Real Character and a Philosophical Language* (1668); see Bennett and Mandelbrote 1998, pp. 92–101.

49 J. B. Fisher von Erlach, *Entwurff einer Historischen Architectur* (1721); see Soo 1998, pp. 132–3. Von Erlach visited England in 1704.

50 Smaller Roman examples include the Temple of Diana at Baiae in Italy.

51 See R. Burns, *Origins of the Colonnaded Streets in the Cities of the Roman East* (2017).

52 For these writings see Wren 1750; Soo 1998.

53 See K. Downes, 'Sir Christopher Wren', *Oxford Dictionary of National Biography*, ed. H. C. G. Matthew, vol. 60 (2004), pp. 406–19; C. S. L. Davies, 'The Youth and Education of Christopher Wren', *English Historical Review*, vol. 123 no. 501 (2008), pp. 300–27.

54 See the Introduction. This lecture was delivered in Latin; it is recorded in its English version in Wren 1750, pp. 24–33 (Herodotus on p. 28). For the Latin version see www.philological.bham.ac.uk/wren2/text.html (accessed 7 April 2019). He also refers to Herodotus three times in the 'Discourse'; see Soo 1998, pp. 189, 190, 193; p. 119 for Wren's early studies.

55 'Parentalia', British Library, Add. MS 25,071 (without the Tracts). See J. A. Bennett, 'Christopher Wren: The Natural Causes of Beauty', *Architectural History*, vol. 15 (1972), pp. 5–8; Bennett, 'A Study of *Parentalia*, with Two Unpublished Letters of Sir Christopher Wren', *Annals of Science*, vol. 30 (1973), pp. 129–47; Soo 1998 pp. 8–12.

56 On Wren's other possible travels in Europe, see L. Jardine, *On a Grander Scale: The Outstanding Career of Sir Christopher Wren* (2002), pp. 72–4, 76, 79, 81–2, 85–7.

57 For Wren's library see Watkin 1972, pp. 135–91. This sale included books owned by Wren's son, so some caution is required. Wren's enthusiasm for purchasing books is recorded in a letter to his son of 1705, in L. Phillimore, *Sir Christopher Wren: His Family and His Times: with Original Letters and a Discourse on Architecture Hitherto Unpublished* (1881), p. 303.

58 On the large library of Hooke (more than 2,600 volumes) see *Bibliotheca Hookiana* (1703), facsimile in H. A. Feisenberger, ed., *Sale Catalogue of Libraries of Eminent Persons*, vol. 11: *Scientists* (1972), pp. 57–116. See now the searchable online catalogue www.hookesbooks.com; see also A. Geraghty, 'Robert Hooke's Collection of Architectural Books and Prints', *Architectural History*, vol. 47 (2004), pp. 113–25. For Evelyn's library (more than 1,700 volumes) see Evelyn, *Evelyn Library* (1977).

59 On Hooke see S. Inwood, *The Man who knew Too Much: The Strange and Inventive Life of Robert Hooke 1635–1703* (2002); M. Cooper, *'A More Beautiful City': Robert Hooke and the Rebuilding of London after the Great Fire* (2003); J. A. Bennett et al., eds, *London's Leonardo: The Life and Work of Robert Hooke* (2003); L. Jardine, *The Curious Life of Robert Hooke: The Man who measured London* (2003); M. Cooper and M. Hunter, eds, *Robert Hooke, Tercentennial Studies* (2006).

60 'Descriptio Constantinopolis', Cotton MSS Vitellius, A.xx, British Library; see www.bl.uk/reshelp/findhelprestype/manuscripts/cottonmss/cottonmss.html (accessed 7 April

2019). Wren owned Thomas Smith's *Catalogus Librorum Manuscriptorum Bibliothecae Cottonianae* (1696) (Lot 149).

61 See nn. 31, 33 above. For a scan of Diary 1671–83 (London Metropolitan Archives MS 01758) including the years January 1681–May 1683, untranscribed in Hooke 1935 see: https://search.lma.gov.uk/scripts/mwimain.dll/144/LMA_OPAC/web_detail/REFD+CLC~2F495~2FMS01758?SESSIONSEARCH (accessed 7 April 2019); Evelyn 1959; S. Pepys, *The Diary of Samuel Pepys*, ed. H. B. Wheatley (1893); see www.pepysdiary.com (accessed 7 April 2019).

62 Hooke, Diary, pp. 179 (Solomon's Temple, 6 September 1675), 328 (Hagia Sophia, 14 November 1677); see Soo 1998, p. 124; du Prey 2000, p. 154 n. 90.

63 Sweetman 1988, p. 46.

64 K. Downes, *Hawksmoor* (1959), p. 29.

65 Soo 1998, pp. 37 (Saracens), 128–30 (Tyrian). See also L. Soo, 'Reconstructing Antiquity: Wren and his Circle and the Study of Natural History, Antiquarianism, and Architecture at the Royal Society', PhD thesis, Princeton University (1989).

66 Soo 2012, pp. 209–31.

67 L. Soo, 'The Architectural Setting of "Empire": The English Experience of Ottoman Spectacle in the Late 17th Century and its Consequences', in M. Keller and J. Irigoyen-Garcia, eds, *The Dialectics of Orientalism in Early Modern Europe* (2017), pp. 217–45.

68 Du Prey 2000, p. 10.

69 See P. Coles, *The Ottoman Impact on Europe* (1968); Sweetman 1988 on the trade in carpets pp. 11–14, silk pp. 40–1; L. Jardine, *Worldly Goods: A New History of the Renaissance* (1996); G. MacLean and N. Matar, *Britain and the Islamic World, 1558–1713* (2011), pp. 16–20, 68–71, 198–229.

70 See Wren 1750, p. 211.

71 See A. C. Wood, *A History of the Levant Company* (1935); P. Lawson, *The East India Company: A History, 1600–1857* (1993); J. Mather, *Pashas: Traders and Travellers in the Islamic World* (2009), pp. 1–15; W. Dalrymple, *The Anarchy* (2019). Hooke was a frequent visitor to East India House in Leadenhall Street, where news and the fruits of the Company's trade with the East and China were discussed; Hooke, Diary, pp. 63, 258 (3 October 1673, 20 November 1676). On 9 November 1676 Hooke noted 'At court of Aldermen about East India Company', on 17 November 'east india committee where nothing was done', and on 12 December 'To Guildhall gave in Report of East India Company', pp. 255, 257, 262.

72 See N. Matar, *Islam in Britain, 1558–1685* (1998); G. MacLean, *The Rise of Oriental Travel: English Visitors to the Ottoman Empire, 1580–1720* (2004); MacLean and Matar 2011; E. W. Said, *Orientalism: Western Conceptions of the Orient* (1978) (for a critique see D. M. Varisco, *Reading Orientalism: Said and the Unsaid* [2007]). See also R. Fedden, *English Travellers in the Near East* (1958); Sweetman 1988, esp. on Said on pp. 8–9 and more generally pp. 10–57; D. Banks and M. Frassetto, eds, *Western Views of Islam in Medieval and Early Modern Europe: Perception of Other* (1999).

73 Matar 1998, pp. 13–14.

74 See esp. ibid., pp. 13, 19; MacLean and Matar 2011.

INTRODUCTION

1 M. Hunter, *The Royal Society and its Fellows 1660–1700* (1994); D. Carey, 'Compiling Nature's History: Travellers and Travel Narratives in the Early Royal Society', *Annals of Science*, vol. 54 (1997), p. 275.

2 See e.g. L. Soo, 'Reconstructing Antiquity: Wren and his Circle and the Study of Natural History, Antiquarianism, and Architecture at the Royal Society', PhD thesis, Princeton University (1989); Carey 1997, pp. 269–92; R. Iliffe, 'Foreign Bodies and the Early Royal Society of London. Part 1: Englishmen on Tour', *Canadian Journal of History*, vol. 33 (1998), pp. 357–85; J. Schleck, 'Forming Knowledge: Natural Philosophy and English Travel Writing', in J. A. Hayden, ed., *Travel Narratives, the New Science and Literary Discourse, 1659–1750* (2012), pp. 53–70; M. F. Walker, 'Francis Vernon, the Early Royal Society and the First English Encounter with Ancient Greek Architecture', *Architectural History*, vol. 56 (2016), pp. 39–40; L. Soo, 'The English in the Levant: Social Networks and the Study of Architecture', in O. Horsfall Turner, ed., *'The Mirror of Great Britain': National Identity in Seventeenth-Century British Architecture*, Proceedings of the 2010 Annual Symposium of the Society of Architectural Historians of Great Britain (2012), pp. 211–12 (on Turkish steel); Soo, 'The Architectural Setting of "Empire": The English Experience of Ottoman Spectacle in the Late 17th Century and its Consequences', in M. Keller and J. Irigoyen-Garcia, eds, *The Dialectics of Orientalism in Early Modern Europe* (2017), pp. 217–45.

3 K. Parker, ed., *Early Modern Tales of Orient: A Critical Anthology* (1999), p. 13; G. MacLean and N. Matar, *Britain and the Islamic World, 1558–1713* (2011), esp. pp. 156–97.

4 J. Nieuhof, *Legatio batavica ad magnum Tartariae chamum Sungteium, modernum Sinae imperatorem* (1668); A. Kircher, *China Monumentis illust. & Fig. ornat.* (1667); see J. Rykwert, *The First Moderns* (1980), p. 65; Carey 1997, pp. 281, 283; L. Soo, 'The Study of China and Chinese Architecture in Restoration England', *Architectura: Zeitschrift für Geschichte der Baukunst*, vol. 31 (2001), pp. 169–84. The architect John Webb's *An Historical Essay Endeavoring a Probability that the Language of the Empire of China is the Primitive Language* (1669) was informed by the reports of Jesuit missionaries; see J. Bold, *John Webb:*

Architectural Theory and Practice in the Seventeenth Century (1989). Hooke owned Webb's book, as well as many others on China including Alvaro Semedo's *History of China* (1655); 'English Books in Octavo', lot 108, p. 47, 'English Books in Folio', lot 14, p. 38: see www.hookesbooks.com/hookes-books-database/browse-bh-in-full (accessed 12 April 2019). Hooke also owned John Ogilby's translation of Nieuhof (1668) and his work on Japan (1670): see www.hookesbooks.com; he noted on 20 March 1673, Diary, p. 35: 'bought Ogylbys china for 12sh', and on 11 October 1673, p. 64: 'Received from Ogilby second part of china unbound'. Wren observed in a letter concerning the visit of Charles II to the Society in 1661 that 'the Chinese have their Compass swimming in Water instead of Circles'; Wren 1750, p. 59. Listed in the sale catalogue of Wren and his son's books is 'Histoire de la Chine' in octavo (Lot 4); see D. J. Watkin, ed., *Sale Catalogues of Libraries of Eminent Persons*, vol. 4: *Architects* (1972), 'Wren', pp. 135–91. The philosopher John Locke, in his catalogue of books describing voyages and travels, noted concerning China: 'many books of that empire have appeared writ by missioners, who have resided there many years'; catalogue in J. Locke, *The Works of John Locke*, vol. 9 (1824); see https://oll.libertyfund.org/titles/locke-the-works-of-john-locke-vol-9-letters-and-misc-works (accessed 12 April 2019).

5   See R. T. Gunther, ed., *Early Science in Oxford*, vol. 7 (1930), p. 592.

6   On Jones's library see V. Hart, *Inigo Jones: The Architect of Kings* (2011), pp. 32–6.

7   For Wren's library see Watkin 1972.

8   Martin Lister, *A Journey to Paris in the year 1698* (1699; Lot 160); Charles Patin, *Travels through Germany, Bohemia, Switzerland, Holland and other parts of Europe* (1696; Lot 157); Johann Jakob Scheuchzer, *Itinera Alpina tria* (1708, with dedication to the Royal Society; Lot 86); de la Combe de Vrigny, *Travels through Denmark and Some Parts of Germany* (1707; Lot 457).

9   Daniel Beeckman, *Voyage to and from the Island of Borneo in the East Indies* (1718; Lot 305); Acarete du Biscay, *Relation of Mr R. M's Voyage to Buenos Ayres* (1716; Lot 157); Willem Bosman, *A New and Accurate Description of the Coast of Guinea* (1705; Lot 209); Edward Cook, *A Voyage to the South Sea and round the World* (1712; Lot 452); Baudelot de Dairval, *De l'utilité des Voyages* (1696; Lot 320); William Dampier, A *Voyage to New Holland…Wherein are described, the Canary-Islands, the Isles of Mayo and St Jago. The Bay of All Saints, with the forts and town of Bahia in Brasil* (1699; Lot 439); Amédée-François Frézier, *A Voyage to the South Seas, and Along the Coasts of Chili and Peru* (1717; Lot 238); François Leguat, *A new voyage to the East Indies* (1708; Lot 452); Hiob Ludolf, *Historia Aethiopica* (1681; Lot 419); John Ogilby, *Africa: Being an Accurate Description of the Regions of Aegypt, Barbary, Lybia, and Billedulgerid, the Land of Negroes, Gunee, Aethiopia and the Abyssines* (1679 edn; Lot 539); John Oldmixon, *The British Empire in America* (1708; Lot 458); du Perier, *A general history of all voyages and travels throughout the old and new world, from the first ages to this present time* (probably the English edition published in 1708; Lot 207); Charles-Jacques Poncet, *A Voyage to Ethiopia made in the years 1698, 1699, and 1700* (1709; Lot 439); Woodes Rogers, *A Cruising Voyage Round the World: First to the South-Seas, Thence to the East-Indies, and Homewards by the Cape of Good Hope* (1712; Lot 309). Wren owned two copies of *The Agreement of the Customs of the East-Indians with those of the Jews, and other ancient people* (1705; Lots 59 and 198) trans. John Toland from de la Créquinière's French original of 1704; this included discussion of Indian and Mogul customs, the ancient reports of which were corrected through de la Créquinière's first-hand experience.

10 Sandys, *Travels containing a history of the original and present state of the Turkish Empire* (1670 edn; Lot 109); Spon, *Voyage d'Italie, de Dalmatie, du Grèce, et du Levant, fait aux annés 1675 & 1676. Par Jacob Spon & George Wheler* (1679 edn; Lot 318); Wheler, *A Journey into Greece by George Wheler, Esq., in Company of Dr Spon of Lyons in Six Books* (1682; Lot 114); Chardin, *Journal du Voyage du Chevalier Chardin en Perse et aux Indes Orientales* (1686; Lot 145); Thévenot, *The Travels of Monsieur de Thevenot into the Levant* (1687; Lot 143); Grelot (1683 and 1689 edns; Lots 207, 367); Hacke, *A Collection of Original Voyages…IV Mr. Roberts's Adventures among the corsairs of the Levant; his account of their way of living…with maps, draughts* (1699; Lot 207); de Bruyn (Le Brun), *Voyage to the Levant* (1702; Lot 140); Maundrell, *A Journey from Aleppo to Jerusalem at Easter* (1703; Lot 471); Lucas, *Voyage d'Italie dans la Grèce, l'Asie Mineure, la Macédoine et l'Afrique* (1712; Lot 319); Ferriol, *Explication des Cent Estampes qui Représentent différentes Nations du Levant* (1715; Lot 559); Tournefort, *Relation d'un Voyage du Levant* (1718; Lot 366). Note also *A collection of voyages undertaken by the Dutch East-India Company* (1703; Lot 455).

11 Hooke's library, Sandys ('English Books in Folio', lot 41, p. 39), Grelot ('Libri in Albiis, &c. in Duodecimo', lot 1, p. 56), Chardin ('Libri Latini, &c. in Duodecimo', lot 37, p. 33, and 'English Books in Folio', lot 44, p. 39), Thévenot ('Libri Latini, &c. in Quarto', lot 274, p. 14, and 'Libri Latini, &c. in Octavo', lot 38, p. 22) and see Hooke, Diary, p. 145, Blount ('English Books in Duodecimo', lot 19, p. 52), d'Alquié ('Libri Latini, &c. in Duodecimo', lot 36, p. 33). His persistent interest in Greece, Turkey and Syria in ancient times is shown by his purchase in 1693 of Philostratus the Elder's *Life of Apollonius Tyanaeus* (1680), in Hooke, Diary 2, p. 255 ('English Books in Folio', lot 126, p. 40); see www.hookesbooks.com.

12 Hooke, Diary, pp. 45, 138, 139; Monconys, *Journal des Voyages* was listed in his library: 'Libri Latini, &c. in Quarto', lot 30, p. 8; see www.hookesbooks.com.

13 Hooke, Diary 2, pp. 172, 174.
14 T. Fuller, *The Holy State and the Profane State* (1642), Book III, ch. 24, pp. 226–8.
15 Hooke, Diary 2, p. 262.
16 See Walker 2016, pp. 39–40; see also G. MacLean, *The Rise of Oriental Travel: English Visitors to the Ottoman Empire, 1580–1720* (2004), p. 52.
17 M. Hunter, *Science and Society in Restoration England* (1981), pp. 90–1; K. H. Ochs, 'The Royal Society of London's History of Trades Programme: An Early Episode in Applied Science', *Notes and Records of the Royal Society of London*, vol. 39 no. 2 (1985), pp. 129–58; see also Wren 1750, pp. 51–6.
18 P. Rycaut, *The Present State of the Ottoman Empire* (1667), p. 318; see n. 75 below.
19 J. Harvey, 'Coronary Flowers and their "Arabick" Background', in G. A. Russell, ed., *The 'Arabick' Interest of the Natural Philosophers in Seventeenth-Century England* (1994), p. 300. John Varney collected seeds and plants in Aleppo to send home for planting on his estates; see MacLean and Matar 2011, p. 101. On the use of Oriental flower motifs in ceramics see J. Sweetman, *The Oriental Obsession: Islamic Inspiration in British and American Art and Architecture 1500–1920* (1988), pp. 50–3.
20 J. Evelyn, *Directions for the Gardiner at Says Court*, ed. G. Keynes (1932), pp. 35–6; Harvey 1994, p. 300.
21 J. Evelyn, *The Diary of John Evelyn*, ed. E. S. de Beer (1959), p. 753.
22 See A. R. Hall and M. B. Hall, eds, *The Correspondence of Henry Oldenburg*, vol. 7 (1965), pp. 85–9; see also pp. 61–2, 141, 216–20, 239–42; these works appeared as F. Bernier, *The History of the Late Revolution of the Empire of the Great Mogul* (1671) and *A Continuation of the Memoires of Monsieur Bernier, Concerning the Empire of the Great Mogul* (1672).
23 Hall 1965, vol. 7, pp. 219–20; see also vol. 9, p. 340.
24 Ibid., vol. 7, p. 241 (perhaps Oldenburg singled out buildings in Persia because visiting there was more difficult than Turkey, although it is unclear if de Monceaux had actually travelled in the country).
25 See G. Meynell, 'André de Monceaux, F.R.S. 1670', *Notes and Records of the Royal Society in London*, vol. 47 no. 1 (1993), pp. 11–15.
26 'A Narrative of some Observations lately made by certain Missionaries in the *Upper Egypt*; communicated in a Letter written from *Cairo* the sixth of January 1670', *Philosophical Transactions*, 6 no. 71 (22 May 1671), pp. 2151–3. On the general interest of the Society in Egypt see Carey 1997, pp. 289–90.
27 [R. Huntington], 'A Letter from Dublin to the Publisher of these Tracts, concerning the Porphyry Pillars in Egypt', *Philosophical Transactions*, 14 no. 161 (20 July 1684), pp. 624–9; 'An Explanation of the Cutts of Two Porphyry Pillars in Ægypt', ibid., 15 no. 178 (December 1685), p. 1252 and pl. 1; J. M. Vansleb (Wansleben), *The Present State of Egypt; or, A new Relation of a late Voyage into that Kingdom* (1678).
28 Hooke's Kircher books on China: Kircher 1667 ('Libri Latini, &c. in Folio', lot 41, p. 2 and 'Libri Latini, &c. in Folio', lot 42, p. 2); Kircher, *Prodromus Coptus sive Aegyptianus* (1636; 'Libri Latini, &c. in Quarto', lot 308, p. 15). On Egypt see Hooke, Diary, p. 221. In January 1679 and in May 1689 he purchased Wansleben's *The present state of Egypt, or, A new relation of a late voyage into that kingdom performed in the years 1672 and 1673*, the 1678 edition of which is also recorded in his library: Hooke, Diary, p. 394; Diary 2, p. 125, 'English Books in Octavo', lot 72, p. 46; see www.hookesbooks.com.
29 Hooke, Diary, p. 286; Diary 2, p. 188. On 28 January 1688 he borrowed and read a book entitled *Sphynx*; Diary 2, p. 87 and see p. 88.
30 See Carey 1997, pp. 278–9.
31 Ochs 1985, p. 134.
32 S. Kusukawa, 'Picturing Knowledge in the Early Royal Society: The Examples of Richard Waller and Henry Hunt', *Notes and Records: The Royal Society Journal of the History of Science* (2011); see http://rsnr.royalsocietypublishing.org/content/early/2011/05/10/rsnr.2010.0094#xref-fn-19-1 (accessed 12 April 2019).
33 [H. Oldenburg], 'A Preface to the Seventh Year of these Tracts', *Philosophical Transactions*, 6 no. 69 (25 March 1671), pp. 2087–92; see also Ch. One.
34 L. Soo, *Wren's 'Tracts' on Architecture and Other Writings* (1998), p. 190.
35 Hooke, Diary, p. 77; for Hooke's 1673 edition of Wyche see www.hookesbooks.com/wp-content/themes/hookesbooks/searchresults.php (accessed 12 April 2019).
36 J. Lobo, *A Short Relation of the River Nile, of its Source and Current, and of its overflowing the Campagnia of Egypt*, trans. P. Wyche (1669), [sig. A4r], Dedication to Henry Lord Arlington: 'The *Royal Society* commanded me to Translate them [the discourses], and ordered the Impression'; see Carey 1997, pp. 290–1.
37 Lobo 1669, Dedication, [sig. A4r].
38 Soo 1998, p. 190.
39 Wren also owned H. Noris, *Annus et Epochae Syromacedonum in Vetustis urbium Syriae Nummis praefertim Mediceis Expositae* (1696 edn; Lot 72).
40 Webb 1669, p. 190.
41 See J. Emerson, 'Sir John Chardin', *Encyclopaedia Iranica*, vol. 5 (1991), pp. 369–77; see www.iranicaonline.org/articles/chardin-sir-john (accessed 12 April 2019).
42 Hooke, Diary, p. 449.
43 R. Hooke, *Hooke Folio*, Royal Society, fol. 456; see Hooke Folio Online, www.livesandletters.ac.uk/cell/Hooke/hooke_folio.php?id=455&option=both (accessed 12 April 2019).
44 Evelyn 1959, pp. 689–90 (30 August 1680).
45 Hooke to O. Pulleyn, 9 August 1680; Chardin is mentioned

46 again in Hooke to Henri Justel, 10 August 1680: Gunther 1930, vol. 7, pp. 561, 562.
46 See Walker 2016, pp. 39–40.
47 Evelyn 1959, p. 690.
48 Ibid., pp. 595–6.
49 See M. Vickers, 'The Views of Persepolis by William Marshall and Wenceslaus Hollar in Sir Thomas Herbert's Travels', in H. Sancisi-Weerdenburg and J. W. Drijvers, eds, *Achaemenid History VII Through Travellers' Eyes* (1991), pp. 59–69; L. E. Semler, 'The Ruins of Persepolis: Grotesque Perception in Thomas Herbert's Travels', in L. E. Semler and E. Kelly, eds, *Word and Self Estranged in English Texts, 1550–1660* (2010), pp. 33–60.
50 Evelyn 1959, p. 690.
51 Ibid., pp. 763, 769.
52 J. Evelyn, *The Evelyn Library: Sold by Order of the Trustees of the Wills of J. H. C. Evelyn, deceased and Major Peter Evelyn, deceased*, vol. 1 (1977), no. 332, p. 98 (French edn, recording the inscription).
53 N. Matar, *Islam in Britain, 1558–1685* (1998), p. 3; J. Grogan, *The Persian Empire in English Renaissance Writing, 1549–1622* (2014). On the picture *A Woman in Persian Dress*, c.1600, attributed to Marcus Gheeraerts the Younger, at Hampton Court Palace, see Sweetman 1988, pp. 23, 27 and p. 30 for the interest by Charles I and William Laud in Persian manuscripts; see also MacLean and Matar 2011, p. 102.
54 T. Herbert, *Relation of some Yeares Travaile* (1634); see Parker 1999, pp. 195–220; Evelyn, *Evelyn Library*, vol. 2 (1977), no. 727, p. 95; Hooke's 1667 edn, 'English Books in Folio', lot 43, p. 39: see www.hookesbooks.com.
55 Herbert 1677 edn, p. 147; see Vickers 1991, pp. 59–69; Semler 2010, pp. 33–60.
56 See Sweetman 1988, pp. 28, 260 n. 34 (citing *Country Life*, vol. 132, 29 November 1962, pp. 1359–61). A reproduction hangs in the Merchant Adventurers' Hall, York.
57 S. Pepys, *The Diary of Samuel Pepys*, ed. H. B. Wheatley (1893): see www.pepysdiary.com/diary/1666/11/21 (accessed 12 April 2019); MacLean and Matar 2011, pp. 216, 221.
58 Evelyn 1959, p. 501.
59 Ibid. Evelyn, *Tyrannus, or the Mode* (1661), p. 29 (with vest and cloak praised but not identified as Persian).
60 On Persian miniatures and Charles II's vest, see J. Uglow, *A Gambling Man: Charles II and the Restoration* (2009), p. 399; see also E. S. de Beer, 'King Charles II's Own Fashion: An Episode in Anglo-French Relations 1666–1670', *Journal of the Warburg Institute*, vol. 2 (1938), pp. 105–15; D. de Marly, 'King Charles II's Own Fashion: The Theatrical Origins of the English Vest', *Journal of the Warburg and Courtauld Institutes*, vol. 37 (1974), pp. 378–82; A. Geczy, *Fashion and Orientalism: Dress, Textiles and Culture from the 17th to the 21st Century* (2013), pp. 31–3.
61 See S. Orgel, 'Inigo Jones's Persian Entertainment', *Art and Archaeology Research Papers*, vol. 2 (1972), pp. 59–69. Persian costume had been illustrated by Cesare Vecellio in his *Degli habiti antichi et moderni di diverse parti del mondo* (1590) and *Habiti antichi et moderni di tutto il mondo* (1598). On the Eastern influences in masques see Sweetman 1988, pp. 24–5. Later, Jones's pupil John Webb represented Persian captives as caryatids, in interpretation of the Persian colonnade mentioned by Vitruvius (I.i.6), in the courtyards to their jointly designed but unrealised Whitehall Palace scheme for Charles I of c.1638. See G. Worsley, *Inigo Jones and the European Classicist Tradition* (2007), pp. 168–99.
62 See Sweetman 1988, pp. 28–30.
63 See Parker 1999, pp. 61–82, and 106–27 for John Cartwright's *The Preachers Travels. Wherein is set downe a true Journall to the confines of the East Indies, through the great countreyes of Syria, Mesopotamia, Armenia, Media, Hircania and Parthia. With the Authors returne by the way of Persia, Susiana, Assiria, Chaldaea, and Arabia...Also a true relation of Sir Anthonie Sherleys Entertainment there* (1611).
64 Hooke, Diary 2, p. 87; 'Libri Latini, &c. in Folio', lot 160, p. 4; see www.hookesbooks.com.
65 Hooke's Chardin: 'English Books in Folio', lot 44, p. 39 and 'Libri Latini, &c. in Duodecimo', lot 37, p. 33; Olearius: 'English Books in Folio', lot 46, p. 39; Tavernier: 'English Books in Folio', lot 47, p. 39; Hooke also owned two volumes of John Fryer's *Travels into East India and Persia, with Figures* (1698): 'English Books in Folio', lot 45, p. 39 and 'English Books in Quires in Folio', lot 1, p. 56; and John Ogilby's *Asia or Description of Persia, &c. with Maps* (1673): 'English Books in Folio', lot 141, p. 41; see www.hookesbooks.com. On Tavernier see Sweetman 1988, p. 47.
66 'Observations concerning some of the most considerable parts of Asia', *Philosophical Transactions*, 11 no. 129 (20 November 1676), pp. 711–15.
67 Hooke, Diary, pp. 313, 346 (February 1678).
68 Hooke, Diary 2, pp. 72, 129.
69 Pepys 1893; see www.pepysdiary.com/diary/1663/09/22/ (accessed 12 April 2019). The Turkish army was eventually defeated at the gates of Vienna in 1683.
70 Hall 1965, vol. 11, p. 481. On this episode see G. Scholem, *Sabbatai Sevi: The Mystical Messiah, 1626–1676*, trans. R. J. Zwi Werblowsky (2016 edn), pp. 334–7. See also C. Littleton, 'Ancient Languages and New Science: The Levant in the Intellectual Life of Robert Boyle', in A. Hamilton, M. H. van den Boogert and B. Westerweel, eds, *The Republic of Letters and the Levant* (2005), pp. 151–72.
71 Hooke owned Nicolay's *Le Navigationi, &c. nella Turchia* (1576 edn), first published in French in 1567: 'Libri Latini, &c. in Quarto', lot 272, p. 14; see www.hookesbooks.com.
72 Francesco Sansovino produced two works on the Turkish empire, *Dell'Historia universale dell'origine, et impero de'Turchi* (1560) and *Gl'Annali overo le Vite de principi et signori della casa Othomana* (1570): F. Sansovino, *Sansovino's Venice*, trans. V. Hart and P. Hicks (2017), p. 16.

73 W. Biddulph, *The Travels of certaine Englishmen into Africa, Asia, Troy, Bythinia, Thracia, and to the Blacke Sea* (1609): see Parker 1999, pp. 83–105; J. Foxe, *Actes and Monuments* (1570 edn), Book 6, p. 895; H. Marsh, *A New Survey of the Turkish Empire and Government* (1633).

74 H. Blount, *A Voyage into the Levant…by way of…Egypt, unto Gran Cairo* (1636), p. 2. See MacLean 2004, pp. 51–114 on Biddulph, 115–76 on Blount. On these English early modern histories of the Turks, see Matar 1998, esp. p. 158. On the depiction of the Turk in Lodowick Carlell's *Osmond, the Great Turk* (1637–42) see Keller and Irigoyen-Garcia 2017, pp. 144–7.

75 See S. Anderson, *An English Consul in Turkey: Paul Rycaut at Smyrna, 1667–1678* (1996); Soo 2012, p. 213; T. Seccombe, 'Paul Rycaut', *Dictionary of National Biography*, ed. L. Stephen, vol. 50 (1885–1900), pp. 38–40, https://en.wikisource.org/wiki/Rycaut,_Paul_(DNB00) (accessed 12 April 2019).

76 Pepys 1893; see www.pepysdiary.com/diary/1667/05/03 (accessed 12 April 2019).

77 Hooke: 'English Books in Folio', lot 32, p. 39; Hooke also owned Prospero Alpini's *De Medicina Aegyptiorum* (1591), 'Libri Latini, &c. in Quarto', lot 220, p. 12; see www.hookesbooks.com; Alpini's work dealt primarily with Turkish medical practices observed during a three-year sojourn in Egypt. Evelyn, *Evelyn Library*, vol. 3 (1977), no. 1274, p. 128.

78 Evelyn 1959, p. 524.

79 A. C. Wood, *A History of the Levant Company* (1935); P. Lawson, *The East India Company: A History, 1600–1857* (1993); J. Mather, *Pashas: Traders and Travellers in the Islamic World* (2009); see also D. J. Vitkus, 'Trafficking with the Turk: English Travellers in the Ottoman Empire during the Early Seventeenth Century', in I. Kamps and J. Singh, eds, *Travel Knowledge: European 'Discoveries' in the Early Modern Period* (2001), pp. 41–2; Soo 2012, pp. 209–31.

80 Samuel Hartlib in 'The Hartlib Papers', Sheffield University, Digital Humanities Institute (1995), 43/33A; see www.dhi.ac.uk/hartlib (accessed 12 April 2019).

81 Henry Oldenburg to John Finch, 28 November 1672, in Hall 1965, vol. 9, p. 388. On Oldenburg and travel accounts see Carey 1997, p. 281. On John Finch's embassy see G. F. Abbott, *Under the Turk in Constantinople: A Record of Sir John Finch's Embassy, 1675–1681* (1920); MacLean and Matar 2011, pp. 112–21.

82 On the chaplains in general see J. B. Pearson, *A Biographical Sketch of the Chaplains to the Levant Company maintained at Constantinople, Aleppo and Smyrna 1611–1706* (1883).

83 H. Finch, *A narrative of the success of the voyage of the Rt. Hon. H. F.… his majesties Ambassadour Extraordinary to the…Sultan Mamet Han, emperour of Turkey, from Smyrna to Constantinople; his arrival there, the manner of his entertainment and audience with the Grand Visier and Grand Seignior* (1661). See C. Wylde, 'Charles Wylde's Journal of a Voyage from England unto the Straights, or Mediterranean Sea, being bound to Constantinople with Sir John Finch, Ambassador, and in his Majesty's ship, the Centurion, 1672/3, and back again, with colored draughts' (1672), British Library, Sloane MS 2439; see also D. Goffman, *Britons in the Ottoman Empire, 1642–1660* (1998); more generally see D. Banks and M. Frassetto, eds, *Western Views of Islam in Medieval and Early Modern Europe: Perception of Other* (1999).

84 MacLean and Matar 2011, pp. 79–123.

85 See J. Covel, 'Autograph Journal of Dr John Covel during his travels in Asia and Italy', British Library, Add. MS 22912, partly transcribed in J. T. Bent, ed., *Early Voyages and Travels in the Levant* (1893) and J.-P. Grèlois, ed., *Voyages en Turquie, 1675–1677* (1998). On Covel see MacLean and Matar 2011, pp. 113–14; on this festival see pp. 116–19; Soo 2017.

86 Soo 2017.

87 The excommunication of Elizabeth I by Pope Pius V in 1570 allowed her to act outside the papal edicts forbidding Christian trade with Muslims and create commercial and political alliances with various Islamic states, including the Moroccan Sa'adian dynasty, the Ottoman empire and the Shi'a Persian Empire; see MacLean and Matar 2011, pp. 42–78; see also L. Jardine and J. Brotton, *Global Interests: Renaissance Art between East and West* (2000); J. Brotton, *This Orient Isle: Elizabethan England and the Islamic World* (2016); N. Yildiz, 'Turkish Britons and Ottoman Turks in England during the Eighteenth Century', in M. Hüttler and H. E. Weidinger, eds, *Ottoman Empire and European Theatre: The Time of Joseph Haydn: From Sultan Mahmud I to Mahmud II (r.1730–1839)*, vol. 2 (2014), pp. 539–86. On trade with the East see P. Coles, *The Ottoman Impact on Europe* (1968); Sweetman 1988, pp. 11–14 on the trade in carpets, 40–1 in silk; L. Jardine, *Worldly Goods: A New History of the Renaissance* (1996); MacLean and Matar 2011, pp. 16–20, 68–71, 198–229.

88 S. Gilliat-Ray, *Muslims in Britain: An Introduction* (2010); J. Selwood, *Diversity and Difference in Early Modern London* (2010).

89 See Matar 1998, pp. 10–11; MacLean and Matar 2011, pp. 16–20, 68–71, 198–229.

90 According to John Aubrey, the first coffee house in London 'was in St. Michael's Alley, in Cornhill, opposite to the Church, which was sett up by one…Bowman (coachman to Mr. Hodges, a Turkey merchant, who putt him upon it) in or about the yeare 1652'; Aubrey, 'Life of Sir Henry Blount', in J. Walker, ed., *Letters Written by Eminent Persons in the Seventeenth and Eighteenth Centuries*, vol. 2 (1813), p. 244. See R. S. Hattox, *Coffee and Coffeehouses: The Origins of a Social Beverage in the Medieval Near East* (1985), pp. 38–40, 81–2; Matar 1998, pp. 110–19; S. A. Özkoçak, 'Coffeehouses: Rethinking the Public and Private

in Early Modern Istanbul', *Journal of Urban History*, vol. 33 no. 6 (2007), pp. 966–7. For the many coffee houses cited in Hooke, Diary, see pp. 463–70. See also A. Tinniswood, *His Invention so Fertile: A Life of Christopher Wren* (2001), p. 245.

91   Evelyn 1959, p. 229: 'There being at the time a ship bound for the Holy Land, I had now resolved to imbarke myself, intending to see Jerusalem, & other parts of Syria, Egypt, & Turky', but that the ship 'happnd to be press'd for the service of the State' which 'altogether frustrated my designe, to my greate sorrow'.

92   On William Lithgow see Parker 1999, pp. 149–74. On Blount and the dangers of travel see MacLean 2004, p. 164.

93   See A. Cohen, *Economic Life in Ottoman Jerusalem* (1986), p. 4; J. J. Moscrop, *Measuring Jerusalem: The Palestine Exploration Fund and British Interests in the Holy Land* (2000), p. 215.

94   On Aldersey see MacLean and Matar 2011, p. 171. A. Shirley, *Sir Antony Sherley His Relation of His Travels into Persia. The Dangers, and Distresses, which befell him* (1613), p. 9; see Parker 1999, pp. 61–82. J. Sanderson, *A Discourse of the most notable things of the famous Citie Constantinople: both in ancient and late time*, in Purchas 1625; Sanderson, *The travels of John Sanderson in the Levant, 1584–1602: with his autobiography and selections from his correspondence*, ed. W. Foster (1930), pp. 95–121. H. Timberlake, *A True and Strange Discourse on the Travailes of two English Pilgrims* (1603), repub. in *Two journeys to Jerusalem: Containing First, A Strange and True Account of the Travels of Two English Pilgrims* (1685).

95   Biddulph 1609, p. 127; on his visit to Jerusalem see MacLean 2004, pp. 100–14.

96   MacLean and Matar 2011, p. 180.

97   Rycaut quoted in T. Birch, *The History of the Royal Society of London, for Improving of Natural Knowledge*, vol. 2 (1756–7), p. 270.

98   Anderson 1996, pp. 210–11; MacLean and Matar 2011, pp. 101–2.

99   Soo 2012, p. 216.

100 Hooke, Diary, p. 220.

101 See Birch 1756–7, vol. 3, p. 357; Walker 2016, pp. 29–61; E. Mitsi, *Greece in Early English Travel Writing, 1596–1682* (2017), pp. 156–7.

102 'Mr. Francis Vernons Letter…giving a short account of some of his Observations in his Travels from Venice through Dalmatia…to Smyrna', *Philosophical Transactions*, vol. 11 no. 124 (24 April 1676), pp. 575–82; see Walker 2016, pp. 29–61.

103 Hooke, Diary, p. 292.

104 F. Vernon, 'Journal of Travels in the Eastern Mediterranean', Royal Society, London, MS 73; the opening letter dated July 15 1709 notes: 'found these papers among Dr Hooke's collections'; see G. le G. Norgate, 'Francis Vernon', *Dictionary of National Biography*, vol. 58 (1885–1900), pp. 273–4, https://en.wikisource.org/wiki/Vernon,_Francis_(DNB00) (accessed 12 April 2019); F. Henderson, 'Robert Hooke's Archive', *Script & Print: Bulletin of the Bibliographical Society of Australia and New Zealand*, 33, nos 1–4 (2009), p. 106; see www.bsanz.org/download/script-and-print/script_and_print_vol._33_nos._1-4_(2009)/SP_2009-Vol33-Nos1-4_pp92-108.pdf (accessed 12 April 2019); see also Walker 2016; Ch. One.

105 Hooke, Diary, pp. 321, 322, 324; see Henderson 2009, p. 106. Hooke took great pains to transcribe and sometimes translate correspondence and journals related to travel. He noted, Diary, p. 383, 2 November 1678, somewhat cryptically (apparently in reference to Syria): 'transcribed Ecl: C [Hooke's sign for the Moon or silver] from Mr. —— at Aleppo'. He also translated two letters by the Jesuit Father Ferdinand Verbiest describing the Chinese Emperor's travels in Tartary in 1682 and 1683, published in French; these translations were printed anonymously in *Philosophical Transactions* in 1686, and are now in London Metropolitan Archives, MS 01757, fols 82r–86v; *Philosophical Transactions*, 16 no. 180 (1 January 1687), pp. 39–51, 52–62; pp. 62–3, 'An Explanation, *necessary to justify the* Geography *supposed in these* Letters', is presumably also by Hooke.

106 For Hooke and Wren's discussions on Turkish culture, see e.g. Ch. Three.

107 Vernon, 'Journal', fols 31*v* (Odeon of Herodes Atticus), 34*v* (Propylaea and Erechtheion), 58*r* where he noted on 22 April 1676: 'walls of the Seraglio, lower fountains and Turkish inscriptions', as well as 'cushions' and a 'cloth of gold'; he also noted on 24 April a visit to 'Santa Sophia', and made brief descriptive notes.

108 'Hartlib Papers' 1995, 39/3/25A.

109 Evelyn 1959, p. 949 (6 January 1692). Attempts were made through Oldenburg to coordinate Seaman's project with a separate one in Holland, promoted by Comenius, allotting the Old Testament to the former and the New to the latter. Seaman's Turkish New Testament was published in 1666, but the Dutch-commissioned translation remained in manuscript for more than 150 years; see N. Malcolm, 'Comenius, Boyle, Oldenburg, and the Translation of the Bible into Turkish', *Church History and Religious Culture*, vol. 87 no. 3 (2007), pp. 327–62; H. L. Thomson, 'William Seaman', *Dictionary of National Biography*, vol. 51 (1885–1900), p. 163, https://en.wikisource.org/wiki/Seaman,_William_(DNB00) (accessed 12 April 2019); see also Matar 1998, p. 143. On Pocock see MacLean and Matar 2011, pp. 102, 160.

110 Thomas Sprat quoted in Wren 1750, p. 100. On other aspects of Ottoman culture criticised by English visitors see Soo 2017, p. 235.

111 The explanation of Wren's work on purely rational grounds is epitomised by Bennett 1982 and more recently A. Gerbino and S. Johnston, *Compass and Rule: Architecture as Mathematical Practice in England 1500–1750* (2009).

112 On the overlap between the old (occult) and the new (scientific) experiments into natural phenomena see W. Eamon, *Science and the Secrets of Nature: Books of Secrets in Medieval and Early Modern Culture* (1994). On esoteric interests see P. K. Monod, *Solomon's Secret Arts: The Occult in the Age of Enlightenment* (2013); also M. Bloch, *The Royal Touch: Sacred Monarchy and Scrofula in England and France* (1973); L. Principe, *The Aspiring Adept: Robert Boyle and his Alchemical Quest* (1998), pp. 181–213, esp. p. 187. See also C. Webster, *From Paracelsus to Newton: Magic and the Making of Modern Science* (1982); Webster, 'Christopher Wren', *Contemporary Physics*, vol. 26 no. 2 (1985), pp. 169–70 (review of Bennett 1982); A. Mendelsohn, 'Alchemy and Politics in England 1649–1665', *Past & Present*, no. 135 (1992), pp. 30–78; M. K. Schuchard, *Restoring the Temple of Vision: Cabalistic Freemasonry and Stuart Culture* (2002), esp. ch. 10, '"The Pleasant Theatre of Naturall Things", Rosicrucianism, Freemasonry, and the Royal Society (1660–1673)', pp. 595–668.

113 On the Eastern, especially Arab, origin of the hermetic tradition see Matar 1998, pp. 89–102.

114 See Webb 1669; J. A. Bennett and S. Mandelbrote, *The Garden, the Ark, the Tower, the Temple* (1998), pp. 114–18. Hooke discussed the 'Universall Language, of temporall promise in the old testament' on 14 December 1675, Diary, p. 200; on 23 July 1676 he notes: 'With Dr. Johnson about philosophers stone, about universal Language', p. 244. See also Ch. Two.

115 See Keller and Irigoyen-Garcia 2017, p. 205; see also Webster 1982.

116 See C. S. L. Davies, 'The Youth and Education of Christopher Wren', *English Historical Review*, vol. 123 no. 501 (2008), pp. 300–27. Anthony Wood, 'The Life of Anthony à Wood', in T. Hearne, ed., *Thomæ Caii… Vindiciae Antiquitatis Academiae Oxoniesnsis*, vol. 2 (1730), p. 559, recorded: 'the noted Chymist and Rosicrucian Peter Sthael, of Strasburgh, in Royal-Prussia, was brought to Oxford by the honourable Mr. Robert Boyle, An. 1659. Among the chiefest of his Scholars were Dr John Wallis, Mr. Christopher Wren, afterwards a Knight, and an eminent Virtuoso, with others of great Names in Physick and Learning'. Stahl founded a laboratory after his arrival in Oxford, holding at least five classes between 1660 and 1663 with Locke and Wren attending: see N. Tyacke, ed., *The History of the University of Oxford*, vol. 4: *Seventeenth-century Oxford* (1997), p. 432. Some of Wren's experiments listed in *Parentalia* (Wren 1750, p. 22), such as into speaking organs and perpetual motion, were among the norms of hermetic enquiry, as too his '*Chymical Furnaces*' mentioned in R. Plot, *The Natural History of Oxford-Shire* (1677), p. 231. Rykwert 1980, p. 211 n. 103 and p. 135, notes concerning Wren that, 'it is not often noticed that, like many of his contemporaries, he also had an interest in occult literature, particularly in alchemy and "natural magic"'.

117 Wren 1750, p. 28. For the Latin original see Wren, 'Oratio Inauguralis Habita Londini in Collegio Greshamensi': www.philological.bham.ac.uk/wren2/text.html (accessed 12 April 2019).

118 See F. Lenorman, *Chaldean Magic: Its Origins and Development* (1877); D. Levitin, *Ancient Wisdom in the Age of the New Science: Histories of Philosophy in England, c.1640–1700* (2016).

119 G. Vasari, *Vite de' più eccellenti architetti, pittori, et scultori italiani, da Cimabue insino a' tempi nostri* (1568 edn), preface; see *Lives of the most eminent painters, sculptors & architects, by Giorgio Vasari*, trans. G. du C. de Vere, vol. 1 (1912), https://ebooks.adelaide.edu.au/v/vasari/giorgio/lives/complete.html#preface3 (accessed 12 April 2019). Hooke borrowed Vasari from the Royal Society Library at Arundel House on 9 April 1673: Diary, p. 38.

120 R. Hooke, *Micrographia: or some Physiological Descriptions of Minute Bodies made by Magnifying Glasses* (1665), 'Preface', n.p., quoted in Wren 1750, p. 49.

121 Wren 1750, p. 26. See Vitruvius, *De Architectura*, Book IX, chs 2, 6, 8, trans. F. Granger, vol. 2 (1931), pp. 227, 245–7; p. 255: 'Berosus the Chaldaean is said to have invented the semicircular dial hollowed out of a square block and cut according to the latitude'. The Dial of Ahaz is mentioned in 2 Kings 20:5–11 and Isaiah 38:8.

122 See K. Thomas, *Religion and the Decline of Magic* (1971), pp. 151–3, 286, 768–9; M. Haeffner, *Dictionary of Alchemy: From Maria Prophetissa to Isaac Newton* (1991), p. 108.

123 'Hartlib Papers' 1995, 25/19/1A.

124 J. Aubrey, *Miscellanies: A Collection of Hermetick Philosophy* (1696), ch. 5, p. 52.

125 Wren 1750, p. 234. Wren was clearly familiar enough with Egyptian palm and dates to dream about them.

126 Ibid., p. 28.

127 On this astrological belief stemming from Egypt see V. Hart, *Art and Magic in the Court of the Stuarts* (1994), pp. 186–7.

128 Wren 1750, pp. 32–3.

129 Ashmole calculated a horoscope for the foundation of the Royal Exchange (designed by Edward Jarman), which was led by Charles II on 23 October 1667; see E. Conder, 'King Charles II at the Royal Exchange, London in 1667', *Ars Quatuor Coronatorum*, vol. 11 (1898), pp. 138–51. On Ashmole's interest in horoscopes see M. Hunter, *Science and the Shape of Orthodoxy: Intellectual Change in Late Seventeenth Century Britain* (1995), pp. 25–30. On 30 June 1696, Evelyn 1959, p. 1010, noted: 'I went with a select committee of the Commissioners for the fabri[c]k of Greenwich Hospital, & with Sir Chr: Wren the Surveyor, where with him I laied the first [corner] stone of that intended foundation; precisely at 5 a clock in the Evening after we had dined together: Mr. Flamsted the Kings Astronomical Profes[s]or observing the punctual time by Instruments'.

130 See J. M. Levine, *Between the Ancients and the Moderns:*

Baroque Culture in Restoration England (1999), on Wren pp. 161–209.
131 T. Sprat, *The History of the Royal Society of London, For the Improving of Natural Knowledge* (1667), p. 5.
132 Ibid., p. 6.
133 Oldenburg, 'A Preface to the Seventh Year' (25 March 1671), pp. 2087, 2092.

1 CLASSICAL ORDERS AND LANTERNS

1 L. Soo, *Wren's 'Tracts' on Architecture and Other Writings* (1998), pp. 157–8.
2 Wren's view of the history of classical architecture has largely escaped the detailed attention of commentators but see ibid., pp. 128–31; P. R. du Prey, *Hawksmoor's London Churches: Architecture and Theology* (2000), esp. pp. 10, 17.
3 See M. Whinney, *Wren* (1971), pp. 66–79; P. Jeffery, 'Originals or Apprentice Copies? Some recently found Drawings for St Paul's Cathedral, All Saints, Oxford and the City Churches', *Architectural History*, vol. 35 (1992), pp. 118–34; A. Geraghty, 'Nicholas Hawksmoor and the Wren City Church Steeples', *The Georgian Group Journal*, vol. 10 (2000), pp. 1–14. On Hawksmoor's steeples see V. Hart, *Nicholas Hawksmoor: Rebuilding Ancient Wonders* (2002).
4 Soo 1998, p. 157.
5 Ibid.
6 Hooke, Diary, p. 234.
7 See T. Birch, *The History of the Royal Society of London, for Improving of Natural Knowledge*, vol. 3 (1756–7), p. 357; M. F. Walker, 'Francis Vernon, the Early Royal Society and the First English Encounter with Ancient Greek Architecture', *Architectural History*, vol. 56 (2016), pp. 29–61, who gives a less likely explanation that the sketches in question were 'probably' two plans by Capuchin monks, but one of these was not brought out of the Levant until after 1685 and the other formed the basis for a plan in G. Guillet, *Athènes Ancienne et Nouvelle* (1675), which Hooke already owned (Diary, pp. 165, 167): this book had been discredited in Vernon's Royal Society letter (see the Introduction, n. 102). See J. R. Wheeler, 'Notes on the So-Called Capuchin Plans of Athens', *Harvard Studies in Classical Philology*, vol. 12 (1901), pp. 221–30; E. Mitsi, *Greece in Early English Travel Writing, 1596–1682* (2017), pp. 156–7.
8 Hooke, Diary, p. 217 (25 February 1676).
9 See the Introduction. On Vernon's detailed measurements of the Parthenon, e.g., in his Journal see Walker 2016.
10 Soo 1998, p. 173; on Flitcroft's engraving see pp. 14–15.
11 See Thomas Smith's life of Huntington in *Robert Huntingtoni...Epistole* (1704), trans. in *The Gentleman's Magazine*, vol. 95 (1825), pp. 11–15.
12 Soo 1998, p. 299 n. 102; see J. Rykwert, *The First Moderns* (1980), pp. 263–6; C. Knight, 'The Travels of the Rev. George Wheler (1650–1723)', *The Georgian Group Journal*, vol. 10 (2000), pp. 21–35; E. Mitsi, 'Travel, Memory and Authorship: George Wheler's "A Journey into Greece" (1682)', *Restoration: Studies in English Literary Culture, 1600–1700*, vol. 30 no. 1 (2006), pp. 15–29; Walker 2016, pp. 29–61; Mitsi 2017, esp. ch. 6, 'The Rediscovery of Athens in George Wheler's *Journey into Greece*', pp. 151–84.
13 J. Evelyn, *The Diary of John Evelyn*, ed. E. S. de Beer (1959), p. 762; see also p. 855 (24 October 1686), 'coming from his travels out of Greece, of which he has published a very learn'd & ingenious book...He is a very worthy, learned, ingenious, person, a little formal, and particular, but exceedingly devout.'
14 Soo 1998, p. 167.
15 On this need see M. Wilson Jones, *Origins of Classical Architecture* (2014).
16 Following Sebastiano Serlio in *Regole Generali di Architettura di Sebastiano Serlio Bolognese* (1537), Book 4, e.g. on the title-page and fol. III*v*: see S. Serlio, *Sebastiano Serlio on Architecture* [Books I–'VIII'], trans. V. Hart and P. Hicks, vol. 1 (1996), p. 254.
17 Soo 1998, p. 154.
18 Ibid., p. 169.
19 Ibid., p. 167.
20 See K. H. Dannenfeldt, 'The Renaissance and the Pre-Classical Civilizations', *Journal of the History of Ideas*, vol. 13 no. 4 (1952), pp. 435–40; Wilson Jones 2014.
21 L. B. Alberti, *On the Art of Building in Ten Books*, trans. J. Rykwert, N. Leach and R. Tavernor (1988), Book 6, ch. 3, p. 157.
22 W. B. Fleming, *The History of Tyre* (1915); M. Woolmer, *Ancient Phoenicia: An Introduction* (2011).
23 Wren 1750, p. 29.
24 Herodotus, *The Histories*, trans. A. de Selincourt (1954), Book 1.1–2.
25 Tyre is mentioned in Isaiah (23), Jeremiah (25:22, 47.4), Ezekiel (26–28), Joel (3.4–8), Amos (1.9–10) and the Psalms, and Zechariah (9.3–4) predicts its destruction.
26 Herodotus 1954, Book 2.44.
27 Josephus, *Jewish Antiquities*, trans. H. St. J. Thackeray et al., Loeb Classical Library, vol. 3 (1930–65), Book 8; see Fleming 1915.
28 Strabo, *The Geography of Strabo*, trans. H. L. Jones et al., Loeb Classical Library, vol. 7 (1928–32), Book 16, 2.23.
29 Strabo, *Rerum Geographicarum libri XVII Isaacus Casaubonus recensuit...Geographum* (1620).
30 Hooke, Diary, p. 453; 'Libri Latini, &c. in Folio', lot 63, p. 2, 'Libri Latini, &c. in Octavo', lot 58, p. 23; see www.hookesbooks.com/hookes-books-database/browse-bh-in-full (accessed 14 April 2019).
31 Hooke, 'Libri Latini, &c. in Octavo', lot 97, p. 24; see www.hookesbooks.com.
32 Hooke, 'Libri Latini, &c. in Octavo', lot 102, p. 24; see ibid.

33 J. Evelyn, *Navigation and Commerce, their Original and Progress containing a Succinct Account of Traffick in General: Its Benefits and Improvements* (1674), p. 26.

34 J. Twyne, *De Regus Albionicis, Britannicis atque Anglicis, commentariorum libri duo* (1590). See J. Ganim, *Medievalism and Orientalism: Three Essays on Literature, Architecture and Cultural Identity* (2005), p. 70.

35 'Britannia Antiqua Illustrata', *Philosophical Transactions* 11 no. 124 (24 April 1676), p. 596. Wren's son referred to 'Mr Samms' in Wren 1750, p. 168.

36 W. Stukeley, 'Stonehenge', [n.d.], Cardiff Central Library, MS 253, first leaf; see Soo 1998, p. 125 ('El Shaddai' is conventionally translated as God Almighty).

37 G. Wheler, *An Account of the Churches, or Places of Assembly, of the Primitive Christians…with a Seasonable Application* (1689), pp. 12–38 (plan on p. 12).

38 Wren would also have seen a reference to Eusebius and the history of Syria in Humphrey Prideaux's *Marmora Oxoniensa ex Arundellianis, Seldenianis, aliisque conflata* (1676; Lot 102); Eusebius, *Eusebius: The Church History*, trans. P. L. Maier (2007 edn). Evelyn owned two editions of Eusebius, 1544 and 1659: J. Evelyn, *The Evelyn Library: Sold by Order of the Trustees of the Wills of J. H. C. Evelyn, deceased and Major Peter Evelyn, deceased*, vol. 2 (1977), nos 549, 550, pp. 38–9.

39 Roger North, 'Cursory Notes of Building occasioned by the Repair, or rather Metamorfosis, of an old house in the Country', British Library, Add. MS 32540, fols 74v–80v: see R. North, *Of Building*, ed. H. Colvin and J. Newman (1981), p. 119.

40 R. North, *The Lives of the Right Hon. Francis North, Baron Guilford, The Hon. Sir Dudley North, and the Hon. and Rev. Dr. John North*, vol. 3 (1826 edn); G. MacLean and N. Matar, *Britain and the Islamic World, 1558–1713* (2011), p. 113.

41 North 1981, p. xvii; see North 1826, vol. 3, p. 208.

42 See A. Wragge-Morley, 'Restitution, Description and Knowledge in English Architecture and Natural Philosophy, 1650–1750', *Architectural Research Quarterly*, vol. 14 (2010), pp. 247–54.

43 Soo 1998, p. 168.

44 For Wren's interest in Solomon's Temple see Soo 1998, p. 123; du Prey 2000, pp. 42–5; R. Griffith-Jones, '"An Enrichment of Cherubims": Christopher Wren's Refurbishment of the Temple Church', in R. Griffith-Jones and D. Park, *The Temple Church in London: History, Architecture, Art* (2010), esp. pp. 160–4.

45 Soo 1998, p. 169, repeated in the 'Discourse', p. 191.

46 J. B. Villalpando, *In Ezechielem Explanationes et Apparatus Urbis ac Templi Hierosolymitani* (1596–1605); see J. A. Bennett and S. Mandelbrote, *The Garden, the Ark, the Tower, the Temple* (1998), pp. 140–2; S. Kravtsov, 'Juan Bautista Villalpando and Sacred Architecture in the Seventeenth Century', *Journal of the Society of Architectural Historians*, vol. 64 (2005), pp. 312–39.

47 Soo 1998, p. 169.

48 J. Evelyn, *A Parallel of the Ancient Architecture with the Modern* (1664 edn), pp. 63–6. On Wren's ownership of this edition see du Prey 2000, pp. 18, 148 n. 36 (letter from Evelyn to Wren, 4 April 1665).

49 Hooke, Diary, p. 209; 30 shillings was an appropriate price for the three volumes of Villalpando's work: for comparison see the prices in ibid., p. 253: 'Evelins *Parallel* 13sh'.

50 'The Hartlib Papers', Sheffield University, Digital Humanities Institute (1995), 29/3/8A; see www.dhi.ac.uk/hartlib (accessed 14 April 2019).

51 Evelyn 1664, p. 66.

52 Hooke, Diary, p. 179.

53 Hooke, Diary, pp. 210, 211 ('Faild saboth being begun').

54 C. Huygens to Wren, 7 October 1674; copy of the letter preserved in Koninklijke Bibliotheek, The Hague, MS KAXLVIII; see C. Huygens, *De Briefwisseling van Constantijn Huygens (1608–1687)*, ed. J. A. Worp, vol. 6 (1917), pp. 356–7 (no. 6954). Letters of introduction were also sent to Henry Bennet, 1st Earl of Arlington, and Oldenburg; see H. Rosenau, *Vision of the Temple: The Image of the Temple of Jerusalem in Judaism and Christianity* (1979), p. 141 n. 4; Soo 1998, p. 123; du Prey 2000, p. 19; M. K. Schuchard, *Restoring the Temple of Vision: Cabalistic Freemasonry and Stuart Culture* (2002), pp. 698–9, 704–5; Kravtsov 2005, p. 332; T. Morrison, 'Isaac Newton and the Architectural Models of Solomon's Temple', *Avello Publishing Journal*, vol. 1 no. 3 (2013), pp. 6–7.

55 Wren 1750, p. 212: All Souls College, Oxford, Wren Collection II.95; see A. Geraghty, *The Architectural Drawings of Sir Christopher Wren at All Souls College, Oxford: A Complete Catalogue* (2007), p. 195 no. 297. On this mausoleum see Ch. 4. Twisting, 'Solomonic' columns featured in an unexecuted design by Grinling Gibbons for a catafalque for Mary II at Westminster Abbey (c.1694): see All Souls, Wren Collection I.5, in Geraghty 2007, p. 279 no. 438. Wren used two such columns in a design for a reredos canopy to the altar at St Paul's, a design preserved in a timber model by Charles Hopson (c.1693; after the baldacchino by Bernini in St Peter's, Rome); see A. T. Bolton and H. D. Hendry, eds, *Wren Society Volumes*, vol. 13 (1924–43), pl. 27.

56 In evoking the image of the 'glorious Temple of *Salomon*', Bishop John King continued: 'This Church is your Sion indeed, others are but *Synagogues*, this your *Jerusalem the mother to them all*': J. King, *A Sermon at Paules Crosse, on behalf of Paules Church* (1620), pp. 19, 47; see J. Williams, *Great Britains SALOMON* (1625), pp. 25, 29.

57 On James I as Solomon see V. Hart, *Inigo Jones: The Architect of Kings* (2011), pp. 41, 46–8, 195–201; Charles II was sometimes compared to Solomon, especially at the time of the Restoration in 1660. The king was depicted as Solomon on the title-page to John Ogilby's *The Holy Bible…Illustrated w[i]th Chorographical Sculp[ture]s by*

58 *J. Ogilby* (1660). Charles II was compared to Solomon in an anonymous work, only identified by the initials R.H., entitled *New Atlantis, begun by the lord Verulam, viscount of St. Albans and continued by R.H. Esquire, wherein is set forth a platform of the monarchical government with a pleasant intermixture of divers rare inventions and wholesome customs, fit to be introduced into all kingdoms, states, and commonwealths* (1660).

58 E. Ashmole and F. Stanford, *The entire ceremonies of the coronations of His Majesty King Charles II. and of her Majesty Queen Mary, Consort to James II: As published by those learned heralds Ashmole and Sandford. With the prayers at full length. To which is prefix'd, an introduction historical and critical; likewise an appendix, containing many curious particulars* (1761), pp. 6, 13, 16.

59 On the consecration service see A. Tinniswood, *His Invention so Fertile: A Life of Christopher Wren* (2001), p. 315.

60 Martial, *De Spectaculis*, I: see www.thelatinlibrary.com/martial/mart.spec.shtml (accessed 14 April 2019). See also K. Jeppesen, *Paradeigmata: Three Mid-Fourth Century Main Works of Hellenic Architecture, Reconsidered* (1958), p. 10.

61 Soo 1998, p. 184; Pliny, *Natural History*, trans. H. Rackham, Loeb Classical Library (1938), Book 36, 4.30–2 (Pliny does not mention the Doric Order).

62 Soo 1998, p. 185.

63 Serlio 1537, Book 4, fol. XVIIr, in Serlio 1996, vol. 1, p. 281.

64 G. Sandys, *A relation of a Journey begun an: Dom: 1610. Foure bookes. Containing a description of the Turkish Empire, of Ægypt, of the Holy Land, of the remote parts of Italy, and ilands adjoining* (1615), Book III, p. 189.

65 See D. H. Brewer, 'Secret History and Allegory', in R. Bullard and R. Carnell, eds, *The Secret History in Literature, 1660–1820* (2017), pp. 60–73. Other, more minor, works had also drawn on the story, e.g. E. Settle, *Absalom Senior: or, Achitophel Transpros'd. A Poem* (1682); see also R. F. Jones, 'The Originality of Absalom and Achitophel', *Modern Language Notes*, vol. 46 no. 4 (1931), pp. 211–18.

66 Soo 1998, p. 169.

67 Ibid.

68 Ibid., p. 191.

69 F. Moryson, F., *An Itinerary* (1617), p. 224.

70 There was a possible confusion with another of Absalom's monuments, described by Josephus and 2 Samuel (18:17–18) as a commemorative pillar built of marble: Josephus 1930–65, vol. 3, Book 7, 241–3. See Soo 1998, p. 296 n. 88; M. F. Walker, *Architects and Intellectual Culture in Post-Restoration England* (2017), pp. 183–4.

71 I. Basire, *The Correspondence of Isaac Basire, D.D.*, ed. W. N. Darnell (1831), pp. 116–17; see N. Matar, *Islam in Britain, 1558–1685* (1998), pp. 164–5.

72 Evelyn 1959, p. 430.

73 Ibid., p. 447.

74 See J. Meggitt, 'George Robinson', in D. Thomas and J. Chesworth, eds, *Christian–Muslim Relations: A Bibliographical History*, vol. 8: *Northern and Eastern Europe, 1600–1700* (2016), pp. 392–401; D. J. Vitkus, 'Trafficking with the Turk: English Travellers in the Ottoman Empire during the Early Seventeenth Century', in I. Kamps and J. Singh, eds, *Travel Knowledge: European 'Discoveries' in the Early Modern Period* (2001), pp. 41–2; L. Soo, 'The English in the Levant: Social Networks and the Study of Architecture', in O. Horsfall Turner, ed., *'The Mirror of Great Britain': National Identity in Seventeenth-Century British Architecture*, Proceedings of the 2010 Annual Symposium of the Society of Architectural Historians of Great Britain (2012), pp. 209–31. On George Fox's praise for Quakers in Jerusalem see Matar 1998, p. 132.

75 Evelyn 1959, p. 580.

76 Smith 1704; 1825.

77 Sandys 1615, Book III, p. 189 (1670, p. 147). Absalom's tomb enjoyed some prominence through the publisher Nathaniel Crouch's compilation *Two Journeys to Jerusalem* [by Henry Timberlake in 1603] …*secondly, The travels of fourteen Englishmen in 1669 from Scanderoon to Tripoly, Joppa, Ramah, Jerusalem, Bethlehem, Jericho, the River Jordan, the Lake of Sodom and Gomorrah, and back again to Aleppo by T.B.; with the rare antiquities, monuments, and memorable places and things mentioned in holy Scripture; and an exact description of the old and new Jerusalem* (1st pub. 1683), p. 91: '*Absaloms* Pillar or Sepulchre, which is cut out of the Rock, and about the bigness of a small Chamber, with Pillars round about; like a Room built for some single Person: it is of a good Height, and hath some Carving about it'.

78 J. Aubrey, 'Monumenta Britannica', Bodleian Library, Oxford, MSS Top.Gen.c.24–25: see Aubrey, *Monumenta Britannica; or, A Miscellany of British antiquities*, ed. R. Legg et al., vol. 2 (1980–2), pp. 670–1.

79 Soo 1998, pp. 193, 194.

80 Herodotus 1954, Book 1.94.5–7; see P. Fane-Saunders, *Pliny the Elder and the Emergence of Renaissance Architecture* (2016), p. 392 n. 65.

81 Pliny 1938, Book 36: 'The Natural History of Stones', 19, Labyrinths, pp. 91ff, from Varro's *De novem disciplinis*, a lost work on the liberal arts.

82 Pliny 1938, Book 36, 19, Labyrinths, pp. 91ff.

83 Soo 1998, pp. 193–4.

84 Evelyn, *Evelyn Library*, vol. 2 (1977), no. 656, p. 68 (noting annotations); Hooke, Diary, p. 67 (and see n. 119 below); Greaves, 'English Books in Octavo', lot 89, p. 46; see www.hookesbooks.com.

85 Hooke's Pliny, 'Libri Latini, &c. in Quarto', lot 23, p. 8; 'Libri Latini, &c. in Folio', lot 131, p. 4; 'Libri Latini, &c. in Folio, lot 132, p. 4; 'English Books in Folio', lot 10, p. 38; see www.hookesbooks.com. Hooke mentions the purchase of Pliny in 1678 in his Diary, pp. 388, 390, and

86 Hooke, Diary, p. 320; see du Prey 2000, p. 15.
87 Hooke, Diary, p. 317.
88 This steeple type had been used e.g. in the medieval lantern spire on the Cathedral of St Nicholas in Newcastle (1448) and, less closely, on St Giles Cathedral in Edinburgh (1495) and on the chapel tower at King's College in Aberdeen (c.1508). On the 'imperial crown' see Soo 1998, p. 218. his restoration (presumably the binding) of the English edition (in 1688) in Hooke, Diary 2, p. 71; a five-vol. set is also mentioned (in 1689), p. 111.
89 Aubrey 1980–2, vol. 2, pp. 670–1, 674–5; see K. J. Williams, *The Antiquary: John Aubrey's Historical Scholarship* (2016), p. 89.
90 Hooke, Diary, pp. 320–1.
91 Birch 1756–7, vol. 4, p. 315.
92 Aubrey, 'Monumenta Britannica', [marked fol. 9br], in Aubrey 1980–2, vol. 2, p. 677; Aubrey added at the bottom: 'In ye E Indies such another Monument is mentioned in a Book, wch Mr R. Hook hath'.
93 Hooke, Diary, p. 322.
94 All Souls, Wren Collection II.91–95, in Geraghty 2007, pp. 193–5, nos 293–7; Hart 2002, pp. 51, 261 n. 66.
95 Hart 2002, p. 51. On Gibbons's design see n. 55 above.
96 D. J. Watkin, ed., *Sale Catalogues of Libraries of Eminent Persons*, vol. 4: *Architects* (1972), 'Hawksmoor', pp. 45–105, Lot 153; see Hart 2002, p. 51.
97 G. Webb, ed., 'The Letters and Drawings of Nicholas Hawksmoor relating to the Building of the Mausoleum at Castle Howard, 1726–1742', *Walpole Society*, vol. 19 (1930–1), p. 117, 3 September 1726. 'Mrs Hawksmoor's Bill', in K. Downes, *Hawksmoor* (1959), p. 223, App. C, p. 266.
98 Alberti 1988, Book 8, ch. 5, p. 257.
99 Soo 1998, p. 113.
100 See Ch. Three.
101 P. Jeffery, *The City Churches of Sir Christopher Wren* (1996), p. 141; All Souls, Wren Collection IV.88, in Geraghty 2007, p. 109, no. 154. A pineapple tops each of the two western towers at St Paul's.
102 All Souls, Wren Collection II.13, in Geraghty 2007, p. 62, no. 74.
103 Vitruvius, *Di Lucio Vitruvio Pollione De architectura libri dece traducti de latino in vulgare* (1521), fol. XXIIII*v*. The Tower of the Winds after Cesariano was a five-storey octagonal form. It was more accurately described and illustrated by Jacob Spon and then George Wheler in *A Journey into Greece by George Wheler, Esq., in Company of Dr Spon of Lyons in Six Books* (1682), Book V, pp. 395–7 (Lot 114). For Hawksmoor's drawing of St Bride's steeple see All Souls, Wren Collection IV.85–86, in Geraghty 2007, p. 110, no. 157. Hooke was also involved, noting on 2 October 1677, Diary, p. 316, 'to St Brides about measuring steeple'.
104 See Hart 2002, pp. 151–3.
105 See Hart 2011, pp. 82–4; E. B. Smith, *Architectural Symbolism of Imperial Rome and the Middle Ages* (1956), pp. 28–9; the pine cone in St Peter's is now in the Cortile della Pigna ('pinecone') in the Vatican: see Fane-Saunders 2016, p. 177. See also Vitruvius 1521, fol. LXIX*v*.
106 See Hart 2002, pp. 157–60.
107 On Hawksmoor as the designer of the steeple see S. Bradley and N. Pevsner, *The Buildings of England. London: The City Churches* (1998 edn), pp. 33–4, 117. On early drawings with variant designs for this steeple, possibly dated to *c*.1700, see Jeffery 1992, pp. 118–34; Jeffery suggests, p. 125, the towers in Rome of St Agnes in Agone and Bernini's bell towers on St Peter's, but these are square. The influence of Borromini's St Ivo della Sapienza in Rome is also possible: see Whinney 1971, p. 74.
108 G. B. Montano, *Li Cinque Libri di Architettura* (1691), Book III, no. 12 (a fanciful temple in Tivoli [of Vesta?]), no. 41 (an antique sepulchre); Book IV, nos 3, 23 (fanciful tabernacles).
109 H. Oldenburg to John Finch, 28 November 1672, in A. R. Hall and M. B. Hall, eds, *The Correspondence of Henry Oldenburg*, vol. 9 (1965), p. 340.
110 H. Maundrell, *Journey from Aleppo to Jerusalem at Easter, A.D. 1697* (1703), pp. 133–4.
111 J. Marot, *Le grand oeuvre d'architecture de Jean Marot* [*c*.1665: 'le Grand Marot'], who considered Baalbek to be 'en Grèce' perhaps because Syria had been part of the Hellenistic world.
112 Hawksmoor to Lord Carlisle, 3 October 1732, in Webb 1930–1, p. 136: 'Dr. Lisle told me he measur'd it [the Temple of Bacchus] so did Dr. Mandrell'; see Hart 2002, p. 39.
113 The Temple of Bacchus formed Hawksmoor's model for Oxford's University church in his ideal plan for the city drawn in 1713–14, about the time of the lantern design and the republication of Maundrell in that city. According to Stukeley, Hawksmoor went on to choose the portico of the temple as his model for that on St George, Bloomsbury, of 1716–31; see Hart 2002, pp. 47, 212.
114 Downes 1959, p. 219.
115 See Soo 1998, p. 217; Hart 2002, p. 52. See also the drawings by Edward Woodroofe for the lantern design at St Paul's, All Souls, Wren Collection II.26, II.28, in Geraghty 2007, p. 53, nos 57–8.
116 All Souls, Wren Collection IV.61–64, in Geraghty 2007, pp. 120–1, nos 175–8. Equally Wren's steeple at St Michael, Queenhithe of 1676–86 had a Halicarnassus-like stepped base, and closely resembled a monument in the *Hypnerotomachia Poliphili* of 1499 that was itself described as a rival to the seven ancient Wonders; see Hart 2002, p. 89.
117 St Dunstan-in-the-East's steeple replaced a leaded spire that had stood before the Fire; see Bradley and Pevsner 1998, p. 80. An early design is illustrated in Bolton and Hendry 1924–43, vol. 10, pl. 3. On St Dunstan-in-the-East see K. Downes, *The Architecture of Wren* (1982), p. 90; Soo 1998, p. 218.

118 On Hawksmoor's involvement see Jeffery 1996, p. 140; M. Cooper, *'A More Beautiful City': Robert Hooke and the Rebuilding of London after the Great Fire* (2003). Hooke was certainly involved with the building of the City churches and their steeples. Nearly all are mentioned in his Diary, those he visited most frequently being St Benet Fink, St Laurence, St Magnus, St Stephen Walbrook, St Anne & St Agnes and St Martin Ludgate. The entries are continuous and record him visiting with and without Wren, passing accounts and attending meetings of the parish councils; e.g. on 22 December 1673: 'agreed with Russell to take down St. Antholins Steeple to the water table'; on 22 June 1674: 'Ordered pulling down St. Bartholomew Tower'; on 28 July 1674: 'With Mr. Prig at Garaways from St. Martins Parish about Steeple, 5 Guineys'; on 29 April 1676: 'agreed with Marshall about St. Bride's Church Tower'; Diary, pp. 76, 109, 114, 158–9, 229, 393.

119 Hooke, Diary 2, pp. 257 (St Dunstan); 178–9, 190 (Pliny: see also the Preface n. 33 above); 186 (purchase of C. Saumaise, *Plinianae exercitationes*, 1689); 226 (Greaves).

120 Ibid., p. 234.

121 The old steeple of St Mary-le-Bow is illustrated in E. F. Sekler, *Wren and his Place in European Architecture* (1956), pl. 10b.

122 Soo 1998, p. 193.

123 See Fane-Saunders 2016, p. 293; see also pp. 282–3.

124 See Whinney 1971, p. 72. See also www.metmuseum.org/collection/the-collection-online/search/403672 (accessed 15 April 2019).

125 Fane-Saunders 2016, p. 255.

126 Soo 1998, p. 195.

127 Ibid.

128 Ibid., p. 187.

2 GOTHIC ARCHES AND TOWERS

1 K. Downes, *Hawksmoor* (1959), p. 27: 'Wren's remarks on gothic, in the opening of the *Discourse* and elsewhere, are disparaging'; P. Jeffery, *The City Churches of Sir Christopher Wren* (1996), p. 149: 'William Dickinson, who had a great deal more sympathy for the gothic style than either Wren or Hawksmoor'; L. Soo, *Wren's 'Tracts' on Architecture and Other Writings* (1998), p. 37: 'Generally he gives a negative appraisal of the style, although it is mild in comparison to those of some of his contemporaries.'

2 See R. Wittkower, *Gothic vs Classic: Architectural Projects in Seventeenth-Century Italy* (1974), pp. 18–20. Not all architectural theorists were hostile to Gothic. The style was used to promote Roman architectural principles by Cesare Cesariano in his Vitruvius of 1521 through illustrations of the yet to be completed Gothic Milan Cathedral, ordered through a grid of circles and triangles (illustrations republished in Ryff's Vitruvius of 1575, owned by Hooke); see Vitruvius, *Di Lucio Vitruvio Pollione De architectura libri dece traducti de latino in vulgare* (1521), fols XVr–v. See D. Hui, 'Ichnographia, Orthographia, Scaenographia: An Analysis of Cesare Cesariano's Illustration of Milan Cathedral in his Commentary of Vitruvius, 1521', *Knowledge and/or/of Experience: The Theory of Space in Art and Architecture* (1993), pp. 77–97; P. Fane-Saunders, *Pliny the Elder and the Emergence of Renaissance Architecture* (2016), 'Mixing Traditions', pp. 170–94. Gothic's virtues were also extolled by Jean-François Félibien in an appendix to an edition of Pliny the Younger's description of Roman villas (Paris, 1699, which Hawksmoor collected): see V. Hart, *Nicholas Hawksmoor: Rebuilding Ancient Wonders* (2002), pp. 63–4.

3 S. Serlio, *Il terzo libro di Sebastiano Serlio Bolognese* (1540), Book 3, p. VIII; see S. Serlio, *Sebastiano Serlio on Architecture*, [Books I–'VIII'], trans. V. Hart and P. Hicks, vol. 1 (1996), p. 102.

4 G. Vasari, *Vite de' più eccellenti architetti, pittori, et scultori italiani, da Cimabue insino a' tempi nostri* (1568 edn), preface; see *Lives of the most eminent painters, sculptors & architects, by Giorgio Vasari*, trans. G. du C. de Vere, vol. 1 (1912); see https://ebooks.adelaide.edu.au/v/vasari/giorgio/lives/complete.html (accessed 17 April 2019).

5 See F. Sansovino, *Sansovino's Venice*, trans. V. Hart and P. Hicks (2017), App. One, p. 234.

6 See S. Orgel and R. Strong, *Inigo Jones: The Theatre of the Stuart Court*, vol. 1 (1973), p. 160, ll. 40–1.

7 'The letter to Leo X by Raphael and Baldassare Castiglione', published in A. Palladio, *Palladio's Rome*, trans. V. Hart and P. Hicks (2006), App., p. 184. See E. Panofsky, *Renaissance and Renascences in Western Art* (1960), pp. 23–4; P. Draper, 'Islam and the West, the Early Use of the Pointed Arch Revisited', *Architectural History*, vol. 48 (2005), p. 2. William Stukeley, *Itinerarium Curiosum: Or, An Account of the Antiquities, and Remarkable Curiosities in Nature or Art, Observed in Travels through Great Britain* (1776 edn), p. 68, made this association on visiting Gloucester Cathedral: 'The Cloisters of this Cathedral are beautiful…Nothing could have ever made me so much in love with Gothic Architecture…the idea of it is taken from a walk of trees, whose branching heads are curiously imitated by the roof'.

8 H. Wotton, *The Elements of Architecture…collected from the Best Authors and Examples* (1624), p. 51.

9 J. Aubrey, 'Chronologia Architectonica', c.1671, in 'Monumenta Britannica', Bodleian Library, Oxford, MSS Top.Gen. c.25, fol 151r. See J. Ganim, *Medievalism and Orientalism: Three Essays on Literature, Architecture and Cultural Identity* (2005), p. 21; K. J. Williams, *The Antiquary: John Aubrey's Historical Scholarship* (2016).

10 J. Evelyn, 'An Account of Architects and Architecture', in *A Parallel of the Ancient Architecture with the Modern* (1707 edn), p. 9.

11　Ibid., p. 10.
12　Ibid.
13　See Soo 1998, p. 37; Hart 2002, p. 27.
14　See e.g. B. Fletcher, *A History of Architecture* (1975), pp. 1022–3; ch. 32, 'Renaissance Architecture in Britain', for the churches; J. Summerson, *Architecture in Britain 1530–1830* (1991 edn), churches in Part three, ch. 13, 'Wren and the Baroque (1660–1710)', pp. 187–202. A number of church schemes had porticoes but were not built: see an early scheme for St Clement Danes, in Jeffery 1996, p. 65, fig. 13, and an unbuilt scheme for a church in Lincoln's Inn Fields, in P. Jeffery, 'The Church that never was: Wren's St Mary, and Other Projects for Lincoln's Inn Fields', *Architectural History*, vol. 31 (1988), pp. 136–44.
15　A few free-standing antique towers did exist, such as the Roman tomb of the Julii at Saint-Rémy in Provence to which Hawksmoor turned for his tower to All Saints, Oxford (*c.*1713–20); see Hart 2002, pp. 157–9. And further east, the eleventh-century minaret of the Great Mosque in Aleppo was a square structure with a mixture of columns and Gothic (ogee) arches.
16　Wren's use of the term 'Saracen' for the Arab (which since the Crusades had included the Turk) was unremarkable, because at that time it was the more common name for an Arab than terms of faith such as 'Islamic' or 'Muslim'; see N. Matar, *Islam in Britain, 1558–1685* (1998), pp. 155, 157; J. Brotton, *This Orient Isle: Elizabethan England and the Islamic World* (2016).
17　See J. Sweetman, *The Oriental Obsession: Islamic Inspiration in British and American Art and Architecture 1500–1920* (1988), p. 56.
18　Soo 1998, p. 50.
19　Ibid., p. 154.
20　Ibid., p. 155.
21　Ibid., pp. 54, 113.
22　Wren 1750, p. 178. A presentation drawing by Hawksmoor is at All Souls College, Oxford, Wren Collection II.49, in A. Geraghty, *The Architectural Drawings of Sir Christopher Wren at All Souls College, Oxford: A Complete Catalogue* (2007), p. 107, no. 151.
23　Spires in various forms were also used at St Benet Gracechurch of 1681–7 (possibly by Hooke, demolished in 1868), St Augustine Old Change of 1695–6 (probably by Hawksmoor), St Margaret Lothbury of 1698–1700, St Margaret Pattens of 1698–1702, St James Piccadilly of 1699 (by Wren's office or Edward Wilcox) and St Magnus the Martyr of 1703–6. St Mary-le-Bow of 1670–80, St Mildred Bread Street of 1681–7 (destroyed in 1941) and St Vedast Foster Lane of 1695–9 were all given less conventional obelisk-spires, while St Peter Cornhill of 1677–84 has a tower, cupola and obelisk-steeple.
24　Wren 1750, p. 177. Wren noted in a letter to the Church Commissioners in 1681, quoted in Jeffery 1996, p. 193: 'and the Tower also carried up from ye ground to the highth of the Church for ye Summe of £1850'.
25　See H. Colvin, 'The Church of St Mary Aldermary and its Rebuilding after the Great Fire of London', *Architectural History*, vol. 24 (1981), pp. 24–31; Jeffery 1996, p. 276.
26　Soo 1998, pp. 62–3.
27　Ibid., p. 84.
28　On the description by Wren's son of St Paul's visit to Britain see Soo 1998, p. 39. Joseph of Arimathea was also said to have visited England: see V. Hart, *Art and Magic in the Court of the Stuarts* (1994), pp. 50, 65.
29　On the survival of medieval practices and Gothic forms in the Stuart period see G. Addleshaw and F. Etchells, *The Architectural Setting of Anglican Worship* (1948); J. F. Merritt, 'Puritans, Laudians and the Phenomenon of Church-building in Jacobean London', *The Historical Journal*, vol. 41 (1998), pp. 935–60; P. Guillery, 'Suburban Models, or Calvinism and Continuity in London's Seventeenth-Century Church Architecture', *Architectural History*, vol. 48 (2005), pp. 69–106; M. Howard, *The Building of Elizabethan and Jacobean England* (2007), pp. 70–1, who cites e.g. the private chapel at Groombridge in Kent built by John Packer in 1625 (with pointed-arched tripartite lights).
30　On Laudian church architecture see P. Lake, 'The Laudian Style: Order, Uniformity and the Pursuit of the Beauty of Holiness in the 1630s', in K. Fincham, ed., *The Early Stuart Church 1603–1642* (1993), pp. 161–85; Guillery 2005, pp. 71–2.
31　See R. Sweet, *Antiquaries: The Discovery of the Past in Eighteenth-Century Britain* (2004) pp. 237–76; O. Horsfall Turner, 'Perceptions of Medieval Buildings in England, *c.*1640–*c.*1720', PhD thesis, University College London (2009).
32　Aubrey's 'Chronologia Architectonica' of *c.*1671 attempted to categorise different styles of medieval architecture through recording the evolving design of windows but he also undertook chorographic studies of county histories, which record his early interest in architecture; see O. Horsfall Turner, '"The Windows of This Church Are of Several Fashions": Architectural Form and Historical Method in John Aubrey's "Chronologia Architectonica"', *Architectural History*, vol. 54 (2011), pp. 171–93; Williams 2016, pp. 84–7. Stukeley wrote essays on the design and construction of Gothic architecture late in his life: see S. Piggott, *William Stukeley: An Eighteenth-Century Antiquary* (1985 edn). Willis was interested in church building as well as Church history and published a number of surveys of English and Welsh cathedrals.
33　Wren owned other key antiquarian studies, notably Aylett Sammes, *Britannia Antiqua Illustrata, or the Antiquities of Ancient Britain derived from the Phœnicians* (1676; Lot 287) and John Webb, *Vindication of Stone-Heng Restored* (1665; Lot 530). He also owned John Selden's 1623 edition of Eadmer's *Historia Novarum* (Lot 389), which included in

appendices information from the Domesday Book that was unpublished at the time and could only be consulted in the original at Westminster. As well as Dugdale's study of Warwickshire, Wren owned Charles Leigh, *The Natural History of Lancashire, Cheshire, and the Peak in Derbyshire* (1700; Lot 37); Robert Plot, *The Natural History of Oxford-Shire* (1677; Lot 105); Plot, *Natural History of Staffordshire* (1686; Lot 106).

34 Aubrey, 'Chronologia Architectonica', fol. 153r. See M. K. Schuchard, *Restoring the Temple of Vision: Cabalistic Freemasonry and Stuart Culture* (2002), p. 664.

35 On Jones's refacing of the nave and transepts at old St Paul's see V. Hart, *Inigo Jones: The Architect of Kings* (2011), pp. 211–25, Appendix I, pp. 240–6. At the Banqueting House, Whitehall, the proximity of the medieval Holbein gate and palace played no part in Jones's design. But the assimilation of medieval and classical architectural forms had found an important expression at the White Tower of the Tower of London ordered by Charles I in 1638: see G. Worsley, *Inigo Jones and the European Classicist Tradition* (2007), p. 159; A. Keay and R. Harris, 'The White Tower, 1485–1642', in E. Impey, ed., *The White Tower* (2008), pp. 176–7.

36 In the case of the Honywood Library (1674) at Lincoln Cathedral, which can (at least in part) be attributed to Wren, he chose a plain style of classicism with an arcade of eight Doric columns (which possibly he considered had some relationship with the original Romanesque building, still evident on the west front). The library formed a self-contained range on the north of the cloister. K. Downes, *The Architecture of Wren* (1982), p. 125 n. 159, considered that 'the London mason John Tompson was almost certainly responsible for the design'; see also D. N. Griffiths, *Lincoln Cathedral Library* (1970). However, the contract for the building works (between Dean Michael Honywood and a builder, William Evison) dated 2 June 1674 stated that the building was to be constructed 'according to Sir Christopher Wren's directions and Mr Tompson's modell', Lincolnshire Archives Office, Dean and Chapter Records (c iij 31/1/1).

37 See H. Colvin, *The History of the King's Works, 1660–1782*, vol. 5 (1976), p. 318; V. Hart, *Sir John Vanbrugh: Storyteller in Stone* (2008), p. 63, figs 95, 96.

38 See Wittkower 1974.

39 On decorum, esp. as developed by Serlio, see Hart 2002, pp. 167–8; Hart 2011, pp. 153–4.

40 Evelyn, 'Account of Architects and Architecture' 1664, p. 122; 1707, p. 45.

41 Wren to John Fell, 26 May 1681, in A. T. Bolton and H. P. Hendry, eds, *Wren Society Volumes*, vol. 5 (1924–43), p. 17; see W. Douglas-Caroë, *Tom Tower, Christ Church, Oxford: Some Letters of Christopher Wren to John Fell, Bishop of Oxford hitherto Unpublished* (1923); see also V. Fürst, *The Architecture of Sir Christopher Wren* (1956), p. 51; Soo 1998, pp. 218–19.

42 For a brief history of Christ Church see www.chch.ox.ac.uk/sites/default/files/Visitor_Information-gb.pdf (accessed 17 April 2019).

43 Wren 1750, p. 226.

44 Wren to Fell, 3 December 1681, in Douglas-Caroë 1923, p. 31; see also Fürst 1956, pp. 51, 193 n. 277.

45 Soo 1998, p. 159.

46 Ibid., p. 154.

47 Ibid. See J. Summerson, 'The Mind of Wren', in *Heavenly Mansions and Other Essays on Architecture* (1949), pp. 51–86; J. A. Bennett, 'Christopher Wren: The Natural Causes of Beauty', *Architectural History*, vol. 15 (1972), pp. 5–22; V. Hart, *St Paul's Cathedral: Sir Christopher Wren* (1995), pp. 10–13. For the idea that Wren took a more positive view of 'customary beauty' see J. Bikker, 'Re-reading Wren's Mind in Light of the Bookish Evidence', in P. R. du Prey, ed., *Architects, Books & Libraries: A Collection of Essays published in Conjunction with the Exhibition of the Same Name* (1995), pp. 16–23.

48 See M. Cranston, *John Locke, a Biography* (1957); J. M. Levine, *Between the Ancients and the Moderns: Baroque Culture in Restoration England* (1999), p. 168.

49 J. Locke, *An Essay Concerning Human Understanding*, ed. J. W. Yolton, vol. 1 (1965 edn), based on the expanded 5th edition of 1706; A. Geraghty, 'Nicholas Hawksmoor's Drawing Technique of the 1690s and John Locke's *Essay Concerning Human Understanding*', in H. Hills, ed., *Rethinking the Baroque* (2011), pp. 125–41.

50 Locke 1965, p. 109.

51 Ibid., p. 232. Wren's observation in the first Tract, Soo 1998, p. 155, that 'An Architect ought to be jealous of Novelties, in which Fancy blinds the judgment' resonated with Locke's comment, 1965, p. 123, on the role of fancy or imagination in the composition of ideas: 'For *wit* lying most in the assemblage of *ideas*, and putting those together with quickness and variety, wherein can be found any resemblance or congruity, thereby to make up pleasant pictures and agreeable visions in the fancy; *judgment*, on the contrary, lies quite on the other side, in separating carefully, one from another, ideas wherein can be found the least difference, thereby to avoid being misled by similitude, and by affinity to take one thing for another.'

52 Locke 1965, p. 167.

53 Hooke noted, Diary 2, June 1693, pp. 252, 253: 'To Sr C. Wren he viwed Abbey North Gable, approvd bricking up …I spake with Dr. Busby, B.[ishop] of Rochester and the Chapter. They desird a note from Sr Christ. Wren, signd by us both, about the Abby north end.'

54 Soo 1998, p. 90.

55 See W. Rodwell, *The Lantern Tower of Westminster Abbey 1060–2010* (2010), pp. 29–33.

56 Westminster Abbey Muniments (WAM) (P) 900; see also P. Binski, *Westminster Abbey and the Plantagenets* (1995),

57 Soo 1998, p. 91.
58 WAM (P) 907, 909; see Rodwell 2010, pp. 34–6.
59 Soo 1998, pp. 91–2.
60 Jeffery 1996, pp. 194, 239, 276; see also Colvin 1981.
61 See Hart 2002, pp. 57–64.
62 Downes 1959, p. 241, letter no. 58; see Hart 2002, pp. 79–80.
63 Downes 1959, p. 278, drawing no. 217.
64 Ibid., p. 256, letter no. 147.
65 See the account of Wren's views in M. Mateo, 'The Making of the Saracen Style: The Crusades and Medieval Architecture in the British Imagination of the 18th and 19th Centuries', in K. I. Semaan, ed., *The Crusades: Other Experiences, Alternate Perspectives. Selected Proceedings from the 32nd Annual CEMERS Conference* (2003), pp. 115–40; see also Mateo, 'In Search of the Gothic: Thomas Pitt's Travel in Spain in 1760', *Journal of Art Historiography*, vol. 15 (2016), pp. 1–21.
66 Wren 1750, p. 172.
67 Binski 1995, pp. 13–27.
68 Soo 1998, pp. 82–3.
69 Hooke, Diary, p. 141 (14 January 1675); for Magnus, 'English Books in Folio', lot 15, p. 38, see www.hookesbooks.com/hookes-books-database/browse-bh-in-full (accessed 17 April 2019).
70 Henry III in fact never joined a Crusade himself, unlike his son Edward I; see C. Tyerman, *England and the Crusades, 1095–1588* (1988).
71 Soo 1998, pp. 83, 85. Wren's 1525 edition of Froissart's *Chronicles* (Lot 265) contained an account of the later Crusades.
72 Wren 1750, p. 172.
73 See R. Hachili, 'The Niche and the Ark in Ancient Synagogues', *Bulletin of American School of Oriental Research*, vol. 222 (1976), pp. 43–53; see also Schuchard 2002, p. 47. On Islamic motifs woven into the texture of European Gothic see R. A. Jairazbhoy, *Oriental Influences in Western Art* (1965).
74 Draper 2005, pp. 6–7.
75 A. Stokes and J. Strzygowski, 'A Study in the Aesthetics and Historiography of Orientalism', *Art History*, vol. 26 no. 4 (2003), pp. 505–33.
76 See 'Arch' in J. Bloom and S. Blair, eds, *Grove Encyclopedia of Islamic Art & Architecture*, vol. 1 (2009), p. 67.
77 Also illustrated were the domes at Sultaniyeh which J. Chardin, *Travels into Persia and the East Indies, with Figures* (1686), p. 353, highlighted as 'beautiful *Duomo's*'.
78 See R. Willis, *Remarks on the Architecture of the Middle Ages, especially of Italy* (1835), p. 154; Jairazbhoy 1965; R. Sweet, *Cities and the Grand Tour: The British in Italy, c.1690–1820* (2012), p. 244. On its use in Venice, Deborah Howard in *Venice & the East: The Impact of the Islamic World on Venetian Architecture 1000–1500* (2000), p. 142, has observed that 'the intention behind the introduction of the ogee arch and its adoption as a trademark by the Venetian merchant class was to allude to a mental image of the Orient'; see also pp. 143–6. On the arabesque see Sweetman 1988, pp. 16–22.
79 Evelyn 1664, p. 137 noted, when defining the members of the classical entablature, 'the *Ovolo* or *Echinus* forms an *Ogee* by a turn under the *Planceere*'.
80 Perhaps the best-known were those added by Henry VIII to the White Tower in the Tower of London in 1530, but they could also be found on the turrets of country houses such as Wollaton Hall and Burghley House.
81 Hawksmoor's drawings of schemes for a new tower, nave and transepts to St Mary in Warwick, produced in Wren's office in c.1695–7, included ogee domes: see All Souls, Wren Collection IV.35–38, 42–46, in Geraghty 2007, pp. 111–17, nos 158–69. In one of these schemes, Tom Tower is recognisable as the inspiration for a crossing tower (IV.43, Geraghty, p. 114, no. 164). Wren also used this form of dome in his steeple to St Michael Crooked Lane of 1711–14; see Jeffery 1996, p. 308. And it was used in another gate design for an Oxford college, this time by Hawksmoor at All Souls in 1720; see Hart 2002, pp. 79–80, fig. 109.
82 See L. Slater, 'Imagining Places and Moralizing Space: Jerusalem at Medieval Westminster', *British Art Studies*, vol. 6 (2017); see http://britishartstudies.ac.uk/issues/issue-index/issue-6/moralizing-space (accessed 17 April 2019). Many of the medieval tombs in the Abbey were of Crusader knights, including Edmund 'Crouchback', William de Valence and Edward I.
83 F. W. D. Brie, ed., *The Brut or The Chronicle of England*, Early English Text Society, vol. 2 (1908), p. 372.
84 Inside the Temple Church these knights were celebrated through the tomb effigies in 'the Round', the last addition to which of c.1682 coincided with Wren's direct involvement with the church: see R. Griffith-Jones, '"An Enrichment of Cherubims": Christopher Wren's Refurbishment of the Temple Church', in R. Griffith-Jones and D. Park, *The Temple Church in London: History, Architecture, Art* (2010), App. II, p. 171.
85 See ibid., pp. 135–74.
86 See R. Krautheimer, *Early Christian and Byzantine Architecture* (1986 edn), pp. 60–3.
87 E. Ashmole, *The Institution, Laws & Ceremonies of the Most Noble Order of the Garter* (1672), pp. 20–1. Wren's father was the Register of the Garter, as well as Dean of Windsor, and Wren had moved there in 1636 when he was four. This experience too must have suggested links between Gothic buildings and the Crusaders; see L. Jardine, *On a Grander Scale: The Outstanding Career of Sir Christopher Wren* (2002), pp. 9–10; on Wren and the Garter see pp. 209, 478–9.
88 G. Sandys, *A relation of a Journey begun an: Dom: 1610. Foure bookes. Containing a description of the Turkish Empire, of Ægypt, of the Holy Land, of the remote parts of Italy, and ilands adjoining* (1615), p. 168.

89 F. Moryson, *An Itinerary* (1617), pp. 228–31; W. Biddulph, *The Travels of certaine Englishmen into Africa, Asia, Troy, Bythinia, Thracia, and to the Blacke Sea* (1609), pp. 127–8.

90 Evelyn 1707, pp. 10–11.

91 Four other circular churches of the twelfth century associated with the Knights Templar and Knights Hospitaller survive in England – those of the Holy Sepulchres at Cambridge and at Northampton, that at Little Maplestead in Essex and the chapel of Ludlow Castle. In Paris, the (rectangular) Sainte-Chapelle is thought to have been modelled on the Chapel of the Franks in the Holy Sepulchre in Jerusalem.

92 The twelfth–thirteenth-century Hospital of St John in Acre, built by Crusaders, has pointed arches: see J. Folda, *The Art of the Crusaders in the Holy Land, 1098–1187* (1995); Folda, *Crusader Art in the Holy Land: From the Third Crusade to the Fall of Acre, 1187–1291* (2005).

93 J. Rykwert, *The First Moderns* (1980), p. 134, observes that in the seventeenth century, chivalry and the crafts, masonry in particular, 'were still understood as secret societies, with roots in hoary traditions' and that 'the link between chivalry and masonry still seemed easy enough to establish'; see also pp. 135–6.

94 For medieval visions of the Temple in Gothic form see H. Rosenau, *Vision of the Temple: The Image of the Temple of Jerusalem in Judaism and Christianity* (1979), pp. 33–64; O. von Simson, *The Gothic Cathedral* (1956), p. 11. See also Nicolas de Lyre, *Postilla super totam Bibliam* (1471–2). The imaginary view of Jerusalem by Jakob Zeller from the early seventeenth century pictured a medley of Gothic and classical forms and even incorporated elements found in Regensburg Cathedral in Germany.

95 See J. A. Bennett and S. Mandelbrote, *The Garden, the Ark, the Tower, the Temple* (1998), p. 145; P. R. du Prey, *Hawksmoor's London Churches: Architecture and Theology* (2000), pp. 26–9.

96 Hooke's Lightfoot: 'English Books in Quarto', lot 45, p. 42; see www.hookesbooks.com.

97 Lightfoot, 'The Temple', in *The Works of the Reverend and Learned John Lightfoot*, vol. 1 (1684), p. 1065; see du Prey 2000, p. 29.

98 Hooke's Lee: 'English Books in Folio', lot 7, p. 38, see www.hookesbooks.com; Lee's Temple was an English vernacular version of the image of the Temple as an Italian Renaissance church complete with campanile that had appeared in a Polyglot Bible of 1572; see Rosenau 1979, pp. 94, 107; Bennett and Mandelbrote 1998, pp. 78, 134.

99 See Bennett and Mandelbrote 1998, pp. 146–8; du Prey 2000, pp. 127–8.

100 See also Hubert van Eyck's *The Three Marys at the Tomb* (c.1410–26; Museum Boijmans van Beuningen, Rotterdam), with its view of Jerusalem complete with a medieval castle.

101 J. de Sigüenza, *Segunda parte de la Historia de la Orden de San Geronimo* (1600); see Rykwert 1980, p. 222 n. 191.

102 F. Fénelon, *Dialogues sur l'Éloquence* (1718; 1st edn, 1717), Second Dialogue, p. 156. This dialogue dates back to 1679: see Mateo 2016, p. 9 n. 19. Other French authors who echoed this theory are Augustin Charles Davilier, 'Dictionnaire d'Architecture', in *Cours d'architecture* (1693); Florent Le Comte and Rowland Burdon, 'Sommaire historique d'Architecture et des architectes, dont les ouvrages ont le plus éclaté dans la France', *Cabinet des singularitez d'architecture, peinture, sculpture, et gravure*, vol. 1 (1699). See also P. Frankl, *The Gothic: Literary Sources and Interpretations through Eight Centuries* (1960), pp. 346, 376; Draper 2005, p. 3.

103 Evelyn 1707, pp. 9–10.

104 Downes 1959, p. 256, letter no. 147; see Hart 2002, pp. 58, 62.

105 The traditional English understanding of the Saracen was as the enemy of the Christian knight, not least of the most legendary of them all, King Arthur; see Thomas Malory, *Most ancient and famous history of the renowned prince Arthur King of Britaine: Wherein is declared his life and death, with all his glorious battailes against the Saxons, Saracens and pagans* (1634). On the distinction made by some between Arab (positive) and Saracen (negative) see Matar 1998, p. 155. On John Foxe see G. MacLean and N. Matar, *Britain and the Islamic World, 1558–1713* (2011), p. 27.

106 Biddulph 1609, 'Of the Arabians', pp. 69–71; see G. MacLean, *The Rise of Oriental Travel: English Visitors to the Ottoman Empire, 1580–1720* (2004), pp. 92–6.

107 On Wren's house see a report on the Saracen Head inn's demolition in *The Builder*, vol. 2 (1844), p. 71. On the Saracen's head sign see N. Yildiz, 'Turkish Britons and Ottoman Turks in England during the Eighteenth Century', in M. Hüttler and H. E. Weidinger, eds, *Ottoman Empire and European Theatre*, vol. 2 (2014), pp. 553–4. Pepys mentions visiting the Saracen's Head (on the north side of Snow Hill in Farringdon Ward Without) in his Diary on 11 November 1661: see S. Pepys, *The Diary of Samuel Pepys*, ed. H. B. Wheatley (1893), www.pepysdiary.com/diary/1661/11/11 (accessed 18 April 2019).

108 Wren 1750, p. 172.

109 Matar 1998, pp. 92–102; see also G. A. Russell, ed., *The 'Arabick' Interest of the Natural Philosophers in Seventeenth-Century England* (1994); G. J. Toomer, *Eastern Wisdom and Learning: The Study of Arabic in Seventeenth-Century England* (1996); D. Banks and M. Frassetto, eds, *Western Views of Islam in Medieval and Early Modern Europe: Perception of Other* (1999).

110 Hooke's Jabir: 'Libri Latini, &c. in Quarto', lot 230, p. 13; see www.hookesbooks.com. On Gerber see Matar 1998, pp. 88, 93; on the decline of the study of Arabic, with the decline in interest in esoteric subjects on the rise of Baconian science, see p. 118.

111 Ulugh Beg completed his astronomical tables, the *Zij al-Sultani* or *Zij-i Ulugh Beg*, in c.1441. Based largely on

observations carried out at his observatory in Samarkand, Uzbekistan, this work became the standard star table well into the following century. Sections from the *Zij-i Ulugh Beg* were translated by John Greaves (1602–1652) and Thomas Hyde (1636–1703) and printed at Oxford University Press in London in 1655.

112 J. Milton, 'Prolusion 7', in *Complete Prose Works of John Milton*, ed. D. M. Wolfe, vol. 1 (1953), p. 299. On Milton's condemnation of the Turks see Matar 1998, p. 104.

113 See A. Hamilton, *William Bedwell the Arabist 1563–1632* (1985); Toomer 1996; Matar 1998, esp. pp. 74–5, 77 (on Samuel Purchas's and Ephraim Pagitt's surveys of Muslim theology), 83–6; Brotton 2016; G. Astengo, 'The Rediscovery of Palmyra and its Dissemination in *Philosophical Transactions*', *Notes and Records: The Royal Society Journal of the History of Science* (16 March 2016); see http://rsnr.royalsocietypublishing.org/content/early/2016/03/12/rsnr.2015.0059 (accessed 17 April 2019).

114 Letter to Thomas Adams from the Heads of Houses (colleges?), 1632, in R. Bidwell, 'Middle Eastern Studies in British Universities', *British Society for Middle Eastern Studies*, vol. 1 no. 2 (1975), p. 84.

115 The first incumbent of the Chair at Oxford was Edward Pococke, a former chaplain in Aleppo (see the Introduction); see M. Feingold, 'Patrons and Professors: The Origins and Motives for the Endowment of University Chairs – in Particular the Laudian Professor of Arabic', in Russell 1994, pp. 109–27. Laud's Arabic manuscripts are now in the Bodleian Library, Oxford, GB 161 MSS Laud Or; see https://archiveshub.jisc.ac.uk/search/archives/f95d440c-5254-3338-9417-d1f290471378 (accessed 18 April 2019).

116 See J. R. Jacob, *Henry Stubbe, Radical Protestantism and the Early Enlightenment* (1983). William Beveridge's interest in the ancient languages of the East led to his *De linguarum orientalium, praesertim hebraicae, chaldaicae, syriacae, arabicae, & samaritanae praestantia… & utilitate* (1658; 2nd edn 1664).

117 J. Evelyn, *The Diary of John Evelyn*, ed. E. S. de Beer (1959), p. 423.

118 Hooke, Diary 2, p. 234; p. 151, 24 September 1689: 'Receivd from Capn. Knox 2 books: one in Arabic, another in Malabaric characters'; Diary, pp. 109, 112, 347, 10 July 1674: 'Sent by Harry the arabick manuscript for Mr. Bernard' (previously borrowed from the Royal Society library at Arundel House on 29 June), adding on 5 March 1678: 'Arundell Library…[Dr Thomas] Gale took out thence two Arabick books for Mr. [Edward] Barnard'. These were probably works on astronomy, since Bernard was the Savilian Professor of Astronomy at Oxford and was working on the Greek astronomer Apollonius of Perga (and, in the 1680s, an edition of Josephus).

119 On the library deposits of 1614 at the Escorial see O. Zhiri, 'A Captive Library Between Morocco and Spain', in M. Keller and J. Irigoyen-Garcia, eds, *The Dialectics of Orientalism in Early Modern Europe* (2017), pp. 17–31.

120 H. Oldenburg to S. Hartlib, July 1659, in 'The Hartlib Papers', Sheffield University, Digital Humanities Institute (1995), 39/3/25A; see www.dhi.ac.uk/hartlib (accessed 18 April 2019).

121 On Olearius see Keller and Irigoyen-Garcia 2017, pp. 51–66; on Hooke's ownership see the Introduction.

122 M. B. Hall, 'Arabick Learning in the Correspondence of the Royal Society', in Russell 1994, pp. 147–57.

123 Evelyn 1959, p. 297. Arabian tents were also discussed in A. Shirley, *Sir Antony Sherley His Relation of His Travels into Persia. The Dangers, and Distresses, which befell him* (1613), p. 12.

124 Rycaut in T. Birch, *The History of the Royal Society of London, for Improving of Natural Knowledge*, vol. 2 (1756–7), p. 268: 'Mummies are certainly found in the sands of Arabia, that is, the flesh of men dried and hardened by the sun, and driness of the sands.'

125 S. Ockley, *Conquest of Syria, Persia, and Egypt by the Saracens* (1708), p. 328.

126 S. Ockley, *An Account of South-West Barbary: containing what is most Remarkable in the Territories of the King of Fez and Morocco* (1713); Wren also owned a copy of Dominick Busnot, *The history of the reign of Muley Ismael: the present king of Morocco, Fez, Tafilet, Sous, &c.* (1714; Lot 156). On Ockley's work see MacLean and Matar 2011, p. 151. Tangier was an isolated foothold in Muslim territory that was ceded to the British in 1661 as part of Charles II's dowry from his Portuguese bride; see Matar 1998, p. 13. It was under constant threat of attack from the Moors and was finally evacuated in 1684 during which Pepys visited the city; see M. Lincoln, 'Samuel Pepys and Tangier, 1662–1684', *Huntington Library Quarterly*, vol. 77 no. 4 (2014), pp. 417–34.

127 Hooke, Diary 2, pp. 389, 393.

128 A. du Ryer, trans., *L'Alcoran de Mahomet* (1649 edn); Hooke's: 'Libri Latini, &c. in Duodecimo', lot 13, p. 32; 'English Books in Octavo', lot 22, p. 45; see www.hookesbooks.com. On Ross's translation see Matar 1998, pp. 73, 76–9; on the Koran in England see ch. 3, pp. 73–119; MacLean and Matar 2011, pp. 34–7.

129 Soo 1998, p. 83.

130 Ibid.

131 Ibid., p. 154. All Souls, Wren Collection II.60, in Geraghty 2007, p. 55, no. 61.

132 Wren 1750, p. 173.

133 Sandys 1615, p. 31.

134 T. Herbert, *A Relation of Some Yeares Travaile: begunne anno 1626* (1677 edn), p. 129.

135 Wren 1750, p. 173.

136 Ibid.

137 Ibid.

138 Soo 1998, p. 162.

139 Ibid., p. 166.
140 Given that the content of Wren's Tracts reflected much Masonic teaching on the importance of geometry and Eastern archetypes, most notably Solomon's Temple, it has even been proposed that they were designed as lectures to Masonic meetings; see Schuchard 2002, p. 706.
141 Rykwert 1980, p. 135; Schuchard 2002. On early Masonry see D. Stevenson, *The Origins of Freemasonry: Scotland's Century 1590–1710* (1988). See also the account of Wren and Freemasonry and the East in Mateo 2003, pp. 115–40.
142 See Stevenson 1988, pp. 18–25.
143 The Halliwell Manuscript also known as the Regius Poem, 'Constituciones artis gemetrie secundum Euclyde: a poem on the craft of Masonry', British Library, MS Royal 17 A I.
144 Matthew Cooke Manuscript, dated slightly later than 1450, British Library, Add. MS 23198.
145 Schuchard 2002, p. 108.
146 The so-called 'Grand Lodge No. 1' of 25 December 1583 (the first of these *Charges* actually to bear a date), held in the library of the United Grand Lodge of England at Freemason's Hall, London.
147 J. Campbell, *Was Sir Christopher Wren a Mason?* (2011), p. 7, notes 'Wren knew or had worked with…Ashmole, Sir William Wilson, Mr William Grey, Mr Samuel Taylour, Mr Thomas Wise, Mr Thomas Shorthose, Mr Nicholas Young, Mr John Shorthose, Mr William Hamon, Mr John Thompson and Mr William Stanton'; Elias Ashmole's diary entry for 10 March 1682: 'About 5 p. m. I received a summons, to appear at a Lodge to be held the next day at Mason's Hall London…Accordingly I went, and about noon were admitted into the Fellowship of Free-Masons, Sir William Wilson, Knight, Captain Richard Borthwick, Mr. William Woodman, Mr. William Grey, Mr. Samuel Taylour, and Mr. William Wise. I was the Senior Fellow among them (it being 35 years since I was admitted)': see E. Ashmole, *The Diary and Will of Elias Ashmole*, ed. R. T. Gunther (1927), pp. 119–20.
148 Schuchard 2002, pp. 630, 667, 727.
149 Hooke, Diary, p. 45. See K. H. Ochs, 'The Royal Society of London's History of Trades Programme: An Early Episode in Applied Science', *Notes and Records of the Royal Society of London*, vol. 39 no. 2 (1985), p. 132.
150 See Stevenson 1988, p. 223; J. Hamill, *The History of Freemasonry* (1994), p. 41; Jardine 2002, pp. 468–70; Anderson even identified Wren as a Deputy Grand Master from as early as 1666: see Schuchard 2002, p. 654.
151 Campbell 2011, e.g. p. 19: notice of funeral in 1723, 'London. March 5, this evening the corpse of that Worthy Free Mason, Sir Christopher Wren, Knight, is to be interr'd in the church of St Paul's'.
152 J. Aubrey, 'Naturall Historie of Wiltshire', 1685, additional notes in Aubrey's hand 1691, Bodleian Library, MS Aubrey 2. fol. 72v. When the Royal Society ordered their clerk, B. G. Cramer, to produce a copy, Aubrey made many additions and emendations and he oversaw their inclusion into the new text. Aubrey was still active in the Society in 1691, the date of Cramer's copy, Royal Society archives, Misc. MS 92, fol. 277, repr. in B. Williamson and M. Baigent, 'Sir Christopher Wren and Freemasonry: New Evidence', *Ars Quatuor Coronatorum*, vol. 109 (1996), pp. 188–9; see Schuchard 2002, pp. 777–8.
153 Campbell 2011, p. 33: he concludes that there are plenty of suggestions that Wren belonged to this lodge, 'but we cannot say with any certainty that he was a member, or that he was a regular attendee or a keen mason, nor can we say that he was ever Master of this Lodge although he might have been'.
154 Wren 1750, p. 173.

3 GREEK CROSSES AND DOMES

1 P. Jeffery, *The City Churches of Sir Christopher Wren* (1996), pp. 121–6.
2 Drawing attributed to Wren from an extra-illustrated edition of Thomas Pennant, *Some Account of London*, vol. 4 (1825 edn, City of Westminster Archives Centre), p. 299. See P. Jeffery, 'The Church that never was: Wren's St Mary, and Other Projects for Lincoln's Inn Fields', *Architectural History*, vol. 31 (1988), pp. 136–44.
3 See V. Hart, *Inigo Jones: The Architect of Kings* (2011), p. 147.
4 M. Whinney, 'John Webb's Drawings for Whitehall Palace', *Walpole Society*, vol. 31 (1946), pp. 45–107. Ch. Two noted that in Elizabethan architecture, small onion-shaped cupolas (a three-dimensional version of the ogee arch) sometimes featured on the skyline.
5 S. Serlio, *Il terzo libro di Sebastiano Serlio Bolognese* (1540), Book 3, pp. XVIII–XXI; see Serlio, *Sebastiano Serlio on Architecture* [Books I–'VIII'], trans. V. Hart and P. Hicks, vol. 1 (1996), pp. 112–14.
6 Bramante's scheme for St Peter's as illustrated in Serlio 1540, p. XL; 1996, p. 130.
7 J. Evelyn, *The Diary of John Evelyn*, ed. E. S. de Beer (1959), p. 223.
8 Ibid., p. 494.
9 L. Soo, *Wren's 'Tracts' on Architecture and Other Writings* (1998), pp. 53–4.
10 See M. Whinney, *Wren* (1971), pp. 28–30; K. Downes, *The Architecture of Wren* (1982), pp. 9, 47.
11 On St Peter's as a model see Whinney 1971, p. 31.
12 Soo 1998, pp. 155–6.
13 Ibid., pp. 177–8.
14 A. Palladio, *I quattro libri dell'architettura* (1570), Book IV, chs VI–VII; see *The Four Books on Architecture*, trans. R. Tavernor and R. Schofield (1997), pp. 221–31. On Wren's interpretation of these two temples see C. van Eck, 'Understanding Roman Architecture from a Distance:

Sir Christopher Wren on the Temples of Peace and of Mars the Avenger', in A. Payne, ed., *The Companions to the History of Architecture*, vol. 1: *Renaissance and Baroque Architecture* (2017), pp. 498–523.

15 Soo 1998, p. 172.

16 Eusebius, *De vita Constantini*, Book 3, ch. 38, in Eusebius, *Life of Constantine*, trans. A. Cameron and S. G. Hall (1999), p. 136. See R. Krautheimer, *Early Christian and Byzantine Architecture* (1986 edn), pp. 61–3.

17 On decorum, esp. as developed by Serlio, see V. Hart, *Nicholas Hawksmoor: Rebuilding Ancient Wonders* (2002), pp. 167–8; Hart 2011, pp. 153–4.

18 Soo 1998, p. 178; see also van Eck 2017, pp. 498–523.

19 Wren 1750, pp. 137, 139.

20 Ibid., p. 153.

21 Soo 1998, p. 54.

22 E.g. the many-domed temple in Hartmann Schedel's 1493 woodcut of the Temple from the *Liber Cronicarum* ('Nuremberg Chronicle'): see A. Balfour, *Solomon's Temple: Myth, Conflict, and Faith* (2012), pp. 220–1 and fig. 8.2; see also H. Rosenau, *Vision of the Temple: The Image of the Temple of Jerusalem in Judaism and Christianity* (1979), pp. 65, 71.

23 J. A. Bennett and S. Mandelbrote, *The Garden, the Ark, the Tower, the Temple* (1998), pp. 189–91.

24 This dome of the Holy Sepulchre was rebuilt in the eleventh century; see Krautheimer 1986, pp. 60–3.

25 In fact Hagia Sophia was built by Justinian, clarified in Evelyn's later versions with the addition 'or rather, that at present, by the Emperor Justinian, (one Anthemius of Trales, and Isador the Miletan being the Architects)': see J. Evelyn, *The Miscellaneous Writings of John Evelyn, Esq.*, ed. W. Upcott (1825), p. 416.

26 J. Evelyn, 'An Account of Architects and Architecture', in *A Parallel of the Ancient Architecture with the Modern* (1664 edn), p. 140.

27 R. North, 'Cursory Notes of Building occasioned by the Repair, or rather Metamorfosis, of an old house in the Country', British Library Add. MS 32540, fols 31–36v; see R. North, *Of Building*, ed. H. Colvin and J. Newman (1981), pp. 113–14.

28 On English interest in the various Christian communities living in Islamic countries (including the Greek-speaking patriarchate of Constantinople) see G. MacLean and N. Matar, *Britain and the Islamic World, 1558–1713* (2011), pp. 158–74.

29 S. Purchas, *Hakluytus Posthumus, Purchas, his Pilgrimage*, vol. 1 (1625), p. 247. Hooke: 'English Books in Folio', lot 51, p. 39; see www.hookesbooks.com/hookes-books-database/browse-bh-in-full (accessed 26 April 2019).

30 E. Pagitt, *Christianography: or, the Description of the Multitude and Sundary sort of Christians in the World* (1674 edn), p. 57.

31 F. H. W. Sheppard, ed., *Survey of London: Volume 33 and 34, St Anne Soho* (1966); see *British History Online*, www.british-history.ac.uk/survey-london/vols33-4/pp278-287 (accessed 26 April 2019). On Turkish oppression of Christians in Constantinople following the fire of 1660 see M. D. Baer, 'The Great Fire of 1660 and the Islamization of Christian and Jewish Space in Istanbul', *International Journal of Middle East Studies*, vol. 36 no. 2 (2004), pp. 159–81.

32 See C. Knight, 'The Travels of the Rev. George Wheler (1650–1723)', *The Georgian Group Journal*, vol. 10 (2000), pp. 21–35; see also J. Rykwert, *The First Moderns* (1980), p. 266; P. M. Doll, *After the Primitive Christians* (1997); D. H. Smart, 'Primitive Christians: Baroque Architecture and Worship in Restoration London', PhD thesis, University of Toronto (1997); J. Loach, 'Anglicanism in London, Gallicanism in Paris, Primitivism in Both', in N. Jackson, ed., *Plus ça change…Architectural Interchange between France and Britain: Papers from the Annual Symposium of the Society of Architectural Historians of Great Britain* (1999), pp. 9–32; P. R. du Prey, *Hawksmoor's London Churches: Architecture and Theology* (2000), esp. p. 38; M. Delbeke and A. F. Morel, 'Metaphors in Action: Early Modern Church Buildings as Spaces of Knowledge', *Architectural History*, vol. 53 (2010), pp. 110–14; Doll, '"The Reverence of God's House": The Temple of Solomon and the Architectural Setting for the "Unbloody Sacrifice"', in Doll, ed., *Anglicanism and Orthodoxy 300 Years after the 'Greek College' in Oxford* (2006), pp. 193–224.

33 G. Wheler, *An Account of the Churches, or Places of Assembly, of the Primitive Christians…with a Seasonable Application* (1689), p. 55; see also p. 58; Eusebius, *De vita Constantini*, Book 4 chs 58–9; see Eusebius 1999, pp. 176–77; Procopius, *De aedificiis*, Book I, ch. 4, in Procopius, *Buildings, General Index to Procopius*, trans. H. B. Dewing, Loeb Classical Library, vol. 7 (1940), pp. 50–1.

34 Wheler 1689, p. 44; Eusebius, *De vita Constantini*, Book 3, ch. 38, in Eusebius 1999, p. 136; see also Krautheimer 1986, pp. 61–3.

35 See J. Wilkinson, *Jerusalem Pilgrims before the Crusades* (1977); P. Darby and D. Reynolds, 'Reassessing the "Jerusalem Pilgrims": The Case of Bede's De locis sanctis', *Bulletin for the Council for British Research in the Levant*, vol. 9 (2014), pp. 27–31.

36 G. Sandys, *A relation of a Journey begun an: Dom: 1610. Foure bookes. Containing a description of the Turkish Empire, of Ægypt, of the Holy Land, of the remote parts of Italy, and ilands adjoyning* (1615). On Sandys (and the edition owned by Hugh May) see S. Mussells, 'Architects, Travellers and the Revival of the Early Christian Basilica', in P. R. du Prey, ed., *Architects, Books & Libraries: A Collection of Essays published in Conjunction with the Exhibition of the Same Name* (1995), pp. 9–15.

37 See K. B. Moore, *The Architecture of the Christian Holy Land: Reception from Late Antiquity through the Renaissance* (2017), pp. 240–84.

38 F. Moryson, *An Itinerary* (1617), p. 231.
39 Hooke's Fuller: 'English Books in Folio', Lot 120, p. 40; see www.hookesbooks.com.
40 Hooke's Sandys: 'English Books in Folio', Lot 41, p. 39; see www.hookesbooks.com. See also J. Haynes, *The Humanist as Traveler: George Sandys's Relation of a Journey begun An. Dom. 1610* (1986).
41 Soo 1998, p. 153.
42 Ibid., p. 172.
43 T. Birch, *History of the Royal Society of London, for Improving of Natural Knowledge*, vol. 3 (1756–7), p. 337. The model is listed in the two inventories of the Repository made in the eighteenth century, described in the later one, Royal Society MS 417 [1765], item 34, as 'A Model of the holy sepulcher in wood, inlayed with Mother of pearl'.
44 There are seventeenth-century models of the Holy Sepulchre in the Museum of the Order of St John, London (nos LDOSJ:3033, LDOSJ:3034, LDOSJ:3035), the British Museum, London (no. 1983,0107.1), the Museum of Fine Arts, Boston (2019.91), and the collection at Burghley House (EWA08635). On the so-called 'Pearson model', brought to England in the seventeenth century by a merchant called 'Mr Ashby', see www.finch-and-co.co.uk/antiquities/d/the-pearson-model-of-the-church-of-the-holy-sepulchre-jerusalem/57378 (accessed 26 April 2019).
45 See Soo 1998, pp. 124, 132; du Prey 2000, pp. 42–6. See also L. Jardine, *On a Grander Scale: The Outstanding Career of Sir Christopher Wren* (2002), pp. 414–20 (based on du Prey).
46 H. Blount, *A Voyage into the Levant…by way of…Egypt, unto Gran Cairo* (1636), p. 26.
47 See e.g. Metropolitan Museum of Art, New York, 28.85.7a, b, www.metmuseum.org/toah/works-of-art/28.85.7a (accessed 26 April 2019).
48 On Lorck's panorama and other early images of Constantinople see N. Westbrook, K. R. Dark and R. van Meeuwen, 'Constructing Melchior Lorichs's "Panorama of Constantinople"', *Journal of the Society of Architectural Historians*, vol. 69 (2010), pp. 62–87. For Lorck's woodcut of the Suleimaniye mosque see http://germanhistorydocs.ghi-dc.org/sub_image.cfm?image_id=3352 (accessed 26 April 2019). On Lorck see R. D. Radway, 'Christians of Ottoman Europe in Sixteenth-Century Costume Books', in M. Keller and J. Irigoyen-Garcia, eds, *The Dialectics of Orientalism in Early Modern Europe* (2017), pp. 173–93.
49 See P. Ward-Jackson, 'Some Rare Drawings by Melchior Lorichs in the Collection of Mr. John Evelyn of Wotton and now at Stonor Park, Oxfordshire', *The Connoisseur*, vol. 135 (1955), pp. 83–93; now in the Royal Collection of Graphic Art, National Gallery of Denmark (SMK), Copenhagen (inv. no. KKS1966 14–18). Lorck served as a member of the Imperial embassy at the court of Sultan Suleiman I (r. 1520–66) from 1555 to 1559. He composed numerous studies of the architecture and the people of the Ottoman empire, which were later used as the basis for drawings and prints.
50 Pieter van den Keere's panorama was in the collection of the Swedish statesman Count Magnus Gabriel de la Gardie (1622–1686): see www.wdl.org/en/item/14391 (accessed 26 April 2019).
51 Trinity College Library, Cambridge, R.14.23; see also an album of *c.*1620 in the British Museum, London, 1928,0323,0.46.
52 See Baer 2004, pp. 159–81.
53 On the travellers to Turkey see D. Goffman, *Britons in the Ottoman Empire, 1642–1660* (1998); G. MacLean, *The Rise of Oriental Travel: English Visitors to the Ottoman Empire, 1580–1720* (2004); L. Soo, 'The Architectural Setting of "Empire": The English Experience of Ottoman Spectacle in the Late 17th Century and its Consequences', in Keller and Irigoyen-Garcia 2017, pp. 217–45. On Russian pilgrims see G. P. Majeska, *Russian Travelers to Constantinople in the Fourteenth and Fifteenth Centuries* (1984).
54 See H. G. Rawlinson, 'The Embassy of William Harborne to Constantinople, 1583–8', *Transactions of the Royal Historical Society*, vol. 5 (1922), pp. 1–27; Hooke's Hakluyt: 'English Books in Folio', lot 50, p. 39; see www.hookesbooks.com; see K. Parker, ed., *Early Modern Tales of Orient: A Critical Anthology* (1999), pp. 48–53.
55 H. Cavendish, 'Mr. Harrie Cavendish his Journey To and From Constantinople 1589, by Fox, His Servant', *Camden Miscellany of the Offices of the Royal Historical Society*, XVIII, 3rd series, ed. A. C. Wood, vol. 64 (1940), pp. 1–29; for R. Wragge, 'A Description of a Voiage to Constantinople' (1598) see Parker 1999, pp. 54–60.
56 T. Coryat, *Master Coryats Constantinopolitan Observations Abridged*; J. Sanderson, *A Discourse of the most notable things of the famous Citie Constantinople: both in ancient and late time*, both in Purchas 1625; see also Sanderson, *The travels of John Sanderson in the Levant, 1584–1602: with his autobiography and selections from his correspondence*, ed. W. Foster (1930); J. T. Bent, ed., *Early Voyages and Travels in the Levant: Part II, 'Extracts from the Diaries of Dr John Covel. 1670–1679'* (1893); R. Fedden, *English Travellers in the Near East* (1958).
57 W. Biddulph, *The Travels of certaine Englishmen into Africa, Asia, Troy, Bythinia, Thracia, and to the Blacke Sea* (1609), p. 17; see Parker 1999, pp. 83–105. On Biddulph see MacLean 2004, pp. 49–114.
58 Moryson 1617, pp. 260–7.
59 Blount 1636, pp. 24–6; see MacLean 2004, pp. 115–76; Parker 1999, pp. 128–48 (Moryson), 175–94 (Blount).
60 G. Wheler, *A Journey into Greece by George Wheler, Esq., in Company of Dr Spon of Lyons in Six Books* (1682), Book II, pp. 181–2.
61 Sandys 1615, p. 31.
62 Early Stuart works such as the Hebraist Joseph Mede's

Churches, that is, Appropriate Places for Christian worship both in and ever since the Apostles Times (1638) and the anonymous 'R.T.', *De templis, a treatise of temples wherein is discovered the ancient manner of building, consecrating, and adorning of churches* (1638) had sought a basis for Anglican practices in ancient times. The Laudians too studied textual sources both ancient and modern: see J. Newman, 'Laudian Literature and the Interpretation of Caroline Churches in London', in D. Howarth, ed., *Art and Patronage in the Caroline Courts: Essays in honour of Sir Oliver Millar* (1993), pp. 176–80; P. Guillery, 'Suburban Models, or Calvinism and Continuity in London's Seventeenth-Century Church Architecture', *Architectural History*, vol. 48 (2005), p. 71; du Prey 2000, pp. 31–5.

63 *De templis* 1638, pp. 45–6.
64 On the legend of Justinian's exclamation see G. Scheja, 'Hagia Sophia und Templum Salomonis', *Istanbuler Mitteilungen*, vol. 12 (1962), pp. 47–8; W. Rosen, *Justinian's Flea: Plague, Empire, and the Birth of Europe* (2007). See n. 25 above.
65 Wren 1750, p. 153.
66 Queen's University at Kingston, Ontario, pasted down at the back of a copy of Julien-David Leroy, *Histoire de la disposition et des formes différentes que les chrétiens ont données à leurs temples* (1764). First attributed to Wren by Kerry Downes in 1988 for the London bookseller Hugh Pagan: see Downes, 'Julien-David Leroy', *Hugh Pagan Limited: Catalogue No. 3* (1988), pp. 18–20; attribution repeated in Mussells 1995, pp. 14–15; du Prey 2000, pp. 42–5, 154 n. 88; Soo 2017, p. 240. But Jardine 2002, p. 551 n. 96, describes them as 'associated with Wren (possibly in Hawksmoor's hand)' following a reattribution by Geraghty.
67 Leroy's book has an inscription by Robert Mylne (Cathedral Surveyor from 1766) which recorded that the drawings had first been 'among some Drawings of Sr C:r Wren which were evidently *Studios* for St. Pauls, London'; see Mussells 1995, p. 14; du Prey 2000, pp. 42–3.
68 Hooke, Diary, p. 328.
69 See the Introduction, n. 90 above.
70 Soo 1998, p. 124; du Prey 2000, p. 154 n. 90; Soo, 'The English in the Levant: Social Networks and the Study of Architecture', in O. Horsfall Turner, ed., *'The Mirror of Great Britain': National Identity in Seventeenth-Century British Architecture, Proceedings of the 2010 Annual Symposium of the Society of Architectural Historians of Great Britain* (2012), pp. 213, 223, 226; A. Cadwallader, 'The Reverend Dr. John Luke and the Churches of Chonai', *Greek, Roman and Byzantine Studies*, vol. 48 (2008), pp. 326–8. On 1 January 1690 Hooke noted in his Diary, p. 176: 'Smith going for Smyrna' (Izmir), possibly referring to Thomas Smith.
71 T. Smith, *Syntagma de Druidum Moribus ac Institutis* (1664).
72 'Historical Observations Relating to Constantinople. By the Reverend and Learned Tho. Smith D.D. Fellow of Magd. Coll. Oxon, and of the Royal Society', *Philosophical Transactions*, 13 no. 152 (20 October 1683), pp. 335–46; 'An Account of the City of Prusa in Bithynia, and a Continuation of the Historical Observations Relating to Constantinople, by the Reverend and Learned Tho. Smith D.D. Fellow of Magd. Coll. Oxon. and of the Royal Society', *Philosophical Transactions*, 14 no. 155 (20 January 1684), pp. 431–54.
73 See R. Griffith-Jones, '"An Enrichment of Cherubims": Christopher Wren's Refurbishment of the Temple Church', in R. Griffith-Jones and D. Park, eds, *The Temple Church in London: History, Architecture, Art* (2010), pp. 157–8; Loach 1999, pp. 13–14.
74 Hooke, Diary, p. 384; 'Libri Latini, &c. in Octavo', lot 16, p. 22; see www.hookesbooks.com (*De Graecae ecclesiae hordierno statu epistola*, also published in Oxford in 1676).
75 Hooke too had contact with people who had lived in Constantinople. On 25 June 1680 he noted in his Diary, p. 447: 'Leonard an ingenious German mechanic servant to [Franciscus Mercurius] Van Helmont, the Butler who had lived 3 years in Constantinople'.
76 P. H. Osmond, *Isaac Barrow: His Life and Times* (1944); see also C. Webster, *The Great Instauration* (1975), p. 134; J. J. O'Connor and E. F. Robertson, 'Isaac Barrow' (1998), www-groups.dcs.st-and.ac.uk/history/Biographies/Barrow.html (accessed 18 April 2019).
77 Barrow quoted in Wren 1750, pp. 230–1.
78 Hooke mentions Barrow on frequent enough occasions in the early 1670s in his Diary, e.g. Diary, pp. 10 ('met Dr. Barrow'), 11 ('Dind…with Dr. Barrow'), 56, 58. See also D. McKitterick, *The Making of the Wren Library: Trinity College, Cambridge* (1995), p. 39.
79 As recorded in Hooke, Diary, p. 252.
80 All Souls College, Oxford, Wren Collection I.39, I.40–2, in A. Geraghty, *The Architectural Drawings of Sir Christopher Wren at All Souls College, Oxford: A Complete Catalogue* (2007), pp. 32–4, nos 23–6; see also Whinney 1971, p. 135; McKitterick 1995, pp. 32–3.
81 Evelyn 1959, p. 1001 (23 November 1695).
82 See the leather-bound volume with Arabic and Turkish vocabulary in Covel's hand, now in Westminster College, Cambridge. His *Some Account of the present Greek Church* finally appeared in 1722, with a plan of Hagia Sophia.
83 See J. Covel, 'Autograph Journal of Dr John Covel during his travels in Asia and Italy', British Library, Add. MS 22912 (Yeni Camii in Constantinople, fol. 118r; Selimiye in Adrianople, fol. 477v); partly transcribed in Bent 1893, and J.-P. Grèlois, ed., *Voyages en Turquie, 1675–1677* (1998); Soo 2012, pp. 213–29; Soo 2017, p. 240.
84 Covel, 'Autograph Journal', fol. 236r.
85 Ibid., fols 120r–123v; Soo 2012, p. 217.
86 Covel, 'Autograph Journal', fol. 266r.
87 R. North, *The Lives of the Right Hon. Francis North, Baron Guilford, The Hon. Sir Dudley North, and the Hon. and Rev.*

	Dr. John North, vol. 3 (1826 edn), pp. 40–1; see Soo 1998, p. 125.	100	Du Prey 2000, p. 44; see also Soo 1998, p. 124.
88	Covel, 'Autograph Journal', fol. 76r; Soo 2012, pp. 215, 217 (on two other plans of Constantinople owned by Covel, including one by Grelot).	101	Wren to unknown, 9 August 1681; see T. Thorpe, *Catalogue of a Most Interesting Series of Autograph Letters* (1836), p. 118, no. 1157; Sotheby sale, 25 January 1955, Lot 493, as quoted in K. Downes, *Hawksmoor* (1959), p. 29 n. 51 (the date incorrectly identified as 1680).
89	H. Finch, *A narrative of the success of the voyage of the Rt. Hon. H. F.… his majesties Ambassadour Extraordinary to the…Sultan Mamet Han, emperour of Turkey, from Smyrna to Constantinople; his arrival there, the manner of his entertainment and audience with the Grand Visier and Grand Seignior* (1661); see the Introduction.	102	R. Hooke, *Hooke Folio, Royal Society*, fol. 449; see Hooke Folio Online, www.livesandletters.ac.uk/cell/Hooke/hooke_index.php?ref=451&option=both (accessed 26 April 2019).
90	See T. Seccombe, 'Paul Rycaut', *Dictionary of National Biography*, ed. L. Stephen, vol. 50 (1885–1900), pp. 38–40; see https://en.wikisource.org/wiki/Rycaut,_Paul_(DNB00) (accessed 26 April 2019); S. Anderson, *An English Consul in Turkey: Paul Rycaut at Smyrna, 1667–1678* (1996); M. Birchwood, *Staging Islam in England: Drama and Culture, 1640–1685* (2007).	103	Soo 1998, p. 163; see also p. 294 n. 62.
		104	Ibid., p. 163.
		105	Procopius, *De aedificiis*, Book I, ch. 1, in Procopius 1940, p. 21.
		106	Ibid., ch. 4, p. 51.
		107	Du Prey 2000, p. 44.
		108	Soo 1998, p. 163.
91	Seccombe 1885–1900, p. 39; Anderson 1996, pp. 29–30.	109	See G. Necipoglu, *Architecture, Ceremonial, and Power: The Topkapi Palace in the Fifteenth and Sixteenth Centuries* (1991), pp. 3–4, 79–84.
92	Rycaut was the author of several early works on the Turks: *The Present State of the Ottoman Empire* (1667, with a 'particular description of the Seraglio', of which Hooke owned a 1668 edition), and *The History of the Turkish Empire from 1623 to 1677, containing the reigns of the last three emperors (Amurath IV–Mahomet IV)* (1680). Rycaut's work on the Greek Church was entitled *The Present State of the Greek and Armenian Churches, Anno Christi 1678* (1679; Hooke owned this edition). Hooke also owned Tavernier's *Six Voyages…Through Turkey into Persia*: see Introduction n. 65 above.	110	Hooke's Bon: 'English Books in Octavo', lot 71, p. 46; see www.hookesbooks.com.
		111	Soo 2012, p. 217.
		112	The second Tract must be post-1680 given its reliance on Grelot's book; see du Prey 2000, p. 154 n. 86. And the reference to St Paul's must post-date the final, revised design of c.1685–7. On the construction of St Paul's see K. Downes, *Sir Christopher Wren: The Design of St Paul's Cathedral* (1988), esp. p. 50, chronology.
93	G. J. Grelot, *Relation Nouvelle d'un Voyage de Constantinople enrichie de plans levés par l'auteur sur les lieux* (1680), p. 264: 'ils en ont pris le modele sur ceux qu'ils avoient enlevez aux Chrétiens…C'est pour ce sujet que toutes les Mosquées de Constantinople sont comme autant de copies tres-imparfaites de la belle Eglise de sainte Sophie.'	113	Saucer domes carry the thrust in all directions, rather than concentrating it in four as with cross-vaults. The Byzantine domes Wren cited, including at Hagia Sophia, cover square areas; rectangles such as at St Paul's are more problematic to cover because the semi-circular arches on the short sides will be smaller and lower than on the longer ones. K. Downes, 'Wren and the New Cathedral', in D. Keene, A. Burns and A. Saint, eds, *St Paul's: The Cathedral Church of London 604–2004* (2004), p. 206, notes: 'That is what happens in the aisles; in the main vaults Wren ingeniously adapted the system, making the clerestory lunettes tall half-ovals and thus as high as the semi-circular cross arches. Decorative spandrels link them to the saucer-domes and fill in the pendentives.'
94	J. Evelyn, *The Evelyn Library: Sold by Order of the Trustees of the Wills of J. H. C. Evelyn, deceased and Major Peter Evelyn, deceased*, vol. 2 (1977), no. 661, p. 69. The English octavo edition was reduced from the quarto of 1680, and used reworked versions of the original thirteen engraved plates. Perhaps for the benefit of clergymen, this edition contained a new part on the past and present state of the Greek Orthodox Church.		
95	Hooke's Grelot: 'Libri in Albiis, &c. in Duodecimo', lot 1, p. 56; see www.hookesbooks.com.	114	On Serlio's woodcut as a source for the dome of St Paul's see V. Hart, *St Paul's Cathedral: Sir Christopher Wren* (1995), pp. 22–3. Jardine 2002, p. 417, mis-describes Wren's section of Hagia Sophia as showing a 'double dome' construction.
96	See S. Lang, 'By Hawksmoor out of Gibbs', *Architectural Review*, vol. 105 (1949), pp. 186–7; Hart 2002, pp. 37–8.	
97	See Mussells 1995, p. 15; du Prey 2000, p. 43.	115	North 1826, vol. 3, pp. 41–2; see Soo 1998, p. 125; Jardine 2002, pp. 418–20; H. Caygill, 'Ottoman Baroque: The Limits of Style', in H. Hills, ed., *Rethinking the Baroque* (2011), p. 73.
98	On Grelot and Chardin see Soo 2012, p. 214.	
99	Hooke's Chardin: 'Libri Latini, &c. in Duodecimo', lot 37, p. 33; 'English Books in Folio', lot 44, p. 39; see www.hookesbooks.com; Hooke, Diary 2, pp. 78, 80 (here Chardin is italicised, indicating his book).	116	Hooke, Diary 2, p. 80.
		117	North 1826, vol. 3, p. 208; see Ch. One.
		118	Wren 1750, p. 123.

119 L. Allatius, *The Newer Temples of the Greeks*, ed. and trans. A. Cutler (1969); see A. Cutler, 'A Baroque Account of Byzantine Architecture: Leone Allacci's *De templis Graecorum recentioribus*', *Journal of the Society of Architectural Historians*, vol. 25 (1966), pp. 79–89; W. Beveridge, *Synodikon sive Pandectae Canonum SS. Apostolorum, et Conciliorum ab Ecclesia Graeca receptorum*, vol. 2 (1672), opp. p. 71 (Allatius cited in prologue, pp. xviii, xix); see du Prey 2000, pp. 34–5.

120 All Souls, Wren Collection I.101, I.7, in Geraghty 2007, pp. 254–6, nos 395, 396.

121 The narthex on Wren's small plan of St Paul's on the City plan (clearer on the revised version) was not Jones's portico repaired, as was the initial intention, because this portico had ten columns to the front, not six as shown here.

122 See G. Worsley, *Inigo Jones and the European Classicist Tradition* (2007), pp. 132–3.

123 L. Allatius, *De templis Graecorum recentioribus* (1645), Letter I, fols 5–6, in Cutler 1969, pp. 7–8; W. Cave, *Primitive Christianity: Or, The Religion of the Ancient Christians in the first ages of the Gospel in three parts* (1672), p. 138; Allatius is cited p. 140 and in a list of 'Late Writers' at the end, n.p.

124 See Whinney 1971, pp. 84–5; Downes 1982, pp. 52–3. On a copy of a lost drawing by Wren see Geraghty 2007, p. 49 n. 51.

125 Wren 1750, p. 137.

126 All Souls, Wren Collection II.60, in Geraghty 2007, p. 55, no. 61, note: 'The design has been convincingly traced to the following Roman precedents: to Santa Costanza for the ring of columns, and to the Baths of Constantine for the apsidal openings.'

127 Serlio 1540, pp. XVIII–XXI, in 1996, pp. 112–14; Palladio 1570, pp. 85–6, in 1997, pp. 297–8. Palladio, *Descritione de le chiese…in la città de Roma* (1554), p. 57, trans. V. Hart and P. Hicks, *Palladio's Rome* (2006), pp. 146–7, had also noted that 'Costanza was buried in the said church in an exceedingly beautiful porphyry tomb'.

128 All Souls, Wren Collection II.61–62, in Geraghty 2007, pp. 56–7, nos 62, 63.

129 Allatius's *De templis Graecorum recentioribus* is listed in J. Evelyn, *Evelyn Library*, vol. 1 (1977), no. 20, p. 12 (Cave's works are nos 319–21, pp. 94–5). It is listed at Oxford in the Bodleian Library at or before 1674: see T. Hyde, *Catalogus impressorum librorum Bibliothecae Bodlejanae in Academia Oxoniensi* (1674), p. 20; in Trinity College (R.2.4, with contemporary inscription recording the purchase with funds from Richard Rands, who had gifted money in 1640); at Cambridge in Trinity College (L.8.111[1], bequeathed by James Duport, Dean of Peterborough, who died in 1679); in Gonville and Caius College Library (M.25.14, in catalogue of 1679, so available at or before this date); Corpus Christi College, Parker Library (A.9.8, bookplate dated 1670).

130 Allatius 1645, Letter I, fols 7, 9 (vault), 21 (gallery); Letter II, fol. 4 (barrel-vault), in Allatius 1969, pp. 10 (vaulted space), 20–1 (gallery), 27 (barrel-vault); see Cutler 1966, p. 85: 'It is remarkable that both plans of the "newer temples" show only the single apse that characterised the post-Byzantine architecture of Chios and not the triple form common at Mistra and elsewhere in continental Greece.'

131 See du Prey 2000, pp. 34–5.

132 Jeffrey 1996, pp. 230–1; All Souls, Wren Collection II.54–7, in Geraghty 2007, pp. 101–2, nos 139–42. On this church plan, and a similar one of an unidentified church, both in the Bute collection, see du Prey 2000, pp. 72–3.

133 See Griffith-Jones 2010, pp. 159–60.

134 Ibid., p. 160; Eusebius, *Historia Ecclesiastica*, Book 10, ch. 4, 41, in Eusebius, *Eusebius: The Church History*, trans. P. L. Maier (2007 edn), pp. 310–32.

135 Griffith-Jones 2010, p. 160.

136 Cave 1672, pp. 137, 151; W. Beveridge, *A sermon concerning the excellency and usefulness of the Common-prayer. Preach'd by William Beveridge, D.D. (late Lord Bishop of St. Asaph) at the opening of the parish-church of St. Peter's Cornhill, London, the 27th of November, 1681* (1682); see du Prey 2000, pp. 32–6; Delbeke and Morel 2010, p. 112; C. Stevenson, *The City and the King: Architecture and Politics in Restoration London* (2013), pp. 280–1.

137 Allatius 1645, Letter I, fols 7, 11, in Allatius 1966, pp. 8, 13.

138 Cave 1672, pp. 141, 150; see Loach 1999, pp. 13–14.

139 Wheler 1689, pp. 37, 103.

140 Soo 1998, p. 113.

141 Wheler 1689, p. 27: 'the Platform must be an exact Square, with a great *Cupalo*, or *Dome* in the middle, sustained by four great Pilasters, as that of *Jovian* at *Corfu*; which to my best Remembrance hath but four *Pilasters* sustaining the *Cupalo*; and I think *Sancta Sophia*, at *Constantinople* hath no more'.

142 Procopius, *De aedificiis*, Book I, ch. 1, in Procopius 1940, pp. 19–21.

143 Wheler 1689, p. 57.

144 G. Addleshaw and F. Etchells, *The Architectural Setting of Anglican Worship* (1948).

145 C. Mango, *Byzantine Architecture* (1978), pp. 7, 35–46; Krautheimer 1986, esp. ch. 7, 'The Latin West', pp. 167–99.

146 For Byzantine 'cross-in-square' plans see Mango 1978, pp. 96, 104, 118, 184; Krautheimer 1986, p. 520.

147 See J. A. Bennett, *The Mathematical Sciences of Christopher Wren* (1982), p. 94.

148 See Jeffery 1996, pp. 112–16.

149 St Mary Abchurch (1681–6) and St Mildred Bread Street (1681–7, now destroyed) have internal domes carried on pendentives over square central areas. At St Mildred the internal dome was in plaster, with short barrel-vaults filling the east and west ends of the rectangular plan. The use of a dome in this case, despite its not filling the rectangular site, has proved puzzling but might be explained by the

dome's importance to Wren as an early Christian form. Jeffery 1996, p. 316, notes: 'The choice of a domed ceiling can hardly have been obvious for a rectangular building.' Jeffrey claims, pp. 121–3, figs 35, 36, that the original design for St Mary Abchurch was rectangular with a dome resting on four central columns and two to one side, but see All Souls, Wren Collection I.60, in Geraghty 2007, p. 87, no. 113 where the design is unidentified.

150 On the French Protestant church in the Savoy see Jeffery 1996, pp. 116, 349; on St Mary's in Lincoln's Inn Fields see P. Jeffery, 'The Church that never was: Wren's St Mary, and Other Projects for Lincoln's Inn Fields', *Architectural History*, vol. 31 (1988), pp. 136–44; Jeffery 1996, pp. 125–6, 348.

151 Jeffery 1996, p. 126. Wren also used small domes on corner abutments at the north-east façade of St Andrew in Holborn (1684–92) and the south-west (front) façade of St Clement Danes (1679–85).

152 Hooke, Diary, pp. 315, 441, notes on 25 September 1677, 'With Sir Ch. Wren to Paules. And St. Stephens, Walbrooke', and on 22 March 1680, 'At St. Stephens, Walbrook view'.

153 See Krautheimer 1986, p. 518; see e.g. in Greece the Katholikon of Daphni, within the Nea Moni of Chios and the Katholikon monastery of Hosios Loukas cited by Wheler (see fig. 130).

154 See e.g. M. Trachtenberg and I. Hyman, *Architecture: From Prehistory to Post-Modernism* (1986), p. 382.

155 Soo 2012, p. 229.

156 See ibid.

157 Evelyn, *Evelyn Library*, vol. 4 (1977), no. 1569, p. 48.

158 Whinney 1971, pp. 61, 63. More recently, Adrian Tinniswood, *His Invention so Fertile: A Life of Christopher Wren* (2001), p. 221, observed: 'Hooke seems to have been particularly interested in the cross contained within a square' and that the idea 'first appeared in Jacob van Campden's Nieuwe Kerk in Haarlem'.

159 Jeffery 1996, p. 111.

160 K. Downes, 'Sir Christopher Wren', *Oxford Dictionary of National Biography*, ed. H. C. G. Matthew, vol. 60 (2004), pp. 406–19, republished in K. Downes, *Christopher Wren* (2007), ch. 3, p. 35.

161 S. Kravtsov, 'Juan Bautista Villalpando and Sacred Architecture in the Seventeenth Century', *Journal of the Society of Architectural Historians*, vol. 64 (2005), pp. 332–4, esp. 333: 'Nevertheless, it remains difficult to explain the similarity between the Dutch and English church architecture by these contacts, since the construction of St. Mary-at-Hill and St. Stephen's, Walbrook, was already under way in 1674.'

162 Downes, *Hawksmoor* (1970), p. 18, asserts that 'Hooke may have visited Holland' but without offering any evidence. Hooke was certainly aware of Dutch architecture. He produced a drawing, of unknown date, of the Nieuwe Kerk in the Hague (1649–56), British Library, Add. MS 5238 fol. 47 (not that in Haarlem, as Tinniswood claims, in the course of his Dutch attribution, see n. 158 above): however, this church does not have a dome and is not of the cross-in-square type. Hooke, Diary, p. 111, noted on 7 July 1674 (in the only reference of its kind): 'Saw Mr. [Abraham] Storey who returned from Holland Saturday last. Told me of the new Lutheran church 70 foot Diameter [drawing: '70' within a circle] and 70 foot over at Amsterdam [the Ronde Lutherse Kerk, 1671]. Of the Burghers hiordiage [New Town Hall of 1655]. Of the Jews new Synagogue 100 foot square [the Grote Sjoel, the Ashkenazi Great Synagogue of 1670–1]'. None of these provides a model of the Byzantine plan 'type' and the date is in any case too late to influence St Mary-at-Hill. See in general A. Stoesser-Johnston, 'Robert Hooke and Holland: Dutch Influence on his Architecture', *Bulletin KNOB* (2002), pp. 121–37; Guillery 2005, pp. 92–3.

163 In A. Labacco, *Libro d'Antonio Labacco appartenente a l'architettura nel qual si figurano alcune notabili antiquità di Roma* (1572 edn), pl. IV. The folio engraving, as the sale catalogue records (Lot 560), is inscribed: 'Sacelli S. Crucis ab Hilaro Papa apud baptisterium Constantini exaedificati et marmorea incrustione emblebatisque ornati deformatio Romae'; dated 1568, so the date in the catalogue (1658) was incorrectly transcribed; see M. Johnson, 'The Fifth-Century Oratory of the Holy Cross at the Lateran in Rome', *Architectura: Zeitschrift für Geschichte der Baukunst*, vol. 25 (1995), esp. pp. 137 n. 42 and 139, fig. 11.

164 Amico's *Trattato* (1620) is listed at Oxford: Bodleian Library in or before 1674: see Hyde 1674, p. 26; Worcester College (Special Collections, Worc. 636), provenance George Clarke (Hawksmoor's patron); at Cambridge: acquired by Christ's College (D.10.21) in *c*.1630 (with money from Henry Burrell, as recorded in 'Old Library, Donors' Register 1' of that date).

165 Allatius 1645, Letter II, fols 3–4, in Allatius 1969, pp. 25–7; see Cutler 1966, esp. pp. 87–9; du Prey 2000, pp. 3, 34–5. Byzantine architecture was also discussed by Desiderio Spreti, *Della grandezza, della ruine e della restaurazione di Ravenna* (1575).

166 See Goffman 1998; MacLean 2004; MacLean and Matar 2011.

167 On Rycaut's book see n. 92 above.

168 See Soo 2012, pp. 217, 223. On Salter and Luke see Cadwallader 2008, p. 327 (Salter), pp. 328–38 (Luke). On the chaplains in general see Introduction, n. 82 above.

169 See Cadwallader 2008, pp. 326–7; see T. Smith, *Epistolae Duae, quarum altera de moeibus ac institutis Turcarum agit* (1672), trans. as *Remarks upon the Manners, Religion and Government of the Turks. Together with a Survey of the Seven Churches of Asia as they now lye in their Ruines: and a Brief Description of Constantinople* (1678).

170 Evelyn 1959, p. 399 (30 August 1659), who met Blount again on 10 July 1660, p. 409. S. Pepys, *The Diary of*

Samuel Pepys, ed. H. B. Wheatley (1893) (19 September 1664); see www.pepysdiary.com/diary/1664/09/19/ (accessed 26 April 2019).

171 Hooke, Diary, p. 200 (13 December 1675); Diary 2, pp. 78, 90, for Blount's work (1 December 1688, 14 January 1689).
172 Blount 1636, pp. 21–2.
173 George Wheler to Thomas Seymour, n.d. [*c*.1692], transcribed in T. Zouch, *The Works of the Rev. Thomas Zouch*, vol. 2 (1820), p. 180; see also 'The Estate of the Whelers of Charing and Otterden', in F. H. W. Sheppard, ed., *Survey of London: Volume 27, Spitalfields and Mile End New Town* (1957), pp. 100–7; see *British History Online* www.british-history.ac.uk/survey-london/vol27/pp100-107 (accessed 26 April 2019).
174 See Jardine 2002, pp. 7–14.
175 Wren 1750, p. 172.
176 All Souls, Wren Collection II.21–23, in Geraghty 2007, pp. 49–50, nos 52–4.
177 Wren 1750, p. 139.
178 Whinney 1971, pp. 88–90.
179 Lambeth Palace Library, London, MS 2750/16; see du Prey 2000, pp. 60–3; Hart 2002, pp. 42–5.
180 See J. J. Keevil, 'The Bagnio in London, 1648–1725', *Journal of the History of Medicine and Allied Sciences*, vol. 7 no. 3 (1952), pp. 250–7; D. Cruickshank, *The Secret History of Georgian London: How the Wages of Sin shaped the Capital* (2009), pp. 215–27; N. Yildiz, 'Turkish Britons and Ottoman Turks in England during the Eighteenth Century', in M. Hüttler and H. E. Weidinger, eds, *Ottoman Empire and European Theatre: The Time of Joseph Haydn: From Sultan Mahmud I to Mahmud II (r. 1730–1839)*, vol. 2 (2014), pp. 555–7.
181 A. W. Hakewill, 'Charles the Second's Bath, Bath Street, Newgate Street, Sir Christopher Wren, Architect', *The Civil Engineer and Architects Journal*, vol. 13 (October 1850), pp. 348–50; N. Avcioğlu, *Turquerie and the Politics of Representation, 1728–1876* (2011), pt III, ch. 4, 'The Royal Bagnio and the Legacy of Sir Christopher Wren', pp. 189–98. Irrespective of Wren's involvement or otherwise in the Royal Bagnio, his interest in the tradition of hot bathing in England is shown by his ownership of Thomas Guidotti, *De Thermis Britannicis Tractatus* (1691; Lot 377).
182 E. Hatton, *A New View of London*, vol. 2 (1708), p. 797.
183 J. Aubrey, 'Life of Sir Henry Blount', in J. Walker, ed., *Letters Written by Eminent Persons in the Seventeenth and Eighteenth Centuries*, vol. 2 (1813), p. 244.
184 Evelyn 1959, p. 220.
185 Wheler 1682, Book II, p. 193. Wheler's visit was in 1675, so he is either referring to an earlier Bagnio or implying an earlier opening date for the Royal Bagnio than 1679, which is possible; see Yildiz 2014, p. 555.
186 S. Haworth, *Description of the Duke's Bagnio, and of the Mineral Bath, and New Spaw thereunto belonging* (1683), pp. 33–4.
187 *A True Account of the Royal Bagnio, with a Discourse of its Virtues* (1680), p. 3.
188 Ibid., pp. 4, 6.
189 Ibid., p. 6.
190 Hatton 1708, pp. 784–6, 793, 797.
191 Sir William Jennens, '"Sworn Servant to His Majesty for the Bagnio", Advertisement for the King's Bath, March 25, 1686', Yale Center for British Art, New Haven, Connecticut, B1977.14.11017.
192 Haworth 1683, pp. 3–4; see Cruickshank 2009, p. 220; p. 221 notes: 'The Duke's Bagnio, with its cupola, colonnades, walks paved with marble, courts and service buildings, sounds like an authentic Ottoman-style bath complex combined with Renaissance monastic architecture.'
193 Haworth 1683, pp. 4–5.
194 Other tokens include British Museum, London, *c*.1667, nos J.2988, M.7576.
195 Haworth 1683, p. 17.
196 See Hart 2011, pp. 46–8.
197 Laud's views are recorded in W. Prynne, *Canterburies Doome: or, The first part of a Compleat History of the Commitment, Charge, Tryall, Condemnation and Execution of William Laud* (1646), pp. 126, 497–9. On the foundation ceremony at old St Paul's see Hart 2011, p. 218; on that at Wren's Cathedral see Hart 1995, p. 20.
198 J. Howell, *Londonopolis... The Imperial Chamber, and Chief Emporium of Great Britain* (1657), p. 4. This idea of an ancient Constantinian city had archaeological evidence to support it. Wren dug up Roman artefacts in the course of his building in the city: on a Roman urn discovered by Wren in Spitalfields in 1678 and presented to the Royal Society see the report by Wren's son, 'Of *London* in ancient Times, and the Boundary of the *Roman* Colony, discern'd by the *Surveyor*, after the *great Fire*', published in Wren 1750, pp. 113–16; Soo 1998, pp. 28–30. In Winchester Wren unearthed 'Coins of Constantine the Great, and others': Wren 1750, p. 202; see also J. Aubrey, 'Monumenta Britannica', Bodleian Library, Oxford, MSS. Top. Gen.c.24–25: see Aubrey, *Monumenta Britannica; or, A Miscellany of British antiquities*, ed. R. Legg et al., vol. 2 (1980–2), pp. 978–9; Soo 1998, p. 252 n. 3.
199 Wren 1750, p. 123.
200 See Geoffrey of Monmouth, *The History of the Kings of Britain*, trans. S. Evans (1963 edn), Book 5, ch. 6.
201 The Stuart apologist John Gordon, in justifying their imperial ambitions, asserted in 1604: 'by all these victories this Britaine King became Emperour, King, and Monarche of the whole world'. Since Constantine represented the archetype of the British Christian prince, James I necessarily became 'our newe *Constantinus*': Gordon, *ENOTIKON: Or, A Sermon of the Union of Great Brittannie in antiquite of language, name, religion and Kingdome* (1604), p. 46. Roy Strong, *Van Dyck: Charles I on Horseback* (1972), p. 47, observed that the 'English Reformation

was carried through on the imperial status of the kings of England, and both Tudor and Stuart monarchs were built up in succession as images of Constantine revived'; see also F. Yates, *Astraea: The Imperial Theme in the Sixteenth Century* (1975), pp. 42–3. This idea found expression in prominent examples of Stuart art. In Whitehall, on the Banqueting House ceiling painted by Paul Rubens, the king is pictured under what appears to be a dome and in the presence of figures identified as Brute (or Brutus), Lucius and Constantine. And a design by Jones for a triumphal arch at Temple Bar (1636–8) was based on the Arch of Constantine in Rome, thereby emphasising the Stuart monarch's role as the 'British Constantine'; see Strong, *Britannia Triumphans: Inigo Jones, Rubens and Whitehall Palace* (1980), pp. 24, 28; Hart 2011, pp. 76–7. On references to the Arch in connection with Charles II, and his triumphal entry at the time of his coronation in 1661, see Stevenson 2013, p. 112.

202 See J. R. Jacob, *Henry Stubbe, Radical Protestantism and the Early Enlightenment* (1983), pp. 124–6; see also N. Jose, *Ideas of the Restoration in English Literature 1660–1671* (1984), p. 44; M. Howard, 'Self-Fashioning and the Classical Moment in Mid-Sixteenth-Century English Architecture', in L. Gent and N. Llewellyn, eds, *Renaissance Bodies: The Human Figure in English Culture c.1540–1660* (1990), pp. 210–12.

203 Evelyn 1959, pp. 139, 371 (19 November 1644, 8 July 1656).

204 E. Stillingfleet, *Origines Britannicae: or the Antiquities of the British Churches* (1685), p. 90; Eusebius, *De vita Constantini*, Book 3, ch. 19, in Eusebius 1999, p. 129. Wren's own interest in the early British Church is shown by his ownership of Henry Spelman's *Concilia Ecclesiastica Orbis Britannici*, a comprehensive edition of the proceedings of the early church councils in Britain, vol. 1 published in 1639 (Lot 388).

205 See Griffith-Jones 2010, p. 165.

206 C. Reynell, *The Fortunate Change: Being a Panegyrick to His Sacred Majesty, King Charles the Second* (1661), p. 6.

207 Evelyn 1959, p. 330.

4 MONUMENTAL COLUMNS AND COLONNADES

1 L. Soo, *Wren's 'Tracts' on Architecture and Other Writings* (1998), p. 188.

2 See R. Lynche, trans., *An Historical Treatise of the Travels of Noah into Europe* (1601), sig. Br.

3 Soo 1998, p. 153.

4 Ibid., p. 193; Herodotus, *The Histories*, trans. A. de Selincourt (1954), Book 1.178–81.

5 Soo 1998, p. 157.

6 J. Evelyn, *The Diary of John Evelyn*, ed. E. S. de Beer (1959), p. 202.

7 See W. Hollar and J. Leake, *An exact surveigh of the streets, lanes and churches contained within the ruines of the City of London* (1667); facsimile, London Topographical Society (1908–9); Hollar, *A true and exact prospect of the famous Citty of London from S. Marie Overs steeple in Southwarke in its flourishing condition before the Fire. Another Prospect of the sayd city taken from the same place as it appeareth now, after the sad calamitie and destruction by Fire, in the year of 1666* (1666); facsimile (*c*.1792).

8 Evelyn 1959, p. 495.

9 See 'Letter concerning the Great Fire in London Sept. 1666', Bodleian Library, Oxford, MS Gough London 14, fol. 38r. Thomas Vincent in *Gods Terrible Voice in the City* (1667) presented the destruction of old St Paul's as akin to the day of Judgement; see C. Stevenson, 'Robert Hooke, Monuments and Memory', *Art History*, vol. 28 no. 1 (2005), p. 48; A. Balfour, *Solomon's Temple: Myth, Conflict, and Faith* (2012), p. 199.

10 See V. Hart, *Inigo Jones: The Architect of Kings* (2011).

11 All Souls College, Oxford, Wren Collection I.101, I.7, in A. Geraghty, *The Architectural Drawings of Sir Christopher Wren at All Souls College, Oxford: A Complete Catalogue* (2007), pp. 254–6, nos 395, 396.

12 Wren 1750, pp. 117–21; A. T. Bolton and H. D. Hendry, eds, *Wren Society Volumes*, vol. 12 (1924–43), pls 24, 25; R. T. Reddaway, 'The Rebuilding of London', *Town Planning Review*, vol. 17 (1937), pp. 205–11; Reddaway, *The Building of London after the Great Fire* (1951); J. Summerson, *Sir Christopher Wren* (1953), pp. 68–74; E. F. Sekler, *Wren and his Place in European Architecture* (1956), pp. 59–62; K. Downes, *Christopher Wren* (1971), pp. 60–3; M. Whinney, *Wren* (1971), pp. 38–9; Downes, *The Architecture of Wren* (1982), pp. 11, 50–1; Downes, *Sir Christopher Wren: An Exhibition selected by Kerry Downes at the Whitechapel Art Gallery* (1982), p. 63; Downes, *Sir Christopher Wren and the Making of St Paul's* (1991), p. 20; P. Jeffrey, *The City Churches of Sir Christopher Wren* (1996), pp. 17–30; L. Jardine, *On a Grander Scale: The Outstanding Career of Sir Christopher Wren* (2002), pp. 247–67.

13 See Whinney 1971, p. 39. Work on the radial plan of the palace at Versailles was also under way by the time of Wren's visit, a year before the fire, in 1665; see Soo 1998, pp. 103–4.

14 Despite the fact that some churches had also survived the Fire, these were to be demolished and new ones built on fresh sites related to the grid.

15 See Geraghty 2007, p. 256 note; city illustrated in Cesariano's Vitruvius, *Di Lucio Vitruvio Pollione De architectura libri dece traducti de latino in vulgare* (1521), fol. XXVIv, republished in Ryff's Vitruvius of 1575, owned by Hooke. Wren's library listed the 1684 French edition of Vitruvius by Perrault (Lot 545), although his reliance

16   on Vitruvius for sections of the 1657 lecture at Gresham College indicates that he also owned an earlier one.
16   Vitruvius, *De Architectura*, trans. F. Granger, vol. 1 (1931), pp. 59–61.
17   Wren 1750, pp. 32, 120.
18   Ibid., p. 52, records that the Royal Society aspired to advance '1. Knowledge. 2. Profit. 3. Health; and Convenience of Life'.
19   The camp was illustrated in Fra Giocondo's Vitruvius of 1511.
20   Polybius, *The Histories*, trans. W. R. Paton, vol. 3 (1967–8), Book VI, pp. 329–67; see also Guillaume du Choul, *Veterum Romanorum religio, castrametatio, disciplina militaris ut & balneae* (1686, Lot 77).
21   On Serlio's drawings of the camp's layout, and the interest of students of military planning such as Niccolò Machiavelli, see S. Serlio, *Sebastiano Serlio on Architecture*, trans. V. Hart and P. Hicks, vol. 2 (2001), esp. pp. xxxvii–xliv.
22   On the grid see R. Burns, *Origins of the Colonnaded Streets in the Cities of the Roman East* (2017), p. 29; see also in general J. Ward-Perkins, *Cities of Ancient Greece and Italy: Planning in Classical Antiquity* (1974).
23   All Souls, Wren Collection II.101, in Geraghty 2007, p. 285, no. 450. Comparing the Wren drawing to the Roman camp, the barracks in both occupy half the area and are arranged in rectangular rows (as in his city plan), while the public buildings occupy the other half. And in both, the camp is enclosed by a wall with gates and towers. In Wren 1750, p. 215, a list of Wren's drawings for unexecuted designs includes a 'Plan of Barracks proposed in Hyde-park, for a Body of Guards of 1000 Horse, with Houses for Officers, Commissary, Farriers, Sadlers, Courts of Guard, Haybarns, Granaries, &c. by Order'; also listed is a 'Plan of Barracks in Hyde-park, for 2000 private Men, and Officers, and Infirmary for 160 Men, a Chapel, & all Accommodations. By Order, in 1713; the Estimate of the whole computed at £48,118'.
24   Wren 1750, p. 121, noted 'he propos'd to build all the Houses uniform', quoting James Ralph's *Critical Review of the Buildings of London* (1734), p. 2.
25   See P. Lombaerde and C. van den Heuval, eds, *Early Modern Urbanism and the Grid: Town Planning in the Low Countries in International Context. Exchanges in Theory and Practice 1550–1800* (2011).
26   Wren 1750, pp. 113–16; see Soo 1998, p. 26. The immediate aftermath of the Fire allowed for archaeological investigations that previously had been impossible.
27   Wren 1750, p. 33.
28   See e.g. T. Sprat, *The History of the Royal Society of London, For the Improving of Natural Knowledge* (1667), p. 149: 'They [the Society] have begun an exact *Survey of the Heavens*: and Saint *Jameses Park* may witness, that *Ptolomey* and *Alphonso* were not the only *Monarchs*, who observ'd the motions, and appearances of the *Stars*.'
29   Ibid., p. 150; see J. Evelyn, *Navigation and Commerce, their Original and Progress containing a Succinct Account of Traffick in General: Its Benefits and Improvements* (1674).
30   Wren 1750, p. 201; see Whinney 1971, p. 42.
31   On Jerman's design see A. Saunders, ed., *The Royal Exchange* (1997), pp. 127–33.
32   Wren 1750, p. 118.
33   Vitruvius, *De Architectura*, Book V, ch. 1, trans. F. Granger, vol. 1 (1931), p. 255.
34   A. Palladio, *I quattro libri dell'architettura* (1570), Book III, ch. XVII, in *The Four Books on Architecture*, trans. R. Tavernor and R. Schofield (1997), p. 194.
35   See Geraghty 2007, p. 256 note.
36   Wren 1750, p. 118.
37   On the Thames waterside see e.g. Hollar 1666.
38   Edward Browne to his father, Sir Thomas Browne, September 1665, in S. Wilkin, ed., *Sir Thomas Browne's Works, including his Life and Correspondence*, vol. 1 (1836), pp. 111–12. These 'quays' were the embankments of the College of the Four Nations facing the Louvre, by Louis Le Vau. See M. Whinney, 'Sir Christopher Wren's Visit to Paris', *Gazette des Beaux-Arts*, vol. 51 (1958), p. 233; J. Rykwert, *The First Moderns* (1980), p. 143.
39   Wren 1750, p. 121, quoting Ralph 1734, p. 2.
40   Wren 1750, p. 214.
41   Soo 1998, p. 156.
42   Wren 1750, p. 207.
43   Soo 1998, p. 158.
44   Wren to Isaac Barrow, *c*.1675, in Bolton and Hendry 1924–43, vol. 5, p. 32; see Soo 1998, pp. 290–1 n. 36.
45   On Wren's Stoicism see J. Douglas Stewart, 'A Militant, Stoic Monument: The Wren-Cibber-Gibbons Charles I Mausoleum Project: Its Authors, Sources, Meaning, and Influence', in G. W. Marshall, ed., *The Restoration Mind* (1997), pp. 21–64.
46   Sprat 1667, pp. 6–7.
47   Soo 1998, p. 158.
48   On this drawing of the precinct at St Paul's, with copies held in the Sir John Soane Museum, London, and St Paul's Cathedral Library, see http://collections.soane.org/OBJECT7062 (accessed 29 April 2019).
49   The Corinthian columnar façade of Rome's Septizonium (destroyed in 1588) was partly illustrated in Serlio and apparently studied by Wren in 1679: S. Serlio, *Il terzo libro di Sebastiano Serlio Bolognese* (1540), Book 3, p. LXXXII; see also the 'Portico of Pompeo', pp. LVII–LIX: see Serlio 1996, pp. 172, 147–9. Hooke, Diary, p. 432, noted on 6 December 1679: 'Dined with Sir Ch. Wren. Saw his Septizonium Severi. See figure A.' See also the 'Edifice des Tuteles', a Roman colonnaded structure described and illustrated in Perrault's *Vitruvius, Les dix livres d'architecture de Vitruve* (1684), pp. 217–19, which influenced Hawksmoor: see V. Hart, *Nicholas Hawksmoor: Rebuilding Ancient Wonders* (2002), pp. 146, 147, fig. 198.

50 Soo 1998, pp. 167–8.
51 See Burns 2017, pp. 38–51.
52 H. Blount, *A Voyage into the Levant…by way of…Egypt, unto Gran Cairo* (1636), p. 33, Alexandria on pp. 34–5; see G. MacLean, *The Rise of Oriental Travel: English Visitors to the Ottoman Empire, 1580–1720* (2004), pp. 120–1, 160.
53 See G. MacLean, *Looking East: English Writing and the Ottoman Empire before 1800* (2007), pp. 73–4.
54 Soo 1998, p. 190.
55 Strabo, *The Geography of Strabo*, trans. H. L. Jones et al., Loeb Classical Library (1932), 17.1.8–10: 'In short, the city of Alexandria abounds with public and sacred buildings. The most beautiful of the former is the Gymnasium, with porticos exceeding a stadium in extent. In the middle of it are the court of justice and groves…The wide street extends in length along the Gymnasium from the Necropolis to the Kanopic gate'; Diodorus Siculus, *Library of History*, 17.52.1–3, trans. C. H. Oldfather et al., Loeb Classical Library (1967); Pliny, *Natural History*, Book 5. 11.62–3, trans. H. Rackham, Loeb Classical Library (1938); Josephus, *The Wars of the Jews*, 2.487–8; Josephus, *Against Apion*, 2.35, trans. H. St. J. Thackeray, Loeb Classical Library (1926).
56 Soo 1998, p. 167.
57 Ibid., p. 168.
58 Strabo 1928–32, 14.5.9.
59 Burns 2007, p. 1.
60 See ibid., pp. 18–19, 142–3.
61 Tadmor was identified with Solomon in 2 Chronicles 8.4; Josephus, *Jewish Antiquities*, trans. H. St. J. Thackeray et al., Loeb Classical Library, vol. 3 (1930–65), Book 8, 6; see also Pliny 1938, Book 5.21.
62 Evelyn 1959, p. 1001.
63 W. Halifax, 'A Relation of a Voyage from Aleppo to Palmyra in Syria; sent by the Reverend Mr. William Halifax to Dr. Edw Bernard (late) Savilian Professor of Astronomy in Oxford, and by him communicated to Dr. Thomas Smith, Reg. Soc. S', *Philosophical Transactions*, 19 no. 217 (November 1695), pp. 83–110; T. Lanoy and A. Goodyear, 'An Extract of the Journals of two Several Voyages of the English Merchants of the Factory of Aleppo, to Tadmor, anciently call'd Palmyra', ibid. no. 218 (December 1695), pp. 129–60; E. Halley, 'Some Account of the Ancient State of the City of Palmyra, with Short remarks upon the Inscriptions Found there. By E. Halley', ibid., pp. 160–75. See G. Astengo, 'The Rediscovery of Palmyra and its Dissemination in *Philosophical Transactions*', *Notes and Records: The Royal Society Journal of the History of Science* (16 March 2016); see http://rsnr.royalsocietypublishing. org/content/early/2016/03/12/rsnr.2015.0059 (accessed 29 April 2019); M. F. Walker, *Architects and Intellectual Culture in Post-Restoration England* (2017), pp. 129–30.
64 Halifax 1695, p. 95.
65 Halley 1695, p. 160.
66 On Hooke and Halley and biblical paradigms see W. Poole, *The World Makers: Scientists of the Restoration and the Search for the Origins of the Earth* (2010), esp. pp. 85–114; see also the Preface above.
67 See Astengo 2016, p. 223 (with incorrect publication date).
68 R. Huntington, 'A Letter from Dublin to the Publisher of these Tracts, concerning the Porphyry Pillars in Egypt, by R H', *Philosophical Transactions*, 14 no. 161 (20 July 1684), p. 629; see Astengo 2016, p. 211.
69 Soo 1998, pp. 167–8.
70 Soo 1998, p. 156.
71 P. della Valle, *Viaggi di P. della V.… divisi in tre parti, cioè la Turchia, la Persia, e l'India*, vol. 2 (1658); see M. D. Davis, 'Della Valle's Exploration of the Ruins of Persepolis in 1621', *Fontes 66* (2012), http://archiv.ub.uni-heidelberg. de/artdok/1868/1/Davis_Fontes66.pdf (accessed 29 April 2019). A fanciful illustration of Persepolis appeared in Jan Janszoon Struys's *Drie aanmerkelijke en seer rampspoedige Reysen* (1676).
72 M. Vickers, 'The Views of Persepolis by William Marshall and Wenceslaus Hollar in Sir Thomas Herbert's Travels', in H. Sancisi-Weerdenburg and J. W. Drijvers, eds, *Achaemenid History VII: Through Travellers' Eyes* (1991), pp. 59–69; L. E. Semler, 'The Ruins of Persepolis: Grotesque Perception in Thomas Herbert's Travels', in Semler and E. Kelly, eds, *Word and Self Estranged in English Texts, 1550–1660* (2010), pp. 33–60. On Hooke's ownership of Herbert see the Introduction, n. 54 above.
73 'Inquiries for Persia', *Philosophical Transactions*, 2 no. 23 (11 March 1667), p. 423.
74 T. Herbert, *A Relation of Some Yeares Travaile: begunne anno 1626* (1677 edn), p. 142.
75 Hooke, Diary, p. 321.
76 Evelyn 1959, p. 690.
77 J. Chardin, *Voyages de Monsieur le Chevalier Chardin en Perse et autres lieux de l'Orient*, vol. 3 (1711), pp. 99–126.
78 Evelyn 1959, pp. 762, 768.
79 'A Letter from Monsieur N. Witsen to Dr. Martin Lister, with Two Draughts of the Famous Persepolis', *Philosophical Transactions*, 18 no. 210 (May 1694), pp. 117–18, republished in J. Lowthorp, ed., *The Philosophical Transactions and Collections*, vol. 3 (1705), p. 527, pl. 6. The engravings were based on drawings by Engelbert Kämpfer, who visited Persepolis in 1684, supplied to Witsen by Ludvig Fabritius; see www.iranicaonline.org/articles/ kaempfer-engelbert (accessed 29 April 2019).
80 Naturally enough, Wren was credited with the design in Wren 1750, p. 197. Aubrey, however, listed the column as among Hooke's works: *Brief Lives*, ed. O. Lawson Dick (1958), p. 165. The design is attributed to Hooke alone in M. Cooper, *'A more beautiful city': Robert Hooke and the Rebuilding of London after the Great Fire* (2003), pp. 197, 198–205 (see also J. E. Moore's 2005 review, at www.history.ac.uk/reviews/paper/moore.html), and in M.

F. Walker, 'The Limits of Collaboration: Robert Hooke, Christopher Wren and the Designing of the Monument to the Great Fire of London', *Notes and Records: The Royal Society Journal of the History of Science* (16 February 2011); see http://rsnr.royalsocietypublishing.org/content/65/2/121.full#sec-4 (accessed 29 April 2019). For a joint attribution see Jardine 2002, pp. xii, 307–21; Stevenson 2005, pp. 49–52.

81. Evelyn 1959, p. 705; see also Evelyn, *Numismata: A Discourse of Medals, Ancient and Modern* (1697), p. 162.

82. All Souls, Wren Collection II.71, in Geraghty 2007, p. 259, no. 400. This design includes all the Monument's key features, namely the bas-relief panel in the western pedestal, the heraldic dragons and royal arms on its cornice, Doric shaft and a crowning emblem that in this case is a phoenix. Wren was most directly involved in creating designs for this emblem, through being asked by the City Lands Committee in 1675 to produce a report proposing a number of alternatives; see Walker 2011, p. 6; see also J. Moore, 'The Monument, or, Christopher Wren's Roman Accent', *The Art Bulletin*, vol. 80 no. 3 (1998), pp. 516–21. These designs were his own version of a phoenix, a heraldic statue, a fire-ball and the flaming urn ornamented with heraldry that was eventually built, albeit to a variant design by Hooke: phoenix, British Museum, 1881,0611.205; statue, flaming urn, fire-ball, British Library, Add MS 5238 fols 70, 71, 77. Hooke studied Wren's urn before designing his own: Walker 2011, fig. 8 and nn. 67, 72; Hooke, Diary, p. 180 (11 September 1675) records that he had been 'To Sir Chr. Wrens. Received Draught of Urne'.

83. Wren 1750, pp. 200–1.

84. Ibid., p. 200; Moore 1998, p. 506.

85. Wren 1750, p. 201.

86. The column of Theodosius was in the Forum of Theodosius. Its shaft was carved with reliefs depicting this emperor's victory over the barbarians and a statue of him stood at the top. In discussing the Monument in *Parentalia*, Wren's son repeated the comparisons made in the draft inscription when observing that the column 'much exceeds in Height the Pillars at Rome, of the Emperors Trajan, and Antoninus, the stately Remains of Roman Grandeur; or that of Theodosius at Constantinople'; Wren 1750, p. 197.

87. J. Evelyn, *A Parallel of the Ancient Architecture with the Modern* (1664) p. 89; (1707), p. 93.

88. G. Wheler, *A Journey into Greece by George Wheler, Esq., in Company of Dr Spon of Lyons in Six Books* (1682), Book II, p. 189; see L. Soo, 'The English in the Levant: Social Networks and the Study of Architecture', in O. Horsfall Turner, ed., *'The Mirror of Great Britain': National Identity in Seventeenth-Century British Architecture, Proceedings of the 2010 Annual Symposium of the Society of Architectural Historians of Great Britain* (2012), p. 217.

89. On the heraldic aspects of the Monument's design see V. Hart, 'London's Standard: Christopher Wren and the Heraldry of the Monument', *RES: Journal of Anthropology and Aesthetics*, vol. 73/74 (forthcoming 2020).

90. Josephus 1930–65, Book I, pp. 69–71; see W. Adler, 'Did the Biblical Patriarchs practice Astrology? Michael Glykas and Manuel Komnenos I on Seth and Abraham', in P. Magdalino, ed., *The Occult Sciences in Byzantium* (2006), p. 250.

91. On Wren's ownership of more Josephus editions than this of 1693 see the Preface.

92. Soo 1998, pp. 188–9.

93. See V. Hart, *Art and Magic in the Court of the Stuarts* (1994), p. 61.

94. 'N.W.', in S. Daniel, *The worthy tract of Paulus Iovius, contayning a discourse of rare inventions, both militarie and amorous called imprese, whereunto is added a preface by S. Daniell* (1585), n.p; see M. Corbett and R. Lightbown, *The Comely Frontispiece: The Emblematic Title-Page in England 1550–1660* (1979), p. 22. Unsurprisingly, associations between heraldry and hieroglyphics became the norm in English books on heraldry, e.g. in Edmund Bolton's *The Elements of Armories* (1610), where heraldry is called 'the hieroglyphicks of Nobility', dedicatory poem, entitled 'H.C. To the Gentleman Reader'.

95. Soo 1998, pp. 177–8; see C. van Eck, 'Understanding Roman Architecture from a Distance: Sir Christopher Wren on the Temples of Peace and of Mars the Avenger', in A. Payne, ed., *The Companions to the History of Architecture*, vol. 1: *Renaissance and Baroque Architecture* (2017), pp. 498–523.

96. Hooke's Maier ('Libri Latini, &c. in Quarto', lot 37, p. 8), Valeriano ('Libri Latini, &c. in Folio', lot 96, p. 3), Caussin ('Libri Latini, &c. in Quarto', lot 68, p. 9), Kircher ('Libri Latini, &c. in Quarto', lot 308, p. 15); see www.hookesbooks.com/hookes-books-database/browse-bh-in-full (accessed 29 April 2019).

97. Evelyn 1959, p. 237.

98. Thomas Sprat cited in Wren 1750, p. 100.

99. All Souls, Wren Collection II.95, in Geraghty 2007, p. 195, no. 297. The sketch is not in Wren's hand: see R. A. Beddard, 'Wren's Mausoleum for Charles I and the Cult of the Royal Martyr', *Architectural History*, vol. 27 (1984), p. 46 n. 59. On the use of Ripa see Douglas Stewart 1997, p. 33, nn. 32, 36, 39, 41.

100. Wren 1750, p. 212; see Douglas Stewart 1997, pp. 21–64. Emblems were used elsewhere in Wren's work. King William identified with Hercules, and extensive reference to this identity is made at Hampton Court: in Hercules trampling on Superstition, Envy and Fury in the east pediment, in the lion skins in Portland stone round the windows in Fountain Court, in the 'Labours of Hercules' painted by Laguerre on the south side of that court and in the two snakes (those strangled by the infant Hercules, a Dutch emblem of liberation) over the gateways in the east front; see Downes, *Architecture of Wren*, 1982, p. 100.

101 All Souls, Wren Collection II.91, in Geraghty 2007, p. 193, no. 293; see Douglas Stewart 1997, p. 41.
102 See van Eck 2017.
103 See Hart 2020.
104 Intertwined dragons were illustrated in E. Ashmole, *Theatrum Chemicum Britannicum* (1652), in a treatise by Thomas Vaughan on pp. 342, 354. Hooke transcribed from this book an account of the life and works of John Dee, the Elizabethan polymath and magus, which included both alchemy and heraldry, *The Posthumous Works of Robert Hooke. Containing his Cutlerian lectures* (1705), p. 203. The image of the phoenix being reborn from flames at the apex of a structure can be found in any number of alchemical emblems, even those with dragons at the base (e.g. in Andreas Libavius's *Alchymia* of 1606); see A. Roob, *Alchemy and Mysticism* (1997), pp. 299, 301, 303; M. K. Schuchard, *Restoring the Temple of Vision: Cabalistic Freemasonry and Stuart Culture* (2002), pp. 710–11.
105 As noted in Chapter Two, Wren owned three separate copies of Ashmole's history of the Garter (Lots 259, 412, 478). For Ashmole on heraldry and the Garter see M. Hunter, *Science and the Shape of Orthodoxy: Intellectual Change in Late Seventeenth Century Britain* (1995), p. 33. The image of St George and his dragon had appeared elsewhere in Wren and his associate's work: among the 'Wren Office' drawings at All Souls is one by Hawksmoor of a monument, for an unknown location, in which both are raised on a pedestal flanked by a pair of crouching captives: Wren Collection IV.75, in Geraghty 2007, p. 283, no. 446.
106 Hooke, Diary, pp. 38, 270, 319; 'Libri Latini, &c. in Quarto', lot 48, p. 9; see www.hookesbooks.com.
107 On this use of Ripa see C. Stevenson, *The City and the King: Architecture and Politics in Restoration London* (2013), pp. 229–31.
108 See the description of the relief in R. Seymour, *A survey of the cities of London and Westminster, borough of Southwark, and Parts Adjacent*, vol. 1 (1733), pp. 451–2. See also Moore 1998, pp. 503–5.
109 London Metropolitan Archives, CLC/281/MS00184/004; see Moore 1998, pp. 511, 530 nn. 31, 41, 112; P. Ward-Jackson, *Public Sculpture of the City of London* (2003), p. 263.
110 'An Act for Rebuilding the City of London', 8 February 1667, *Statutes of the Realm*, vol. 19 (1810–28), Charles II, p. 8; see Cooper 2003, pp. 129–31.
111 Wren 1750, p. 198.
112 The two columns were a major feature of the Temple and were fequently illustrated. They were shown in Martin van Heemskerk's version of the destruction of the Temple, as engraved by Philip Galle in 1557; Samuel Lee illustrated them in his *Orbis miraculum; or, the Temple of Solomon Pourtrayed by Scripture-Light* (1659), discussed in Chapter Two; see J. A. Bennett and S. Mandelbrote, *The Garden, the Ark, the Tower, the Temple* (1998), p. 148.
113 See Moore 1998, p. 504.
114 Ibid.
115 On the subsequent appropriation of the Monument as a religious icon see N. Smith, '"Making Fire": Conflagration and Religious Controversy in Seventeenth-Century London', in J. F. Merritt, ed., *Imagining Early Modern London: Perceptions and Portrayals of the City from Stow to Strype 1598–1720* (2001), pp. 273–93, esp. p. 280.

CONCLUSION

1 Wren 1750, p. 235: '*In eundum, Astronomum et Architectum, Basilicae Divi Pauli, et Urbis Londini Conditorem.* / Astra polumque suo concepit pectore Wrennus, / Paulinam mira qui struit arte domum. / Ista manus Triviae templi revocasset honores; / Seu Mausolei; seu Babylonis opus. / Grandior ex flammis *Augusta renascitur, artem / Stantia non poterant tecta probare suam.'
2 Martial, *Epigrams*, trans. D. R. Shackleton Bailey, Loeb Classical Library, vol. 2 (1993), Book V.7: 'To Vulcan, on the Restoration of the City after being partially destroyed by Fire'; see www.tertullian.org/fathers/martial_epigrams_book05.htm ; see also https://archive.org/stream/martialepigrams01martiala/martialepigrams01martiala_djvu.txt (both accessed 30 April 2019).
3 Wren 1750, p. 235: '*De Londino post Incendium Restaurato.* / Qualiter Assyrios renovant incendia nidos, / Una decem quoties saecula vixit avis: / Taliter exuta est veterem *Nova Troja senectam, / Et sumpsit vultus Principis ipsa sui.'
4 V. Hart, *Inigo Jones: The Architect of Kings* (2011), pp. 41–5; C. Stevenson, *The City and the King: Architecture and Politics in Restoration London* (2013), pp. 73, 107, 155, 181.
5 See Stevenson 2013, pp. 155, 169, 202.
6 See E. Visconsi, 'Trojan Originalism: Dryden's *Troilus and Cressida*', in M. Novak, ed., *The Age of Projects* (2008), p. 75.
7 Wren 1750, p. 232: Martial 1993, Book X.63: *Marmora parva quidem sed non cessura, viator,* / *Mausoli saxis pyramidumque legis*; see J. Elmes, *Sir Christopher Wren and his Times* (1852), p. 411.
8 G. Sandys, *A relation of a Journey begun an: Dom: 1610. Foure bookes. Containing a description of the Turkish Empire, of Ægypt, of the Holy Land, of the remote parts of Italy, and ilands adjoyning* (1615), [sig. A2].
9 See Chapter Three; P. R. du Prey, *Hawksmoor's London Churches: Architecture and Theology* (2000), pp. 60–3; V. Hart, *Nicholas Hawksmoor: Rebuilding Ancient Wonders* (2002), pp. 42–5.
10 See S. Lang, 'By Hawksmoor out of Gibbs', *Architectural Review*, vol. 105 (1949), pp. 186–7; Hart 2002, pp. 22, 37–9, 42, 45, 47, 51–2, 83, 85, 89, 144–5.
11 See V. Hart, *Sir John Vanbrugh: Storyteller in Stone* (2008), esp. pp. 148–56.

12 See E. W. Said, *Orientalism: Western Conceptions of the Orient* (1978); J. Sweetman, *The Oriental Obsession: Islamic Inspiration in British and American Art and Architecture 1500–1920* (1988).
13 L. Soo, *Wren's 'Tracts' on Architecture and Other Writings* (1998), p. 153.
14 See N. Canny, ed., *The Origins of Empire: British Overseas Enterprise to the Close of the Seventeenth Century*, Oxford History of the British Empire, vol. 1 (1998).
15 On the use of the Ottoman empire as a model for a renewed British nation, with its own national style, see L. Soo, 'The English in the Levant: Social Networks and the Study of Architecture', in O. Horsfall Turner, ed., *'The Mirror of Great Britain': National Identity in Seventeenth-Century British Architecture, Proceedings of the 2010 Annual Symposium of the Society of Architectural Historians of Great Britain* (2012), pp. 209–31; Soo, 'The Architectural Setting of "Empire": The English Experience of Ottoman Spectacle in the Late 17th Century and its Consequences', in M. Keller and J. Irigoyen-Garcia, eds, *The Dialectics of Orientalism in Early Modern Europe* (2017), pp. 217–45.
16 See in general L. Jardine, *On a Grander Scale: The Outstanding Career of Sir Christopher Wren* (2002).
17 Soo 1998, p. 168 (repeated in the 'Discourse', p. 191).
18 J. Evelyn, *The Diary of John Evelyn*, ed. E. S. de Beer (1959), p. 501 (October 1666).

BIBLIOGRAPHY

MANUSCRIPTS

All Souls College, Oxford, Wren Collection
Aubrey, J., 'Monumenta Britannica', Bodleian Library, Oxford, MSS Top.Gen.c.24–25 (including the 'Chronologia Architectonica'); see Aubrey 1980–2
——, 'Naturall Historie of Wiltshire', 1685, additional notes in Aubrey's hand, 1691, Bodleian Library, Oxford, MS Aubrey 2
——, 'Naturall Historie of Wiltshire', transcript by the clerk to the Royal Society, Mr B. G. Cramer, Royal Society, London, Misc. MS 92
British Museum, London, album 1928,0323,0.46
Calendar of State Papers (Domestic), 1660–1720
Covel, J., 'Autograph Journal of Dr John Covel during his travels in Asia and Italy' (1670–8), British Library, Add. MSS 22912 and 22914; see Bent 1893 and Grélois 1998
The Dryden Album, Trinity College Library, Cambridge, R.14.23
Grünenberg, C., 'Beschreibung der Reise von Konstanz nach Jerusalem' (1487), MS Cod. St. Peter, pap.32, Badische Landesbibliothek, Karlsruhe
Hartlib, S., 'The Hartlib Papers', Sheffield University, Digital Humanities Institute (1995); see www.dhi.ac.uk/hartlib
Hooke, R., 'Diary, 1672–1683', London Metropolitan Archives, MS 01758; see Hooke 1935 and https://search.lma.gov.uk/scripts/mwimain.dll/144/LMA_OPAC/web_detail/REFD+CLC~2F495~2FMS01758?SESSIONSEARCH
——, 'Diary, 1688 to 1693', British Library, MS Sloane 4024; see Hooke 1935
——, Hooke Folio, Extracts from the Royal Society's Journal Books 1661–7 and Minutes 1677–91, Royal Society, London; see Hooke Folio Online, www.livesandletters.ac.uk/projects/hooke-folio-online
'Journal Book of the Royal Society' (containing the minutes of the Society's meetings), vol. 11 (1702–14), GB 117
'Letter concerning the Great Fire in London Sept. 1666', Bodleian Library, Oxford, MS Gough London 14
Lincolnshire Archives Office, Dean and Chapter Records
London Metropolitan Archives, CLC/281/MS00184/004
North, R., 'Cursory Notes of Building occasioned by the Repair, or rather Metamorfosis, of an old house in the Country', British Library, Add. MS 32540; see North 1981
Repository inventory, Royal Society MS 417 [1765]
Stukeley, W., 'Stonehenge', Cardiff Central Library, MS 253
Vernon, F., 'Journal of Travels in the Eastern Mediterranean' (1675–6), Royal Society, London, MS 73
Wren, C., 'Tracts', one–four, in Wren 1750; transcribed in Bolton and Hendry, vol. 19 (1942), pp. 126–39, and in Soo 1998, pp. 153–87
——, 'Discourse on Architecture' (Tract five), inserted in the Royal Institute of British Architects' 'Heirloom' copy of Wren 1750, with drawing of the elevation of the

Mausoleum of Halicarnassus by Hawksmoor; transcribed in Bolton and Hendry, vol. 19 (1942), pp. 140–5, and in Soo 1998, pp. 188–95

——, 'Letter to a Friend on the Commission for Building Fifty New Churches', in Wren 1750; transcribed in Bolton and Hendry, vol. 19 (1942), pp. 15–18, and in Soo 1998, pp. 112–18

——, 'Parentalia', British Library, Add. MS 25,071

Wylde, C., 'Charles Wylde's Journal of a Voyage from England unto the Straights, or Mediterranean Sea, being bound to Constantinople with Sir John Finch, Ambassador, and in his Majesty's ship, the Centurion, 1672/3, and back again, with colored draughts' (1672), British Library, Sloane MS 2439

Royal Society Transactions

Philosophical Transactions, 1667–1710; see http://rstl.royalsocietypublishing.org/content/by/year:

'Inquiries for Persia', 2 no. 23 (11 March 1667), p. 423

[H. Oldenburg], 'A Preface to the Seventh Year of these Tracts', 6 no. 69 (25 March 1671), pp. 2087–92

'A Narrative of some Observations lately made by certain Missionaries in the *Upper Egypt*; communicated in a Letter written from *Cairo* the sixth of January 1670', 6 no. 71 (22 May 1671), pp. 2151–3

'Mr. Francis Vernons Letter…giving a short account of some of his Observations in his Travels from Venice through Dalmatia…to Smyrna', 11 no. 124 (24 April 1676), pp. 575–82

'Britannia Antiqua Illustrata', 11 no. 124 (24 April 1676), p. 596

'Observations concerning some of the most considerable parts of Asia', 11 no. 129 (20 November 1676), pp. 711–15

[T. Smith], 'Historical Observations Relating to Constantinople. By the Reverend and Learned Tho. Smith D.D. Fellow of Magd. Coll. Oxon, and of the Royal Society', 13 no. 152 (20 October 1683), pp. 335–46

[T. Smith], 'An Account of the City of Prusa in Bithynia, and a Continuation of the Historical Observations Relating to Constantinople, by the Reverend and Learned Tho. Smith D.D. Fellow of Magd. Coll. Oxon. and of the Royal Society', 14 no. 155 (20 January 1684), pp. 431–54

[R. Huntington], 'A Letter from Dublin to the Publisher of these Tracts, concerning the Porphyry Pillars in Egypt, by R[obert] H[untington]', 14 no. 161 (20 July 1684), pp. 624–9

'An Explanation of the Cutts of Two Porphyry Pillars in Ægypt', 15 no. 178 (December 1685), p. 1252 and pl. 1

[R. Hooke, trans.], 'A Voyage of the Emperor of China into the Eastern Tartary, Anno. 1682', and 'A Voyage of the Emperor of China, into the Western Tartary, in the Year, 1683', 16 no. 180 (1 January 1687), pp. 39–51, 52–62

[N. Witsen], 'A Letter from Monsieur N. Witsen to Dr. Martin Lister, with Two Draughts of the Famous Persepolis', 18 no. 210 (May 1694), pp. 117–18

[W. Halifax], 'A Relation of a Voyage from Aleppo to Palmyra in Syria; sent by the Reverend Mr. William Halifax to Dr. Edw Bernard (late) Savilian Professor of Astronomy in Oxford, and by him communicated to Dr. Thomas Smith, Reg. Soc. S', 19 no. 217 (November 1695), pp. 83–110

[T. Lanoy and A. Goodyear], 'An Extract of the Journals of two Several Voyages of the English Merchants of the Factory of Aleppo, to Tadmor, anciently call'd Palmyra', 19 no. 218 (December 1695), pp. 129–60

[E. Halley], 'Some Account of the Ancient State of the City of Palmyra, with Short remarks upon the Inscriptions Found there. By E. Halley', 19 no. 218 (December 1695), pp. 160–75

PRIMARY SOURCES

'An Act for Rebuilding the City of London', 8 February 1667, *Statutes of the Realm*, London (1810–28), vol. 19, Charles II

Adrichem, C. van, *Theatrum Terrae Sanctae et Biblicarum Historiarum*, Cologne (1600 edn)

Alberti, L. B., *On the Art of Building in Ten Books*, trans. J. Rykwert, N. Leach and R. Tavernor, Cambridge, Mass. (1988)

Allatius, L., *De septem orbis spectaculis*, Rome (1640)

——, *De templis Graecorum recentioribus*, Cologne (1645); *The Newer Temples of the Greeks*, ed. and trans. A. Cutler, London (1969)

Alpini, P., *De Medicina Aegyptiorum*, Venice (1591)

Amico, B., *Trattato delle piante et imagini de sacri edificii di Terra Santa, disegnate in Gierusalemme secondo le regole della prospettiua, & vera misura della lor grandezza, etc.*, Rome (1609); enlarged edn, Florence (1620)

Ashmole, E., *Theatrum Chemicum Britannicum*, London (1652)

——, *The Institution, Laws & Ceremonies of the Most Noble Order of the Garter*, London (1672; 2nd edn 1715)

——, *The Diary and Will of Elias Ashmole*, ed. R. T. Gunther, Oxford (1927)

——, and F. Stanford, *The entire ceremonies of the coronations of His Majesty King Charles II. and of her Majesty Queen Mary, Consort to James II: As published by those learned heralds Ashmole and Sandford. With the prayers at full length. To which is prefix'd, an introduction historical and critical; likewise an appendix, containing many curious particulars*, London (1761)

Aubrey, J., *Miscellanies: A Collection of Hermetick Philosophy*, London (1696)

———, *Brief Lives*, ed. O. Lawson Dick, London (1958)

———, *Aubrey's Brief Lives*, Harmondsworth (1972)

———, *Monumenta Britannica; or, A Miscellany of British antiquities*, ed. R. Legg et al., 2 vols, Sherborne (1980–2)

Bacon, F., *Instauratio Magna*, London (1620)

Banks, J., *The Destruction of Troy a Tragedy*, London (1679)

Basire, I., *The Correspondence of Isaac Basire, D.D.*, ed. W. N. Darnell, London (1831)

Beauvau, H. de, *Relation journalière du voyage du Levant*, Nancy (1615)

Bedloe, W., *A Narrative and Impartial Discovery of the Horrid Popish Plot: Carried on for the Burning and Destroying of the Cities of London and Westminster*, London (1679)

Bernier, F., *The History of the Late Revolution of the Empire of the Great Mogul*, London (1671)

———, *A Continuation of the Memoires of Monsieur Bernier, Concerning the Empire of the Great Mogul*, London (1672)

Beveridge, W., *De linguarum orientalium, praesertim hebraicae, chaldaicae, syriacae, arabicae, & samaritanae praestantia… & utilitate*, London (1658; 2nd edn 1664)

———, *Synodikon sive Pandectae Canonum SS. Apostolorum, et Conciliorum ab Ecclesia Graeca receptorum*, 2 vols, Oxford (1672)

———, *A sermon concerning the excellency and usefulness of the Common-prayer. Preach'd by William Beveridge, D.D. (late Lord Bishop of St. Asaph) at the opening of the parish-church of St. Peter's Cornhill, London, the 27th of November, 1681*, London (1682)

Biddulph, W., *The Travels of certaine Englishmen into Africa, Asia, Troy, Bythinia, Thracia, and to the Blacke Sea*, London (1609)

Birch, T., *History of the Royal Society of London, for Improving of Natural Knowledge*, 4 vols, London (1756–7)

Blount, H., *A Voyage into the Levant… by way of… Egypt, unto Gran Cairo*, London (1636)

Bolton, E., *The Elements of Armories*, London (1610)

Bon, O., *A Description of the grand Signor's Seraglio, or Turkish Emperours Court*, London (1650)

Braun, G., and F. Hogenberg, *Civitates Orbis Terrarum*, vol. 1, Cologne (1572)

Bruyn, C. de, *Voyage to the Levant*, London (1702)

Burnet, T., *The sacred theory of the earth: containing an account of the original of the earth*, London (1684)

Busnot, D., *The history of the reign of Muley Ismael: the present king of Morocco, Fez, Tafilet, Sous, &c.*, London (1714)

Cange, C. du F. du, *Historia Byzantina duplici commentario illustrata*, Paris (1680)

Cartwright, J., *The Preachers Travels. Wherein is set downe a true Journall to the confines of the East Indies, through the great countreyes of Syria, Mesopotamia, Armenia, Media, Hircania and Parthia. With the Authors returne by the way of Persia, Susiana, Assiria, Chaldaea, and Arabia…Also a true relation of Sir Anthonie Sherleys Entertainment there*, London (1611)

Caussin, N., *Symbolica Aegyptiae Sapientia*, Paris (1647)

Cave, W., *Primitive Christianity: Or, The Religion of the Ancient Christians in the first ages of the Gospel in three parts*, London (1672); see https://quod.lib.umich.edu/e/eebo/A31421.0001.001?rgn=main;view=fulltext

Cavendish, H., 'Mr. Harrie Cavendish his Journey To and From Constantinople 1589, by Fox, His Servant', *Camden Miscellany of the Offices of the Royal Historical Society*, XVIII, 3rd series, ed. A. C. Wood, vol. 64 (1940), pp. 1–29

Chardin, J., *Travels into Persia and the East Indies, with Figures*, London (1686)

———, *Journal du Voyage du Chevalier Chardin en Perse et aux Indes Orientales*, London (1686)

———, *Voyages de Monsieur le Chevalier Chardin en Perse et autres lieux de l'Orient*, 3 vols, Amsterdam (1711)

Choul, G. du, *Veterum Romanorum religio, castrametatio, disciplina militaris ut & balneae*, Amsterdam (1686)

Colonna, F. [?], *Hypnerotomachia Poliphili*, Venice (1499)

Coryat, T., *Master Coryats Constantinopolitan Observations Abridged*, see Purchas 1625, vol. 3

Covel, J., *Some Account of the present Greek Church*, Cambridge (1722)

Crouch, N., *Two Journeys to Jerusalem… secondly, The travels of fourteen Englishmen in 1669 from Scanderoon to Tripoly, Joppa, Ramah, Jerusalem, Bethlehem, Jericho, the River Jordan, the Lake of Sodom and Gomorrah, and back again to Aleppo by T.B.; with the rare antiquities, monuments, and memorable places and things mentioned in holy Scripture; and an exact description of the old and new Jerusalem*, London (1683)

Davilier, A. C., 'Dictionnaire d'Architecture', in *Cours d'architecture*, Paris (1693)

Dickinson, E., *Delphi Phenicizantes*, Oxford (1655)

Diodorus Siculus, *Library of History*, trans. C. H. Oldfather et al., Loeb Classical Library, Cambridge, Mass. (1967)

Dryden, J., *The Works of John Dryden*, ed. V. A. Dearing et al., 20 vols, Oakland, Cal. (1972–90)

Dugdale, W., *Monasticon Anglicanum, or the History of the Ancient Abbies, and other Monasteries, Hospitals, Cathedral and Collegiaye Churches in England and Wales*, 3 vols, London (1655; 1718)

———, *The Antiquities of Warwickshire*, London (1656)

———, *The History of St. Paul's Cathedral in London*, London (1658)

———, *The History of St Paul's Cathedral in London… Whereunto is added, a Continuation thereof, setting forth what *was done in the structure of the new church, to the Year 1685*, ed. T. Herbert, London (1716 edn)

Eusebius, *Thesaurus temporum, Eusebii Pamphili Caesarae Palaestinae Episcopi, Chronicorum canonum ominimodae historiae libri duo*, Leiden (1606)

——, *De vita Constantini*; trans. A. Cameron and S. G. Hall, *Life of Constantine*, Oxford (1999)

——, *Historia Ecclesiastica*; see Eusebius 2007

——, *Eusebius: The Church History*, trans. P. L. Maier, Grand Rapids, Mich. (2007 edn)

Evelyn, J., *Tyrannus, or the Mode: in a Discourse on Sumptuary Lawes*, London (1661)

——, *A Parallel of the Ancient Architecture with the Modern*, London (1664; 1707): see Fréart 1650

——, *The history of the three late, famous impostors, viz. Padre Ottomano, Mahomed Bei and Sabatai Sevi the one, pretended son and heir to the late Grand Signior, the other, a prince of the Ottoman family, but in truth, a Valachian counterfeit, and the last, the suppos'd Messiah of the Jews, in the year of the true Messiah, 1666*, London (1669)

——, *Navigation and Commerce, their Original and Progress containing a Succinct Account of Traffick in General: Its Benefits and Improvements*, London (1674)

——, *Numismata: A Discourse of Medals, Ancient and Modern*, London (1697)

——, 'An Account of Architects and Architecture', in *A Parallel of the Ancient Architecture with the Modern*, London (1664; 1707)

——, *The Miscellaneous Writings of John Evelyn, Esq.*, ed. W. Upcott, London (1825)

——, *Directions for the Gardiner at Says Court*, ed. G. Keynes, London (1932)

——, *The Diary of John Evelyn*, ed. E. S. de Beer, London and New York (1959)

——, *The Evelyn Library: Sold by Order of the Trustees of the Wills of J. H. C. Evelyn, deceased and Major Peter Evelyn, deceased*, 4 vols, London (1977)

Fénelon, F., *Dialogues sur l'Éloquence*, Paris (1717; 2nd edn 1718)

Finch, H., *A narrative of the success of the voyage of the Rt. Hon. H. F. ... his majesties Ambassadour Extraordinary to the ... Sultan Mamet Han, emperour of Turkey, from Smyrna to Constantinople; his arrival there, the manner of his entertainment and audience with the Grand Visier and Grand Seignior*, London (1661); see https://quod.lib.umich.edu/e/eebo2/A52655.0001.001?rgn=main;view=fulltext

Fisher von Erlach, J. B., *Entwurff einer Historischen Architectur*, Vienna (1721)

Fontana, C., *Templum Vaticanum et Ipsius Origo cum Ædificiis Maximè conspicuis antiquitus, & recèns ibidem constitutes*, Rome (1694)

Foxe, J., *Actes and Monuments*, London (1570 edn); see www.johnfoxe.org/index.php

Foy-Vaillant, J., *Seleucidarum imperium, sive, Historia regum Syriae ad fidem numismatum accommodate*, Paris (1681)

——, *Historia Ptolemaeorum Ægypti Regum*, Amsterdam (1701)

Fréart, R., *Parallèle de l'Architecture antique et de la moderne*, Paris (1650); see Evelyn 1664

Fryer, J., *Travels into East India and Persia, with Figures*, London (1698)

Fuller, T., *The Historie of the Holy Warre*, Cambridge (1639)

——, *The Holy State and the Profane State*, Cambridge (1642)

——, *Pisgah-sight of Palestine and the confines thereof: with the history of the Old and New Testaments acted thereon*, London (1650)

Geoffrey of Monmouth, *The History of the Kings of Britain*, trans. S. Evans, London (1963 edn)

——, *The History of the Kings of Britain*, trans. L. Thorpe, Harmondsworth (1966)

Gilles, P., *De Bosporo Thracio libri III*, London (1561)

——, *De Topographia Constantinopoleos et de illius antiquitatibus, libri IV*, London (1561)

Giovio, P., *Dialogo dell'imprese militari et amorose*, Lyon (1559); trans. S. Daniel, *The worthy tract of Paulus Iovius, contayning a discourse of rare inventions, both militarie and amorous called imprese, whereunto is added a preface by S. Daniell*, London (1585); see https://quod.lib.umich.edu/e/eebo/A01764.0001.001/1:3?rgn=div1;view=fulltext

Gordon, J., *ENOTIKON: Or, A Sermon of the Union of Great Brittannie in antiquite of language, name, religion and Kingdome*, London (1604)

Greaves, J., *Pyramidographia: or a description of the pyramids in Egypt*, London (1646)

Grelot, G.-J., *Relation Nouvelle d'un Voyage de Constantinople enrichie de plans levés par l'auteur sur les lieux*, Paris (1680); see https://archive.org/details/gri_relationnouvoogrel

——, *A Late Voyage to Constantinople*, trans. J. Philips, London (1683)

Grimeston, E., *The history of Polybius the Megalopolitan*, London (1633)

Gruterus, S., *Funeralia Mariae II Britanniarum*, Haarlem (1695)

Guidotti, T., *De Thermis Britannicis Tractatus*, London (1691)

Guillet, G., *Athènes Ancienne et Nouvelle*, Paris (1675)

Hakluyt, R., *The Principal Navigations, Voyages, Traffiques and Discoveries of the English Nation*, 2 vols, London (1599 edn)

Hall, A. R., and M. B. Hall, eds, *The Correspondence of Henry Oldenburg*, 13 vols, Madison, Wis. (1965)

Hatton, E., *A New View of London*, 2 vols, London (1708)

Haworth, S., *A Description of the Duke's Bagnio, and of*

the Mineral Bath, and New Spaw thereunto belonging, London (1683); see https://quod.lib.umich.edu/e/eebo/A43109.0001.001/1:3?rgn=div1;view=fulltext

Herbert, T., *A Relation of Some Yeares Travaile: begunne anno 1626. Into Afrique and the greater Asia, especially the Territories of the Persian Monarchie*, London (1634; 1677)

Herodotus, *Herodoti Halicarnassei Historiarum lib. IX… Ejusdem narratio de vita Homeri… Ctesiae quaedam de rebus Persarum et Indiarum*, Geneva (1592)

——, *The Histories*, trans. A. de Selincourt, Harmondsworth (1954)

Herwarth von Hohenburg, J. G., *Thesaurus Hieroglyphicorum*, Augsburg (1610)

Hobbes, T., *Leviathan*, ed. C. B. Macpherson, Harmondsworth (1951)

Hollar, W., and J. Leake, *An exact surveigh of the streets, lanes and churches contained within the ruines of the City of London* (1667); facsimile, London Topographical Society (1908–9)

Hooke, R., *Micrographia: or some Physiological Descriptions of Minute Bodies made by Magnifying Glasses*, London (1665)

——, *The Diary of Robert Hooke: 1672–1680*, ed. H. W. Robinson and W. Adams, London (1935)

——, 'Diary, 1688 to 1693', in R. T. Gunther, ed., 'Life and Work of Robert Hooke (Part IV)', *Early Science in Oxford*, vol. 10, Oxford (1935)

——, *Bibliotheca Hookiana*, London (1703); facsimile in H. A. Feisenberger, ed., *Sale Catalogue of Libraries of Eminent Persons*, vol. 11: *Scientists*, London (1972), pp. 57–116; see www.hookesbooks.com

——, *The Posthumous Works of Robert Hooke. Containing his Cutlerian lectures*, London (1705)

Howell, J., *Londonopolis… The Imperial Chamber, and Chief Emporium of Great Britain*, London (1657)

Huygens, C., *De Briefwisseling van Constantijn Huygens (1608–1687)*, ed. J. A. Worp, 6 vols, The Hague (1911–17)

Hyde, T., *Catalogus impressorum librorum Bibliothecae Bodlejanae in Academia Oxoniensi*, Oxford (1674)

Jabir Ibn Hayyan, *Alchemiae*, Bern (1545)

Josephus, *Against Apion*, trans. H. St. J. Thackeray, vol. 1, Loeb Classical Library, Cambridge, Mass. (1926)

——, *The Wars of the Jews*; see www.perseus.tufts.edu/hopper/text?doc=J.%20BJ

——, *Jewish Antiquities*, trans. H. St. J. Thackeray et al., 9 vols, Loeb Classical Library, Cambridge, Mass. (1930–65)

King, J., *A Sermon at Paules Crosse, on behalf of Paules Church*, London (1620)

Kircher, A., *Prodromus Coptus sive Aegyptianus*, Rome (1636)

——, *China Monumentis illust. & Fig. ornat.*, Antwerp (1667)

——, *Arca Noë*, Amsterdam (1675)

——, *Sphinx Mystagoga*, Amsterdam (1676)

——, *Turris Babel*, Amsterdam (1679)

——, *Physiologia Kircheriana experimentalis*, Amsterdam (1680)

Knolles, R., *The Generall Historie of the Turkes*, London (1603)

Labacco, A., *Libro d'Antonio Labacco appartenente a l'architettura nel qual si figurano alcune notabili antiquità di Roma*, Rome (1572 edn)

Labrosse, J. [Ange de Saint-Joseph], *Gazophylacium Linguae Persarum, Clari Italicae, Lat. & Gallicae Linguae reseratum*, Amsterdam (1684)

Le Comte, F., and R. Burdon, 'Sommaire historique d'Architecture et des architectes, dont les ouvrages ont le plus éclaté dans la France', *Cabinet des singularitez d'architecture, peinture, sculpture, et gravure*, vol. 1 (1699)

Lee, S., *Orbis miraculum; or, the Temple of Solomon Pourtrayed by Scripture-Light*, London (1659)

Leigh, C., *The Natural History of Lancashire, Cheshire, and the Peak in Derbyshire*, Oxford (1700)

Lenorman, F., *Chaldean Magic: Its Origins and Development*, London (1877); see www.masseiana.org/lenormant.htm

Leo Africanus, J., *Totius Africae Descriptio*, Antwerp (1556)

Lightfoot, J., *The Temple: Especially as it stood in the Days of Our Savior*, London (1650)

——, *The Works of the Reverend and Learned John Lightfoot*, 2 vols, London (1684)

Lithgow, W., *The Totall Discourse, of the Rare Adventures, and Painfull Peregrinations of Long Nineteene Yeares Travayles, From Scotland, to the Most Famous Kingdomes in Europe, Asia and Africa*, London (1632)

Lobo, J., *A Short Relation of the River Nile, of its Source and Current, and of its overflowing the Campagnia of Egypt*, trans. P. Wyche, London (1669)

Locke, J., *The Works of John Locke*, 9 vols, London (1824); see http://oll.libertyfund.org/titles/locke-the-works-of-john-locke-in-nine-volumes

——, *An Essay Concerning Human Understanding*, ed. J. W. Yolton, 2 vols, London (1965 edn)

——, *The Correspondence of John Locke*, ed. E. S. de Beer, 8 vols, Oxford (1976–89)

Lorck, M., *Wolgerissene und Geschnittenes Figuren, zu Ross und Fus, sampt schönen Türckischen Gebäwen*, Hamburg (1626 [not 1619 as on the title-page])

Lord, H., *A Display of two forraigne sects in the East Indies: sect of the Banians… and sect of the Persees*, London (1630)

Lowthorp, J., ed., *The Philosophical Transactions and Collections, to the end of the year 1700. Abridg'd and dispos'd under general heads*, 3 vols, London (1705)

Lynche, R., trans., *An Historical Treatise of the Travels of Noah into Europe*, London (1601)

Magnus, O., *A compendious history of the Goths, Swedes, & Vandals, and other Northern nations*, London (1658 edn)

Maier, M., *Arcana Arcanissima hoc est Hieroglyphica Aegyptio-Graeca*, London (1613)

Malory, T., *Most ancient and famous history of the renowned prince Arthur King of Britaine: Wherein is declared his life and death, with all his glorious battailes against the Saxons, Saracens and pagans…also, all the noble acts, and heroicke deeds of his valiant knights of the Round Table*, London (1634)

Marot, J., *Le grand oeuvre d'architecture de Jean Marot*, Paris [c.1665]

Marsh, H., *A New Survey of the Turkish Empire and Government*, London (1633)

Martial, *Epigrams*, trans. D. R. Shackleton Bailey, 2 vols, Loeb Classical Library, Cambridge, Mass. (1993); see www.tertullian.org/fathers/martial_epigrams_book05.htm; https://archive.org/stream/martialepigrams01martiala/martialepigrams01martiala_djvu.txt

——, *De Spectaculis*; see www.thelatinlibrary.com/martial/mart.spec.shtml

Maundrell, H., *Journey from Aleppo to Jerusalem at Easter, A.D. 1697*, Oxford (1703; 3rd edn 1714)

Mede, J., *Churches, that is, Appropriate Places for Christian worship both in and ever since the Apostles Times*, London (1638)

Milton, J., *Complete Prose Works of John Milton*, ed. D. M. Wolfe, 7 vols, New Haven and London (1953–83)

Molinet, C. du, *Le cabinet de la Bibliothèque de Sainte Geneviève: divisé en deux parties: contenant les antiquitez de la réligion des chrétiens, des Egyptiens, & des Romains*, Paris (1692)

Monconys, B. de, *Journal des Voyages*, Lyon (1665)

Montano, G. B., *Li Cinque Libri di Architettura*, Rome (1691)

Moryson, F., *An Itinerary…containing his ten yeeres travell*, London (1617)

Nicolas de Lyre, *Postilla super totam Bibliam*, Rome (1471–2)

Nicolay, N. de, *Les quatre premiers livres des navigations et pérégrinations orientales*, Lyon (1567)

Nieuhof, J., *Legatio batavica ad magnum Tartariae chamum Sungteium, modernum Sinae imperatorem*, Amsterdam (1668)

Noorthouck, J., *A New History of London Including Westminster and Southwark*, London (1773), in British History Online, www.british-history.ac.uk/no-series/new-history-london/pp560-566

Noris, H., *Annus et Epochae Syromacedonum in Vetustis urbium Syriae Nummis praefertim Mediceis Expositae*, Leipzig (1696 edn)

North, R., *The Lives of the Right Hon. Francis North, Baron Guilford, The Hon. Sir Dudley North, and the Hon. and Rev. Dr. John North*, 3 vols, London (1826 edn)

——, *Of Building*, ed. H. Colvin and J. Newman, Oxford (1981)

Ockley, S., *The Conquest of Syria, Persia, and Egypt by the Saracens…Giving an account of their most remarkable battles, sieges…Illustrating the religion, rites, customs and manner of living of that warlike people. Collected from the most Authentick Arabick Authors, especially Manuscripts, not hitherto publish'd in any European language*, London (1708)

——, *An Account of South-West Barbary: containing what is most Remarkable in the Territories of the King of Fez and Morocco*, London (1713)

Ogilby, J., *The Holy Bible…Illustrated w[i]th Chorographical Sculp[ture]s by J. Ogilby*, Cambridge (1660)

——, *Asia or Description of Persia, &c. with Maps*, London (1673)

Olearius, A., *Beschreibung der muscowitischen und persischen Reise*, Schleswig-Holstein (1647)

——, *The Voyages and Travels of the Ambassadors sent by Frederick Duke of Holstein, to the Great Duke of Muscovy, and the King of Persia*, trans. J. Davies, London (1662)

Pagitt, E., *Christianography: or, the Description of the Multitude and Sundary sort of Christians in the World*, London (1674 edn)

Palladio, A., *Descritione de le chiese…in la città de Roma*, Rome (1554); trans. V. Hart and P. Hicks, *Palladio's Rome*, New Haven and London (2006)

——, *I quattro libri dell'architettura*, Venice (1570); *The Four Books on Architecture*, trans. R. Tavernor and R. Schofield, Cambridge, Mass. (1997)

——, *Commentari di Giulio Cesare*, Venice (1575)

Pennant, T., *Some Account of London*, vol. 4, London (1825 edn, City of Westminster Archives Centre)

Pepys, S., *The Diary of Samuel Pepys*, ed. H. B. Wheatley, London (1893); see www.pepysdiary.com/diary

Perrault, Charles, *Parrallèle des anciens et des modernes*, Paris (1688–97)

Perrault, Claude, *Ordonnance des cinq espèces de colonnes selon la methode des Anciens*, Paris (1683); *A Treatise of the Five Orders of Columns*, trans. J. James, London (1708)

Pliny the Elder, *Natural History*, trans. H. Rackham, Loeb Classical Library, Cambridge, Mass. (1938)

Plot, R., *The Natural History of Oxford-Shire*, Oxford (1677)

——, *Natural History of Staffordshire*, Oxford (1686)

Polybius, *The Histories*, trans. W. R. Paton, 6 vols, Loeb Classical Library, Cambridge, Mass. (1967–8)

Pratt, R., 'St Paul's and the New Way of Architecture for Churches' (1672), in *The Architecture of Sir Roger Pratt*, ed. R. T. Gunther, Oxford (1928)

Prideaux, H., *Marmora Oxoniensa ex Arundellianis, Seldenianis, aliifque conflata*, Oxford (1676)

——, *The true nature of imposture fully display'd in the life of Mahomet with a discourse annexed for the vindicating of Christianity from this charge*, London (1697)

Procopius, *Buildings, General Index to Procopius*, trans. H. B. Dewing, vol. 7, Loeb Classical Library, Cambridge, Mass. (1940)

Prynne, W., *Canterburies Doome: or, The first part of a Compleat History of the Commitment, Charge, Tryall, Condemnation and Execution of William Laud*, London (1646)

Purchas, S., *Hakluytus Posthumus, Purchas, his Pilgrimage*, 5 vols, London (1625); see http://archive.org/stream/hakluytusposthum01purcuoft/hakluytusposthum01purcuoft_djvu.txt

Ralph, J., *Critical Review of the Buildings of London*, London (1734)

Rawlinson, R., *The history and antiquities of the Cathedral-Church of Salisbury, and the abbey-church of Bath*, London (1719)

Reynell, C., *The Fortunate Change: Being a Panegyrick to His Sacred Majesty, King Charles the Second*, London (1661)

[R.H.], *New Atlantis, begun by the lord Verulam, viscount of St. Albans and continued by R.H. Esquire, wherein is set forth a platform of the monarchical government with a pleasant intermixture of divers rare inventions and wholesome customs, fit to be introduced into all kingdoms, states, and commonwealths*, London (1660)

Ripa, C., *Iconologia, overo, Descrittione dell'imagini universali cavate dall'antichita et da altri Ivoghi da Cesare Ripa Perugino*, Rome (1593); see https://archive.org/details/iconologia00ripa/page/n1

[R.T.], *De templis, a treatise of temples wherein is discovered the ancient manner of building, consecrating, and adorning of churches*, London (1638)

Rycaut, P., *The Present State of the Ottoman Empire containing the maxims of the Turkish politie, the most material points of the Mahometan religion, their sects and heresies, their convents and religious votaries, their military discipline…illustrated with divers pieces of sculpture, representing the variety of habits among the Turks*, London (1667)

——, *The Present State of the Greek and Armenian Churches, Anno Christi 1678*, London (1679)

——, *The History of the Turkish Empire from 1623 to 1677, containing the reigns of the last three emperors (Amurath IV–Mahomet IV)*, London (1680)

Ryer, A. du, trans., *L'Alcoran de Mahomet*, Paris (1647, 1649 edn); trans. A. Ross, London (1649)

Sammes, A., *Britannia Antiqua Illustrata, or Antiquities of Ancient Britain, derived from the Phoenicians: wherein the original trade of this island is discovered…with the antiquities of the Saxons, as well as Phoenicians, Greeks, and Romans*, London (1676)

Sanderson, J., *A Discourse of the most notable things of the famous Citie Constantinople: both in ancient and late time*; see Purchas 1625, vol. 3

——, *The travels of John Sanderson in the Levant, 1584–1602: with his autobiography and selections from his correspondence*, ed. W. Foster, London (1930)

Sandys, G., *A relation of a Journey begun an: Dom: 1610. Foure bookes. Containing a description of the Turkish Empire, of Ægypt, of the Holy Land, of the remote parts of Italy, and ilands adjoyning*, London (1615); 6th edn *Sandys Travels: containing an history of the original and present state of the Turkish Empire…a description of Constantinople, the Grand Signior's seraglio, and his manner of living*, London (1670)

Sansovino, F., *Dell'Historia universale dell'origine, et impero de' Turchi*, Venice (1560)

——, *Gl'Annali overo le Vite de principi et signori della casa Othomana*, Venice (1570)

——, *Venetia città nobilissima et singolare*, Venice (1581)

——, *Sansovino's Venice*, trans. V. Hart and P. Hicks, New Haven and London (2017)

Saumaise, C., *Plinianae exercitationes*, Utrecht (1689)

Schedel, H., *Liber Chronicarum* (the 'Nuremberg Chronicle'), Nuremberg (1493)

Seller A., *The Antiquities of Palmyra*, London (1696)

Serlio, S., *Regole Generali di Architettura di Sebastiano Serlio Bolognese*, Venice (1537): see Serlio 1996

——, *Il terzo libro di Sebastiano Serlio bolognese*, Venice (1540): see Serlio 1996

——, *Sebastiano Serlio on Architecture* [Books I–'VIII'], trans. V. Hart and P. Hicks, 2 vols, New Haven and London (1996, 2001)

Settle, E., *Absalom Senior: or, Achitophel Transpros'd. A Poem*, London (1682)

Seymour, R., *A survey of the cities of London and Westminster, borough of Southwark, and Parts Adjacent*, 2 vols, London (1733)

Shakespeare, W., *William Shakespeare: The Complete Works*, ed. S. Wells and G. Taylor, Oxford (1988)

Shepherd, T., *London and its Environs in the Nineteenth Century*, London (1829)

Shirley, A., *Sir Antony Sherley His Relation of His Travels into Persia. The Dangers, and Distresses, which befell him*, London (1613)

Sigüenza, J. de, *Segunda parte de la Historia de la Orden de San Geronimo*, Madrid (1600)

Sleidan, J., *A Briefe Chronicle of the foure principall Empyres. To witte of Babilon, Persia, Grecia and Rome*, London (1563)

Smith, T., *Syntagma de Druidum Moribus ac Institutis*, London (1664)

——, *Epistolae Duae, quarum altera de moeibus ac institutis Turcarum agit: altera septem Asiae Ecclesiarum notitiam continent*, Oxford (1672); trans. *Remarks upon the Manners, Religion and Government of the Turks. Together with a Survey of the Seven Churches of Asia as they now lye in their Ruines: and a Brief Description of Constantinople*, London (1678)

——, *De Graecae ecclesiae hodierno statu epistola*, Oxford (1676); trans. *An Account of the Greek Church as to its doctrine and rites of worship*, London (1680)

——, *Robert Huntingtoni...Epistole*, London (1704); trans. in *The Gentleman's Magazine*, vol. 95 (1825), pp. 11–15

Spon, J., *Voyage d'Italie, de Dalmatie, du Grèce, et du Levant, fait aux annés 1675 & 1676. Par Jacob Spon & George Wheler*, Lyon (1678); see Wheler, 1682

——, *Recherches curieuses d'antiquité*, Lyon (1683)

——, *Miscellanea Eruditae Antiquitatis*, Lyon (1685 edn)

Sprat, T., *The History of the Royal Society of London, For the Improving of Natural Knowledge*, London (1667)

Spreti, D., *Della grandezza, della ruine e della restaurazione di Ravenna*, Pesaro (1575)

Stephanus of Byzantium, *De urbibus et populis fragmenta*, Leiden (1674)

Stevin, S., *Materiae Politicae: Burgherlicke Stoffen; vervanghende ghedachtenissen der oeffeninghen des doorluchtichsten Prince Maurits van Orangie*, Leiden (1650)

Stillingfleet, E., *Origines Britannicae: or the Antiquities of the British Churches*, London (1685)

Strabo, *Rerum Geographicarum libri XVII Isaacus Casaubonus recensuit...Geographum*, Paris (1620)

——, *The Geography of Strabo*, trans. H. L. Jones et al., 8 vols, Loeb Classical Library, Cambridge, Mass. (1928–32)

Struys, J. J., *Drie aanmerkelijke en seer rampspoedige Reysen*, Amsterdam (1676)

——, *Les Voyages de Jan Struys en Moscovie, en Tartarie, en Perse, aux Indes*, Amsterdam (1681)

Stukeley, W., *Itinerarium Curiosum: Or, An Account of the Antiquities, and Remarkable Curiosities in Nature or Art, Observed in Travels through Great Britain*, London (1776 edn)

Tavernier, J. B., *Nouvelle Relation de l'intéreur du Sérail du Grand Seigneur contenant plusieurs singularitez qui jusqu'icy n'ont point esté mises en Lumière*, Paris (1675)

——, *Voyages thro' Turkey into Persia and the East Indies, with Figures*, London (1678)

Thévenot, J., *The Travels of Monsieur de Thevenot in the Levant*, trans. A. Lovell, London (1687 edn)

Thorpe, T., *Catalogue of a Most Interesting Series of Autograph Letters*, London (1836)

Timberlake, H., *A True and Strange Discourse on the Travailes of two English Pilgrims*, London (1603)

——, *Two journeys to Jerusalem: Containing First, A Strange and True Account of the Travels of Two English Pilgrims*, London (1685)

Troia Redeviva, or, The Glories of London Surveyed: in an heroick Poem, London (1674)

A True Account of the Royal Bagnio, with a Discourse of its Virtues, London (1680)

Twyne, J., *De Regus Albionicis, Britannicis atque Anglicis, commentariorum libri duo*, London (1590)

Ussher, J., *The Annals of the World*, London (1658 edn)

Valeriano, P., *Hieroglyphica sive sacris Aegyptiorum literis commentarii*, Basel (1556)

Valle, P. della, *Viaggi di P. della V....divisi in tre parti, cioè la Turchia, la Persia, e l'India*, vol. 2, Rome (1658)

Vansleb (Wansleben), J. M., *The Present State of Egypt; or, A new Relation of a late Voyage into that Kingdom*, London (1678)

Vasari, G., *Vite de' più eccellenti architetti, pittori, et scultori italiani, da Cimabue insino a' tempi nostri*, Florence (1568 edn)

——, *Lives of the most eminent painters, sculptors & architects, by Giorgio Vasari*, trans. G. du C. de Vere, 10 vols, London (1912–15); see https://ebooks.adelaide.edu.au/v/vasari/giorgio/lives/complete.html

Vecellio, C., *Degli habiti antichi et moderni di diverse parti del mondo*, Venice (1590)

——, *Habiti antichi et moderni di tutto il mondo*, Venice (1598)

Veen, O. van, *Quinti Horatii Flacci emblemata Imaginibus in oes incisis, notisq[ue], illustrata, studio Othonis Voeni, Batauolugdunensis*, Brussels (1682 edn)

Vegetius, F. R., *De Re Militari*, Wesel (1670 edn)

Villalpando, J. B., *In Ezechielem Explanationes et Apparatus Urbis ac Templi Hierosolymitani*, 3 vols, Rome (1596–1605)

Vincent, T., *Gods Terrible Voice in the City*, London (1667)

Vitruvius, *Di Lucio Vitruvio Pollione De architectura libri dece traducti de latino in vulgare*, Como (1521)

——, *Zehen Bücher von der Architectur und künstlichem Bawen...per D. Gualtherum H. Rivium, cum Fig.*, trans. W. H. Ryff, Basel (1575)

——, *Architecture...en Abrege par M. Perrault*, Amsterdam (1681)

——, *Les dix livres d'architecture de Vitruve*, trans. C. Perrault, Paris (1684)

——, *De Architectura*, Books I–X, trans. F. Granger, 2 vols, Loeb Classical Library, Cambridge, Mass., and London (1931)

Walker, J., ed., *Letters Written by Eminent Persons in the Seventeenth and Eighteenth Centuries*, 2 vols, London (1813); repub. Cambridge (2015)

Wansleben, see Vansleb

Watkins, R., *Newes from the Dead, or a true and exact narration of the miraculous Deliverance of Anne Greene, who being executed at Oxford Dec. 14, 1650, afterwards revived; and by the care of certain Physicians there is now perfectly recovered*, Oxford (1651)

Webb, J., *Vindication of Stone-Heng Restored*, London (1665)

——, *An Historical Essay Endeavoring a Probability that the Language of the Empire of China is the Primitive Language*, London (1669)

Wheler, G., *A Journey into Greece by George Wheler, Esq., in Company of Dr Spon of Lyons in Six Books*, London (1682); see Spon 1678 and https://quod.lib.umich.edu/e/eebo2/A65620.0001.001

——, *An Account of the Churches, or Places of Assembly, of the Primitive Christians…with a Seasonable Application*, London (1689); see https://quod.lib.umich.edu/e/eebo/A65619.0001.001

Wilkin, S., ed., *Sir Thomas Browne's Works, including his Life and Correspondence*, 4 vols, London (1836)

Wilkins, J., *An Essay Towards a Real Character and a Philosophical Language*, London (1668)

Williams, J., *Great Britains SALOMON*, London (1625)

Wood, A., 'The Life of Anthony à Wood', in T. Hearne, ed., *Thomæ Caii…Vindiciae Antiquitatis Academiae Oxoniesnsis*, Oxford (1730), vol. 2, pp. 438–603; see https://babel.hathitrust.org/cgi/pt?id=nyp.33433079892109;view=1up;seq=134

Wotton, H., *The Elements of Architecture…collected from the Best Authors and Examples*, London (1624)

Wren, C., 'Oratio Inauguralis Habita Londini in Collegio Greshamensi', 1657, trans. in Wren 1750, pp. 24–33; see: www.philological.bham.ac.uk/wren2/text.html; alternative trans. (with additional material): www.philological.bham.ac.uk/wren2/trans.html#1

Wren, S., ed., *Parentalia: Or, Memoirs of the Family of the Wrens*, London (1750); repr. *Life and Works of Sir Christopher Wren from the Parentalia, or Memoirs by His Son Christopher*, ed. E. J. Enthoven, London (1903)

Zouch, T., *The Works of the Rev. Thomas Zouch*, 2 vols, London (1820)

SECONDARY SOURCES

Abbott, G. F., *Under the Turk in Constantinople: A Record of Sir John Finch's Embassy, 1675–1681*, London (1920)

Addleshaw, G., and F. Etchells, *The Architectural Setting of Anglican Worship*, London (1948)

Adler, W., 'Did the Biblical Patriarchs practice Astrology? Michael Glykas and Manuel Komnenos I on Seth and Abraham', in P. Magdalino, ed., *The Occult Sciences in Byzantium*, Geneva (2006), pp. 245–64

Anderson, S., *An English Consul in Turkey: Paul Rycaut at Smyrna, 1667–1678*, Oxford (1996)

Arnold, D., and S. Bending, eds, *Tracing Architecture: The Aesthetics of Antiquarianism*, Chichester (2003)

Astengo, G., 'The Rediscovery of Palmyra and its Dissemination in *Philosophical Transactions*', *Notes and Records: The Royal Society Journal of the History of Science* (16 March 2016); see http://rsnr.royalsocietypublishing.org/content/early/2016/03/12/rsnr.2015.0059

Aurenhammer, H., *J. B. Fischer von Erlach*, London (1973)

Avcıoğlu, N., *Turquerie and the Politics of Representation, 1728–1876*, Farnham (2011)

Baer, M. D., 'The Great Fire of 1660 and the Islamization of Christian and Jewish Space in Istanbul', *International Journal of Middle East Studies*, vol. 36 no. 2 (2004), pp. 159–81

Balfour, A., *Solomon's Temple: Myth, Conflict, and Faith*, Chichester (2012)

Banks, D., and M. Frassetto, eds, *Western Views of Islam in Medieval and Early Modern Europe: Perception of Other*, New York (1999)

Baxandall, M., *Shadows and Enlightenment*, New Haven and London (1995)

Beard, G., *The Works of Christopher Wren*, Edinburgh (1982)

Beddard, R. A., 'Wren's Mausoleum for Charles I and the Cult of the Royal Martyr', *Architectural History*, vol. 27 (1984), pp. 36–49

Beer, E. S. de, 'King Charles II's Own Fashion: An Episode in Anglo-French Relations 1666–1670', *Journal of the Warburg Institute*, vol. 2 (1938), pp. 105–15

Bennett, J. A., 'Christopher Wren: The Natural Causes of Beauty', *Architectural History*, vol. 15 (1972), pp. 5–22

——. 'A Study of *Parentalia*, with Two Unpublished Letters of Sir Christopher Wren', *Annals of Science*, vol. 30 (1973), pp. 129–47

——, 'Christopher Wren: Astronomy, Architecture and the Mathematical Sciences', *Journal for the History of Astronomy*, vol. 6 (1975), pp. 149–84

——, *The Mathematical Sciences of Christopher Wren*, Cambridge (1982)

——, and S. Mandelbrote, eds, *The Garden, the Ark, the Tower, the Temple: Biblical Metaphors of Knowledge in Early Modern Europe*, Oxford (1998)

Bennett, J. A., et al., eds, *London's Leonardo: The Life and Work of Robert Hooke*, Oxford (2003)

Bent, J. T., ed., *Early Voyages and Travels in the Levant: Part II, 'Extracts from the Diaries of Dr John Covel. 1670–1679'*, London (1893)

Bidwell, R., 'Middle Eastern Studies in British Universities', *British Society for Middle Eastern Studies*, vol. 1 no. 2 (1975), pp. 84–6; see www.tandfonline.com/doi/abs/10.1080/13530197508705115?journalCode= cbjm19

Bikker, J., 'Re-reading Wren's Mind in Light of the Bookish Evidence', in P. R. du Prey, ed., *Architects, Books and Libraries: A Collection of Essays published in conjunction with the Exhibition of the Same Name*, Kingston, Ontario (1995), pp. 16–23

Binski, P., *Westminster Abbey and the Plantagenets*, New Haven and London (1995)

Birchwood, M., *Staging Islam in England: Drama and Culture, 1640–1685*, Cambridge (2007)

Bloch, M., *The Royal Touch: Sacred Monarchy and Scrofula in England and France*, Montreal (1973)

Bloom, J., and S. Blair, eds, *Grove Encyclopedia of Islamic Art & Architecture*, 3 vols, Oxford (2009)

Bold, J., *John Webb: Architectural Theory and Practice in the Seventeenth Century*, Oxford (1989)

Bolton, A. T., and H. D. Hendry, eds, *Wren Society Volumes*, 20 vols, Oxford (1924–43): vols 1–3 Cathedral drawings, vol. 5 city design, vols 8–16, 18, 19 accounts

Bradley, S., and N. Pevsner, *The Buildings of England. London: The City Churches*, New Haven and London (1998 edn)

Brewer, D. H., 'Secret History and Allegory', in R. Bullard and R. Carnell, eds, *The Secret History in Literature, 1660–1820*, Cambridge (2017), pp. 60–73

Brie, F. W. D., ed., *The Brut or The Chronicle of England*, Early English Text Society, 2 vols, London (1908); see https://quod.lib.umich.edu/c/cme/APG1531

'A Brief History of Christ Church', Oxford, n.d; see www.chch.ox.ac.uk/sites/default/files/Visitor_Information-gb.pdf

Brotton, J., *This Orient Isle: Elizabethan England and the Islamic World*, London (2016)

Burns, R., *Origins of the Colonnaded Streets in the Cities of the Roman East*, Oxford (2017)

Cadwallader, A., 'The Reverend Dr. John Luke and the Churches of Chonai', *Greek, Roman and Byzantine Studies*, vol. 48 (2008), pp. 319–38

Campbell, C., et al., *Bellini and the East*, London (2005)

Campbell, J., *Building St Paul's*, London (2007)

——, *Was Sir Christopher Wren a Mason?*, Prestonian Lecture for 2011, London (2011)

Canny, N., ed., *The Origins of Empire: British Overseas Enterprise to the Close of the Seventeenth Century*, Oxford History of the British Empire, vol. 1, Oxford (1998)

Carey, D., 'Compiling Nature's History: Travellers and Travel Narratives in the Early Royal Society', *Annals of Science*, vol. 54 (1997), pp. 269–92

Caygill, H., 'Ottoman Baroque: The Limits of Style', in H. Hills, ed., *Rethinking the Baroque*, Farnham (2011), pp. 65–79

Chapman, A., *England's Leonardo: Robert Hooke and the Seventeenth Century Scientific Revolution*, London (2005)

Cohen, A., *Economic Life in Ottoman Jerusalem*, Cambridge (1986)

Coles, P., *The Ottoman Impact on Europe*, London (1968)

Colvin, H., *The History of the King's Works, 1660–1782*, vol. 5, London (1976)

——, 'The Church of St Mary Aldermary and its Rebuilding after the Great Fire of London', *Architectural History*, vol. 24 (1981), pp. 24–31

Conder, E., 'King Charles II at the Royal Exchange, London in 1667', *Ars Quatuor Coronatorum*, vol. 11 (1898), pp. 138–51

Cooper, M., *'A More Beautiful City': Robert Hooke and the Rebuilding of London after the Great Fire*, Stroud (2003); see also Moore 2005

——, and M. Hunter, eds, *Robert Hooke, Tercentennial Studies*, Aldershot (2006)

Corbett, M., and R. Lightbown, *The Comely Frontispiece: The Emblematic Title-Page in England 1550–1660*, London (1979)

Cottingham, J., *The Cambridge Companion to Descartes*, Cambridge (1992)

Cranston, M., *John Locke, a Biography*, New York (1957)

Cruickshank, D., *The Secret History of Georgian London: How the Wages of Sin shaped the Capital*, London (2009)

Cutler, A., 'A Baroque Account of Byzantine Architecture: Leone Allacci's *De templis Graecorum recentioribus*', *Journal of the Society of Architectural Historians*, vol. 25 (1966), pp. 79–89

Dalrymple, W., *The Anarchy: The Relentless Rise of the East India Company*, London (2019)

Dannenfeldt, K. H., 'The Renaissance and the Pre-Classical Civilizations', *Journal of the History of Ideas*, vol. 13 no. 4 (1952), pp. 435–40

Darby, P., and D. Reynolds, 'Reassessing the "Jerusalem Pilgrims": The Case of Bede's De locis sanctis', *Bulletin for the Council for British Research in the Levant*, vol. 9 (2014), pp. 27–31

Davies, C. S. L., 'The Youth and Education of Christopher Wren', *English Historical Review*, vol. 123 no. 501 (2008), pp. 300–27; see http://ehr.oxfordjournals.org/content/CXXIII/501/300.abstract

Davis, M. D., 'Della Valle's Exploration of the Ruins of Persepolis in 1621', *Fontes 66* (2012); see http://archiv.ub.uni-heidelberg.de/artdok/1868/1/Davis_Fontes66.pdf

Delbeke, M., and A. F. Morel, 'Metaphors in Action: Early Modern Church Buildings as Spaces of Knowledge', *Architectural History*, vol. 53 (2010), pp. 99–122

Dew, N., *Orientalism in Louis IV's France*, Oxford (2009)

Doll, P. M., *After the Primitive Christians*, Cambridge (1997)

——, '"The Reverence of God's House": The Temple of Solomon and the Architectural Setting for the "Unbloody Sacrifice"', in Doll, ed., *Anglicanism and Orthodoxy 300 Years after the 'Greek College' in Oxford*, Oxford (2006), pp. 193–224

Douglas-Caroë, W., *Tom Tower, Christ Church, Oxford: Some Letters of Christopher Wren to John Fell, Bishop of Oxford hitherto Unpublished*, Oxford (1923)

Douglas Stewart, J., 'A Militant, Stoic Monument: The Wren-Cibber-Gibbons Charles I Mausoleum Project: Its Authors, Sources, Meaning, and Influence', in G. W. Marshall, ed., *The Restoration Mind*, Newark, Del. (1997), pp. 21–64

Downes, K., *Hawksmoor*, London (1959)

——, *Hawksmoor*, London (1970)

——, *Christopher Wren*, London (1971)

——, *The Architecture of Wren*, London (1982; 2nd edn, 1988)

——, *Sir Christopher Wren: An Exhibition selected by Kerry Downes at the Whitechapel Art Gallery*, London (1982)

——, *Sir Christopher Wren: The Design of St Paul's Cathedral*, London (1988)

——, 'Julien-David Leroy', *Hugh Pagan Limited: Catalogue No. 3*, London (1988), pp. 18–20

——, *Sir Christopher Wren and the Making of St Paul's*, exh. cat., Royal Academy of Arts, London (1991)

——, 'Wren and the New Cathedral', in D. Keene, A. Burns and A. Saint, eds, *St Paul's: The Cathedral Church of London 604-2004* (2004), pp. 191–206

——, 'Sir Christopher Wren', *Oxford Dictionary of National Biography*, ed. H. C. G. Matthew, Oxford, vol. 60 (2004), pp. 406–19; see www.oxforddnb.com/view/10.1093/ref:odnb/9780198614128.001.0001/odnb-9780198614128-e-30019; republished as *Christopher Wren*, Oxford (2007)

Draper, P., 'Islam and the West, the Early Use of the Pointed Arch Revisited', *Architectural History*, vol. 48 (2005), pp. 1–20

Dutton, R., *The Age of Wren*, London (1951)

Eamon, W., *Science and the Secrets of Nature: Books of Secrets in Medieval and Early Modern Culture*, Princeton, N.J. (1994)

Eck, C. van. ed., 'Sir Christopher Wren', in *British Architectural Theory 1540–1750*, Aldershot (2003), pp. 217–23

——, 'Understanding Roman Architecture from a Distance: Sir Christopher Wren on the Temples of Peace and of Mars the Avenger', in A. Payne, ed., *The Companion to the History of Architecture*, vol. 1: *Renaissance and Baroque Architecture*, Chichester (2017), pp. 498–523

Elmes, J., *Sir Christopher Wren and his Times*, London (1852)

Emerson, J., 'Sir John Chardin', *Encyclopaedia Iranica*, vol. 5 (1991), pp. 369–77; see www.iranicaonline.org/articles/chardin-sir-john

Fane-Saunders, P., *Pliny the Elder and the Emergence of Renaissance Architecture*, Cambridge (2016)

Faroqhi, S., and C. Neumann, eds, *Ottoman Costumes: From Textile to Identity*, Istanbul (2004)

Fedden, R., *English Travellers in the Near East*, London (1958)

Feingold, M., 'Patrons and Professors: The Origins and Motives for the Endowment of University Chairs – in Particular the Laudian Professor of Arabic', in Russell 1994, pp. 109–27

Fleming, W. B., *The History of Tyre*, New York (1915)

Fletcher, B., *A History of Architecture*, London (1975)

Folda, J., *The Art of the Crusaders in the Holy Land, 1098–1187*, Cambridge and New York (1995)

——, *Crusader Art in the Holy Land: From the Third Crusade to the Fall of Acre, 1187–1291*, Cambridge (2005)

Frankl, P., *The Gothic: Literary Sources and Interpretations through Eight Centuries*, Princeton, N.J. (1960)

Fürst, V., *The Architecture of Sir Christopher Wren*, London (1956)

Ganim, J., *Medievalism and Orientalism: Three Essays on Literature, Architecture and Cultural Identity*, New York and Basingstoke (2005)

Geczy, A., *Fashion and Orientalism: Dress, Textiles and Culture from the 17th to the 21st Century*, London (2013)

Geraghty, A., 'Nicholas Hawksmoor and the Wren City Church Steeples', *The Georgian Group Journal*, vol. 10 (2000), pp. 1–14

——, 'Wren's Preliminary Design for the Sheldonian Theatre', *Architectural History*, vol. 45 (2002), pp. 275–88

——, 'Robert Hooke's Collection of Architectural Books and Prints', *Architectural History*, vol. 47 (2004), pp. 113–25

——, *The Architectural Drawings of Sir Christopher Wren at All Souls College, Oxford: A Complete Catalogue*, Aldershot (2007)

——, 'Nicholas Hawksmoor's Drawing Technique of the 1690s and John Locke's *Essay Concerning Human Understanding*', in H. Hills, ed., *Rethinking the Baroque*, Farnham (2011), pp. 125–41

——, *The Sheldonian Theatre: Architecture and Learning in Seventeenth-Century Oxford*, New Haven and London (2013)

Gerbino, A., and S. Johnston, *Compass and Rule: Architecture as Mathematical Practice in England 1500–1750*, New Haven and London (2009)

Gilliat-Ray, S., *Muslims in Britain: An Introduction*, Cambridge (2010)

Goffman, D., *Britons in the Ottoman Empire, 1642–1660*, Washington, D.C. (1998)

Gombrich, E. H., *Shadows: The Depiction of Cast Shadows in Western Art*, London (1995)

Grafton, A., *New Worlds, Ancient Texts: The Power of Tradition and the Shock of Discovery*, Cambridge, Mass. (1992)

Granston, M., *John Locke, A Biography*, London (1957)

Grogan, J., *The Persian Empire in English Renaissance Writing, 1549–1622*, London (2014)

Grèlois, J.-P., ed., *Voyages en Turquie, 1675–1677*, Paris (1998)

Griffith-Jones, R., '"An Enrichment of Cherubims": Christopher Wren's Refurbishment of the Temple Church', in R. Griffith-Jones and D. Park, ed., *The Temple Church in London: History, Architecture, Art*, Woodbridge (2010), pp. 135–74

Griffiths, D. N., *Lincoln Cathedral Library*, Lincoln (1970)

Grimstone, A. V., *Building Pembroke Chapel: Wren, Pearce and Scott*, Cambridge (2009)

Guillery, P., 'Suburban Models, or Calvinism and Continuity in London's Seventeenth-Century Church Architecture', *Architectural History*, vol. 48 (2005), pp. 69–106

Gunther, R. T., ed., *Early Science in Oxford*, vol. 7, Oxford (1930)

Hachili, R., 'The Niche and the Ark in Ancient Synagogues', *Bulletin of American School of Oriental Research*, vol. 222 (1976), pp. 43–53

Haeffner, M., *Dictionary of Alchemy: From Maria Prophetissa to Isaac Newton*, London (1991)

Hakewill, A. W., 'Charles the Second's Bath, Bath Street, Newgate Street, Sir Christopher Wren, Architect', *The Civil Engineer and Architects Journal*, vol. 13 (October 1850), pp. 348–50

Hall, M. B., 'Arabick Learning in the Correspondence of the Royal Society', in Russell 1994, pp. 147–57

Hamill, J., *The History of Freemasonry*, Addlestone (1994)

Hamilton, A., *William Bedwell the Arabist 1563–1632*, Leiden (1985)

Harris, E., *British Architectural Books and Writers 1556–1785*, Cambridge (1990), pp. 503–8

Hart, V., *Art and Magic in the Court of the Stuarts*, London (1994)

——, 'London, St Paul's Architecture', *Macmillan Dictionary of Art*, London (1995)

——, *St Paul's Cathedral: Sir Christopher Wren*, London (1995)

——, *Nicholas Hawksmoor: Rebuilding Ancient Wonders*, New Haven and London (2002)

——, *Sir John Vanbrugh: Storyteller in Stone*, New Haven and London (2008)

——, *Inigo Jones: The Architect of Kings*, New Haven and London (2011)

——, 'London's Standard: Christopher Wren and the Heraldry of the Monument', *RES: Journal of Anthropology and Aesthetics*, vol. 73/74 (forthcoming 2020)

Harvey, J., 'Coronary Flowers and their "Arabick" Background', in Russell 1994, pp. 297–303

Hattox, R. S., *Coffee and Coffeehouses: The Origins of a Social Beverage in the Medieval Near East*, Washington, D.C. (1985)

Haynes, J., *The Humanist as Traveler: George Sandys's Relation of a Journey begun An. Dom. 1610*, London and Toronto (1986)

Henderson, F., 'Robert Hooke's Archive', *Script & Print: Bulletin of the Bibliographical Society of Australia and New Zealand*, vol. 33 nos 1–4 (2009), pp. 92–108; see www.bsanz.org/download/script-and-print/script_and_print_vol._33_nos._1-4_(2009)/SP_2009-Vol33-Nos1-4_pp92-108.pdf

Horsfall Turner, O., 'Perceptions of Medieval Buildings in England, c.1640–c.1720', PhD thesis, University College London (2009)

——, '"The Windows of This Church Are of Several Fashions": Architectural Form and Historical Method in John Aubrey's "Chronologia Architectonica"', *Architectural History*, vol. 54 (2011), pp. 171–93

Howard, D., *Venice & the East: The Impact of the Islamic World on Venetian Architecture 1000–1500*, New Haven and London (2000)

Howard, M., 'Self-Fashioning and the Classical Moment in Mid-Sixteenth-Century English Architecture', in L. Gent and N. Llewellyn, eds, *Renaissance Bodies: The Human Figure in English Culture c.1540–1660*, London (1990), pp. 198–217

——, *The Building of Elizabethan and Jacobean England*, New Haven and London (2007)

Howarth, D., *Images of Rule: Art and Politics in the English Renaissance, 1485–1649*, Berkeley and Los Angeles, Cal. (1997)

Hui, D., 'Ichnographia, Orthographia, Scaenographia: An Analysis of Cesare Cesariano's Illustration of Milan Cathedral in his Commentary of Vitruvius, 1521', *Knowledge and/or/of Experience: The Theory of Space in Art and Architecture*, Brisbane (1993), pp. 77–97

Hunter, M., *Science and Society in Restoration England*, Cambridge (1981)

——, *The Royal Society and its Fellows 1660–1700*, London (1994)

——, *Science and the Shape of Orthodoxy: Intellectual Change in Late Seventeenth Century Britain*, Woodbridge (1995)

Hutchison, H., *Sir Christopher Wren, A Biography*, London (1976)

Iliffe, R., 'Foreign Bodies and the Early Royal Society of London. Part 1: Englishmen on Tour', *Canadian Journal of History*, vol. 33 (1998), pp. 357–85

Inwood, S., *The Man who knew Too Much: The Strange and Inventive Life of Robert Hooke 1635–1703*, London (2002)

Jacob, J. R., *Henry Stubbe, Radical Protestantism and the Early Enlightenment*, Cambridge (1983)

Jairazbhoy, R. A., *Oriental Influences in Western Art*, Bombay and New York (1965)

Jardine, L., *Worldly Goods: A New History of the Renaissance*, London (1996)

——, *On a Grander Scale: The Outstanding Career of Sir Christopher Wren*, London (2002)

——, *The Curious Life of Robert Hooke: The Man who measured London*, London (2003)

——, and J. Brotton, *Global Interests: Renaissance Art between East and West*, Ithaca, N.Y. (2000)

Jeffery, P., 'The Church that never was: Wren's St Mary, and Other Projects for Lincoln's Inn Fields', *Architectural History*, vol. 31 (1988), pp. 136–44

——, 'Originals or Apprentice Copies? Some recently found Drawings for St Paul's Cathedral, All Saints, Oxford and the City Churches', *Architectural History*, vol. 35 (1992), pp. 118–34

——, *The City Churches of Sir Christopher Wren*, London (1996)

Jeppesen, K., *Paradeigmata: Three Mid-Fourth Century Main Works of Hellenic Architecture, Reconsidered*, Aarhus (1958)

Johnson, M., 'The Fifth-Century Oratory of the Holy Cross at the Lateran in Rome', *Architectura: Zeitschrift für Geschichte der Baukunst*, vol. 25 (1995), pp. 128–55; see www.academia.edu/4116172/The_Fifth-Century_Oratory_of_the_Holy_Cross_at_the_Lateran_in_Rome

Jones, R. F., 'The Originality of Absalom and Achitophel', *Modern Language Notes*, vol. 46 no. 4 (1931), pp. 211–18

Jose, N., *Ideas of the Restoration in English Literature 1660–1671*, Cambridge, Mass. (1984)

Josten, C. H., *Elias Ashmole (1617–1692)*, 2 vols, Oxford (1966)

Kantorowicz, E., *The King's Two Bodies*, Princeton, N.J. (1957)

Keay, A., and R. Harris, 'The White Tower, 1485–1642', in E. Impey, ed., *The White Tower*, New Haven and London (2008), pp. 160–77

Keene, D., A. Burns and A. Saint, eds, *St Paul's: The Cathedral Church of London 604–2004*, New Haven and London (2004)

Keevil, J. J., 'The Bagnio in London, 1648–1725', *Journal of the History of Medicine and Allied Sciences*, vol. 7 no. 3 (1952), pp. 250–7

Keller, M., and J. Irigoyen-Garcia, eds, *The Dialectics of Orientalism in Early Modern Europe*, London (2017)

Knight, C., 'The Travels of the Rev. George Wheler (1650–1723)', *The Georgian Group Journal*, vol. 10 (2000), pp. 21–35

Krautheimer, R., *Early Christian and Byzantine Architecture*, New Haven and London (1986 edn)

Kravtsov, S., 'Juan Bautista Villalpando and Sacred Architecture in the Seventeenth Century', *Journal of the Society of Architectural Historians*, vol. 64 (2005), pp. 312–39

Kusukawa, S., 'Picturing Knowledge in the Early Royal Society: The Examples of Richard Waller and Henry Hunt', *Notes and Records: The Royal Society Journal of the History of Science* (2011); see http://rsnr.royalsocietypublishing.org/content/early/2011/05/10/rsnr.2010.0094#xref-fn-19-1

Lake, P., 'The Laudian Style: Order, Uniformity and the Pursuit of the Beauty of Holiness in the 1630s', in K. Fincham, ed., *The Early Stuart Church 1603–1642*, London (1993), pp. 161–85

Lang, J., *Rebuilding St Paul's after the Great Fire of London*, Oxford (1956)

Lang, S., 'By Hawksmoor out of Gibbs', *Architectural Review*, vol. 105 (1949), pp. 183–90

Lawson, P., *The East India Company: A History, 1600–1857*, Studies in Modern History, London and New York (1993)

Levine, J. M., *Between the Ancients and the Moderns: Baroque Culture in Restoration England*, New Haven and London (1999)

Levitin, D., *Ancient Wisdom in the Age of the New Science: Histories of Philosophy in England, c.1640–1700*, Cambridge (2016)

Lincoln, M., 'Samuel Pepys and Tangier, 1662–1684', *Huntington Library Quarterly*, vol. 77 no. 4 (2014), pp. 417–34

Littleton, C., 'Ancient Languages and New Science: The Levant in the Intellectual Life of Robert Boyle', in A. Hamilton, M. H. van den Boogert and B. Westerweel, *The Republic of Letters and the Levant*, Leiden (2005), pp. 151–72

Loach, J., 'Anglicanism in London, Gallicanism in Paris, Primitivism in Both', in N. Jackson, ed., *Plus ça change …Architectural Interchange between France and Britain: Papers from the Annual Symposium of the Society of Architectural Historians of Great Britain*, Nottingham (1999), pp. 9–32

Lombaerde, P., and C. van den Heuval, eds, *Early Modern Urbanism and the Grid: Town Planning in the Low Countries in International Context. Exchanges in Theory and Practice 1550–1800*, Turnhout (2011)

McKellar, E., *The Birth of Modern London: The Development and Design of the City 1660–1720*, Manchester and New York (1999)

McKitterick, D., *The Making of the Wren Library: Trinity College, Cambridge*, Cambridge (1995)

MacLean, G., *The Rise of Oriental Travel: English Visitors to the Ottoman Empire, 1580–1720*, New York and Basingstoke (2004)

——, *Looking East: English Writing and the Ottoman Empire before 1800*, New York and Basingstoke (2007)

——, and N. Matar, *Britain and the Islamic World, 1558–1713*, Oxford (2011)

Majeska, G. P., *Russian Travelers to Constantinople in the Fourteenth and Fifteenth Centuries*, Washington, D.C. (1984)

Malcolm, N., 'Comenius, Boyle, Oldenburg, and the Translation of the Bible into Turkish', *Church History and Religious Culture*, vol. 87 no. 3 (2007), pp. 327–62

Mango, C., *Byzantine Architecture*, Milan (1978)

Maré, E., *Wren's London*, London (1975)

Marly, D. de, 'King Charles II's Own Fashion: The Theatrical Origins of the English Vest', *Journal of the Warburg and Courtauld Institutes*, vol. 37 (1974), pp. 378–82

Matar, N., *Islam in Britain, 1558–1685*, Cambridge (1998)

Mateo, M., 'The Making of the Saracen Style: The Crusades and Medieval Architecture in the British Imagination of the 18th and 19th Centuries', in K. I. Semaan, ed., *The Crusades: Other Experiences, Alternate Perspectives. Selected Proceedings from the 32nd Annual CEMERS Conference*, New York (2003), pp. 115–40.

——, 'In Search of the Gothic: Thomas Pitt's Travel in Spain in 1760', *Journal of Art Historiography*, vol. 15 (2016), pp. 1–21; see https://arthistoriography.files.wordpress.com/2016/12/mateo-translation1.pdf

Mather, J., *Pashas: Traders and Travellers in the Islamic World*, New Haven and London (2009)

Meggitt, J., 'George Robinson', in D. Thomas and J. Chesworth, eds, *Christian–Muslim Relations: A Bibliographical History*, vol. 8: *Northern and Eastern Europe, 1600–1700*, Leiden (2016), pp. 392–401

Mendelsohn, A., 'Alchemy and Politics in England 1649–1665', *Past & Present*, no. 135 (1992), pp. 30–78

Merritt, J. F., 'Puritans, Laudians and the Phenomenon of Church-building in Jacobean London', *The Historical Journal*, vol. 41 (1998), pp. 935–60

Meynell, G., 'André de Monceaux, F.R.S. 1670', *Notes and Records of the Royal Society in London*, vol. 47 no. 1 (1993), pp. 11–15

Mitsi, E., 'Travel, Memory and Authorship: George Wheler's "A Journey into Greece" (1682)', *Restoration: Studies in English Literary Culture, 1600–1700*, vol. 30 no. 1 (2006), pp. 15–29

——, *Greece in Early English Travel Writing, 1596–1682*, London (2017)

Monod, P. K., *Solomon's Secret Arts: The Occult in the Age of Enlightenment*, New Haven and London (2013)

Moore, J., 'The Monument, or, Christopher Wren's Roman Accent', *The Art Bulletin*, vol. 80 no. 3 (1998), pp. 498–533

——, review of M. Cooper, *'A More Beautiful City': Robert Hooke and the Rebuilding of London after the Great Fire*, *Reviews in History*, no. 440, March 2005, www.history.ac.uk/reviews/review/440

Moore, K. B., *The Architecture of the Christian Holy Land: Reception from Late Antiquity through the Renaissance*, Cambridge (2017)

Morrison, T., 'Isaac Newton and the Architectural Models of Solomon's Temple', *Avello Publishing Journal*, vol. 1 no. 3 (2013), pp. 1–18

Moscrop, J. J., *Measuring Jerusalem: The Palestine Exploration Fund and British Interests in the Holy Land*, London and New York (2000)

Mussells, S., 'Architects, Travellers and the Revival of the Early Christian Basilica', in P. R. du Prey, ed., *Architects, Books and Libraries: A Collection of Essays published in conjunction with the Exhibition of the Same Name*, Kingston, Ontario (1995), pp. 9–15

Necipoglu, G., *Architecture, Ceremonial, and Power: The Topkapi Palace in the Fifteenth and Sixteenth Centuries*, Cambridge, Mass. (1991)

Newman, J., 'Laudian Literature and the Interpretation of Caroline Churches in London', in D. Howarth, ed., *Art and Patronage in the Caroline Courts: Essays in honour of Sir Oliver Millar*, Cambridge (1993), pp. 176–80

Norgate, G. le G., 'Francis Vernon', *Dictionary of National Biography*, ed. L. Stephen, vol. 58, Oxford (1885–1900), pp. 273–4; see https://en.wikisource.org/wiki/Vernon,_Francis_(DNB00)

Ochs, K. H., 'The Royal Society of London's History of Trades Programme: An Early Episode in Applied Science', *Notes and Records of the Royal Society of London*, vol. 39 no. 2 (1985), pp. 129–58

O'Connor, J. J., and E. F. Robertson, 'Isaac Barrow' (1998), www-groups.dcs.st-and.ac.uk/history/Biographies/Barrow.html

Orgel, S., 'Inigo Jones's Persian Entertainment', *Art and Archaeology Research Papers*, vol. 2 (1972), pp. 59–69

——, and R. Strong, *Inigo Jones: The Theatre of the Stuart Court*, 2 vols, London (1973)

Osmond, P. H., *Isaac Barrow: His Life and Times*, London (1944)

Özkoçak, S. A., 'Coffeehouses: Rethinking the Public and Private in Early Modern Istanbul', *Journal of Urban History*, vol. 33 no. 6 (2007), pp. 965–86; see http://journals.sagepub.com/doi/abs/10.1177/0096144207304018

Panofsky, E., *Renaissance and Renascences in Western Art*, Stockholm (1960)

Parker, K., ed., *Early Modern Tales of Orient: A Critical Anthology*, London (1999)

Payne, A., 'Vasari, Architecture and the Origins of Historicizing Art', *RES. Journal of Aesthetics and Anthropology*, vol. 40 (2001), pp. 51–76

Pearson, J. B., *A Biographical Sketch of the Chaplains to the Levant Company maintained at Constantinople, Aleppo and Smyrna 1611–1706*, Cambridge (1883)

Peck, L. Levy, *Consuming Splendor: Society and Culture in Seventeenth-Century England*, Cambridge (2005)

Phillimore, L., *Sir Christopher Wren: His Family and His Times: with Original Letters and a Discourse on Architecture Hitherto Unpublished*, London (1881)

Piggott, S., *William Stukeley: An Eighteenth-Century Antiquary*, London (1985 edn)

Poole, W., *The World Makers: Scientists of the Restoration and the Search for the Origins of the Earth*, Oxford (2010)

Prey, P. R. du, 'Hawksmoor's "Basilica after the Primitive Christians": Architecture and Theology', *Journal of the Society of Architectural Historians*, vol. 48 (1989), pp. 38–52

——, *Hawksmoor's London Churches: Architecture and Theology*, Chicago (2000)

Principe, L., *The Aspiring Adept: Robert Boyle and his Alchemical Quest*, Princeton, N.J. (1998)

Radway, R. D., 'Christians of Ottoman Europe in Sixteenth-Century Costume Books', in Keller and Irigoyen-Garcia 2017, pp. 173–93

Rawlinson, H. G., 'The Embassy of William Harborne to Constantinople, 1583–8', *Transactions of the Royal Historical Society*, vol. 5 (1922), pp. 1–27

Reddaway, R. T., 'The Rebuilding of London', *Town Planning Review*, vol. 17 (1937), pp. 205–11

——, *The Building of London after the Great Fire*, London (1951)

Rodwell, W., *The Lantern Tower of Westminster Abbey 1060–2010*, Oxford (2010)

Roob, A., *Alchemy and Mysticism*, Cologne and London (1997)

Rosen, W., *Justinian's Flea: Plague, Empire, and the Birth of Europe*, New York (2007)

Rosenau, H., *Vision of the Temple: The Image of the Temple of Jerusalem in Judaism and Christianity*, London (1979)

Russell, G. A., ed., *The 'Arabick' Interest of the Natural Philosophers in Seventeenth-Century England*, Leiden (1994)

Rykwert, J., *The First Moderns*, Cambridge, Mass. (1980)

Said, E. W., *Orientalism: Western Conceptions of the Orient*, New York (1978; rev. 2003)

Saunders, A., ed., *The Royal Exchange*, London Topographical Society Publication No. 152, London (1997)

Scheja, G., 'Hagia Sophia und Templum Salomonis', *Istanbuler Mitteilungen*, vol. 12 (1962), pp. 44–58; see www.mgh-bibliothek.de/dokumente/b/b059865.pdf

Schleck, J., 'Forming Knowledge: Natural Philosophy and English Travel Writing', in J. A. Hayden, ed., *Travel Narratives, the New Science and Literary Discourse, 1659–1750*, Farnham (2012), pp. 53–70

Scholem, G., *Sabbatai Sevi: The Mystical Messiah, 1626–1676*, trans. R. J. Zwi Werblowsky, Princeton, N.J. (2016 edn)

Schuchard, M. K., *Restoring the Temple of Vision: Cabalistic Freemasonry and Stuart Culture*, Leiden (2002)

Seccombe, T., 'Paul Rycaut', *Dictionary of National Biography*, ed. L. Stephen, vol. 50, Oxford (1885–1900), pp. 38–40; see https://en.wikisource.org/wiki/Rycaut,_Paul_(DNB00)

Sekler, E. F., *Wren and his Place in European Architecture*, London (1956)

Selwood, J., *Diversity and Difference in Early Modern London*, Farnham (2010)

Semler, L. E., 'The Ruins of Persepolis: Grotesque Perception in Thomas Herbert's Travels', in L. E. Semler and E. Kelly, eds, *Word and Self Estranged in English Texts, 1550–1660*, London (2010), pp. 33–60

Sheppard, F. H. W., ed., *Survey of London: Volume 27, Spitalfields and Mile End New Town*, London (1957); see *British History Online*, www.british-history.ac.uk/survey-london/vol27/pp100-107#fnn15

——, *Survey of London: Volume 33 and 34, St Anne Soho*, London (1966); see *British History Online*, www.british-history.ac.uk/survey-london/vols33-4/pp278-287

Shiqiao, L., *Power and Virtue: Architecture and Intellectual Change in England, 1660–1730*, London and New York (2007)

Simson, O. von, *The Gothic Cathedral*, Princeton, N.J. (1956)

Slater, L., 'Imagining Places and Moralizing Space: Jerusalem at Medieval Westminster', *British Art Studies*, vol. 6 (2017); see http://britishartstudies.ac.uk/issues/issue-index/issue-6/moralizing-space

Smart, D. H., 'Primitive Christians: Baroque Architecture and Worship in Restoration London', PhD thesis, University of Toronto (1997)

Smith, E. B., *Architectural Symbolism of Imperial Rome and the Middle Ages*, Princeton, N.J. (1956)

Smith, N., '"Making Fire": Conflagration and Religious

Controversy in Seventeenth-Century London', in J. F. Merritt, ed., *Imagining Early Modern London: Perceptions and Portrayals of the City from Stow to Strype 1598–1720*, Cambridge (2001), pp. 273–93

Soo, L., 'Reconstructing Antiquity: Wren and his Circle and the Study of Natural History, Antiquarianism, and Architecture at the Royal Society', PhD thesis, Princeton University (1989)

——, *Wren's 'Tracts' on Architecture and Other Writings*, Cambridge (1998)

—— 'The Study of China and Chinese Architecture in Restoration England', *Architectura: Zeitschrift für Geschichte der Baukunst*, vol. 31 (2001), pp. 169–84

——, 'The English in the Levant: Social Networks and the Study of Architecture', in O. Horsfall Turner, ed., *'The Mirror of Great Britain': National Identity in Seventeenth-Century British Architecture*, Proceedings of the 2010 Annual Symposium of the Society of Architectural Historians of Great Britain, Reading (2012), pp. 209–31

——, 'The Architectural Setting of "Empire": The English Experience of Ottoman Spectacle in the Late 17th Century and its Consequences', in Keller and Irigoyen-Garcia 2017, pp. 217–45

Stevenson, C., *Medicine and Magnificence: British Hospital and Asylum Architecture, 1660–1815*, New Haven and London (2000)

——, 'Robert Hooke, Monuments and Memory', *Art History*, vol. 28 no. 1 (2005), pp. 49–52

——, 'Vantage Points in the Seventeenth-Century City', *The London Journal*, vol. 33 no. 3 (2008), pp. 217–32

——, *The City and the King: Architecture and Politics in Restoration London*, New Haven and London (2013)

Stevenson, D., *The Origins of Freemasonry: Scotland's Century 1590–1710*, Cambridge (1988)

Stoesser-Johnston, A., 'Robert Hooke and Holland: Dutch Influence on his Architecture', *Bulletin KNOB* (2002), pp. 121–37

Stokes, A., and J. Strzygowski, 'A Study in the Aesthetics and Historiography of Orientalism', *Art History*, vol. 26 no. 4 (2003), pp. 505–33

Strong, R., *Van Dyck: Charles I on Horseback*, London (1972)

——, *Britannia Triumphans: Inigo Jones, Rubens and Whitehall Palace*, London (1980)

Summerson, J., 'The Mind of Wren', in *Heavenly Mansions and Other Essays on Architecture*, London (1949), pp. 51–86

——, *Sir Christopher Wren*, London (1953)

——, 'Sir Christopher Wren, PRS (1632–1723)', *Notes and Records of the Royal Society of London*, vol. 15 (1960), pp. 99–105; repr. in *The Unromantic Castle*, London (1990), pp. 63–8

——, 'The Penultimate Design for St Paul's', *Burlington Magazine*, vol. 103 (1961), pp. 83–9: repr. in *The Unromantic Castle*, London (1990), pp. 69–78

——, *Architecture in Britain 1530–1830*, London (1991 edn)

Sweet, R., *Antiquaries: The Discovery of the Past in Eighteenth-Century Britain*, London and New York (2004)

——, *Cities and the Grand Tour: The British in Italy, c.1690–1820*, Cambridge (2012)

Sweetman, J., *The Oriental Obsession: Islamic Inspiration in British and American Art and Architecture 1500–1920*, Cambridge (1988)

Thomas, K., *Religion and the Decline of Magic*, New York (1971)

Thomson, H. L., 'William Seaman', *Dictionary of National Biography*, ed. L. Stephen, vol. 51, Oxford (1885–1900), p. 163; see https://en.wikisource.org/wiki/Seaman,_William_(DNB00)

Tinniswood, A., *His Invention so Fertile: A Life of Christopher Wren*, London (2001)

Toomer, G. J., *Eastern Wisdom and Learning: The Study of Arabic in Seventeenth-Century England*, Oxford (1996)

Trachtenberg, M., and I. Hyman, *Architecture: From Prehistory to Post-Modernism*, Upper Saddle River, N.J. (1986)

Tyacke, N., ed., *The History of the University of Oxford*, vol. 4: *Seventeenth-Century Oxford*, Oxford (1997)

Tyerman, C., *England and the Crusades, 1095–1588*, Chicago (1988)

Uglow, J., *A Gambling Man: Charles II and the Restoration*, London (2009)

Ukers, W. H., *All About Coffee*, New York (1922); see www.web-books.com/Classics/ON/B0/B701/15MB701.html

Varisco, D. M., *Reading Orientalism: Said and the Unsaid*, Washington, D.C. (2007)

Vickers, M., 'The Views of Persepolis by William Marshall and Wenceslaus Hollar in Sir Thomas Herbert's Travels', in H. Sancisi-Weerdenburg and J. W. Drijvers, eds, *Achaemenid History VII: Through Travellers' Eyes*, Leiden (1991), pp. 59–69

Visconsi, E., 'Trojan Originalism: Dryden's *Troilus and Cressida*', in M. Novak, ed., *The Age of Projects*, Toronto (2008), pp. 73–90

Vitkus, D. J., 'Trafficking with the Turk: English Travellers in the Ottoman Empire during the Early Seventeenth Century', in I. Kamps and J. Singh, eds, *Travel Knowledge: European 'Discoveries' in the Early Modern Period*, New York and Basingstoke (2001), pp. 35–52

Walker, M. F., 'The Limits of Collaboration: Robert Hooke, Christopher Wren and the Designing of the Monument to the Great Fire of London', *Notes and Records: The Royal Society Journal of the History of Science* (16 February 2011);

see http://rsnr.royalsocietypublishing.org/content/65/2/121.full#sec-4

———, 'Francis Vernon, the Early Royal Society and the First English Encounter with Ancient Greek Architecture', *Architectural History*, vol. 56 (2016), pp. 29–61

———, *Architects and Intellectual Culture in Post-Restoration England*, Oxford (2017)

Ward-Jackson, P., 'Some Rare Drawings by Melchior Lorichs in the Collection of Mr. John Evelyn of Wotton and now at Stonor Park, Oxfordshire', *The Connoisseur*, vol. 135 (1955), pp. 83–93

———, *Public Sculpture of the City of London*, Liverpool (2003)

Ward-Perkins, J., *Cities of Ancient Greece and Italy: Planning in Classical Antiquity*, New York (1974)

Watkin, D. J., ed., *Sale Catalogues of Libraries of Eminent Persons*, vol. 4: *Architects*, London (1972), 'Hawksmoor', pp. 45–105; 'Wren', pp. 135–91 [*A Catalogue of the Curious and Entire Libraries of that ingenious Architect Sir Christopher Wren, Knt. And Christopher Wren, Esq; his Son*, London (1748)]

Webb, G., ed., 'The Letters and Drawings of Nicholas Hawksmoor Relating to the Building of the Mausoleum at Castle Howard, 1726–1742', *Walpole Society*, vol. 19 (1930–1), pp. 111–63

Webster, C., *The Great Instauration*, London (1975)

———, *From Paracelsus to Newton: Magic and the Making of Modern Science*, Cambridge (1982)

———, 'Christopher Wren', *Contemporary Physics*, vol. 26 no. 2 (1985), pp. 169–70 (review of Bennett 1982)

Wemyss, C., 'A Study of Aspiration: The Scottish Treasury Commission and its Impact upon the Development of Scottish Country House Architecture 1667–1682', PhD thesis, University of Dundee (2008)

Westbrook, N., K. R. Dark and R. van Meeuwen, 'Constructing Melchior Lorichs's "Panorama of Constantinople"', *Journal of the Society of Architectural Historians*, vol. 69 (2010), pp. 62–87

Wheeler, J. R., 'Notes on the So-Called Capuchin Plans of Athens', *Harvard Studies in Classical Philology*, vol. 12 (1901), pp. 221–30

Whinney, M., 'John Webb's Drawings for Whitehall Palace', *Walpole Society*, vol. 31 (1946), pp. 45–107

———, 'Sir Christopher Wren's Visit to Paris', *Gazette des Beaux-Arts*, vol. 51 (1958), pp. 229–42

———, *Wren*, London (1971)

Wilkinson, J., *Jerusalem Pilgrims before the Crusades*, Warminster (1977)

Williams, K. J., *The Antiquary: John Aubrey's Historical Scholarship*, Oxford (2016)

Williamson, B., and M. Baigent, 'Sir Christopher Wren and Freemasonry: New Evidence', *Ars Quatuor Coronatorum*, vol. 109 (1996), pp. 188–9

Willis, R., *Remarks on the Architecture of the Middle Ages, especially of Italy*, Cambridge (1835)

Wilson Jones, M., *Origins of Classical Architecture*, New Haven and London (2014)

Wittkower, R., *Gothic vs Classic: Architectural Projects in Seventeenth-Century Italy*, London (1974)

Wood, A. C., *A History of the Levant Company*, Oxford (1935)

Woolmer, M., *Ancient Phoenicia: An Introduction*, London (2011)

Worsley, G., *Inigo Jones and the European Classicist Tradition*, New Haven and London (2007)

Wragge-Morley, A., 'Restitution, Description and Knowledge in English Architecture and Natural Philosophy, 1650–1750', *Architectural Research Quarterly*, vol. 14 (2010), pp. 247–54

Yates, F., *Astraea: The Imperial Theme in the Sixteenth Century*, London (1975; 1985)

Yildiz, N., 'Turkish Britons and Ottoman Turks in England during the Eighteenth Century', in M. Hüttler and H. E. Weidinger, eds, *Ottoman Empire and European Theatre: The Time of Joseph Haydn: From Sultan Mahmud I to Mahmud II (r. 1730–1839)*, vol. 2, Vienna (2014), pp. 539–86; see www.researchgate.net/publication/262796016_Netice_Yildiz_North_Cyprus_Turkish_Britons_and_Ottoman_Turks_in_England_During_the_Eighteenth_Century

Zhiri, O., 'A Captive Library Between Morocco and Spain', in Keller and Irigoyen-Garcia 2017, pp. 17–31

ONLINE SOURCES

Drawings, Woodcuts, Engravings, Models

Aelst, Pieter Coecke van, woodcut of the procession of Sultan Suleiman through the Atmeidan, a panel from 'Ces Moeurs et fachons de faire de Turcz' (Customs and Fashions of the Turks): www.metmuseum.org/toah/works-of-art/28.85.7a

Hollar, Wenceslaus, *A true and exact prospect of the famous Citty of London from S. Marie Overs steeple in Southwarke in its flourishing condition before the Fire. Another Prospect of the sayd city taken from the same place as it appeareth now, after the sad calamitie and destruction by Fire, in the year of 1666* (1666; facsimile c.1792), engraving, British Museum, London, Q,6.58: www.britishmuseum.org/research/collection_online/collection_object_details.aspx?objectId=1526368&partId=1&people=120831&peoA=120831-2-60&page=1

Keere, Pieter van den, engraving of Constantinople (1616): www.wdl.org/en/item/14391/

Labacco, Antonio, and Antonio Salamanca, engraving of St Peter's, 1547, bound in the *Speculum Romanae Magnificentiae* (1553–63): www.metmuseum.org/art/collection/search/403672

Lorck, Melchior, woodcut of the Suleimaniye mosque in Constantinople (1570): http://germanhistorydocs.ghi-dc.org/sub_image.cfm?image_id=3352

'Pearson model' of the Holy Sepulchre, Jerusalem: www.finch-and-co.co.uk/antiquities/d/the-pearson-model-of-the-church-of-the-holy-sepulchre-jerusalem/57378

Rare Books and Library Catalogues

Cotton Library, British Library, London: www.bl.uk/reshelp/findhelprestype/manuscripts/cottonmss/cottonmss.html

Early English Books: http://quod.lib.umich.edu/e/eebogroup

Robert Hooke's Library: www.hookesbooks.com

William Laud's Arabic Manuscripts, Bodleian Library, Oxford: https://archiveshub.jisc.ac.uk/search/archives/f95d440c-5254-3338-9417-d1f290471378

Wren Office drawings at St Paul's Cathedral: www.stpauls.co.uk/history-collections/the-collections/architectural-archive/wren-office-drawings

Wren Office drawings at Sir John Soane's Museum, London: http://collections.soane.org/OBJECT7062

PHOTOGRAPH CREDITS

Illustrations have been provided by and are reproduced courtesy of the owners or custodians of the works. Images that require additional photographic credit are listed below by their respective figure numbers.

The Warden and Fellows of All Souls College, Oxford 46, 76, 100, 102, 122, 127, 141, 149, 152, 158, 170, 175
Angelo Hornak / Alamy Stock Photo 136
© Ashmolean Museum, University of Oxford 114
© British Library Board 83, 103–5, 168
© The Trustees of the British Museum 44, 58, 96, 140, 144–6
Reproduced by permission of the Chatsworth Settlement Trustees 56

Max Sang, 139 (coffee shop sign removed): https://creativecommons.org/licenses/by-nc-nd/2.0/
© The National Trust 20
RIBA London / *Wren Society Volumes* 36
Royal Collection © 2019, Her Majesty Queen Elizabeth II 84
© The Royal Society 1, 26
St Paul's Cathedral, London / author 52, 125
© Vaughan Hart 2–10, 12–15, 17–19, 22–5, 28–35, 39–41, 47, 51, 54, 62, 67, 71–3, 79–82, 85–91, 95, 97, 106–13, 115, 117, 118, 120, 121, 123, 124, 126, 129, 132, 133, 148, 150, 151, 154, 159, 162–67, 171–73, 178
© Dean and Chapter of Westminster Abbey 63
Yale Center for British Art, New Haven, Paul Mellon Collection 143

INDEX

Figures in *italics* refer to illustration numbers

Abraham, 66
Adam, 141
Adams, Thomas, 62
Adrianople (Edirne), Selimiye, 89, 106, 113
Al-Ukhaidir fortress, 57
Alberti, Leon Battista, 21, 37, 149
alchemy, 17, 62, 141–2, 183 n.104
Aldersey, Laurence, 12
Aleppo, 2, 3, 12, 40, 63
Alexander the Great, xv, 7, 22, 27, 129, 130, 135
Alexandria, x, xii, xvi, xix, 5, 120, 125, 129–30, 133, 149, 181 n.55, *159*
Allatius (Allacci), Leone, xiii, 98, 100–1, 112, 176 n.129, *121*
Amico, Bernardino, xiv, 60, 78, 81, 98, 105, 112, 177 n.164, *3, 7, 132–3*
Amiens Cathedral, 60
Anchiale (Anchialos), 120, 130
Ancients *v* Moderns, x–xi, 16–17
Anderson, James, 66
Andronicus of Cyrrhus, 20
Anglicans, 73, 81, 83, 105, 113, 145
    Primitive Christianity/Eastern Church, xvi, xx, 15, 24, 30, 42, 63, 75, 83, 86, 98, 101, 111–12, 114, 116, 149, *142*
Ani Cathedral, 57

Apamea, 131, *160*
Arabs, xx–xxi, 62–5, 166 n.16; *see also* Saracens
Arculfus, 75
Artemis of Ephesus, 145, *179; see also* Ephesus, Temple of Diana (Artemis)
Arwad, 22
Ashmole, Elias, 17, 59, 66, 160 n.129
Athelstan, 66
Athens, 13, 20, *30*
    Holy Apostles of Solaki, 104
    Kapnikarea, 104
    Odeon of Herodes Atticus, 13, *26*
    Parthenon, 19–20, *31*
    Saint Assomati, 104
    Stoa Poikile, 129
    Tower of the Winds, 20, 37–8, 121, 164 n.103, *47*
Atterbury, Francis, 52–3, 55, 59, 62, 63, 66
Aubrey, John, x, 16, 32, 35, 45, 49, 66, 86, 114, 122, 158 n.90, 166 n.32, 171 n.152, *43*

Baalbek (Heliopolis), 3
    Temple of Bacchus, 40, 164 n.113
    Temple of Venus, 39–40, *51*
Babylon, Hanging Gardens, xii, xv, 17
    Walls, 17, 119, *148*
Bacon, Francis, 3
Bani (Bauni), 91

Banks, John, 148
Baroque, x, xi, 45
Barrow, Isaac, 86, 89, 112, 125, 129, 133
Basel Cathedral, 60
Basire, Isaac, 30, 112,
Bastwick, William, 12
Beale, John, 16
Beauvau, Henry de, *159*
Bede, 75, 147
Bedloe, William, 121
Bedwell, William, 62
Belon, Pierre, 2
Bendish, Thomas, 86
Bernier, François, x, 3
Bernini, Gian Lorenzo, ix
Bethlehem, Basilica of the Nativity, xiv, 98, *120*
Beveridge, William, 63, 98, 101, *126*
Biddulph, William, 10, 12, 60, 62, 63, 82
Blondel, François Nicolas, x
Blount, Henry, x, 1, 10, 81, 82, 112–13, 130, 133
Bochart, Samuel, 23
Bologna, 127
Bon, Ottaviano, 97
Boone, Christopher, 3
Boulter, Robert, 26
Boyle, Robert, 9, 15, 122, 125
Bramante, Donato, 69, 98
Braun, George, 64, 81, *4*
Browne, Edward, 126–7

Brunelleschi, Filippo, xix, 71, 83
Brutus (Brute), 147, 179 n.201
Burchard of Mount Sion, xiv
Burns, Ross, 130
Byblos, 22
Byzantium, 22

Cain, 66, 119
Cambridge, University, 63, 112
   Christ's College, 89, 112
   Peterhouse College chapel, 48, *60*
   Trinity College, 82, 86
      Library, 69, 86, 129, 133, *102*, *157*
Camden, William, 48
Campbell, James, 66
Canterbury Cathedral, 60
Carthage, 22
Casaubon, Isaac, 22
Castiglione, Baldassare, 45
Castle Howard, 35–6
   Carrmire Gate, 36, *45*
   Temple of the Four Winds (Belvedere), 40
Caussin, Nicolas, 141
Cave, William, 98, 101, 112
Cavendish, Henry, 82
Cephalonia, 13
Cesariano, Cesare, xiii, 37–9, 121, 164 n.103, 165 n.2, *5, 47, 150*
Chaldeans, 1, 16, 20, 125, 141
Chambrey, Roland Fréart de, x, 26, 139
Chardin, John, x, 1, 2, 6–9, 12, 57, 59, 64, 91–5, 105, 120, 135–6, *11, 17–19, 67, 165–6*
Charles I, 116, 142; see also Stuarts & Windsor Castle, Mausoleum for Charles I
Charles II, 6, 9, 27, 50, 114, 116–17, 143, 145, 162 n.57, 179 n.201, *179*
Charles VI, xviii
China, x, 1, 12
Chishull, Edmund, 12
Chonai (Colossae), 112
Cibber, Caius Gabriel, 143–5, *177, 179*
Clarke, George, 53
Cole of Colchester (King), 116
Colonna, Francesco, xiii
Compton, Henry, 27, 75
Constantine, xx, 24, 63, 75–6, 83, 100, 101, 112, 114, 116
Constantinople, xii, xvi, xix, 2, 3, 9, 12, 13, 24, 64, 81–3, 86, 91, 139, 140, 148, *4, 112, 145*; see also Hagia Sophia
   Ahmed's mosque (Blue mosque), 82, 91, 105, *97, 110*
   Church of the Holy Apostles, 75, 95, 102, 112, *129*
   Column of Arcadius (the 'Historical column'), 139–40, *171–2*
   Column of Constantine, 139–40, *180*
   Column of Marcian, 140, *173–4*
   Column of Theodosius I, 139–40, 182 n.86
   Great Palace, 39
   Hippodrome, 81, *96*
   Myrelaion monastery (Bodrum mosque), 105, *131*
   Nea Ekklesia ('New Church'), *95*
   St Theodore, 106
   Suleimaniye mosque, 81, 91, *111, 113*
   Topkapi Palace (Seraglio), 3, 13, 82, 95–7, *95, 117–18*
   Yeni Camii ('New mosque'), 89, 91, *103, 109*
Cordinus (Kodinos), George, 82
Corfu, Saint Jason and Sosipater, 105
Corsica, 22
Coryat, Thomas, 82
Cotton, Dodmore, 9
Cotton, Robert, xix
Covel, John, xx, 12, 89–91, 112, 113, 139, 174 n.82, *103–5*
Cranach the Elder, Lucas, 62
Crusaders, 46, 55–65, 149

D'Alquié, François Savinien, 2
Daniel, 17
Daniel, Samuel, 141
David, 25, 27, 30
De Bruyn (Le Brun), Cornelis, 2, 30, 130, 132, *40*
De Hooghe, Romeyn, *44*
De Monconys, Balthasar, 2, 40
Decker, Coenraet, 4
Decorum, 50, 73, 149
Dee, John, 183 n.104
Della Valle, Pietro, 134
Dickinson, Edmund, 22
Dickinson, William, 52, 165 n.1, *63*
Dinocrates of Rhodes, 129
Diocletian, 130, 131
Diodorus Siculus, xiii, 130
Downes, Kerry, xi, xx, 40, 107
Druids, 86
Dryden, John, 27
Dryden, Jonathan, 82
Du Cange, Charles du Fresne, 139
Du Prey, Pierre de la Ruffiniére, xx, 81
Dugdale, William, 49, *62*
Dura-Europos, 122
Dürer, Albrecht, 62

East India Company, xxi, 3, 6
Eastcourt, Giles, 13
Echmiadzin Cathedral, 9, 105, *17, 18*
Egypt, xii, xiii, xvi, xxi, 1, 2, 4–5, 15, 16, 66, 129, 132, 141, 145
   Giza, xii, xiii, 4, *6, 15*
Elizabeth I, 12, 158 n.87
Enos (Enoch), 119
Ephesus, x, 20, 112, *29*
   Temple of Diana (Artemis), xii, xiv, xvi, 20, 26, 27, 32, 73, 142, *28*
Escorial, Madrid, 63
Etruscans, 32
Euclid, 66, 125
Eusebius, 24, 73, 75, 101–2, 112, 117
Evelyn, John, ix, x, xix, 1, 3, 6–7, 9, 12, 15, 20, 22, 26, 30, 34, 37, 45–6, 50, 60, 62, 63, 65, 69, 71, 74, 81, 83, 89, 91, 101, 107, 113, 114, 116–17, 119, 121, 131, 132, 135–6, 139, 141, 150, 152 n.16, 159 n.91, 160 n.129, 172 n.25

Farynor, Thomas, 121
Fell, John, 50
Fénelon, François, 62
Fez, xiv
Filarete (Antonio di Pietro Averlino), xiii
Finch, Heneage, 12, 91, 112
Finch, John, 12, 40
Fischer von Erlach, Johann Bernhard, xviii, 64, *10*
Flitcroft, Henry, 20
Florence, Cathedral, 83
   Pazzi chapel, xix, 71
Foxe, John, 10, 62
Foy-Vaillant, Jean, 5–6
Frampton, Robert, 30
freemasonry, xix, xx, 66, 141, 143, 149, 171 nn.147, 152–3
Fuller, Thomas, xiv, 2, 61, 78, *72, 91*

Gadeira, 22
Gale, Thomas, 136
Garter, Order of the, 59, 142, 168 n.87
Geoffrey of Monmouth, 116, 147
Gibbons, Grinling, 35, 162 n.55
Gilles (Gyllius), Pierre, 82, 139
Giovio, Paolo, 141
Gordon, John, 178 n.201
Gothic, xviii, xxi, 35, 37, 42, 45–67, 94, 98, 149, 165 nn.2, 7, 169 n.94
Goths, 45–6, 55, 62
Greaves, John, 4, 17, 34–5, 42, 97, *15, 41*
Greece, 2, 7, 13, 16, 19–20, 148
Green Mausoleum, Bursa, 57, 64, 66

INDEX   205

Grelot, Guillaume-Joseph, x, 2, 7, 64, 89, 91–7, 101, 105, *106–8, 109–13, 117–18*
Gresham College, ix, xix, 1, 16–17, 22, 34–5, 66, 86, 121, 125, 131, 133, 149
Griffith-Jones, Robin, 101
Grimani, Marco, xiii
Grimeston, Edward, 122
Grotius, Hugo, 15
Grünenberg, Conrad, 30, *38*
Guillet, George, 13

Hagia Sophia, xii, xiv, xvi, xix, xx, 13, 60, 74, 81, 82–6, 89, 94–5, 97–8, 101, 105, 111, 112, 113, 116, 149–50, *93, 94, 98, 99, 101, 104, 106–8*
Hakluyt, Richard, 82
Halicarnassus, Mausoleum of Mausolus, xii, xiii, xvi, xviii, 25, 27, 32, 42–3, 133, *5, 36*
Halifax, William, 131, 132
Halley, Edmond, 2, 131–2
Hampton Court, 182 n.100
Hanmer, Meredith, 24
Hanno, 22
Harborne, William, 82
Hartlib, Samuel, 12, 13, 15, 26, 63
  papers of, 16
Harvey, Daniel, 86
Harwood, John, 23
Hatton, Edward, 49, 114–15
Hawksmoor, Nicholas, ix, xx, 27, 35–6, 37, 39–43, 53–5, 62, 83, 91, 95, 114, 129, 149, 164 n.113, *36, 53, 98–100, 114, 142, 158*
Haworth, Samuel, 114–15
Helena (mother of Constantine), 74, 78, 98, 116
Henry III, 48, 49, 55
Henry IV, 59, 121
Henry of Reyns, 55
heraldry, 141–2
Herbert, Thomas, 7, 9, 64, 134–5 *163–4*
Herculaneum, 119
Hercules, 182 n.100
Herod, 60
Herodotus, xiii, xv, xix, 16, 22, 32, 119, 133, *148*
Herwarth von Hohenburg, Johann Georg, 141
hieroglyphics, 4, 15, 72, 73, 141–2, 145
Hieronymite order, 62
Hill, Abraham, 5
Hippocrates, 16
Hiram (Tyrian architect), 25, 145
Hiram I (King), 25
Hogenberg, Frans, 64, 81, *4*
Holland, 107, 177 n.162

Hollar, Wenceslaus, 49, 52, 134, 136, *62, 164*
Holy Land (Palastine), xii, xiv, xv, xvi, xviii, xx, xxi, 2, 12, 15, 46, 55–65, 74, 79, 82, 148–9; *see also* Jerusalem
Homann, Johann Baptist, 117, 125, *146*
Hooke, Robert, xv, xix, 1, 2, 3, 4, 6–7, 9, 12–13, 15, 19–20, 22, 26, 34–5, 39, 40, 42, 52, 55, 60–4, 66, 75, 78, 82, 84, 86, 91–4, 97, 98, 101, 105–7, 111–14, 121, 130, 134–45, 152 n.33, 159 n.105, 165 n.118, 170 n.118, 174 n.75, 177 n.162, 183 n.104, *42, 101, 170*
Hosios Loukas, monastery of, 104, *130*
Hoskins, John, 6
Houghton, John, 42
Howard, Philip, 9
Howell, James, 116
Hunt, Henry, 4
Huntington, Robert, 4, 20, 30, 132–3
Huygens, Constantijn, 3, 26

India, x
  Kilmanoor, 94
  Mogul, xx
Isac, Jasper, 64
Isfahan, 7, 13, 134
  Shah mosque, 98

Jabal, 66
Jabir ibn Hayyan (Geber Arabs), 62
James I, 26–7, 116, 178 n.201; *see also* Stuarts
James II, 27
Jarman, Edward, 125
Jeffery, Paul, 106–7
Jerusalem, x, xii, xiii, xvi, xviii, xix, 2, 12, 30, 56–7, 111, 112, 119, 148, 150, *3, 25, 38, 72; see also* Solomon, Temple of
  Al-Aqsa mosque, 57, *65*
  Chapel of the Ascension, 60, 75, *70, 88*
  Church of the Holy Sepulchre, xiv, xvi, 59–60, 73, 74, 75–9, 100, 111, 149–50, 173 n.44, *7, 84–7, 92*
  Church of St John the Baptist, 75, *89*
  Dome of the Rock, 57, 64, 74, *64*
  St Anne, 105, *133*
  St James Cathedral, 105, *132*
  Tomb of Absalom, xvi, xx, 25, 27–32, 149, *37–40*
Jones, Inigo, ix, xxi, 1, 9, 39, 50, 69, 116, 121, 127, 136, 140, 141, 148, 167 n.35, 179 n.201, *56*
Jonson, Ben, 45, *56*
Josephus, xiii, xiv, xvi, 22, 25, 27, 119, 130, 131, 141, 145
Justinian, 81, 83, 113, 150

Kämpfer, Engelbert, 181 n.79, *167*
Kimbolton Castle, 149
Kircher, Athanasius, xvii, 1, 4, 141, *8, 9, 13*
Knights Templar, 59–60, 150, 169 n.91
Knolles, Richard, 10
Koran, 63–4, 86
Kravtsov, Sergey, 107

Labacco, Antonio, 42, 111, *54, 140*
Labrosse, Joseph, 9
Lafréry, Antonio, 98, 111–12, *140*
Laine, Thomas, *127*
Lamech, 66
Laodicea, 112
Largillière, Nicolas de, *21*
Laud, William, 48, 63, 116
Lee, Samuel, 61–2, 169 n.98, *73*
Lemercier, Jacques, 71
Leo X (Pope), 45
Leo Africanus, xiv
Leon, Jacob Judah, 26
Levant, xi, xii, xx, 2, 3, 12, 19–21, 22, 34, 39, 40, 60, 75, 82, 105, 132, *2*
Levant ('Turkey') Company, xx, xxi, 1, 11, 12, 13, 24, 40, 84–6, 89, 91, 112, 114, 125, 130–1
Lightfoot, John, 60
Lincoln Cathedral, Honywood Library, 167 n.36
Lisle, Samuel, 40
Lithgow, William, 12
Lobo, Jerónimo, 5
Locke, John, 52, 66, 155 n.4, 167 n.51
Lodwick, Francis, 42
London
  All Hallows Bread Street, 46
  All Hallows the Great, 101
  Bagnios (baths), 114–16, *143–4*
  Cheapside, 62
  Chelsea Hospital, 27, 120, 127, 133, *155*
  City churches, xix, 46–7, 53, 69, 101, 105–14
  Custom House, 121, 125
  Greenwich Hospital, 27, 69, 120, 125, 127, 129, 130, 133, *147, 153, 156*
  Monument, xix, 82, 136–45, *168–70, 176–7, 179*
  Old St Paul's Cathedral, ix, xiv, 26, 37, 39, 46, 48, 50, 69, 71, 73–4, 81, 83, 98, 113, 121, 140, *76*
  Queen Anne churches, 37, 47, 101, 149
  Royal Exchange, 121, 125–6
  Savoy, French Protestant church, 106
  St Alban Wood Street, 47, 53, *55*
  St Anne and St Agnes, 105, *134, 136*
  St Antholin Budge Row, 47, 69, 106, *58*
  St Augustine Old Change, 37

St Benet Fink, 69
St Bride Fleet Street, 39, 47, *48*
St Clement Danes, 101, *127–8*
St Dunstan-in-the-East, 19, 42, 47, 53, 164 n.117, *27*
St George Bloomsbury, 41, 43, *53*
St James Garlickhythe, 19, 39
St Lawrence Jewry, 47
St Martin Ludgate, 47, 105, 107, *134, 137*
St Mary Abchurch, 47, 69, 106–7, 176 n.149, *77*
St Mary Aldermanbury, 47
St Mary Aldermary, 47, 53, *59*
St Mary Somerset, 46, *57*
St Mary-at-Hill, 47, 69, 105, 111, *134–5*
St Mary's in Lincoln's Inn Fields, 69, 106, *78*
St Michael Paternoster Royal, 19, 39–40, *49*
St Mildred Bread Street, 69, 176 n.149
St Olave, Old Jewry, 46
St Paul's Cathedral, xxi, 27, 37, 65, 69, 73, 75, 83, 91, 94–5, 98, 129, 147, *46, 75, 100, 116, 119, 158*
　Great Model, 19, 41, 73, 113, 133, *52*
　Greek Cross design, 73, 113, *141*
　'Warrant' design, 37, 73, *46*
St Peter Cornhill, 101
St Stephen Walbrook, 19, 39, 69, 106–7, *134, 138–9*
St Swithin London Stone, 69
Temple Church, 59–60, 78, 100, 101, 168 n.84, *69*
Lorck (Lorichs), Melchior, 81, 139, 173 n.49
Lord, Henry, 9
Louis XIV, x, 3, 7
Lowthorp, John, *167*
Luke, John, 112
Lyon Cathedral, 60

MacLean, Gerald, xx–xxi
Maier, Michael, 141
Mansard, François, 71
Marot, Jean, 40
Marshall, William, 134, *163*
Martel, Charles, 66
Martial, 27, 147–8
Martin, John, 63–4
Mary II, catafalque for, 35, 42, 162 n.55, *44*
Masada, 122
Matar, Nabil, xx–xxi, 62
Maundrell, Henry, 2, 12, 40, 131, *12, 51*
May, Hugh, 50
Mecca, 10
Mehmed I, 57

Merian, Mattheus, 82, 117, *145*
Milan Cathedral, 50
Milton, John, 62
Molinet, Claud du, 141
Monceaux, André de, 1, 3, 40
Montagu, Ralph, 19
Montano, Giovanni Battista, 39
Montepulciano, San Bagio, 42
Moray, Robert, 3, 66
Moryson, Faynes, 30, 60, 78, 82, *90*
Moses, 17
Musgrave, William, xvi
Muslims, xx–xxi, 12, 27, 56–7, 63, 94

Napoleon, Louis, xxi
New Constantinople, London as, 116–17, 121, 147, 178 n.198
New Jerusalem, London as, 26–7, 121, 142, 145
New Troy (Troynovant), London as, 147
Nicholls, Sutton, *168*
Nicolay, Nicolas de, 10
Nieuhof, Jan, 1
Nile, 5, 130
Nimrod, xvii, 66
Nineveh, xvi, 6–7, 17
Noah, 17
　Ark, xvi, xvii, *9*
North, Dudley, 7, 24, 74, 89, 91, 97, 98, 112, 114
North, Francis, 7
North, Roger, 7, 24, 74–5, 91, 98, 101, 104, 114, *83*

Ockley, Simon, 63
Oldenburg, Henry, 3, 4, 9, 12–13, 17, 34, 40, 63, 119, 159 n.109
Olearius, Adam, 9, 63
Orders (columns), 20–1, 24–7, 32, 113, 148, *35*; see also Tyrian, Order of,
Orientalism, xxi, 149
Ottoman empire, xii, xx, xxi, 1, 3, 12, 75, 82, 115, 158 n.87
Oxford, University, 63, 170 n.115
　All Souls, 53–5
　Radcliffe library, 91, *114*
　Sheldonian theatre, ix, 148
　Tom Tower, Christ Church, 46, 47, 49–52, 57–9, 69, *61, 68*
　Wadham College, xix

Padua, baptistery, xix, 71
Pagitt, Epigram, 75
Palladio, Andrea, xxi, 32, 73, 101, 122, 126, 133, 149, *80, 81, 151, 154*

Palmanova, 121
Palmyra (Tadmor), x, xvi, xix, xx, 40, 131–3, 149, *160–1*
Paracelsus, 15
Paris, xix, 121, 149
　Louvre, x
　Place de France, 121
　Sorbonne, church of, 71
　Val-de-Grâce, 71
Paul the Silentiary, xiv
Pausanias, 20
Pearce, Edward, 142, *176*
Pepys, Samuel, xix, 9, 11–12, 113, 169 n.107
Pergamum, 112
Perrault, Charles, x
Perrault, Claude, x
Persepolis, x, xvi, 6–7, 9, 134–6, *16, 163–7*
Persia, 2, 7, 9, 13, 15, 63, 94, 148
Philadelphia (Alaşehir), 112
Philo, xiii
Phocas, John, xiv
Phoenicians, xvi, 21–5, 32, 40, 148, 149, *32*; see also Tyrians
Piranesi, Giovanni Battista, 119
Plato, 43
Pliny the Elder, xiii, xv, xvi, 16, 20, 25, 27, 32–5, 133, 152 n.33
Pococke, Edward, 15, 170 n.115
Poggibonsi, Niccolò da, xiv, 78
Polybius, 120, 122–3, 133
Pompeii, 119
Porsenna, Lars, tomb of, xvi, 25, 32–7, 42–3, 63, *41–3*
Povey, Thomas, 79, 81
Prideaux, Humphrey, 63
Procopius, xiv, 75, 82, 95, 101–2, 112
Ptolemy, 125
Pulleyn, Octavian, 7
Purchas, Samuel, 75
Pythagoras, 43, 66

Qom, tombs, 9, 57, 94, *19, 67, 115*

Raphael, 45
Rauwolf, Leonhard, 3
Rawlinson, Richard, 49
Reynell, Carew, 117
Rhodes, 125
　Colossus, xii
Ripa, Cesare, 141–5, *178*
Robinson, George, 30
Rome, xi, xvii, xix, 116, 119, 121, 129, 135, 147, 149–50
　Baths of Constantine, 142
　Column of Marcus Aurelius, 136

Column of Trajan, 136, 139
Oratory of the Holy Cross (at St John Lateran), 111, *140*
Pantheon, xix, 69, 74, 83, 101
Piazza del Popolo, 121
S. Croce in Gerusalemme, 98
Santa Costanza, 69, 100–1, *79*
Santa Maria di Loreto, 71
St Peter's, 39, 42, 69, 71, 75, 95, 98, *54*
Tempietto, 69
Temple of Mars Ultor, xvi, 32, 73, 142, *81*
Temple of Peace (Basilica of Maxentius), xvi, 72–3, 142, *80*
Ross, Alexander, 64
Royal Society, x, xv, xvi, xix, xxi, 1–17, 19–20, 23, 35, 40, 45, 48, 50, 59, 63, 66, 79, 84, 86, 91–4, 112–13, 121–5, 127, 129, 131–2, 134–6, 141–2, 148, *162, 167*
Rycaut, Paul, 1, 3, 10–13, 59, 63, 91, 112, *22*
Ryer, André du, 64
Ryff, Hermann, 39, 165 n.2

S. Petronio, Bologna, 50
Said, Edward, xxi
Saladin, 78
Salamanca, Antonio, 42, *54*
Salisbury Cathedral, xix, 48–9, 60
Salter, Jerome, 112
Sammes, Aylett, 23, *32*
Samson, xvi, 25
Sanderson, John, 12, 82
Sandys, George, 2, 4, 12, 27, 30–1, 59–60, 64, 75–9, 81, 82–3, 97, 139, 148, *2, 14, 25, 39, 85–9, 120, 171*
Sangallo the Elder, Antonio da, 42
Sangallo the Younger, Antonio da, 42, *54*
Sansovino, Francesco, 10, 45
Saracens, xviii, xxi, 46, 55, 57, 62–5, 83, 113, 149, 166 n.16, 169 n.105; *see also* Arabs & Turks
Sardis, 112
Schedel, Hartmann, 81, 139, 172 n.22, *95*
Scott, James (Duke of Monmouth), 27
Seaman, William, 15
Seiris, 141
Seller, Abednego, 132
Serlio, Sebastiano, xiii, 45, 69, 98, 101, 122, 133, 148, *6, 79*
Seth, xvi, 141
Sevi, Sabbatai, 10, 12
Seymour, Thomas, 113
Shakespeare, William, xvii, 22
Shepherd, Thomas, *58*
Shiraz, Atigh Jame, 64
Shirley, Anthony, 9, 12

Shirley, Robert, 9, *20*
Sidon, 22
Sigüenza, José de, 62
Sinan, 81, 106
Sixtus V (Pope), 121, 136
Sleidan, Johann, 9
Smith, Samuel, 42
Smith, Thomas, 1, 12, 84–6, 101, 112
Smyrna (Izmir), 11, 12–13, 40, 63, 86, 91, 112, *23*
Solomon, xx, 17, 25, 26–7, 40, 60, 83, 131–2, 142
  Temple of, xii, xiii, xvi, xix, xx, 20, 25–7, 32, 56–7, 60–2, 64, 66, 74, 101, 107, 113, 121, 142, 145, 149–50, 183 n.112, *34, 72, 73, 82*
Soo, Lydia, xx, 81, 106
Southwell, Robert, 5
Sparta, 119
Split (Spalatro), 13
  Palace of Diocletian, 122
Spon, Jacob, 2, 13, 20, 75, 132
Sprat, Thomas, 15, 17, 125, 129, 141–2
St Alban, 66
St Paul, 24, 41, 48
St Stephen, 106
Stephanus of Byzantium, 22
Stevens, John, 49
Stevin, Simon, 122
Stillingfleet, Edward, 116–17
Stonehenge, 23
Strabo, 22, 120, 130, 133
Strasburg Cathedral, 60
Struys, Jan, 9
Stuarts, xx, 9, 22, 26, 45, 48, 116, 62, 75, 116, 121, 136, 141, 147–8, 178 n.201, *56*
Stubbe, Henry, 63, 116–17
Stukeley, William, 23, 49, 165 n.7
Suleiman the Magnificent, 13, 81, *96*
Sweetman, John, xix, xx

Tangier, fortifications, ix, 63, 170 n.126
Tarsus, 120, 130, 133
Tartessus, 22
Tavernier, Jean-Baptiste, x, 6, 9, 97, *21*
Temple of Dagon, xvi, 25
Tenison, Thomas, 136
Thebes, 119
Thévenot, Jean de, x, 2
Thyatira, 112
Timberlake, Henry, 12, *24*
Tivoli, 69, 119
Tower of Babel, xv, xvi–xvii, 7, 15, 42, 63, 66, *8*
Trapezeum (Trabzon), 13
Trillia, Pantobasilissa (Kemerli Kilise), 89, *105*

Troy, 147
Turks, 9–12, 62; *see also* Saracens
Turner, Jacob, 112
Twyne, John, 22
Tyre, xiii, xvi, xviii, 22, 43, 82, 101, 112, 125, 131, *33*
Tyrian, Order of, 21–37, 113, 133, 148
Tyrians, xvi, 22–4, 125

Ulugh Beg, 62, 169 n.111
Ussher, James, 74, *82*

Valeriano, Piero, 141
Van Aelst, Pieter, 81, *96*
Van den Keere, Pieter (Petrus Kaerius), 81–2
Van Dyck, Anthony, 9, *20*
Vanbrugh, John, ix, xx, 149
Vansleb, Johann Michael, 4
Varro, 25, 32, 43
Vasari, Giorgio, 16, 45
Veen, Otto van, 141
Vegetius, Flavius Renatus, 122
Venice, 127
  St Mark's, xix, 65, 69, 71, 83, *74*
Vernon, Francis, 1, 13, 19, *26*
Versailles, x, 179 n.13
Vigevano, 127
Villalpando, Juan Bautista, 26, 101, 107, *34, 35*
Vitruvius, ix, x, xii, xiii, xvi, xix, xxi, 16, 19–21, 26, 39, 50, 73, 119, 120–3, 126, 130, 133, 142, *5, 47, 150*

Waller, Richard, 42
Wandesford, John, 63
Ward, Seth, 48
Webb, John, 6, 50, 69, 157 n.61
Westminster Abbey, xviii, xix, 35, 46, 48–9, 52–5, 59, 62, 64, *44, 62, 63*
Westminster School, 63
Wheler, George, 1, 2, 13, 20, 24, 75, 81, 82, 89, 100–1, 104–7, 111, 113, 114, 116, 139–40, *23, 29, 30, 31, 33, 97, 123, 124, 129, 172, 173*
Whinney, Margaret, xi, 107
Whitehall Palace, 69, 127
Wilcocks, Joseph, 55
Wilkins, John, 16, 62
Willis, Brown, 49, 166 n.32
Winchester Palace, 69
Windsor Castle, Mausoleum for Charles I, xxi, 26, 35, 142, *175*
  remodelling, 50
Witsen, Nicholas, 136, 181 n.79

Wolsey, Thomas, 50, 59
Woodroffe, Benjamin, 42
Woodroofe, Edward, 141
Wotton, Henry, 45
Wragge, Richard, 82
Wren, Christopher
  astrology, 16–17
  Chaldeans, 15–16, 142, 149
  general interests, ix, *1*
  Hermeticism / Neo-Platonism, 15–16, 160 n.116
  natural philosophy, 15–17
  Parentalia, xv–xvi, xix, 147–8
  plan for London, 120–7, 136, *149*
  Professor of Astronomy, ix, 1, 17–18, 62
  Surveyor General, ix, 136, 150
  Tracts, xv–xvi, xix, xx, 17, 19–37, 46, 50–1, 59, 65, 72–3, 78–9, 94–5, 97–8, 105, 111, 119, 127–30, 132–3, 150, 171 n.140, 175 n.112, *28*
  visit to Paris, ix, xi, 16, 71, 107, 126–7
Wren, Matthew, 24, 48
Wyche, Peter, 5

Yerevan, mausoleum, 7